ArtScroll® Series

Rabbi Nosson Scherman / Rabbi Meir Zlotowitz

General Editors

Let My

Based on Talmudic
and Midrashic Sources

Published by

ARTSCROLL®
Mesorah Publications, ltd

Nation Live

The Story of Jewish Deliverance in the
Days of Mordechai and Esther

YOSEF DEUTSCH

FIRST EDITION
First Impression ... January 2002
Second Impression ... January 2003
Third Impression ... December 2004
Fourth Impression ... January 2009
Fifth Impression ... February 2011
Sixth Impression ... January 2012
Seventh Impression ... January 2015

Published and Distributed by
MESORAH PUBLICATIONS, LTD.
4401 Second Avenue / Brooklyn, N.Y 11232

Distributed in Europe by
LEHMANNS
Unit E, Viking Business Park
Rolling Mill Road
Jarow, Tyne & Wear, NE32 3DP
England

Distributed in Australia and New Zealand by
GOLDS WORLDS OF JUDAICA
3-13 William Street
Balaclava, Melbourne 3183
Victoria, Australia

Distributed in Israel by
SIFRIATI / A. GITLER — BOOKS
Moshav Magshimim
Israel

Distributed in South Africa by
KOLLEL BOOKSHOP
Northfield Centre
17 Northfield Avenue
Glenhazel 2192, Johannesburg, South Africa

ARTSCROLL® SERIES
LET MY NATION LIVE
© Copyright 2002, by MESORAH PUBLICATIONS, Ltd.
4401 Second Avenue / Brooklyn, N.Y. 11232 / (718) 921-9000 / www.artscroll.com

---

ISBN 10: 1-57819-782-1 / ISBN 13: 978-1-57819-782-8 (hard cover)
ISBN 10: 1-57819-783-X / ISBN 13: 978-1-57819-783-5 (paperback)

Typography by CompuScribe at ArtScroll Studios, Ltd.

Printed in the United States of America by Noble Book Press Corp.
Bound by Sefercraft, Quality Bookbinders, Ltd., Brooklyn N.Y. 11232

In dedication to the life of

David Kreiswirth

דוד בן אהרן קרייזוויררד
תנצב"ה

whose genuine integrity and pure conscience
found him ready to sacrifice everything
for Judaism and for the preservation
of his family's traditional values.

May his memory be a blessing.

בס״ד

שמואל קמנצקי
Rabbi S. Kamenetsky

2018 Upland Way
Philadelphia, Pa 19131

Home: 215-473-2798
Study: 215-473-1212

בס״ד

[handwritten Hebrew text]

דברי המברך

בס"ד

לכבוד וכו' וקירי הרב ר' יוסף שובס הי"ו

חיים וברכה

מאד שמחתי לראות ג' כרכים ענק עצום ונפלא
לגדולי ו מגלות פוסקי הדור הקדמו קדוש ירות "Let my nation Live"
ופלא עלי קשה עלי מאד ומעתיק דבר אחד אחד
ההקבץ ובחומר ומלאכת כביר מלאכת הענקים בקלות
לי יסודות מאמרי גלון והחושבים שמאסקר בכל על אמים
לכבוד זה ועל דבר ודו ...ק מין להאתאק אמה ולאור ה ...פולסומ
ומאספים הבסלום עם אשו ...

...

כ"ט וכ"ט הוכרת החן ... ולך הולאק בג ואש...
מעתתם ולהדריה אלף קדיולק ובוו מינוק וכן א ולאמ
בבו ... ומקף סלה ...ולות וגלות כי מאור עלי קן
פאסב את הכרים סי... קבל ...

הכותב וח.. יאקב גל..ן
כולו הגוחה לה ...
... עראבם גלון

Introduction:
Jewish Deliverance in the
Days of Mordechai and Esther

The first thought that comes to my mind as I prepare to publish my second book is the tremendous debt of gratitude I owe to Hashem. Not only did He give me the privilege of a successful first book, *Let My Nation Go*, He has now given me the privilege of following up with a second book, *Let My Nation Live*. I am humbled by His kindness, and I can only hope and pray that my work will bring honor to His holy Name.

My first book drew on Talmudic and Midrashic sources to describe the Jewish Exodus from Egypt. This second book views the Jewish deliverance in Persia during the days of Mordechai and Esther from a similar perspective. It is a sequel of sorts, although it takes place one thousand years later. The similarities in the two stories are striking. Both involve a wicked king who controls the fate of the Jewish people. Both kings are influenced by a diabolical villain, Bilam in Egypt and Haman in Persia. Both stories begin with roundtable conferences specifically convened to deal with "the Jewish problem." Most ironical of all is that in both stories the liberator of the Jewish people resided in the royal palace (Moshe in Pharaoh's, Queen Esther in Achashverosh's). In the first story, Moshe tells Pharaoh, "Let my nation go!" In the second, Esther tells Achashverosh, "Let my nation live!" Hence the titles of the books.

Compiling the information of this, the second book was quite difficult. My research led me to thousands of *midrashim* and commentaries, of which I chose just a small number to create a cohesive narrative. There are many conflicting views in the Midrash, and on most issues, more than one opinion is offered. For the most part, I have followed the interpretations that appear in the Gemara and the conventional commentaries in the narrative itself, and I have often mentioned other opinions and views in the footnotes.

Once again, as in the first book, I make no claims that the story presented here is the definitive account of what happened in Persia at that time. It is merely one version extrapolated from the vast body of information available. It is meant to give the reader a colorful and vivid picture of the events that took place during that time.

It is important to point out that understanding *midrashim* requires a significant amount of discernment, since they are sometimes meant to be taken literally and at other times metaphorically. I would like to thank RABBI ELIAHU LEVINE who helped me gain understanding of some of the more difficult *midrashim* and helped me determine which *midrashim* to include in the text and which to mention in the footnotes. I would also like to thank RABBI YAAKOV YOSEF REINMAN who edited the entire manuscript with his usual skill and professionalism.

Special thanks to my *rebbe* RABBI YIRMIYAH GUGENHEIMER who gave me support and encouragement when I needed them most. I would also like to express my profound appreciation to CHANAN BACK, who assist me greatly in my research and offered me his time, guidance and unstinting support. I would like to thank SIMCHA BACK for his assistance as well. I also thank RABBI MECHEL GRUSS who gave me access to his library, which contains many obscure *sefarim* I could not find elsewhere.

I would also like to extend a note of appreciation to AARON KREISWIRTH, this book would not have been possible without his direct support and assistance from the beginning of the work to the end.

I would like to take this opportunity to express my deepest gratitude to my dear parents MR. AND MRS. MORDECHAI DEUTCH and my dear grandmother MRS. MARGARET REICHMAN, who have guided me through the obstacle course of life and without whose wisdom and guidance I could never have written these books; my dear parents-in-law MR. AND MRS. MICHAEL LUTZ, who have always given me support, guidance and direction; and my brother GABY, who played an important supportive role in bringing the production of this book to a successful conclusion.

I would like to express my deep thanks to the staff of Mesorah Publications: to my friend, Efraim to ELI KROEN for his aesthetically pleasing page design; MRS. TOVA FINKELMAN for her meticulous proofreading of the manuscript; AVROHOM BIDERMAN and MRS. ZISSEL KELLER for their organization and coordination of this project, in an efficient and cheerful manner; MRS. CHAYA SURI POSNER and LIBBY ZWEIG for their diligent and tireless typing and retyping; and FRADY VORHAND who paginated the entire book. They had collectively outdone themselves in making this book a work of beauty.

Last but not least, I want to thank all the readers who received my first book so warmly, especially those of you who encouraged me to write the second. I hope you enjoy this one as much as you enjoyed the first.

Yossi Deutsch
Rosh Chodesh Shvat, 5762

Table of Contents

Prologue

After Nevuchadnezzar destroyed the *Beis Hamikdash*, he drove the Jewish people into exile in Babylon, the capital of the vast Babylonian Empire. For fifty-one years, they remained under the control of the Babylonians. Then a coalition of Persians and Medes invaded Babylon and toppled the empire.

A new empire arose on the ashes of the old — the Persian-Medean Empire, which had its capital in Shushan, Persia, far to the east of Babylon. Many Jews remained in the old Babylonian capital, but many others migrated to Shushan, the new seat of power.

It was a time of great tension for the Jewish people. Prophecy had promised that the *Beis HaMikdash* would be rebuilt, but after several fits and starts, the reconstruction was halted. In the meantime, the enemies of the Jews grew in number and power until they threatened the very existence of the Jewish people.

At this time, with the guiding hand of divine providence concealed, two great Jewish people came forward to redeem the Jewish people and start the chain of events that would culminate in the reconstruction of the *Beis HaMikdash* and the return to Yerushalayim — Mordechai and Esther. Their wondrous story is told in the *Megillah*. It is the story of Purim.

The Throne Room

Four men approached the Great Palace of Shushan in the early morning light. A glowering guard questioned them briefly and then let them pass. Although they had seen the palace many times before, they stopped for a moment to marvel at the massive, flower-shaped structure.[1] Then they walked past the main entrance, with its immense brass-studded, elaborately carved portals, and came to a modest service door around the side of the building. A caretaker showed them in.

"We've come to work on the throne," said one of the men, an older fellow with a tangled gray beard. "My men will need buckets of soapy water, clean rags and plenty of fragrant oils."

"I know," said the caretaker. "They are waiting for you in the throne room. You know the way, so go straight through. I must be running along. There is no end of work to do." Without another word, he hurried off.

---

1. *Menos HaLevi.*

The gray-bearded man beckoned to his men and set off at a brisk pace. They walked through endless rooms and corridors adorned with colorful paintings and tapestries. Everywhere, servants were removing golden vessels and precious jewels from royal treasure chests and arranging them for public display.

Finally, they reached a small, unobtrusive door. "Here we are," the gray-bearded man said. "The throne room."

"This simple door?" asked one of the men, an apple-cheeked youngster.

"That's right, young fellow," replied another of the men, an extremely thin fellow with a serious look on his face. "The main door is for guests. This one is for Jews like us who come to polish the throne."

"One day, I'll come in through the front door like everyone else," grumbled the fourth man, a rotund redhead. "Just because I'm a Jew doesn't mean I can't get some respect."[2]

"Enough," said the gray-bearded foreman. "Let's get to work."

He opened the door and led them into a dim hallway. One door stood slightly ajar, sunlight streaming through the opening. The youngster reached for the doorknob.

"Wrong door," said the foreman. "Come this way."

"But what's in here?" asked the youngster. He flung open the door and immediately cried out. The others rushed to his side.

For a long moment, they all stood gaping in astonishment.

"I don't believe it," the rotund redhead said at last. "What is this thing?"

The foreman stepped forward for a closer look. "I believe it's Shlomo *Hamelech's* throne," he said reverently. "He supposedly received it as a gift from his father-in-law Sheishak, the Egyptian Pharaoh. Look at this thing! It can't be anything else. Let's get out of here. We have work to do."

"What's the hurry, uncle?" said the thin man with the serious face. "It's early. We have plenty of time. I want to get a good look at this thing. I've never seen anything like it, and I will never again. It is huge!"

The throne indeed towered above them, a structure of majestic beauty decorated with innumerable jewels, pearls and gold inlay. Tall, slender potted date palms on both sides cast soft shadows on

---

2. See *Megillah* 12a, according to both views. See *Tosafos* and *Ben Yehoyada* there; *Einei HaEidah*.

the royal seat. Six steps led up to the throne. On the first, a golden ox and a golden lion crouched menacingly; on the second, a bear and a sheep; on the third, a leopard and a camel; on the fourth, an eagle and a peacock; on the fifth, a cat and a chicken; and on the sixth a young falcon and a dove. Seventy-two golden lions and eagles surrounded the throne.

The rotund redhead edged toward the throne with a surreptitious glance over his shoulder. He started up the steps to the royal seat.

"Where are you going?" snapped the foreman.

"Nobody's looking," he replied. "I'm going to sit down in that seat for a moment. Hey, won't that be something to tell my grand-children? Imagine, I sat on Shlomo *Hamelech's* throne. I'll only be a minute. You can take turns after me." He continued up the steps.

"Stop!" shouted the thin man. "Stop before you get hurt!"

The redhead froze. "W-w-what do you mean?" he stammered.

"Don't you know about this throne?" said the thin man. "Why do you think Achashverosh built himself a new throne when he has this one? About four hundred years ago, after Shlomo passed away, his son Rechavam inherited this throne. Sheishak, the Egyptian Pharaoh, invaded and stripped his treasury bare. He also took back this throne, but when he sat on it, one of the lions bit him in the leg and crippled him. He never fully recov-ered, and from then on, he was known as Pharaoh Necho, the Lame. Eventually, the throne passed into the hands of Nevuchadnezzar, King of Babylon. He also tried to sit on it, and he was also bitten by a lion and crippled. Only the great Cyrus, the second Emperor of the Persian-Medean Empire, the one who ordered the reconstruction of the *Beis HaMikdash*, was able to sit on the throne without coming to harm. Achashverosh has the throne now, but he does not intend to sit on it. He doesn't want to become lame. So, my redheaded friend, do you want to take a chance and sit on it?" He shrugged. "Maybe it only bites kings and emperors. Maybe it won't bother with you. As for me, I'm not taking any chances."

"Neither am I," said the redhead. He spun around and headed down the steps. The man scrambled to his feet and scurried away.

The thin man laughed mirthlessly. "Don't be afraid," he said. "It's not alive. Shlomo *HaMelech* had all these animals and birds set up. When he judged cases, he would have the animals and birds jump up and scream and roar. The litigants and the witnesses were so intimidated that they didn't dare say anything but the truth."[3]

"Amazing," said the youngster. "It's —"

A loud shout interrupted him. "What's going on here?" It was the caretaker. His face was livid. "What are you Jews doing in here? This room is off limits. Get out!"

"We're sorry, sir," said the foreman. "We just took a wrong turn."

"Well, take another turn and get right to work or I'll throw all of you into the dungeon."

The men slipped out silently and went down the dim hallway until they reached the throne room. Achashverosh's new throne stood in the center. It was also incredibly beautiful, but it paled in comparison to Shlomo's throne. Achashverosh had brought the finest artisans in Alexandria and elsewhere and commissioned them to duplicate Shlomo's throne, but try as they might, they could not achieve the same level of beauty and perfection. Still, the new throne was a spectacle to behold in its own right.

As the caretaker had promised, pails of soapy water, rags and oils awaited them. They set to work scrubbing the newly completed throne one section at a time. They wiped away every speck of dust and grime until it gleamed, and then they rubbed in rich oils to give it an opulent luster.

"This is going to be some party," said the youngster. "I wonder what King Achashverosh will be thinking, sitting on this magnificent throne and receiving the delegates from the one hundred and twenty-seven lands of his empire.[4] All these treasures will surely make them feel like ants in front of the mighty king."[5]

"One hundred and twenty-seven lands is not bad," said the thin man, "but it's only half of what he used to have in the beginning of his reign."

"That's right," said the foreman. "Achashverosh began his reign with only seven lands under his control. To these he added twenty more lands and, eventually, another hundred lands until he had one

---

3. *Targum Sheini; Esther Rabbah* 1:12, *Yefei Anaf; Midrash Lekach Tov; Midrash HaGadol; Midrash Panim Acheirim; Midrash Abba Gorion; Aggadas Esther; R' Yosef ibn Nachmiash.* See *Maharal,* who says that Achashverosh wanted the Egyptian magicians to produce a throne like King Solomon's, but was unsuccessful.

4. Eshter became queen over 127 lands in the merit of her ancestor the Matriarch Sarah, who lived 127 years (*Esther Rabbah* 1:8; *Midrash HaGadol* 23:1).

5. See pg. 6.

hundred and twenty-seven lands; some people say that the twenty-seven are actually island nations. Each of these three stages was as difficult as either of the others. By ruling over these nations he also gained control over the lands that adjoined each of them, for a total of two hundred and fifty-two lands. He ruled the world.[6] The saying goes that he rules over one hundred and twenty-seven lands from India to Ethiopia. That means both ways: from India directly to Ethiopia, and also around the circumference of the earth all the way to Ethiopia, thus covering the entire world."[7]

"And he did all this from right here in Shushan?" asked the youngster.

"No, he didn't," said the foreman. "The capital used to be in Babylon, the original capital of the Babylonian Empire. After he lost half his kingdom, Achashverosh moved the seat of the imperial government to Shushan, renaming it Shushan *HaBirah*, Shushan the Capital."[8]

"But why did he make the switch?" asked the youngster.

"It's really quite simple," said the foreman. "Achashverosh wanted all the glory for himself. He did not want to rule in the shadow of the illustrious Babylonian Empire. By moving the capital to Shushan, he felt he had severed the connection in the public perception. He felt he would be recognized and admired for his own achievements. This was very important to him, especially after he lost half his empire."[9]

"Tell us, uncle," said the youngster, "what do the rabbis say? Why did he lose half his kingdom?"[10]

The foreman stroked his gray beard. "Do you know Achashverosh's background, young fellow? Do you know that he stopped the reconstruction of the *Beis HaMikdash*?"

---

6. There are many approaches to reconciling the *gemara* with the *midrash*; it would seem that if Achashverosh was king over the entire world, then he did not rule over only 127 countries. Furthermore, many ask when the 127 were conquered – before or after his loss of half the world? Perhaps the 127 countries *were* the entire world at the time. For clarity's sake, one interpretation has been followed; however, the reader may wish to consider other opinions.

7. *Megillah* 11; see *Menos HaLevi; R' Yosef ibn Nachmiash; Sefer Aruch*, letter 20. *Esther Rabbah* 1:5; *Rokeach* to Esther 1:1; *Taanis* 10a, and *Pirkei d'Rav Eliezer* 11. See *Midrash HaGadol; Me'am Loez.* See also how *Yad HaMelech* explains the *gemara's* argument. Some suggest that there were two places called Hodu and two called Kush (*Tzuf Devash*). R' *Yaakov Emden* relates that he knows of a place that Arabs call Kush that is near Hodu.

8. *Me'am Loez;* see *Rabbeinu Bachai* to Esther 2:5.

9. *Malbim* to Esther 1:2. As will be discussed in later chapters, this was an issue of contention that disturbed Vashti greatly. This would eventually lead to her insolence towards Achashverosh and ultimately her downfall (see *Maharal*).

10. *Megillas Sesarim* 1:2; *Esther Rabbah* 1:5; *Menos HaLevi.*

The youngster fidgeted. "I didn't really pay so much attention when my father told me about it. I was too busy with my friends and games. But here in the palace of the king everything seems so important. Who knows? We may even see the king today. Would you tell us about him?"

"The story really begins fifty-five years ago, in the year 3338 from the creation of the world, when Nevuchadnezzar destroyed the *Beis HaMikdash* and drove the Jewish people into exile in Babylon. Twenty-six years later, in 3364, Nevuchadnezzar died and was succeeded by his son Eveel Merodach. Twenty-three years later, in 3387, Eveel Merodach was succeeded by his son Belshazzar. Two years later, in 3389, Belshazzar lost his life and his empire on the same night."[11]

"Really?" said the youngster. "What happened?"

"Let's backtrack a few years. While the kings ruled their empire in Babylon, two new powers were rising in the east. One was Persia, the great land in which we live, the other was Medea. What I'm about to tell you is not corroborated by eyewitness reports. Some people claim it is only legend. But it is interesting in any case. There was once a Persian king named Astyages. He had a daughter named Mandane who befriended one of the king's courtiers. The furious king killed the courtier and threw his daughter into prison, where she gave birth to a son.

"The king wanted the child to die, but he couldn't bring himself to do it directly. Instead, he gave the order that the child should be left exposed on a mountaintop where it would die in a matter of hours. Miraculously, a dog found the baby and suckled him. The child survived on the mountaintop and grew into a powerful warrior. As he grew older, he drew other warriors to his side until he had his own army. Since he had been raised by a dog, they called him Koresh, which is, as you know, Persian for dog. The Greeks called him Cyrus."

"Hey, isn't he the king who sat on Shlomo *HaMelech's* throne?" asked the youngster. "How did he get to be king?"

"Not bad, young fellow," said the thin man sarcastically. "That's right," said the foreman. "It is one and the same Cyrus. When Astyages, his grandfather, heard he was alive, he sent soldiers to kill him. Cyrus routed the king's soldiers, marched on the capital, killed his grandfather and assumed the throne of Persia. The neighboring kingdom of Medea

---

11. See *Megillah* 11b; *Seder Olam* 25, 28; see *Radak* in *Melachim* II 24:1, 12, 15, and 25:8; see *Daniel* 5:25-30; *Me'am Loez*.

was ruled by King Darius. Cyrus and Darius forged an alliance that was sealed when Cyrus married Darius' daughter. Together, they invaded Babylon in 3389 and conquered it, killing Belshazzar, the last king of Babylon. That was the end of the Babylonian Empire and the beginning of the Persian-Medean.[12] Darius and Cyrus agreed to share power by taking turns; when one held the throne, the other was governor, and vice versa.[13] Darius was the first king. When he died in 3390, Cyrus took the crown. One of the first things he did as emperor was authorize the reconstruction of the *Beis HaMikdash*."

"As Yeshayahu had prophesied," said the thin man.

"Indeed," agreed the foreman as he stroked his gray beard. "Indeed. And he prophesied it a century before it happened. I know the words by heart. 'So said God to His anointed one, to Cyrus whose right hand I held . . . I lifted him up with righteousness, I will straighten all his ways. He shall build My city and free My exiles.' My mother had me memorize these words as a young boy so that I would not despair of ever seeing the rebuilt *Beis HaMikdash*. We had never even heard of Cyrus then."

"So what happened with Cyrus?" asked the youngster. "Why isn't the *Beis HaMikdash* built yet?"

"Good question," said the foreman. "Things started out well. A small group led by Daniel and Mordechai went to *Yerushalayim* first. Zerubavel, a scion of the Davidic dynasty, and Yehoshua ben Yehotzadak followed soon afterward, and construction began. Cyrus himself traveled to the construction site to return the holy vessels Nevuchadnezzar had stolen from the *Beis HaMikdash*."

"How about Ezra?" asked the youngster. "Did he go, too?"

"No, he didn't," said the foreman. "He was afraid his Torah learning would suffer if he left his teacher, Baruch ben Neriah. Many others were also reluctant to make the journey, discouraged by the poverty and desolation that characterized *Eretz Yisrael* at the time and by fear of the hostile peoples who had moved into their vacated homes and towns. They saw the first stirrings of reconstruction as a sign of heavenly favor but not of imminent redemption."

"So what stopped the reconstruction?" asked the youngster.

"Intrigue, lies, intimidation. The Samaritans, or the Kuthim if you please, sent a delegation to Cyrus accusing the Jews of plotting to

---

12. See *Sefer Yuchsin; Seder HaDoros; Shalsheles HaKabbalah* and *Me'am Loez*.
13. *Megillah* 12a.

rebel and of not paying their fair share of taxes. At the same time, they threatened the Jews with physical violence. Cyrus gave in to the pressure. He allowed the Jews who had gone up to *Yerushalayim* to stay there, but he called a halt to further emigration. This was a serious blow to the reconstruction. There simply were not enough people to complete it. In 3393, one year later, he died and was succeeded by his son — our very own beloved King Achashverosh."[14]

3315	Yehoyakim becomes king of Yehudah.
3319	Nevuchadnezzar assumes the throne of Babylon. He subjugates the Kingdom of Yehudah, makes it into a vassal state and exiles its king and the elite.
3327	Yechanyah becomes the Jewish king. Nebuchadnezzar exiles him.
3338	Nevuchadnezzar destroys the *Beis HaMikdash*. King Tzidkiah and the Jewish nation are exiled.
3364	Nevuchadnezzar dies and is succeeded by his son Evil Merodach.
3387	Belshazzar becomes King of Babylon.
3389	Belshazzar dates the "seventy years" of Yirmiah's prophecy from the beginning of the Babylonian Empire. He is, therefore, elated that they have passed without incident. On his night of celebration, Darius I attacks, kills Belshazzar and conquers Babylon. Vashti, Belshazzar's daughter, is twelve years old.
3390	Darius dies. Cyrus becomes King of Persia-Medea. Cyrus orders the reconstruction of the *Beis HaMikdash* seventy years after Nevuchadnezzar's conquest of King Yehoyakim and Yehudah.
3393	Achashverosh becomes king and halts the reconstruction.
3395	Achashverosh makes the great feast; the Jews are not redeemed from exile.
3399	Esther becomes queen.
3400	Darius II is born to Esther and Achashverosh.
3406	Achashverosh dies and is succeeded by Darius II.
3408	Darius II orders the reconstruction of the Second *Beis HaMikdash*; seventy years from the destruction of the first *Beis HaMikdash*.

---

14. See *Maharsha* to *Yoma* 9b; *Shir HaShirim Rabbah* 5:4, 8:9; *Maharsha* to *Megillah* 12a and 16a; *Rashi* to *Pesachim* 87a.

The rotund redhead scratched his head. "Why do you say he is beloved? We don't love him. In my neighborhood, they make a pun of his name and say '*Ach larosh*, woe to my head.' The taxes he imposed on us are driving everyone into the poorhouse. On top of that, he stopped the reconstruction."[15]

"Yes, he did," said the foreman. "The rabbis also used those words as a pun, '*Ach larosh*,' but they translated them as 'brother to the head.' Nevuchadnezzar was the head of the kings, a killer who destroyed the *Beis HaMikdash*. Achashverosh is his brother in evil; he also seeks to kill Jews and destroy the *Beis HaMikdash*.[16] It started from the very beginning, when Achashverosh ascended to the throne. The Samaritans and that rascal Haman, the fellow with a whole bunch of sons, wrote Achashverosh a clever letter accusing the Jews of disloyalty. Haman's son Shimshai is a clever scribe, and he made it seem as if he was interested in promoting peace and harmony in the empire. Achashverosh liked what he heard, but he still wasn't too sure about what to do."

"So why did he decide to stop the reconstruction?" asked the youngster.

"Queen Vashti, his eighteen-year-old bride, persuaded him to do it. She is the daughter of Belshazzar, the Babylonian king who died on the night Babylon fell, the great-granddaughter of Nevuchadnezzar, the one who destroyed the *Beis HaMikdash*. 'Why are you building up,' she asked, 'what my ancestors tore down?' With the support of the haughty queen, Achashverosh issued the decree that put an end to the reconstruction."

"Tell me, uncle," said the thin man, "what do the rabbis say? Why wasn't the *Beis HaMikdash* rebuilt? Didn't the prophet say Cyrus would rebuild it?"

"The rabbis were upset with Cyrus for sending others but not taking part in the reconstruction himself. They were also upset with the Jews who failed to unite for the difficult task of reconstruction. In the opinion of the rabbis, a golden opportunity for redemption was missed."[17]

---

15. See *Maharsha* to *Megillah* 11a; *Me'am Loez* 1:1.
Some suggest that Achashverosh was actually a good king. He was good-hearted by nature and a man of good intentions, but his foolish and gullible character allowed him to be manipulated by others. This influence led to the references to Achashverosh as a wicked Jew-hater, based on his actions towards them (*Eshkol HaKofer, Tzuf Devash*).

16. *Maharsha* to *Megillah* 11a; *Me'am Loez* 1:1; see *Midrash HaGadol* to *Esther* 1:1.

17. *Seder Olam* ch. 29; *Yalkut Shimoni* 1049; *Eliyahu Rabbah* 20; *Yeshayahu* ch. 45; *Daniel* ch. 9; *Ezra* ch. 2, 4 and *Ralbag's* commentary. For further discussion of this matter, see

"How do you know so much?" asked the redhead.

The foreman was about to answer, but he suddenly stood still. He put his finger to his lips to signal the others to be absolutely silent. Then he stepped to the door and listened intently.

"Quick!" he said. "Everyone back to work. I hear footsteps approaching – many of them."

The men grabbed their oil-soaked rags and went back to shining the already gleaming throne. Moments later, a dozen helmeted palace guards marched into the throne room. With a disdainful glance at the four Jewish laborers, they ran a thorough inspection, then they left the room and assumed positions on either side of the door.

In the silence that followed, the four men heard the stamping of heavy feet accompanied by the clank of armor and the rich rustle of silk and satin. Then he appeared, the mighty King Achashverosh himself, a hulking bear-like figure of a man, with bushy eyebrows and a glowering scowl.[18] Two fawning courtiers ran alongside him, holding up the hems of his robe, bowing incessantly and offering to bring him food, drink or anything else his hungry royal heart might desire.

Walking past the Jewish laborers as if they did not exist, the king strode to the throne and ran his hands lovingly over the opulent carvings.

"It looks just about ready," he growled to his courtiers.

"Oh, yes, your majesty, yes," they replied in unison. "It is truly perfect."

"Come, we have to go to the kitchen to check on the preparations for the great feast. I want all my subjects to know that I am giving my personal attention to every detail. It is very important."

"Oh, yes, your majesty, yes," they replied in unison. "It is truly very important."

He glared at the two courtiers, and the blood drained from their faces. He turned to go, and the courtiers snatched up the hems of his robe just as he stamped out of the room.

"Well," said the thin man as soon as they were alone again, "I suppose we should consider ourselves fortunate. Not everyone is privileged to be in the same room with our glorious king."[19]

---

18. See *Megillah* 11a; *Daniel* 7:5; *Krovetz L'Purim*.

19. See *Esther Rabbah* 1:15, 16, 19, 20; *Radal; Yefai Anaf; Megillah* 12a; *Midrash Megillas Esther; Rokeach; Rambam* to *Esther; Rishon LeTzion; Midrash Panim Acheirim; Yalkut Shimoni* 1048; *Yad HaMelech.*

"He doesn't look like a king to me," said the youngster. "He looks more like a bear or a horse trader."[20]

"Interesting that you should say that," said the foreman. "No one is really sure who exactly Achashverosh is. Most believe he is the son of Cyrus, as I told you before. Others think he is the son of Darius.[21] Still others think he is not of the royal blood. You see, Nevuchadnezzar loaded all his treasures onto ships, took them out to sea and had them scuttled. For many years, his treasure sat at some unknown spot on the bottom of the sea. But then Achashverosh managed to find the treasure, and through well-placed bribes, he catapulted himself to the throne."

"I also heard that he is a commoner," said the redhead, "but nothing about Nevuchadnezzar's treasures. Just that he was chosen king because he is more qualified for the position than anyone else.[22] Others say he was chosen because he is a great warrior."[23]

Said the thin man. "If anyone could overhear us, we'd be in trouble for more than half the things we said here today. Having said that, let me add my own little rumor. I heard his father was one of Belshazzar's stable attendants. Can you imagine? A stable boy becomes king?"[24]

"I heard Achashverosh is a fool," said the youngster.

"A fool who can have you killed at any time," said the thin man. "Don't underestimate his abilities and power."

"All right, all right," said the foreman. "Let's bring this thing to a close. Most people would agree that Achashverosh is an ambitious fool. Most people, whether they live close to Shushan or far away, would also agree that he wields tremendous power, and that he strikes equal fear in all their hearts."[25]

---

20. See *Rokeach*; *R' Yosef ibn Yachia*. See *Rinas Yitzchak* for his view.

21. *Yalkut Shimoni* 1049; *Me'am Loez*. It is a matter of debate whether Nevuchadnezzar was Vashti's grandfather or great-grandfather. See *Megillah* 10b, which states the view that she was his granddaughter. See also *Midrash Abba Gorion*; *Esther Rabbah* and *Midrash Panim Acheirim*. *Targum Sheni* and *Seder Olam* suggest that Belshazzar was the son of Eveel Merodach, who was the son of Nevuchadnezzar. Since Vashti was Belshazzar's daughter, according to this she was Nevuchadnezzar's great-grand-daughter. Some reconcile the differences of opinion regarding Vashti's background by explaining that referring to Vashti as Nevuchadnezzar's granddaughter merely means that she was a descendant of his, but she was in fact his great-granddaughter.

22. *Megillah* 11a; *Rashi* to *Esther* 1:1; *Midrash Megillas Esther*; *Esther Rabbah* 2:1; *Matnos Kehunah*. Others suggest that Cyrus found the vast treasure of 680 copper vessels full of gold and precious gems which Nevuchadnezzar had hidden, and this wealth was inherited by Achashverosh. Cyrus merited this treasure for attempting to rebuild the *Beis HaMikdash* (see *Targum Rishon* 1:4).

23. *Yad HaMelech*; *Eshkol HaKofer*.

24. *Esther* 1:1, *Rokeach*; *R' Yosef ibn Yachia*.

25. *Ma'amar Mordechai*; *Shemen HaMaor*.

The Imperial Feast

2

The great feast was a spectacle such as the empire had never seen. The king invited the princes, nobles, governors, legislators, officials, bureaucrats and military officers from Persia, Medea and all the other lands of the empire, near and far, and of course, everyone the king invited came to the feast.[1] He showed special favor to his own aristocracy, but he also showed great honor to the dignitaries of the lands he had conquered in hard-fought wars from Hodu (India) to Kush (Ethiopia). In addition, he circulated among all his guests and mingled with them, seeking to reinforce the loyalty of his subjects to the crown and ensure their eagerness to serve in his wars of conquest.[2]

---

1. *Esther Rabbah* 1:16, 19, 20; *Radal*; *Yefei Anaf*; *Megillah* 12a; *Midrash Megillas Esther*; *Rokeach*; *Rambam* to *Esther*; *Rishon LeTzion*; *Midrash Panim Acheirim*; *Yalkut Shimoni* 1048; *Yad HaMelech*.

2. *Yad HaMelech*; *Eshkol HaKofer*; *Esther* 1:3; *Dana Pishra*; *Megillah* 12a. Others are of the opinion that foreigners were invited to come first and were honored more than local guests. See *Maharsha* and *Iyun Yaakov* for further explanation. There are various opinions regarding where Achashverosh sat at the feast. See *Midrash Panim Acheirim*; *Menos HaLevi* 1:3; *Yishai Elokim*; *Yad HaMelech*; *Yedei Moshe*; *Dana Pishra*.

For one hundred and eighty days, the king entertained his guests. His astrologers had told him that his fortunes would last for a very long time, and that in order to extend his fortune even further he should display his wealth for exactly one hundred and eighty days. Moreover, Achashverosh believed a display of wealth for such a lengthy period of time would show he was master over both the physical and spiritual worlds, over the earth, the heavens and all the celestial denizens.[3]

Achashverosh was so rich that money no longer meant anything to him, but he cared deeply about honor. He decided to use the display of his wealth to increase his honor manifold. He began the exhibition in the spring, when the days are long enough for extensive public viewing.[4] Each day featured a different display of six treasure chests filled with gold, silver and precious gems, for a total of one thousand and eighty chests of priceless treasure. Reportedly, each of these chests contained thirty golden vessels, for a total of five thousand four hundred golden vessels, the exact number of vessels removed from the *Beis HaMikdash*.[5] Afterwards, while he had new treasures displayed for the morrow, he ordered the treasures of the day brought into the street for the local populace to admire. There were also exhibits celebrating the victories of his army and cavalry and the enormous royal wealth throughout the one hundred and twenty-seven lands of his empire.[6]

Achashverosh divided the spectacle into six monthly themes. During the first month, he gave the people a measure of his overall wealth; during the second, he introduced his ministers and dignitaries; during the third, he showcased presents he had received from the subject kings of his empire; during the fourth, he displayed historic documents, rare scrolls and scholarly works; during the fifth, he showed off all his jewels; during the sixth, he showed off other special treasures and beautiful works of art.[7]

---

3. *Megillas Sesarim* 1:4; *Maharal. Ma'amar Mordechai, Yedei Moshe.*

4. *Pirkei d'Rav Eliezer* 49; *Menos HaLevi; Midrash Lekach Tov; Ya'aros Devash; Yad HaMelech.* The *Menos HaLevi* suggests that it was six months plus three days, in order to compensate for the three days when the Jewish people did not participate in the feast: 17 Tammuz, 9 Av and 10 Tishrei, Yom Kippur. Clearly, this view holds that the Jews attended the 180-day feast as well. See *R' Shmuel di Uzida* and *Chasam Sofer*, who suggest that the party began in Tishrei and lasted throughout the winter, followed by the seven-day party in the spring. Some suggest that Achashverosh purposely arranged it so that the final day of the feast was 10 Tishrei; his intention was to prevent the Jews from repenting on Yom Kippur so that Hashem would not forgive them (*Midrash Eliyahu*).

5. *Yalkut Shimoni* 1046; *Shemos Rabbah* 9:7 and commentaries; *Gra* 1:4; *Midrash Abba Gorion, Ya'aros Devash;* see *Targum Sheini* 1:4.

6. *Midrash HaGadol; Pirkei d'Rav Eliezer* 49, see *Radal, Shemos Rabbah* 9:7.

7. *Aggadas Esther* 1:4.

No expense was spared to provide pleasure for the king's guests. The celebration was one long party that lasted one hundred and eighty days without the slightest let-up in the lavish food and beverages; there was as much food on the last day as on the first. Furthermore, the menu was changed every single day and never repeated.[8] The cost of each individual day was equal to what an ordinary king would have spent on a royal party lasting fully one hundred and eighty days. Multiply this amount by one hundred and eighty, and we arrive at a stunning piece of information. An ordinary king would have spent this amount of money on a party lasting thirty-two thousand four hundred days - yet Achashverosh spent it on his guests in just one hundred and eighty days! It was an incredible performance that intimidated the people with the king's mighty power and, at the same time, drew them into the king's good graces.[9]

One day, in a corner of the palace far from the noisy crowd, a group of ministers and prominent personages from across the empire gathered in a brightly lit meeting hall. They did not know the purpose of the meeting, only that it was of utmost importance to the king. A hush fell over the assembly as Achashverosh lumbered into the room and took his seat at the head of the table.

An old minister with a bushy white mustache was the first to address the gathering. "With your majesty's permission," he began with a deferential bow to the king, "I would like to give our guests some background to the historic event taking place in the royal palace. It is now the third year of your most gracious majesty's reign, and it is a time for great celebration in the empire."

He let his gaze sweep over his audience before he continued.

"Our beloved king has brought security, stability and lasting peace to the empire. By his great prowess on the battlefield, he has coalesced all our lands into one mighty empire with one integrated economy and one final arbiter of the law. We have much for which to be grateful."

There was polite applause, and the minister continued.

"Today is the king's birthday. From the depths of our hearts, we all wish him continued glory and success, and much happiness in

---

8. *Alshich; Ma'amar Mordechai, Esther Rabbah* 2:3. Others suggest that Achashverosh divided the party into 18 sessions of 10 days each. At each session various nations participated in the feast. Shushan would be the final one, as he saved his local constituents for last (see *Me'am Loez*).

9. *Pirkei d'Rav Eliezer* 49; *Dana Pishra, Menos HaLevi, Mas'as Moshe* 1:3.

his marriage to Queen Vashti, the illustrious descendant of the Babylonian royal house. Let us show him our good wishes."[10]

All the assembled jumped to their feet, clapping their hands until they rubbed them raw, and cheered wildly, "Long live the king! Long live King Achashverosh!"

The king beamed at them and smiled. He lifted his massive right hand, hairy and bejeweled, and silence was immediately restored.

"My good people," Achashverosh began, "each of you assembled here in this room was selected because of his position of power and influence. This group here is the elite of my empire, and I am relying on you to help me bring peace and prosperity to all our citizens. I want you to know that one of my main reasons for hosting this celebration was to bring this group together and address the important issues of the realm. We will discuss matters of security and military preparedness as well as matters of finance, tax collection and the imperial budget. But there is one overriding issue that concerns me. I would have brought you all together just for this matter alone.

"I want to talk about the Jews," said the king.[11]

There was an audible gasp in the chamber.

"Yes, the Jews," said the king. "They are a dangerous people, untrustworthy, conniving, rebellious. But there is one problem. They have a very powerful God. When He comes to their assistance, they are invincible. All our gods together can do nothing. But when He turns away from them, that is when we can strike.

"My astrologers have told me something disturbing. They have looked at the stars and divined that a Jew will take my crown, sit on my throne and rule as king. Clearly, they are plotting a rebellion against me. They want to take over the empire and rule over all of you. But I will not let them do it. I will crush them and stamp them out, until they are no longer a threat to the empire. But I need your help."

The king fell silent, and instantly the chamber was abuzz with enraged outcries. The king signaled the minister with the bushy mustache, who immediately rose to his feet. He raised his hands to call for silence, but in the rising crescendo of voices, he was ignored.

---

10. *Ibn Ezra; Ma'amar Mordechai.* There are differing views on when Achashverosh got married. Some suggest it was in the first year of his reign; the wedding feast was made three years later. Others suggest he had just recently married. For further insight see *Esther Rabbah 1:15; Etz Yosef; Maharzu; Yefei Anaf; Radal; Targum Rishon; Yad HaMelech; Megillas Sesarim; Rabbeinu Bachyei.*

11. *Midrash Panim Acheirim; Menos HaLevi.*

The minister climbed onto his chair and waved his hands for attention. "Please, gentlemen!" he shouted. "His majesty wants me to tell you important information."

Slowly, the noise subsided to a murmur and then disappeared altogether.

"Gentlemen, gentlemen," said the minister, "I understand your outrage — believe me, I do. But we won't get anywhere unless we deal with the problem with cool logic. That is the point of this conference. His majesty wants to hear your ideas and suggestions. Then we will discuss them and come to a decision. We need a plan that works. Anger alone is not enough."

There was a rumble of approval, and the minister continued.

"As his majesty said, we must be concerned about the God of the Jews. The prophets of the Jews carry His messages, and they always come true. We are well aware of those prophecies, and our wise men study them and seek to interpret them. Even with a prophecy, you see, it can happen that the Jews will ruin it for themselves. We look for indications that the Jews have lost favor and are vulnerable. Does everyone understand?"[12]

A ripple of nods ran around the chamber.

"Good, good. Now then, you all know about the stormy relations between the Kingdom of Yehudah and the Babylonian Empire. In the Jewish year 3319, Nevuchadnezzar conquered the Jewish kingdom and made it a vassal state. In 3327, Yechaniah became King of Yehudah. Nevuchadnezzar sent him into exile in Babylon, and replaced him with Tzidkiyahu. Without going into all the politics and intrigue, it didn't work out. In 3338, Nevuchadnezzar sacked Yerushalayim, destroyed the Temple and carried off the population into captivity."

The minister paused to stroke his mustache and gather his thoughts.

"Now, here is the crux of the matter, my friends. We were talking about prophecy. The Jews had a prophet named Yirmiyahu, a great seer who wrote a whole book of prophecies."

"Is he still alive?" asked a tall dark man in a pearl-studded turban.

"No, he's not," said the minister with the mustache. "He would have been very, very old today if he had survived, but he didn't.

---

12. See *Targum Rishon*; *Megillas Sesarim*; *Esther Rabbah* 7:13, 14; *Ya'aros Devash*; *Einei HaEidah*; *R' Yosef ibn Yachia, Pirkei d'Rav Eliezer*; *Megillas Sesarim*. The Jewish nation would deserve to be killed if they celebrated at the feast, or, as others suggest, sinned by worshipping idols. See *Midrash Eliyahu* for a detailed explanation.

"Well, let me tell you about his prophecy in the year 3331. I'm going to recite it from memory, so don't hold me to the exact accuracy of the text. He said in the name of his God, 'This land shall lay in desolation and waste, and these nations surrounding the Land of Israel shall serve the king of Babylon for seventy years. But when the seventy years come to an end, I will punish the king of Babylon and that nation . . .' The understanding was that in seventy years the Temple would be rebuilt. But when do the seventy years begin? What does it sound like? Well, to me it sounds like seventy years from the Babylonian conquest, which took place in the first year of the Babylonian Empire. That's what the Babylonian wise men also thought, and they waited anxiously to see what would happen."

"Well, Nevuchadnezzar died after forty-five years on the throne. His son Eveel Merodach reigned for twenty-three years, and his son Belshazzar succeeded him — sixty-eight years after the establishment of the Babylonian Empire.[13] Belshazzar was nervous, because he thought he had only two years left to reign. When the two years passed without incident, he was convinced the Jews had been abandoned by their God. Jubilant, he made a great feast, and that very night Darius stormed into the city and put him and his empire to death. The Jews are convinced that Belshazzar died because he defiled the vessels of the Temple. Personally, I have my doubts, but all that is neither here nor there."

"So when did the seventy years of the prophecy begin?" asked a man in a scarlet robe.

"Our wise men are convinced it began eight years later, when Nevuchadnezzar carried off King Yechanyah into exile. These additional eight years came to an end last year. And behold, nothing has happened. In fact, the Jews have suffered a reversal. Koresh had let them do some construction on a new Temple, but our beloved king stopped it completely. And look around you. Has the sky fallen down? Has the ocean risen up to flood our cities? Have wild beasts invaded our beautiful, flower-bedecked capital of Shushan? Have locusts devoured the rich agricultural lands that surround the city? No, no, no and no. Everything is

---

13. See *Metzudas David* to *Yirmiyahu* 25:1,2 and 29:10. See *Shir HaShirim Rabbah* 5:4, 8:9, *Megillah* 11b, 12a; *Rashi* to *Esther* 9:10; *Rashi* to *Megillah* 16a; *Maharsha* and *Rashi* to *Pesachim* 87a; *Seder Olam* ch. 29; *Yalkut Shimoni* 1049, *Eliyahu Rabbah* 20; *Yeshayahu* ch. 45; *Daniel* ch. 9; *Ezra* ch. 2, 4, with *Ralbag*.

wonderful. At last, the Jews are at our mercy. The time has come to strike."[14]

The man in scarlet rose to his feet.

"With your majesty's permission," he began, and bowed to Achashverosh.

Achashverosh inclined his head a fraction of an inch. His expression remained completely inscrutable.

"If I may take the liberty to ask a question," said the man in scarlet. "I am somewhat puzzled. There are not that many Jews in the empire, and those that do live there are unarmed and helpless. Arrayed against them is the mightiest empire on earth. Perhaps the mightiest empire in the history of the world. The Jews are trouble, we all know that. So why don't we just wipe them out, and that will be the end of it? I'm afraid I don't understand."

He sat down to a murmur of assent.

Achashverosh leaned forward and pointed his finger at the man in scarlet. "Stand up."

The man scrambled to his feet, but his knees trembled so violently that he had to lean on the table to keep from falling. His face, especially in contrast to his scarlet robes, had gone completely white.

"What do you know about the Jews?" Achashverosh asked.

"N-n-not very m-much."

"I didn't think so." Achashverosh waved his hand. "Sit down."

The man slumped into his chair, his eyes glued to the ground.

"I'll tell you about the Jews," said Achashverosh. "A thousand years ago, their God just about destroyed Egypt, because the Egyptians had enslaved the Jews. He also destroyed the Canaanite people and gave their land to the Jews. As I told you, it is impossible to fight against this God. If we just attack the Jews, even if we inflict a lot of damage, their God will destroy us. No, we have to outsmart Him. That is our task here tonight. The seventy years have passed. They've apparently lost favor with Him. Belshazzar miscalculated the seventy years. He thought they began with the establishment of the Babylonian Empire. When the seventy years passed quietly, he got cocky, and he paid for it with his life. I know better. I know that the seventy years started with the conquest of Yehudah. Well, seventy years have passed since the conquest, and the Jews are

---

14. *Megillah* 11; *Daniel* 7:5; *Krovetz L'Purim.* See *Esther Rabbah* 1-15.

still in exile. The Jewish God has apparently reneged on His promise to them. We are secure."[15]

"Then what is the problem, your majesty?" asked the man in scarlet.

Achashverosh frowned. "We mustn't become overconfident. It wouldn't be wise to risk a frontal assault against them. We don't know what's going through their God's mind. Maybe He isn't ready to rebuild the Temple but still won't tolerate an attack that threatens their destruction. We need plans, ideas, cleverness. That's why you're all here. Now, let's hear some ideas!"

A deep silence greeted his words. No one stirred. The minister with the white mustache looked around. His gaze settled on the man in scarlet, but he was obviously useless. He pointed to the man with the pearl-studded turban. "You, sir," he said. "Do you have anything to offer? Questions and comments are easy, but what about ideas? Do you have ideas?"

"I have ideas," the man replied, "but they are not fully formed. It would be unseemly to present half-baked ideas in front of his majesty. But I am thinking. I am still thinking."

"I as well," shouted another.

"And I," shouted yet another.

The king tapped on the arm of his chair, his nose scrunched with scorn.

"Has no one anything to offer?" asked the minister with the mustache.

Silence.

"No one?"

A middle-aged man dressed in severe black from head to toe rose to his feet. He bowed to the king. "Your majesty," he murmured.

"Ah, a response at last," said Achashverosh. "Haman, my dear advisor, have you something of value to offer?"

"I believe I do, your majesty. Yes, I believe I do." He rubbed his hands together with relish and squinted. "I have a plan, your majesty, a plan that I believe will work."

"Well, spit it out, Haman," said Achashverosh. "Don't keep it a secret. Speak up, man. We are eager to hear it."

---

15. In truth, Achashverosh was also mistaken. The seventy years did not begin from the conquest of Yehudah but from the destruction of the *Beis HaMikdash*. Daniel had said an earlier prophecy (*Daniel* 9:2), "In the first year of the reign of [Darius II], I, Daniel studied in the books that the number of years about which the word of God had come to the prophet Yirmiyah, to complete the seventy years from the destruction of Yerushalayim."

Haman drew himself to his full height and smiled. Again, he rubbed his hands together and squinted. "My plan is simple, your majesty, if I say so myself. I say we do nothing."

His words were greeted by a mixture of laughter and dismay.

"This is an idea?" said the man in the turban.

This elicited even more uproarious laughter. Haman also roared with delight, too absorbed in his own cleverness to take offense.

"That's right," said Haman when the laughter subsided. "I think we should do nothing. We shouldn't lift a finger against them."

Achashverosh, smiling in spite of himself, pointed his finger. "All right, Haman. You've had your fun with your clever little private idea. Now it's time to share it with us."

"Yes, your majesty," said Haman, suddenly serious. "Forgive me. Our wise men have conducted long-term studies of the Jewish people and have constructed statistical models that have provided invaluable data. There seems to be a very strong statistical correlation between Jewish sin and divine disfavor. It seems that whenever they perform sinful acts, their God either punishes them or at the very least removes His protection from them. As you yourself have pointed out, your majesty, look at the unfulfilled prophecy of the reconstruction of the Temple. They stepped over the line, their God forsook them. That's the way it seems to work."

"True, true," said Achashverosh. "Continue, my good Haman. I like it. I think you're onto something. Proceed."

"Yes, your majesty. Thank you for the encouragement. I believe my idea is brilliant, if I say so myself."

"Well, go on, go on," said Achashverosh impatiently.

"Yes, your majesty. My humble apologies, your majesty. This is my idea. After the celebration is over, perhaps your majesty would invite all the residents of Shushan to a special seven-day celebration exclusively for the residents of the capital city, including all the numerous Jews who live here. We will be very hospitable to them, so hospitable that we will offer them enticements and delights that they never imagined in their lives. Most, if not all of them, will not be able to resist. They will sink irresistibly into the sea of pleasures we offer them. And in the process, they will desecrate their Sabbath, they will eat forbidden foods and they will act inappropriately with the enticements we will provide for their enjoyment. I believe their God hates immorality more than any-

thing else. So we have to lead them down the path to immorality."
Haman looked around the chamber and squinted. "We will drown
them in a sea of enticements and thereby drive a wedge between
them and their God. They will be left defenseless, and then they
will be ours."

Haman bowed to the king and to the assembled dignitaries. As he
sat down, they all applauded.

"Quite a brilliant idea, Haman," said Achashverosh. "I like it."
And a broad smile spread over his bearish face.[16]

---

16. See *Targum Rishon, Megilas Sesarim, Esther Rabbah* 7:13, 14, *Ya'aros Devash, Einei HaEidah, R' Yosef ibn Yachia, Pirkei d'Rav Eliezer.*

Mordechai the Jew

3

Haman harbored in his heart a profound hate for the Jewish people, a hate that stretched back all the way to his ancestor Amalek a thousand years earlier. But ever since embarking on a fateful military expedition to India on behalf of the king, he also came to hold a special personal hatred for the Jews. Specifically, he despised the great Jewish leader known as Mordechai *HaYehudi*, Mordechai the Jew, who came down to Babylon with King Yechanyah's group eleven years before the destruction of the Temple.[1]

Mordechai was an important counselor to the king, although not surprisingly he was not invited to the special conference on the fate of the Jews. The title *HaYehudi* would seem to imply that Mordechai was descended from the tribe of Yehudah, but this was

---

1. See *Targum Rishon; Targum Sheini; Aggadas Esther* to *Esther* 2:6; *Megillah* 13a with *Rashi; Rif; Iyun Yaakov.* For different views on how many times Mordechai was exiled see *Midrash Panim Acheirim; R' Chaim Abulafia; R' Elisha Galico; Gra.* See *Rashi* and *Tosafos* to *Menachos* 64b for a complex discussion of the time frame in which Mordechai lived (*Biurim V'Likutim al Megillas Esther, Gavriel Yosef Levi*).

not so. He was the son of Yair, the grandson of Kish, a descendant
of the tribe of Binyamin. Mordechai was such an illustrious sage that
the tribes of Yehudah and Binyamin both sought to take credit for
him.[2]

The members of Yehudah liked to compare Mordechai to the
patriarch and namesake of their tribe who was willing to become a
slave in place of his younger brother Binyamin when he was
accused of theft in Egypt. They also saw Mordechai as a potential
redeemer of the Jews and therefore called him Yehudi with great
pride. They also pointed to his coming from the Kingdom of
Yehudah together with King Yechaniah as a reason for that title.
There was also another reason for this title.[3]

Centuries before, Mordechai's ancestor Shimi ben Geira of the
tribe of Binyamin had cursed David HaMelech. Avishai, David's
general, wanted to draw his sword and kill Shimi on the spot, but
David stopped him. Prophetically, David foresaw that future
redeemers of the Jewish people were destined to descend from
Shimi. Many years later, when Shimi was already too old to have
more children and David lay on his deathbed, he instructed Shlomo
to kill Shimi for his past insubordination to the crown.

Why was Shimi worthy of a descendant such as Mordechai?
Actually, he was not. His wife was the worthy one. When Avshalom
was pursuing Tzadok and Evyasar to kill them, they sought refuge
in Shimi's home. His wife hid them in a well, then she sat down next
to it with her hair uncovered and her clothing immodestly arranged.
Avshalom's soldiers searched Shimi's house, but when they saw her
sitting immodestly near the well, they did not bother looking in it.
They were sure that the two righteous fugitives would not have
come anywhere near an immodestly dressed woman. They did not
realize that she had hidden them there before disarranging her
clothes deliberately. Because of her great deed, she had the merit of
a grandson such as Mordechai.[4]

In the light of this story, the members of Yehudah took credit for
Mordechai, claiming that it was David's reprieve of Shimi that allowed

---

2. *Megillah* 12b-13a; *Esther* 2:5; *Pirkei d'Rav Eliezer* 50; *Targum Rishon to Esther* 2:5, R'
Yosef ibn Yachia; Yosef Lekach; Yishai Elokim; Esther 2:5.

3. *Midrash Panim Acheirim; Yalkut Shimoni* 1053; *Ibn Ezra*; see *Tosafos to Megillah* 12b;
Midrash HaGadol; R' Chaim Abulafia.

4. See *Megillah* 13a; *Midrash Panim Acheirim to Esther* 2:5; *Aggadas Esther* 2:5; see *Esther
Rabbah; Yalkut Shimoni* 1053; see also *Shmuel* 27 *Minchas Yehudah.*

Mordechai to be born. The people of Binyamin countered that, be that as it may, Mordechai's bloodline was from the tribe of Binyamin.[5]

This good-natured wrangling only underscores Mordechai's greatness. The people compared him to Moshe *Rabbeinu* in humility, patience and kindness, and as a man who spent his whole life spreading the light of Torah among the Jewish people. They also compared him to Avraham *Avinu* for his battle against idol worship and his sanctification of the Name.[6] Although he sat in the royal councils with pagan ministers, surrounded by the trappings of the idolatrous cults, he never compromised his principles. He was proud to be a Jew. He walked the streets of Shushan dressed in *tallis* and *tefillin*.[7] Questionable food never came near his mouth.[8] And when he prayed, one could sense the gates of Heaven opening to receive his fervent prayers.[9]

In actuality, Mordechai's given names were Pesachiah and Bilsham. He was called Mordechai because the name is reminiscent of the myrrh incense as it appears in the Torah. Myrrh in Hebrew is translated as *mar dror*, which Targum translates into Aramaic as *meira dachia*. Hence the name Mordechai.[10] Myrrh is a fragrant incense that is bitter to the taste; Mordechai, too, was fragrant in good deeds yet bitter to the enemies of the Jewish people. Myrrh is the finest of incense spices; Mordechai, too, was the best among his people, the head of the Sanhedrin. Myrrh burned in the *Beis HaMikdash* to abolish evil decrees against the Jewish people; Mordechai also abolished evil decrees with his prayers. Furthermore, the word *dror* also means free, and Mordechai had the ability to free his people from their oppressors. Because of all this

---

5. *Megillah* 13a; see *Rashbam* to *Bava Basra* 91b; *Midrash Panim Acheirim* 2:5.

6. *Esther Rabbah* 6:2, *Yefei Anaf; Pirkei d'Rav Eliezer* 50; *Megillah* 13a; *Midrash Panim Acheirim; Yad HaMelech; Sefer HaAruch,* under letter *nun,* "Namas"). See *R' Yosef ibn Yachiah* on "Yehudi."

   Mordechai was called Pesachiah because he was proficient in all 70 languages. See *Shekalim* 5:1. *Nachal Eshkol* points out that the *gematria* (numerical value) of the words *ish Yehudi* plus 1 equals that of Moshe.

7. *Rokeach; Maharal* to *Esther* 2:5; *Yad HaMelech; Eshkol HaKofer; Ya'aros Devash, derush* 2. Later, after the Jews prevailed over Haman, Mordechai would instruct the Jews to go out in the streets of Shushan publicly wearing their *tefillin*. Haman had decreed that no practices of the Jewish faith may be kept.

8. *Midrash Panim Acheirim; Pirkei d'Rav Eliezer* 50; *Midrash haGadol; Aggadas Esther* 2:5.

9. *Megillah* 12b; *Targum Rishon; Yalkut Shimoni* 1053; see *Sotah* 4a.

10. *Shemos* 30:23; *Megillah* 10b, see *Maharsha; Targum Rishon;* see *Shekalim* 5:1; *Korban HaEidah; Rashi* to *Menachos* 64b and 65a.

symbolism, the very mention of Mordechai's name brought happiness and contentment to Jewish hearts.[11]

In the second year of Achashverosh's reign, there was a rebellion in one of the provinces on the Indian subcontinent. Achashverosh dispatched two armies, each consisting of six thousand imperial troops, to quell the insurrection. He put Mordechai in command of one of these armies and Haman in command of the other. They were to attack the rebels in a classic pincer movement, but there was no guarantee that the objectives would be achieved quickly and easily. There was a real prospect of a long drawn-out siege, and to anticipate all eventualities, Achashverosh gave both armies provisions sufficient for a three-year campaign.

As it turned out, there was indeed a siege in India. Haman's army dug in to the west of the renegade city and Mordechai's to the east. Arrogantly expecting a quick resolution to the conflict, Haman did not conserve his provisions. The man ate freely and copiously, and much food was wasted simply for lack of care. Within a year, Haman's army ran dangerously low on provisions and faced the specter of starvation. Mordechai, however, had husbanded his resources carefully and still had ample provisions in his storehouses.

In desperation, Haman saddled his horse and rode to Mordechai's camp. Mordechai awaited him in the presence of his staff. Haman's staff was also allowed to attend the meeting.

"Mordechai, my good friend," he said, "how is the siege going with you?"

"We are holding our own," Mordechai replied. "Sooner or later, the rebels will run out of food. Starvation will drive them to surrender. And how is your end of the siege going?"

"Oh, wonderful, wonderful, if I say so myself. The morale is high. The troops are fit and in constant training. We are ready to storm the city at any time. What do you say? Do you want to sit here in the hot sun day after day, week after week, month after month, restless and bored? The rebels must be very worn down by now. Let's storm the city. We will come home to Persia covered with glory. What do you say?"

"I say that we continue the siege. Why risk defeat and heavy casualties just because of a little boredom? We have patience. We can wait

---

11. *Maharsha* to *Chulin* 13a, Rashi; *Esther Rabbah* 6:3, *Aggadas Esther* 2:5; see *Iyun Yaakov* to *Megillah* 10b, *Rokeach* to *Esther* 2:5; *Pirkei d'Rav Eliezer* 50, *Radal*; *Vayikra Rabbah* 32:6, *Matnos Kehunah; Yefei To'ar.*

them out and take the city without a fight. If we follow your plan, Haman, I fear we'll come back to Persia covered with more blood than glory. You can do as you wish. I am not storming the city."

"But you know, Mordechai, that I cannot storm the city without you doing the same on the other side."

"Indeed. Then I guess we will both have to wait patiently."

"Ahem." Haman cleared his throat. "Since you advise me to wait, I will need your assistance in waiting."

"How so?"

"How are you on provisions, Mordechai? Are you well-stocked?"

"Not bad. Why do you ask?"

"Well, you see, we are running a little low on provisions, and I wonder if you would share some of yours with us."

"Low on provisions?" said Mordechai. "After only one year? I can't believe it. How do you expect to last for three whole years?"

Haman shrugged. "It just happened. No one noticed that a shortage was developing, and all of a sudden, there it was. Now, if you would agree to storm the city, it really wouldn't make a difference. But since you insist on sitting on your hands and doing nothing, you are creating a real problem for us. The least you could do is help us out."

"I don't have any spare provisions, Haman."

"I suspect you do. In fact, I am sure you do. You're a prudent fellow, Mordechai. I'm sure you counted every grain before you distributed it. You probably have enough food for ten years, let alone three. I'll tell you what, don't give me the food. Just lend it to me. I will pay you back when I replenish my stores. Not only that, I'll pay you back twofold."

"I'm really sorry, Haman, but I can't help you. First of all, you really don't expect me to take interest on a loan to you. Our Torah expressly forbids lending at interest to a brother. And second, I really —"

"Since when are we brothers?" Haman interrupted.

"Well, aren't we brothers in a manner of speaking? Aren't we descended from brothers? You are descended from Eisav through Amalek, and I from Yaakov through Binyamin. If we're not quite brothers, we're certainly cousins. And second, as I was saying before, I really don't have enough to share with you. King Achashverosh assessed the situation quite accurately and decided we might have to lay siege for three years. If I reduced my provision,

I would be compromising the royal mission. That would be very dangerous. And very foolish. Don't you agree?"

"I don't," said Haman, "but I see how stubborn you are. Forget it."

He mounted his horse and rode off with his escort in a cloud of dust.

After Haman was gone, one of Mordechai's lieutenants approached him. "Your excellency, you told Haman we do not have enough provisions for him, but we really could spare some. Would you like to inspect our stores?"

Mordechai smiled. "I inspect the stores every day, young man. I know exactly how much we have. I see you are an intelligent fellow, so I will explain my thinking to you. If we storm the city, we will be rebuffed. We will suffer heavy casualties and perhaps even defeated on the battlefield. Most likely, we would go home in ignominious defeat. So an all-out assault is not really an option for us. We do not have enough men or equipment to be successful. All we can do is sit and wait patiently. They will fall into our hands like a ripe fruit, as the king understood, but we have a long siege ahead of us. If we give Haman some of our provisions, he will waste those like he wasted his own. In a month, he will be back for more, and then what do we do?"[12]

"I see, your excellency," said the lieutenant.

"I have another question," continued the lieutenant. "It appeared to me that Haman has a personal hostility to you. If it does not involve an invasion of privacy, could you explain it to me?"

"Well, you know that I am Jewish, don't you?"

"Of course," said the lieutenant. "Whenever you are not engaged in military business, you always wear that prayer shawl and those black boxes on your head and arm. You don't exactly keep it a secret."

"No, I don't," said Mordechai. "So why are you surprised that Haman hates me? My people are not much beloved in the empire. Don't you agree? How about you? Do you love the Jewish people?"

"I don't know many Jewish people," he said. "In fact, you are one of the only ones I know, and I admire and respect you to no end. I am not naïve, sir. I have bigoted friends and family, and I know there is antipathy to the Jews in the empire. But Haman seems to harbor an especially burning hatred, something way out of the ordinary, much worse than any I have ever seen."

---

12. See *Targum Yerushalmi* as quoted in *Menos HaLevi*; *Me'am Loez*; and *Targum Rishon* (Hermon Press, Ed.); *Megillah* 15a; *Yalkut Shimoni* 1056; *Aggadas Esther* 5:9.

Mordechai thought fully. "You are quite right, young man," he said. "You heard me mention that he is descended from Amalek?"

"Yes, I did."

"Did you appreciate the significance of that ancestry?"

"No. I did not."

"Then I will explain it to you. We have to go far back into history to get to the roots of it. The second patriarch of the Jewish people, a great holy man named Isaac, had two sons, Eisav and Yaakov. Eisav was the older, but Yaakov was the one who followed in the footsteps of his ancestors. Many things happened, and I won't burden you with the details. In the end, Yaakov was designated his father's successor, and Eisav was relegated to second place. Eisav flew into a murderous rage, and Yaakov fled. He came back many years later, and the brothers reached an uneasy accommodation. But Eisav's hatred ran deep, and it was perpetuated most vigorously by his grandson Amalek. Yaakov's descendants ultimately became the Jewish people, and Amalek and his descendants became their archenemies."

"And Amalek is Haman's ancestor?"

"That's right."

"But why Amalek more than the other descendants of Eisav?"

"Good question. There was a young woman named Timnah, a Seirian princess, who offered to become Yaakov's concubine, but he turned her down. Furious at being scorned, she offered herself to Eisav's son Eliphaz as a concubine. He accepted her, and she gave birth to Amalek. This rejected Seirian princess infused her son with her own vitriol in addition to the hatred he inherited from his paternal grandfather. The result was the nemesis of the Jewish people."[13]

"I see."

"Let me continue. Early in our history, we were enslaved in Egypt for hundreds of years, and God brought us forth from bondage with great miracles that stunned the world. Leaving Egypt, we were a large band of exhausted slaves breathing free for the first time in centuries. For so many years, we had worshipped the Egyptian gods, but now, we were loyal to the great almighty God of Israel. How strong was our faith? How strong was the lingering force of habit? How would we react in times of crisis? Would we slip back to the habits of idolatry? These were serious questions. We needed time to strengthen our faith, to break away from the old and

---

13. *Tzror HaMor, Beshalach;* see *Ramban* to *Bereishis* 36:12,20.

embrace the new. But we didn't get it. As soon as we stepped out of Egypt, we were under attack."

"Under attack? By whom? There is nothing but wasteland to the east of Egypt. There is no one in those lands to attack any one."

"You are right, and I'm pleased to see that you know your geography. There is nothing there but wasteland, as you pointed out, but Amalek mounted an attack nonetheless. Within days of the liberation, an Amalekite army had already covered hundreds of miles of wasteland from their homeland to the Jewish encampment and treacherously attacked them."

"But why? Surely they posed no threat to Amalek."

"In a way, they did. The Jewish people represented a new belief in one God, who demanded that mankind live up to His moral standards. The Amalekites wanted to undermine the faith of the newly emancipated Jews and thereby destroy their religion. They also wanted to destroy the Jewish nation because of the deep hatred that was part of their malevolent legacy."

"Weren't they put off by the great miracles the God of the Jews had performed for them?"

"I'm sure they were nervous, but they didn't let that stop them. They called on a celebrated soothsayer and wizard named Bilam for advice. Bilam was an advisor to Pharaoh and a sworn enemy of the Jews, but more than anything he liked money, so I suppose they must have paid him well. He advised them to form an alliance with their neighboring nations and to assemble an army in which sorcerers, wizards and magicians would be heavily represented. The front lines were to be manned by people celebrating their birthdays, since they were unlikely to die on that day. In addition, they were to use their stargazers to identify people who were fated to live through the year. Finally, they were to attack the Jewish camp in the spot manned by the least faithful among the Jews."[14]

"Were they able to form an alliance?"

Mordechai responded to the soldier. "You have a bright future, young man. You go straight to the weak point. The Amalekites did not have an easy time convincing their neighbors to join them. For the most part, they were terrified of the Jews. Because of their God, of course. In the end, they managed to convince five neighbors to

---

14. *Me'am Loez, Beshalach; Esther Rabbah 7;* see *Yalkut Reuveni; Rabbeinu Bachyei* to *Beshalach; Yerushalmi Rosh Hashanah 3:8.*

participate, and they assembled an army of eight hundred thousand men, many of them practitioners of the occult. With great cunning, they attacked the tribe of Dan, which had strayed after the idol a man named Michah had brought out of Egypt. Because of their sinfulness, they were vulnerable to attack. The Amalekites and their allies penetrated the defensive cloud pillars and killed many of them."[15]

"How about the rest of the Jewish people? Were they affected?"

"Unfortunately, some of them were. A number were ritually impure, and they had to stay outside the encampment, unprotected by the cloud pillars.[16] The Amalekites slaughtered many of them. The others were inside the cloud pillars, invulnerable to attack, but the Amalekites drew some of them out with offers of lucrative business ventures. Unaware of what awaited them, these hapless Jews looking for opportunity stepped out of the cloud pillars and were cut down by the enemy. The Jews of stronger faith were not concerned about business opportunities when God had literally taken them under His wing. Uninterested in the blandishments of the Amalekites, they remained inside the cloud pillars, safe from attack."[17]

"So how did all this end?"

"The Amalekites went into a blood frenzy. They castrated the victims and taunted the Jews about the commandment of circumcision. Many of the soldiers, intoxicated by their bloodlust,[18] got down on the ground and lapped the blood of their victims. Moshe, the leader of the Jewish people, called on his disciple Yehoshua and a select group of righteous warriors to engage the Amalekites in battle. Unwilling to stoop to magic to counter the Amalekites' magic, the Jewish defenders singled out soldiers born in the second month of Adar during a leap year. Since they were not governed by any of the signs of the Zodiac, they were impervious to the Amalekite magic spells.[19] These few valiant men engaged the Amalekites on the battlefield, and miraculously, they won. The warriors beheaded the

---

15. *Mechilta Sechel Tov; Targum Yonasan* to *Beshalach; Pesikta d'Rav Kahana.*

16. *Pesikta d'Rav Kahana.*

17. *Pesikta Rabbah* 12; *Pesikta d'Rav Kahana* 3, *Chemdas Yamim.*

18. See *Tanchuma Yashan* to *Yisro* 4; *Pirkei d'Rav Kahana* 3.

For this reason he was referred to as Amalek: *am lak,* a nation that licks. Alternatively, it comes from *am yelek,* a nation swift as the locust called *yelek.*

19. *Chizkuni Beshalach.*

defeated Amalekite generals, along with the women and children. They also chopped off the hands and feet of those warriors that had wrapped themselves in protective spells so that their vital organs could not be reached. Only the weak and the derelict among the Amalekites were spared death or mutilation. The battle was over, but the long, drawn out battle was just beginning."[20]

"You mean throughout history?"

"Yes. After this incident, God commanded the Jewish people to annihilate the Amalekite nation without leaving the slightest trace, no men, no women, no children, not even any livestock; anything at all that carried their memory must be completely eradicated."

"When were they supposed to do this? Right away?"

"Oh, no. God would let them know when the time was right. That time came over four centuries later, during the reign of Shaul, the first king of the Jews. The prophet Shmuel told him, in the name of God, that he was to attack the Amalekites' kingdom and wipe it out, men, women, children and every single animal."

"Why animals?"

"Two reasons. First, animals are known by their owners. Therefore, if the animals survived the memory of Amalek would not be completely obliterated. Second, the Amalekites were heavily into sorcery, and many of their animals were actually Amalekite warriors who, through magic, appeared as animals to the eye of the beholder. Killing the animals would ensure that every last Amalekite was destroyed."

"I see."

"Shaul assembled an army of two hundred thousand men and attacked the Amalekite kingdom, killing the entire population, a total of one half million people. But he did not obey the prophet Shmuel's directions completely. He took pity on Agag, the Amalekite king, and his wife and imprisoned them until he could consult with Shmuel when he arrived the next day. He also failed to destroy all the livestock, which seemed wasteful to him. He reasoned that he could use them as sacrifices to God and to distribute among his soldiers. This was a major blunder, and Shmuel told Shaul that he had forfeited his kingdom through his disobedience. Now let me tell you about Agag."[21]

"May I venture a guess?"

"Sure."

---

20. *Mechilta, Targum Yonasan.*
21. *Shmuel* I, ch. 15; see *Rashi* to *Shmuel* I 15:3; *Sefer Yosifun.*

"Agag was Haman's grandfather," said the lieutenant. "That is why Haman is known as the Agagi."

"Correct. But be patient. I will fill in some of the details about Haman for you in a minute. Let me first tell you about the two imprisoned Amalekites. Agag had used a spell to disguise himself as a bull and his wife as a cow; the cow conceived during the night.[22] When Shmuel arrived in the morning and heard what had happened, he went to see the imprisoned Agag, but he couldn't find him. Shmuel searched all the corrals and stables, but there was no trace of Agag or his wife. Finally, a lone bull and cow somehow caught his attention, he fixed them with a sharp stare, and they were transformed back into their former selves. Seeing Shmuel, they tried to fly away, literally, by using another spell. Agag was caught before he could make good his escape. His wife, however, got away."[23]

"Amazing."

"Agag was brought to Shmuel in chains like a common criminal. He was fuming at this distinctly unroyal treatment. But when he saw the saintly Shmuel, holy as an angel, his heart leaped. Surely this man would take pity on him. At least he would grant him a quick and honorable death. Well, he was mistaken. 'Your sword rendered hundreds of Jewish mothers childless,' Shmuel told the captive king. 'Now my sword shall render your mother childless. Your sword mutilated Jewish women, now you will taste the pain of mutilation.' He had Agag stretched across a frame and killed him. That was the end of Agag."[24]

"But not the end of Amalek. On that one night, his seed was planted and preserved, and the Amalekite nation was reborn. An incredible story."

"Isn't it? Haman the son of Hammedasa is a direct descendant of Agag, as you correctly surmised. His mother's name was Amasla the daughter of Urvasi, which in Hebrew means raven,

---

22. *Midrash Pirush Achashverosh; Esther* 3-1. See *Rashi* to *Shumuel* I 15:3. Some suggest her name was Medasa. Some suggest the woman was his maidservant, while others say she was his concubine. In either case, she was not of Amalekite descent, which explains why she had not been killed earlier. (See *Rambam* on *Esther* 3:1, footnotes.)

23. *Midrash Pirush Achashverosh; Chemdas Yamim, Emor.* Others suggest that Agag and his wife were imprisoned overnight. It was then that the legacy of Agag was perpetuated, leading to the eventual birth of Haman. Some suggest that Agag's son was named Hammedasa. (*Yerushalmi Yevamos* 2:6).

24. *Yalkut Shmuel* 1:15; *Me'am Loez.*

an unkosher bird.[25] Haman himself, as you can see, is a dangerous man. With his snakelike wit, he is cunning and deceitful. He
will do anything to manipulate others to do his bidding.[26] You
saw how he tried to blame me for his food shortage. That is our
Haman. His heart is filled with hate and greed. He is my sworn
enemy."

"Thank you, your excellency. You have given me a solid understanding of the man. I have heard that the Jews see an allusion to
your name in your Torah. Is there also an allusion to the name of
your nemesis Haman?"

"Actually, there is: in the story about Adam and Chavah and the
forbidden fruit of the Garden of Eden. We believe his power is
enhanced when Jewish people eat forbidden food. Haman is just the
type to attack us by getting us to eat forbidden food."

"Interesting. I have one more question. Why does he hate you personally so much? Is it because you are a recognized Jewish leader?"

Mordechai responded to the lieutenant and continued. "You
know, of course, that I am descended from the tribe of Binyamin.
Haman harbors a special hatred for my tribe, because Shaul, the
king that virtually exterminated the Amalekite people, was also a
descendant of Binyamin."

"I see," said the lieutenant. "But at the same time, shouldn't he be
grateful to your tribe? After all, Shaul was the one who spared
Agag's life."

Mordechai smiled. "Hatred knows no logic."

Three days later, a wild-eyed Haman reappeared in Mordechai's
camp. His face was bruised, his clothing ripped and caked with
blood, and he limped as he walked. He demanded to see Mordechai
immediately. The young lieutenant came to fetch him.

"Mordechai, I am desperate," said Haman. "Look at me!"

"I am looking at you. What happened? I imagine your troops are
becoming somewhat unruly."

"Somewhat? Somewhat? Look at me! They tried to kill me, do
you hear? They actually tried to kill me. When I came from visiting
you, I didn't tell them right away that you had turned me down, but

25. *Targum Rishon; Rambam* to *Esther* 3:1; *Maseches Sofrim* 13:6; *Nachalas Yaakov,* and *Gra.
Aggadas Esther, Megillah* 3:1; *Bava Basra* 91. See *Baal HaTurim* on *Bereishis* 22:34 where
he states there were many similarities between Haman and Eisav.

26. See *Rashi* to *Bereishis Rabbah; Matnos Kehunah; Yedei Moshe* 16:4; *Yotzer* to *Parashas
Zachor; Krovetz L'Purim.*

after three days, I couldn't fool them any more. They almost tore me apart. They only let me go because I promised to come here and plead with you for mercy."

"I am sorry to hear that. You need to improve the discipline of your troops."

"Discipline? What does it have to do with discipline? My men are starving. They are convinced they will die here in this forsaken land, far from their homes and families. Mordechai, have pity. Give us food, and I will repay you tenfold for everything you give me."

"But I told once before, Haman, that I simply do not have enough food for both our armies."

"You mean you can't spare anything at all? I can't believe that!"

"And what if I could spare a little? How would it help you? In a few weeks, you would back in the same position. Your men have no discipline. If they have what to eat today, they don't even think about tomorrow."

"You're really blaming me, aren't you?" said Haman. "When you say my men have no discipline, you mean that I can't control our provisions. Under the circumstances, I cannot argue with you. Perhaps you are right. All I can say is that I will try hard to conserve our provisions from now on."

Mordechai stood up and began to pace back and forth, his hands clasped behind his back, his brow knotted in deep thought. Haman barely breathed as he watched Mordechai struggle with the problem, but his eyes blazed with silent hatred.

"How far are you willing to go in order for me to give you provisions?" Mordechai asked at last.

"I'll do anything," said Haman. "As I told you before I'll repay you tenfold. If you want, I will repay you fiftyfold. A hundredfold!"

Mordechai shook his head. "I've already told you that I will accept no interest from you. I had something else in mind."

"What is it?" asked Haman.

"Would you sell yourself as a slave to me?"

Haman's mouth fell open. "You must be joking."

"I'm not."

"But why?"

"That is what I want. Do you agree?"

Haman trembled. "I really have no choice, do I? It's either slavery to you or a horrible death at the hands of my men. I agree to your terms. I am hereby your slave. Now can we have the food?"

"First, we have to formalize our agreement," said Mordechai.

"But I already agreed to your terms. What more do you want?"

"I want a formal sale."

"Well, I give you my word on it. I swear in the presence of your men that I am your slave. Is that sufficient for you?"

"I'm afraid it is not," said Mordechai. "I want a proper deed drawn up. On parchment."

"Very well. Draw one up. I will sign it."

"Your excellency," said the lieutenant to Mordechai, "I don't think we have any parchment in the camp. We did not anticipate the need for any."

Mordechai stroked his beard. "Hmm. So what will we do?"

"Perhaps we can write it on your boot, your excellency," said the lieutenant.

"Very well," said Mordechai. "That is what we will do. We will write the deed on my boot. Lieutenant, go get us some ink. In the meantime, Haman, you can compose the text in your mind. I want you to write, in your own hands, the circumstances that led to this transaction, that you are selling yourself to me for a loaf of bread and that you are doing so of your own free will. Will you do this?"

Haman nodded.

One hour later, Haman took the quill in hand, dipped it into the ink and began to write on the boot in tiny but clear characters. He described the problems he was having with his troops and the need for additional provisions. "Therefore, I, Haman the son of Hammedassa, hereby declare myself to be the slave of Mordechai the son of Kish," he wrote, "and I accept a loaf of bread in full payment thereof. If I fail to perform my duties as a slave or express any resentment or even harbor any ill feelings in my heart, may a beam be pulled from my house, and may I be hanged from it. Unlike my ancestor Eisav who harbored ill feelings against his brother Yaakov after he sold him his birthright, I will never harbor any ill feelings against Mordechai for this transaction. So be it."

After he finished writing, Haman laid aside the quill. He took the boot in his hands and blew on the ink until it dried. Then he handed it to Mordechai with an exaggerated ceremonious flourish.

Mordechai handed Haman a loaf of bread with a similar flourish. The deed was done.

"Now then, Haman," said Mordechai, "now that you are my slave, to whom do all your possessions belong?"

"They belong to you, of course. Whatever belongs to the slave belongs to the master."

"That is correct," said Mordechai. "Therefore, your troops and all their supplies and provisions belong to me. When I give you additional provisions for your army, you will not be in control of them. I will control them. And I will make sure that the food is conserved and the men behave with discipline."[27]

Haman inclined his head with mock obsequiousness. "As you wish."

With Mordechai in control of both armies, the prospects of the siege brightened. Within three months, the rebel stronghold fell and the entire province was subdued. The rebels were slaughtered, and the nobles were brought back to Shushan in chains. Mordechai was hailed as a conquering hero, while Haman was a laughingstock for having sold himself as a slave. "Just as his ancestor Eisav sold his birthright for a pot of red beans," people said, "Haman sold himself into slavery for a loaf of bread."[28]

With typical leniency, Mordechai allowed Haman to work for him only one day of the week and have the rest of the week for himself. This arrangement continued until Haman was elevated to the imperial council as an advisor to the king; it would have been unseemly for Mordechai to exercise the privileges of ownership over a royal advisor.

Haman never forgot his humiliation in India. It kindled a new fire of hatred in his heart, in addition to those that already raged there from before.

---

27. See *Megillah* 15a; *Menos Levi*; *Me'am Loez*; *Yalkut Shimoni* 1056; *Aggadas Esther* to *Esther* 5:9.

28. *Ba'al HaTurim* to *Bereishis* 25:30.

The Shushan Feast

4

On a bright autumn morning, an endless line of fine coaches and carriages rolled out of the royal palace, carrying away the overfed and hungover guests from around the empire who had enjoyed the king's hospitality for six long months. The going was slow, because the roads were all but impassable, clogged with many thousands of the inhabitants of Shushan streaming towards the Great Palace. Here and there, a local dignitary or entrepreneur rode in a carriage or on horseback, but for the most part, the people came on foot. Achashverosh was hosting a special seven-day feast for the common people. Everyone was invited.

For one hundred and eighty days, Achashverosh had flaunted his wealth in front of the nobles and official of the empire to impress them with the vastness of his power. Now Achashverosh turned his attention to the common people in an entirely different mode. Instead of intimidating them, his aim was to make them comfortable, to give them pleasure and enjoyment such as they had never experienced. He wanted the common people in his capital to see that he cared about them, that he held their welfare close to his heart. Above all else, he wanted their undying devotion and loyalty. And of course, he also had a secret ulterior motive. He wanted to entrap the Jewish people by drawing them into sin.[1]

Among the people walking toward the palace were the various Jews who were attending the imperial feast. They walked with a jaunty spring to their steps, with a sense of excitement and anticipation. It promised to be an experience to be remembered and treasured and retold to the grandchildren.

In the vast plaza in front of the main entrance, there were many small tables piled high with lists of the Shushan residents. A protocol officer waited at each table to help the residents find their reserved places. There were more than enough tables to accommodate the huge crowd; there was no need to waste time standing on line.

The four men lined up at one of the tables, and in a few minutes, they found themselves standing in front of a smiling protocol officer.

"Good morning, gentlemen," said the officer. "How are you enjoying this beautiful morning?"

"Very well, thank you," the men replied.

"I greet you in the name of our illustrious king, his royal highness, the powerful and magnanimous King Achashverosh. Welcome! His majesty wants you to have a wonderful time. Seven days of pure pleasure you will never forget. We will cater to your every desire."

"And what must we do?" asked the thin man.

"Oh, the king has very strict demands for you," said the protocol officer, wagging a fat finger at them. "He absolutely demands that you forget all your troubles and all your cares. He absolutely demands that you keep refilling your goblet with his best wines. He absolutely demands that you keep refilling your stomachs with his finest foods. Ahem, let me think. Is there anything else?" He scratched his head. "No, there is nothing else. Those are his demands. Can you meet them?"

"No problem," the youngster declared. "Just point the way."

---

1. *Megillah* 12a; *R' Yosef ibn Nachmiash; Einei HaEidah.* Others posit that the seven-day feast was the last week of the 180-day party and not a separate one (*R' Yosef ibn Yachia; Midrash Talpios*).

The gray-bearded man gave the youngster a sharp look, then he turned to the officer. He shrugged his shoulders and rolled his eyes. "Young people," he remarked. "Older people like me need a little more information. This feast is going to cost the king an incredible amount of money. Why is he doing this? What does he really want from us?"

"Why? You want to know why?" said the officer. He leaned forward and lowered his voice. "Since you ask, I'll tell you why. Do you have any idea how rich the king is? He just finished a huge, one-hundred-and-eighty-day-long feast for important people from all over the empire, and now he is making this seven-day feast for the residents of Shushan. Believe me, when it is all over he won't even feel the pinch. It all means less to him than spending a penny means to you, so rich is he."

"I believe you," said the gray-bearded man, "although it doesn't quite go into my head. But still, why do it? What does he stand to gain?"

"He stands to gain the favor and loyalty of his subjects. He wants to show them that he cares equally for each and every one of them. All his subjects are equal in his eyes. He wants to impress this thought on you in a way that you will always remember it. Can you think of a nicer and more pleasurable way to accomplish this goal than by hosting this wonderful feast?"

"No, I guess not."

"In any case, we need to move along. We don't want the people waiting on line behind you to start fidgeting, do we? We want you to have fun, and we want them to have fun. Fun, fun and only fun! Right?"

"Right."

"By the way, do any of you gentlemen have families? You know, wives or children? Or both?"

"I'm afraid not," said the gray-bearded man. "Why?"

"Because you are invited to bring them with you. We have activities and refreshments for the children, so that the parents can relax and enjoy. But I guess this does not apply to you. Unfortunate.[2] Very well, give me your names. I will direct you to the places in the palace reserved just for you."

---

2. *Esther Rabbah* 2:3; *Menos HaLevi; Ma'amer Mordechai; Einei HaEidah, Malbim* to 1:5. Ironically, when angels later told Achashverosh that they were chopping down his trees at Haman's suggestion (see *Esther* 7:8), he was furious; yet here children were permitted to wreak havoc in the palace with impunity.

They gave their names, and the officer consulted his master list.

"Aha!" he declared triumphantly. "Here you are! I'm sure you'll be pleased to hear that you are all together in the same courtyard. Let's see. It's the Emerald Courtyard. An excellent spot. You'll love it." He marked a small tile and handed it to the gray-bearded man. "Show this to the ushers."

"Are we close to the throne room? Will we see the king?"

"I'm afraid you are not so close to the throne room."

"But didn't you say we are all the king's subjects, all equal in his eyes? Why shouldn't we be allowed to be near the throne room?"

"My dear fellow, not many people can be accommodated near the throne room. There is simply no room. We have to give those places to the higher officials. But to make sure everything is fair, the king ordered that the farther away you are placed, the more luxurious your bed will be. I see here that you four have beds of pure gold."[3]

"Does that mean that we are very far away?" asked the thin man.

The officer laughed and waved them along.

The four men handed their tile to the officer at the main entrance. The officer glanced at the mark and snapped his fingers in the air. An usher instantly appeared at his side. "Show these four honored guests to the Emerald Courtyard," he said.

The usher bowed to them and motioned to them to follow. They stepped into an immense inner courtyard from which numerous gardens and courtyards opened in every direction.[4] The beauty of the central courtyard took their breath away. On the one side were the royal gardens, lush with premium vegetables and abloom with exquisite flowers of every imaginable color and delicate shape. On the other side were the royal orchards, with long, tightly spaced rows of trees laden with succulent fruit begging to be picked and eaten. Gauzy packets of spices and perfumes hung from the branches and sent their sweet scent wafting on the cool breezes that whispered through the freshly cut grass.[5]

They passed into a small courtyard that opened immediately onto a large garden set within a beautiful orchard. Many people were

---

3. *Megillah* 12a, according to both opinions. See *Tosafos* and *Ben Yehoyada* there; also *Einei HaEidah*.

4. See *Megillah* 12a; *Esther Rabbah; Targum Rishon* and *Targum Sheini; R' Saadiah Gaon; R' Yosef ibn Nachmiash.*

5. *Esther Rabbah* 2:6; *Yefai Anaf; Yalkut Shimoni* 1048; *Targum Sheni; Menos HaLevi* 1:5; *R' Yosef ibn Yachia.*

already settling in to this idyllic setting as waiters circulated among them with bottles of spiced wine. Rich tapestries, brocades and drapes of the finest embroidered wool, linen and cotton fabrics billowed like sails among the branches, providing cool shade for the reclining guests. The hangings were all of royal quality, in shimmering whites, purples, blues and greens, studded with pearls and precious stones. Even the cords, pull ropes and rods were made of materials fit for a king and trimmed with strands of gold and silver.[6]

"We will be at your place in a moment, gentlemen," said the usher.

"Are we passing near the Darah Stone?" asked the youngster.

"We can make a short detour to see it if you wish," said the usher.

He led them through a leafy courtyard and a broad corridor to a domed chamber brilliantly illuminated on all sides. Hundreds of people filled the chamber, gawking at a tall pedestal of black marble directly underneath the tip of the dome. On it sat the largest gemstone any of them had ever seen - the celebrated Darah Stone, Achashverosh's prize possession. The stone drew in all the light around it until the innumerable facets on its face glittered and shone with a radiance reminiscent of the midday sun. In fact, the radiance was so powerful that it was equally dazzling to those that stood near it and those that stood far away.

"Have you ever seen anything like this, uncle?" the youngster asked of the gray-bearded man. "It is nice of the king to show it to the people."[7]

"No, I've never seen anything like it," he replied. "But Achashverosh is not showing it to be nice. He wants to compare himself to God. Just as God has a sun that illuminates the world, so does the king have his private sun that illuminates everything around it."[8]

The usher suggested that they continue to their places, and they left the chamber with one last glance at the wonder stone. They walked through hallways and rooms in which residents of the capital reclined with goblets in their hands and engaged in amiable conversation. Children frolicked in the hallways under the watchful eyes of palace attendants.[9]

---

6. See *Megillah* 12a, *Esther Rabbah, Yalkut Shimoni; Pirkei d'Rav Eliezer* 49; *Menos HaLevi.*
7. *Megillah* 12a; see *Sifsei Chachamim* there.
8. *Maharal.*
9. *Menos HaLevi; Ma'amar Mordechai, Einei HaEidah.*

"Can we stop for a moment?" said the rotund redhead. "I want to take a closer look at these carpets on the floor. I've never seen such intricate and beautiful work." He bent down and ran his fingers along the carpet. "And such texture!"

The usher smiled. "You have a discerning eye, sir," he said. "These carpets are worth their weight in gold and diamonds. There are none other like them in the whole world."

The redhead beamed. "Could we get a look at the floor under them?"

The usher shrugged. "Honored guests, your will is my command. Lift the corner of the carpet, and look at the floor. It is indeed something to see."

The carpet was heavy, but the redhead and the thin man pulling together managed to roll it far back. As the floor underneath was exposed, the men gasped. The floor was of gleaming marble tile inlaid with long rows of pearls and gemstones in many colors: green, yellow, white, purple, onyx and sapphire. Without bothering to lift any more of the carpet, the men had no doubt that the rows of gems stretched endlessly across the room and the other rooms as well, and they were flabbergasted by the casual opulence. Even the untrained eye could see that these were extremely precious gems, that anyone who owned even one or two of them would be guaranteed a prosperous, carefree life, a life of privilege and freedom. And yet, these stones were used to decorate the floor upon which people trod and obscured from sight by priceless carpets. It was too much for the ordinary mind to comprehend.

"I see you are impressed by the unusual use of gemstones," said the usher. "To his majesty, gemstones are like ordinary pebbles, so many does he have. In fact, I have heard that the very foundations of the palace and the courtyards are studded with precious stones. I suppose the king wants us all to know that his wealth is unlimited. Difficult to fathom, isn't it? You are not alone. I have led kings and princes through here, and they too have reacted as you did." He shrugged. "Gentlemen, let us proceed."[10]

They retraced their steps through the rest of the rooms and back out into the open areas in the palace complex. In the brief time since they had entered the palace, a flood of humanity had surged into the

10. See *Megillah* 12a; *Esther Rabbah*; *Yalkut Shimoni*; *Pirkei D'Rav Eliezer* 49; *Menos HaLevi*; *Einei HaEidah*; *Yishai Elokim*; *Dana Pishra*.

gardens and courtyards from which they had come just a short time
before. Every available corner was already occupied by revelers.
Hordes of children ran among the carefully manicured plants and
hedges, tearing the sod under their feet and wreaking general havoc
on the products of nature.

"Look what's happening!" exclaimed the redhead. "The king will
have their heads for this."

"Oh, no, sir," said the usher. "The king has given specific instructions that no one is to be rebuked or punished for causing uninten-
tional damage to the royal grounds. His majesty doesn't want his
guests to feel restricted or self-conscious. He wants them to let loose
and have a really good time. Without a care in the world." He lowered his voice. "I wouldn't worry about the grounds. Any damage
can be repaired. It's only a matter of expense, you know, and as you
have seen, his majesty has an unlimited supply of money."[11]

"Don't you think we should be going?" the youngster asked nervously. "There are so many people coming in. They may take our
places."

"Don't worry, sir," said the usher. "Your places are reserved. No
one will take them. Every place in all three sections of the palace is
reserved. We have room for everyone, sir. But we should hurry anyway, so that you can get off your feet and enjoy the king's hospitality."

Five minutes later, they arrived at their destination.

The Emerald Courtyard apparently took its name not from the
green gemstone but from the intense green of its foliage. Expensive
tapestries were hung as canopies across the treetops to screen out
the hot rays of the sun. Here and there, young saplings were bent
towards each other, tied together and bedecked with fine draperies
to form natural arches over the pathways among the trees. And of
course, all the tapestries and hangings glittered with gemstones set
in their embroidery. The men's mouths watered at the sight of the
luscious fruit hanging from the branches and their heads swooned
from the sweetness of the fragrance.

"Here are your couches, gentlemen," said the usher . "Make yourselves comfortable. His majesty has decreed that all of his guests are
to be provided pleasure to delight four of their five senses to the
greatest degree. The exquisite foods and beverages will tingle your
taste buds. The fragrance of the perfume and spices will gratify your

---

11. *Esther Rabbah* 2:3; *Menos HaLevi; Einei HaEidah; Malbim to Esther* 1:5.

sense of smell. The colors and shapes all around you will be a treat to your eyes. And your luxurious couches will indulge your sense of touch. The king has decreed that there will be no music for your ears, because he does not want you to become distracted from your pleasures. You can tickle your sense of hearing with good conversation, if you please. The king has not forbidden that." He smiled at his own witticism. "There will be palace attendants coming through every few minutes. Feel free to ask for anything you please, gentlemen. They are here to serve you in any way they can. Enjoy!" With a wave of his hand, he was gone.

The men were exceedingly pleased with the beds they had been given. Some of the beds they had seen in their tour of the palace were made of silver with gold plated designs, some were of gold with silver bases or legs, and some had little wheels that allowed them to be moved from place to place. But none were as striking as the beds they had been given. Each of these beds was made of solid gold with a tall post rising at each corner to a frame overhead. A canopy draped over the frame provided additional shade, and beautiful curtains enclosed the bed on all sides. Right now the curtains were open, but they could easily be drawn for more privacy. There were also numerous couches for eating and sitting scattered around the courtyard.

"These are excellent," said the thin man, "but I think I might have preferred one of those." He pointed at a cluster of cabins, tents and gazebos across the courtyard. "The beds inside might not be as luxurious as ours, but they probably offer more comfort."

The gray-bearded man laughed. "You will never be satisfied. If you had been assigned one of those, you would have wanted one of these." [12]

A few minutes after the men settled down on their couches, a steward appeared with a bottle of wine and a tray of gold cups. The steward handed a gold cup to each of them, then he uncorked the bottle.

"Good morning, gentlemen," said the steward obsequiously. "Can I offer you some of this wine?"

"What kind of wine is it?" asked the thin man.

"It is sweet spiced wine," said the steward. "A special vintage served at room temperature. A robust fruity wine, with a delicate

---

12. *Midrash Panim Acheirim; Gra; Alshich; Yishai Elokim; Menos HaLevi; Alshich.*

hint of dryness. It is a very rare wine from the royal cellars. This wine is practically priceless, gentlemen, as are all the wines served at this royal feast. We have fifty-year-old wine for adults aged forty and up. We also have some eighty-year-old wine. I will bring you a greater selection later.[13] We have vintages for younger people and for children as well. You can also have your choice of warm or chilled wines, strong wines and weak wines, familiar wines and exotic wines. Your wish is our command. If you want your wine before dinner or after dinner, the choice is yours. In the meantime, let me fill your cups with this wine. It is wonderful. You will like it."

"You mentioned children," said the gray-bearded man. "What if the parents don't want their children to drink?"

"His majesty has commanded that anyone who wants to drink shall drink. Parents are not to stand in the way of their children."

The steward poured for each of them and waited as they tasted it. Smiles of pleasure spread across their faces. Their skin took on a ruddy flush, and their eyes lit up.[14]

"I see you like the wine," said the steward. "You will be pleased to hear that these cups are yours to keep after you drink from them. They are beautiful. Solid gold. Very valuable. We have many different cups, each with its own special design. No two vessels are identical.[15] All the dishes and vessels you will see at this feast are especially produced for this feast by the royal artisans. The quality of the gold cups is so high that you can see your reflection in them, so high that the richness and texture of the wine are not affected by contact with the precious metal. We also have decanters and goblets of the finest crystal, so delicate that any but the most gentle touch will shatter them. These cups, crystal or gold, are yours to keep."[16]

"You're joking, of course," said the redhead.

"Oh, no, sir, I am not joking," said the steward in the same flat, obsequious tone. "I am not permitted to joke with the guests."

The redhead remained doubtful. "Do I get another cup for my second drink?" he asked.

---

13. *Yad HaMelech; Eshkol Hakofer; Iyun Yaakov* to *Megillah* 12a. *Yalkut Shimoni.* Others suggest, however, that they drank wine that was only one year older than they. *Maharal* notes that the numerical value of the Hebrew word *yayin*, 70, is the normal life span of a person. Old wine penetrated the body well.

14. *Esther Rabbah* 2:13; *Lekach Tov* 1:7; *Menos HaLevi, Yad HaMelech; Targum Sheni* 1:7.

15. *Midrash Panim Acheirim.*

16. *Esther Rabbah* 2:10-11; *Midrash R' Zechariah HaRofei; Pirkei d'Rav Eliezer* 49; R' *Yosef ibn Nachmiash; Yad HaMelech; Dana Pishra; Alshich.*

"Yes, sir. You will, and you can keep that one as well."

The redhead laughed. "Now I'm sure you're joking."

"But I am not, sir. I am not permitted to joke."

The redhead's eyes widened as it dawned on him that the steward was telling the truth. He emptied his cup in one gulp and shoved the cup into his pocket. "Give me another cup," he demanded, hand outstretched. "And fill it up. Quick."[17]

"Yes, sir," said the steward. "But I must caution you that his majesty has instructed us to ensure that none of the guests have too much to drink. We are to give you enough to drink to keep you happy and festive all the time, but not to let you become inebriated. The king feels it would be disrespectful to the crown for the guests to get drunk. It would also cause much bedlam and disrupt the pleasures of the feast. And of course, we would not want people getting sick and vomiting."[18]

"That is a good idea," said the thin man. "I can't stand the sight of drunks. They make me nauseous. Tell me, my good fellow, I once heard a legend about the king's enormous goblet. Supposedly, it is many times the size of an ordinary goblet. Is it true? Can we see it?"

"Oh, it is not a legend, sir," said the steward. "I have seen this goblet many times. It is five times the size of an ordinary goblet. I believe it holds about two quarts. Whoever receives this goblet filled with wine from the king is in deep trouble. He has no choice but to drain it, which will either kill him, drive him insane or make him very ill. This goblet has made the royal wine steward rich. People pay him handsomely to make sure that they are not given this goblet. But you will not see it at this feast, sir. The king has commanded that it not be shown. He doesn't want anyone drinking from it and becoming drunk, at the very least. Is there anything else I can tell you about or do for you, gentlemen?"[19]

"I am hungry," said the redhead.

"In a few minutes, they will be bringing out trays of the most delicious food you have ever tasted, more delicious than any ever eaten since the world was created. Eat to your hearts' content. Good day."[20]

17. *Yalkut Shimoni* 1048; *Esther Rabbah; Alshich; Me'am Loez* ; see *Torah Sheleimah.* See *Alshich,* who says that no two sets of dishes were alike, and when one was used, it was replaced by a new set of dishes.

18. *Menos HaLevi* 1:8; *Alshich.*

19. *Targum Sheni; Rashi; Yalkut Shimoni; Esther Rabbah.*

20. *Esther Rabbah* 2:4; *Yalkut Shimoni* above.

For the next hour, the men ate and drank as they reclined on their couches. The wine loosened their tongues, and they told each other jokes and funny stories until they rocked with laughter. All around them, people were indulging their desires and having a thoroughly enjoyable time. Some of them were Jewish, many were not. A rosy haze descended on the courtyard and dulled their senses. They were wholly under the influence of the king's pleasures.

A sudden blast of trumpets shook the people from their alcoholic stupor. A herald ran into the courtyard and shouted at the top of his lungs, "Good people of Shushan! His illustrious majesty, our beloved King Achashverosh approaches. All rise and come forward to honor the king!"

Moments later, five trumpeters appeared. They raised their instruments to their mouths and issued another blast. Then a hush fell over the crowd as the bear-like king strode into the courtyard. He gazed at the overflow crowd from under his bushy eyebrows, but his usual scowl had been replaced by a benign and kindly look. He held a goblet in his hand.

In the place of his customary royal raiment, Achashverosh wore a set of mysterious garments of incredible beauty — a long coat, an intricately embroidered hat, a jewel-studded breastplate and a golden plate across his forehead on which Hebrew letters spelled out the Name of God.

The four Jews looked at each other in confusion. Could it be? Was the king wearing the holy garments of the *Kohein Gadol*? The thought sank into their wine-soaked brains. It could not be anything else. The king was obviously claiming supreme physical and spiritual power in the world.

"My good people," declared Achashverosh. "I hope you are all having a rousing good time."

The people raised their cups and cheered, and the king smiled happily. The Jews were more subdued, shaken by the king's appearance.

"My good people of Shushan," Achashverosh continued, "my good friends and neighbors, welcome to my palace! I have just completed a feast for the nobles and dignitaries of my empire, a feast that lasted for one hundred and eighty days. But believe me, my friends, it was nothing compared to the feast I have prepared for you. You loyal citizens of Shushan are very near and dear to me, and I want to show you my appreciation. Not only have I hosted this feast for you, I have also decreed that for the foreseeable future all sales taxes will be canceled. Plenty of money is pouring into my treasuries from other lands in the empire. You will share the bounty with me. No more taxes!"[21]

The crowd whistled and cheered wildly. The king beamed.

"I have instructed the palace staff to treat each of you as my special honored guest, which you are. Every wish of yours is their command. All I ask is that you do not get drunk. You can go right up to the line, but do not cross it. Drunkenness would ruin the party for the rest of us, and we wouldn't want that."[22]

He neglected to tell them his real reason for wanting them to avoid drunkenness. He wanted God to become angry when they sinned and punish them. If they became drunk, they would not be as responsible for their actions.[23]

"Moreover, my friends, you will all come away rich from this feast, because I have commanded that the cups from which you drink are yours to keep. I did this in order to show you that I care about each and every one of you, not only while you are here as guests in my palace but even after you return to your homes."

And I also want to impress upon you, thought Achashverosh, that just as God sustains the world asking nothing in return, so do I.[24]

"I have provided every enjoyment and pleasure imaginable for you. The only pleasure I did not provide is music. Why? Because music can be a distraction, and I did not want you to limit the indulgence of your pleasures in any way. Besides, there are so many people here, so many noisy children running about, that music would just have added to the din and clamor. It could have been an annoyance rather than a pleasure. And I want you to have only pleasure, pure, uninterrupted, undisturbed pleasure."

Music also tends to inspire people and turn them in a spiritual direction, thought Achashverosh. I certainly did not want my

21. *Sifsei Chachamim* to *Megillah* 12a; *Esther Rabbah*; *Midrash R'Zechariah HaRofei, Menos HaLevi; R' Yosef ibn Nachmiash; Gra; Eshkol Hakofer;* see *Horios* 13a.

22. See *Midrash Panim Acheirim; Rashi* to *Megillah* 1:8.

23. See *Geon Yaakov; Rif* in *Ein Yaakov* on *Megillah* 12a; *Maharal; Ta'ama D'kra.* See *Alshich; Mikra'ei Kodesh* and *Ma'am Loez* for further explanation of the Hebrew term *"Retzon ish va'ish."* Many are of the opinion that most of the God-fearing Jews had left by now, to avoid eating any unkosher food.

24. *Maharal.*

Jewish guests to become inspired and turn away from sin. That would defeat my purpose.[25]

"As for my Jewish friends, I want you to feel as comfortable and as welcome as all my other subjects. I value your presence in my empire, and I want to make you happy and secure. Ask yourselves: Will God prepare a feast for you in the next world to compare with the feast I have prepared for you here? Think about it. I am your king and your friend."[26]

Achashverosh drained the goblet he held in his hand and lifted it high over his head.

"Enjoy yourselves, all my good friends," he bellowed. "Toss away all your cares and worries. Eat, drink and be merry!"

The king strode away, followed by his retinue, and the revelers returned to their pleasures. The four Jews, somber and subdued, sat under a tree.

The youngster tugged at the gray-bearded man's sleeve. "Did you hear what he said, uncle?" he asked. "About his feast being better than the one God will prepare for us in the next world?"

"I heard," he replied. "Terrible words. I suspect that we will never find out. I suspect that those who partake of this feast will be unwelcome in the World to Come."

"Oh, come now," said the redhead. "Don't be such an extremist. What was so terrible about what the king said? He was only joking. He wanted to please us, so he used a framework that we can understand. He meant no harm. Didn't you see the kindness on his face?"

The man with the gray beard shrugged. "I'm not so sure about that. I don't think Achashverosh cares about anything but himself. He has power, wealth and an endless supply of worldly pleasures. That is why he seemed so happy and content. I don't trust him."

"All right," said the thin man. "Don't trust him. But don't go overboard. Let's enjoy the feast. Drink the king's wine. Eat his food. We'll just keep your eyes open, and we'll be just fine."

The men left it at that. Several cups of wine later, their faces turned bright red, and the conversation was forgotten.

---

25. *Menos HaLevi; Yad HaMelech; Yedei Moshe; Dana Pishra.* Some suggest that there *was* music, while others say that for the same reasons mentioned, there was nothing at this feast that catered to the sense of smell for that too would have contributed to the distraction of the guests, which would cause them to eat less. See *Yosef Lekach; R' Yosef ibn Nachmiash; Ma'amar Mordechai; Alshich* and *Maharal.*

26. *Yalkut Shimoni;* see *Esther Rabbah* 2:5; *Yad HaMelech, Maharal.*

Presently, a persistent loud banging intruded on their inebriated haze. They looked up and saw a remarkable sight. Mordechai, the head of the Sanhedrin, was standing at the far end of the courtyard. A number of Jewish guests crowded around him, eager to see the great man and hear him speak. The four men struggled to their feet and stumbled across the courtyard to join their Jewish brethren.

Mordechai waited for them, then he began. "My dear Jewish brothers, we are all in great danger here, terrible danger. The safety of our people depends on our loyalty to God, and I believe that Achashverosh is doing everything he can to undermine that loyalty. I believe that is one of the main motivations for this special feast for Shushan. He wants us to sin. He wants us to turn away from our Father in Heaven. My dear brothers, there is nothing to be gained here. Leave at once. Go back to the safety and sanctity of your Jewish homes. Leave this dangerous place!"

The Jewish audience stirred uneasily. They murmured and grumbled and looked down at their feet, but they made no move to leave.

"I have been running around for hours, seeking out groups of Jewish guests and speaking to them. Do you know how hard that is? There are eighteen and one-half thousand Jewish guests at this feast! But I cannot rest until I have warned all of them. Your souls are in danger. Indeed, your very lives are in danger. Because if you turn away from God, you will have no protection from your enemies. Tell me, my brothers, did you see the king dressed in the priestly garments of the *Kohein Gadol*?"

The audience was unwilling to meet Mordechai's eyes, and remained silent.

"You don't answer me, because you are ashamed. You should be ashamed. Do you know what else he has done? He has brought out the captured vessels of the *Beis HaMikdash* and put them on display. He is even drinking from them. It tickles his fancy to use the holy vessels.[27] He especially enjoys the little cups that miraculously hold tremendous volumes of liquid. I wonder at him. Doesn't he know that Belshazzar was punished for using these selfsame vessels? Doesn't he realize that he will also suffer the consequences of his actions? Many of the members of the Sanhedrin and other Jewish

---

27. Belshazzar used the vessels of the *Beis HaMikdash* to give honor to his idol and to denounce the power of Hashem. Achashverosh, on the other hand, used it for his own sinful pleasures (*Einei HaEidah*).

dignitaries who witnessed this outrage have gone home. You must do the same, my brothers. This is not a place for you."

"With all due respect, Mordechai," said the thin man, "we are sitting here in the courtyard, far from the king and his private displays. We have not seen the vessels of the *Beis HaMikdash*, nor are we likely to see them. Why should we leave this place? Will we ever again in our lifetimes have the opportunity to enjoy a dream experience such as this?"[28]

"I should hope not," snapped Mordechai. "This is not a dream. It is a horrible nightmare. What was yesterday? Do you remember or have you already forgotten? Tell me! What was the day before yesterday?"

"Rosh Hashanah," whispered the thin man.

"Exactly! Rosh Hashanah, the day of judgment. And yesterday was Tzom Gedaliah, a day of fasting in memory of that righteous man who tried to bring together the remnant of the Jewish people left in *Eretz Yisrael* after the destruction of the *Beis HaMikdash*. Did you fast? Did you examine yourselves and do *teshuvah*? If so, why are you here today drinking wine and making merry? Is this where your *teshuvah* has led you? This feast is meant to last seven days, the seven days between Rosh Hashanah and Yom Kippur. Is this how you prepare for atonement? Is this how you persuade the Creator to forgive your sins and bless you with a sweet new year?"[29]

Mordechai paused to allow a response, but no one spoke.

"During these days," he continued, "we are required to be more stringent than usual. We are required to avoid foods cooked by gentiles, even if they are technically kosher. You are going to be here on Shabbos. Will you be able to avoid its desecration?[30] You recline on

---

28. *Targum Rishon; Targum Sheini; Esther Rabbah* 2:2, *Matnos Kehunah; Midrash HaGadol; Menos HaLevi; Esther* 2:5; *Geon Yaakov. Rokeach* notes that the last letters of the Hebrew words *"vehashkos bichlei zahav"* can be rearranged to spell *bayis*, referring to the *Beis HaMikdash*.

29. *Tanchuma Yashan Behar; Pirkei d'Rav Eliezer* 49; *Shir HaShirim Rabbah* 7:8; *Esther Rabbah* 2:13; *Yad HaMelech; Rishon LeTzion.* See *Yalkut Shimoni,* who is of the opinion that the Jews were forced to eat non-kosher food. Many question that view that the Jews partook of non-kosher food and wine; if they had been forced, then the purpose of *"ein oness,"* without coercion, would not have been realized. Achashverosh's intention was for the Jews to sin of their own volition so that they would be liable to punishment. Some suggest that we find here a strong basis for the Rabbinic prohibition against drinking wine with, or touched by, a gentile. It clearly leads to sin, as was the case at the feast (*Yad HaMelech*).

30. *R' Yosef ibn Nachmiash.* See *Menos HaLevi* and *Sha'arai Binah* who hold that they were not present at the feast on Shabbos for this very reason. See *Megillah* 12b; as will be discussed later, Vashti would be punished for forcing the Jewish women to desecrate Shabbos.

these couches. There is no doubt in my mind that the fabric contain *shatnez*.[31] And look at all the children here. Is this proper *chinuch* for them? Why are you allowing your children, so beloved to God, to be corrupted?"[32]

Mordechai paused again, but still no response.

"I tremble at what I see happening here. You have all sinned just by entering this palace. How can you participate in a celebration of the destruction of the *Beis HaMikdash* and the Almighty's abandonment of the Jewish people?[33] You have sinned further by your association with the defiled pagans all around you. Satan has contaminated you. How will you approach God in this state? Even if you survive, it will take years to recover.[34] Look around you. Don't you see the Persian idols sitting in every corner just waiting for you to pay them homage? How long do you think it will be before that happens? Not very long, I assure you. Oh, my poor brothers! All this has come upon you because you neglected learning the Torah. Had you been involved in Torah study, you would never have come to this place. But it is still not too late. Leave this place. Go home. Who has the courage to do what is right? Raise your hands!"[35]

Mordechai swept his gaze over the assembled Jews, but most of them turned away. They were so entrapped in the pleasures of the feast and the prospect of an unforgettable experience that they could not tear themselves away. Only a few raised their hands. Mordechai hugged them and sent them off with his fervent blessings and prayers. The others remained standing there, unable to leave, unwilling to show disrespect to Mordechai.[36]

"My dear brothers," said Mordechai, "my heart weeps for you. You are like flies trapped on a paper spread with honey. A large pit in *Gehinnom* awaits you. My only hope is that God will send a terrible decree against you that will galvanize you and inspire you to do *teshuvah*. That is your only hope, my poor brothers, your only hope."[37]

---

31. *Megillas Sesarim; Melo HaOmer.*

32. *R' Shmuel di Uzidah; Einei HaEidah.*

33. See *Yefei Anaf* to *Shir HaShirim Rabbah* 7:13; see *Rif* to *Ein Yaakov* on *Megillah* 12a.

34. *Kav HaYashar.*

35. *Megillah* 12a and *Ein Yaakov*; see *Esther Rabbah* 7:13 and *Anaf Yosef*; *Shir HaShirim Rabbah* 7:8; *Rokeach*; *Pri Tzaddik* on Purim. See *Alshich* to *Esther* 1:18, where he relates that the Jews committed seven transgressions at the feast.

36. See *Menos HaLevi* to *Esther* 2:5.

37. *Aggadas Esther. Rokeach* points out that the last letters of the Hebrew words *hanimtza'im beShushan HaBirah* can be rearranged to spell *Haman*.

The thin man cleared his throat. The glow of the wine had faded, and tears filled his eyes. "Mordechai, you know that we hold you in the highest esteem, but please understand. We mean no harm. We are still loyal to the Almighty. We still follow His Torah. We will try our hardest not to sin, or at least only to sin a little bit. But we cannot turn away from this spectacular feast. Never again in our lives will we experience such enjoyment. Never again will we walk home with our pockets full of priceless golden cups. Never again will we have the opportunity to have a great king minister to our every whim and desire. How can you ask us to give this up?"

"I am asking you to have the courage to do the right thing," Mordechai replied. "It is not permissible to sin a little bit, as you say. And besides, you will not stop at a little bit. You are already far past a little bit. I am leaving. Who is coming with me?"

Mordechai looked at them and walked away. They did not follow. Only the man with the gray beard seemed to waver for a moment. But then he, too, returned to his luxurious couch.

When Mordechai realized he was walking alone, he headed for the grand ballroom, where Achashverosh was holding court with his cronies and favorites. Hushed whispers greeted his entrance.

"Your majesty," he said, "may I have a private word with you?"

"Why, certainly, Mordechai," said Achashverosh. "You are my guest, and your wish is my command." He waved his hand at the people crowded all around him. "Everyone, back away. Move out of earshot. I must speak privately with our esteemed Jewish friend."

The area around the king's couch was instantly emptied. Only Achashverosh and Mordechai remained.

"Your majesty," said Mordechai, "since you are willing to grant every request today, I would like you to appoint me chief steward for the Jewish guests at this feast."

Achashverosh raised his eyebrows. "Oh? But why? We have plenty of stewards. More than enough for everyone. Your Jewish brothers are being taken care of very well."

"That is exactly what I fear, your majesty. They are so close to overstepping the line of sin. In fairness to me and my people, let me be their steward so that they will at least have a fighting chance."

"Hmm," said Achashverosh. "Let me see. I don't admit to what you are saying, Mordechai. I do not agree that the Jewish people are in any kind of danger at my feast in my palace. Still, you have made a request, and by my own words, I should try to accommodate you. Hmm."

Achashverosh mulled over the question for a minute or two. Then his face brightened.

"I have the answer!" he exclaimed. "I will appoint two chief stewards. You, Mordechai, will be one of them. The other will be Haman. I believe that will be the height of fairness."[38]

Mordechai knew he could not expect to extract any greater concessions from Achashverosh. How foolish Achashverosh is, he thought. Is this what he considers fair, even on the face of it? Can two men marry one woman? Can two ships sail in opposite directions when the wind is blowing only in one direction? Can Haman and I share one position? It is useless.

"Thank you, your majesty," he said. "You are most kind."[39]

As Mordechai had expected, his effectiveness was much reduced by Haman's appointment. Mordechai tried to prevent the Jews from drinking gentile wines and eating non-kosher or gentile foods. He appointed Jews to monitor the preparation of the food and the wine, but Haman managed to substitute non-kosher meats and other products, including untithed produce from *Eretz Yisrael*.[40] They only agreed on one point — to limit the Jews' intake of wine. Haman wanted to make sure that they were fully responsible for all the sins they were committing.[41]

Ultimately, Achashverosh wanted to lure the Jews into immoral sins, and he was successful. The food and the wines went to their heads and caused them to lose all rationality.

By the end of the seven days, the Jews had sinned miserably and repeatedly, bringing down upon themselves the divine wrath, as did

---

38. *Esther Rabbah* 7:13, 14, Rashi; *Megillah* 12a; see *Maharsha* there. See *Targum Rishon* who holds that Mordechai was not even at the feast. Many suggest that although Mordechai was not present at the feast, he had warned the Jews not to attend. Some further suggest that Mordechai was the only Jew in Shushan not to participate in the feast (*R' Elisha Galico*). Mordechai could not protest merely by slipping away from the feast, as some others did. As a leader, he had to take a public stand against it, and he is given specific credit for doing so. Similarly, Chananiah, Mishael and Azariah did not just avoid worshipping Nevuchadnezzar's idol; they took a public stand against it, risking their lives in the furnace, and are also given credit for their act (*Menos HaLevi Esther* 2:5).

39. *Esther Rabbah* 2:14.

40. *Ya'aros Devash*.

41. See *Geon Yaakov; Rif* to *Ein Yaakov* on *Megillah* 12a; *Ta'ama D'kra*.

Achashverosh for his unforgivable desecration of the holy vessels of the *Beis HaMikdash.*[42]

THE FEAST OF ACHASHVEROSH	
THE FEAST OF ACHASHVEIROSH	
ELEMENT OF THE FEAST	**FUNCTION**
COURTYARD	Eating
GARDEN	designed to entice the Jews
TENTS	sleeping and privacy
COUCHES	enticement for sin; also full of shatnez
7 DAYS	included Shabbos
COLORS	enticement to sin
CHILDREN	to involve the youth in sin
VASHTI WEDDING FEAST	similar to idol worship
TIMING	3-10 Tishrei, *Aseres Yemei Teshuvah*
BEIS HAMIKDASH VESSELS	violation of the holy property (*me'ilah*)
WINE	gentile wine
FOOD	non-kosher
FAMILIAR FOOD	was *tevel* (no *maaser* or *terumah* were taken)

---

42. *Megillas Sesarim; Torah Sheleimah; Rokeach; R' Yosef ibn Nachmiash; Esther Rabbah* 7:13; *Yad HaMelech.* See *Baal HaTurim* to *Devarim* 32:28.

Vashti's Feast

5

Vashti was a haughty woman, as one would expect from a pedigreed Babylonian princess, the daughter of Belshazzar and great-granddaughter of Nevuchadnezzar. As a twelve-year-old girl, she had witnessed the destruction of the Babylonian Empire and the death of her father. Her life had been spared, and now, six years later, she was the bride of the mighty King Achashverosh. But she never forgot her origins. She looked down with disdain at her husband as a commoner in comparison to her.

When Achashverosh hosted his lavish, one-hundred-and-eighty-day feast for the nobles and dignitaries of his empire, she was overcome by jealousy. With each passing day, Achashverosh's fame and glory kept rising to unprecedented heights, while she, the noble Vashti, went virtually unnoticed. Surely she, Nevuchadnezzar's sole surviving royal descendant, deserved equal fame and glory. But she wasn't getting it. As the great imperial feast drew to a close and Achashverosh announced an additional seven-day feast for the residents of Shushan, Vashti could contain herself no longer. She decided to act.

"I've had enough," she said to her favorite lady-in-waiting. "We are going to host our own feast for the women of Shushan."

"That is a wonderful idea, your majesty," said the lady-in-waiting. "Shall I have the servants prepare the harem building for the event?"

"The harem building? Perish the thought. We will have our feast right inside the palace, across the way from Achashverosh's feast.[1] Men are such boors, especially my husband. We will show them how to display treasures with style. Right?"

"Er, y-yes, your majesty."

"Good. First, we will decorate the second ballroom as no other ballroom has ever been decorated before. Oh, we will serve the best wines and foods, of course. But we must pay meticulous attention to décor. Men think with their stomachs. Give them enough good food, and they'd be perfectly happy dining in a barn. But women have a more refined esthetic sense. We must create the perfect confluence of color and form, with lighting that is not too harsh nor too soft. The tapestries and painting must be just right, and they must blend with each other in the most pleasing way. Give the instructions!"

"Yes, your majesty." The lady-in-waiting made as if to leave.

"Not so fast," said the queen. "We have more issues to discuss. The wines. Serve only soft, sweet wines, dark red in color. And as for the food, serve things that go down easily without much chewing. Soups would be perfect. Make sure we have a good selection of those. We want to give our guests plenty of choices, but within limits. Understand?"

"Perfectly, your majesty."[2]

"Now then, what to wear? I think I will also wear the garments of the *Kohein Gadol*, as my husband did. They are the most striking garments I have ever seen. And we will also display the captured vessels of the *Beis HaMikdash*. I want to draw the Jewish women into

1. *Yosef Lekach; R' Yosef ibn Nachmiash; Alshich; Maharal; Malbim; Yad HaMelech; R' Shmuel di Uzidah; Yishai Elokim*. Eventually, this lack of respect and struggle for independence would lead to Vashti's downfall and death. Some suggest that Achashverosh encouraged the women to have a feast so that they should not be jealous of the men (*Eshkol HaKofer*).

2. *Esther Rabbah* 3:10; *Yishai Elokim; Midrash Lekach Tov* 1:9. See *Radal*, who writes that it was considered disrespectful for women to drink wine. Achashverosh was motivated by the fact that he knew his wife well. Should she make a party in the company of men, she would surely act inappropriately (*Ben Yehoyada*).

sin, just as my husband is drawing the Jewish men into sin. I want them to join the feast that celebrates the destruction of their holy Temple. I want to complete my grandfather's work. He destroyed their Temple, and I will destroy them."[3]

"Your majesty, what will we tell the king? Why are we making a separate feast? Pardon me, but I need to know what to say if I am asked."

"Tell them we want to give ourselves special attention, since we are often neglected. We will invite all the women of Shushan. Tell them we are doing it to honor the king. Which is not true, of course. I don't care about the honor of that boor who calls himself my husband. We are doing it for my honor. Mine. Mine!

"And for my pleasure, of course," she whispered.

The lady-in-waiting fidgeted. "Yes, your majesty."

The queen laughed. "I want to break all the boundaries of modesty and decorum. I want my husband to see what I am doing, and I want him to be jealous!"

"Yes, your majesty. But I cannot repeat these things."

"I should hope not. But my husband will understand all this on his own. You won't have to tell it to him."

"Do you think the king will object to your plans, your majesty?"

"Achashverosh? That stable boy? Nah! He wouldn't dare!"

The lady-in-waiting turned crimson.

"Very well. Your question. Will my fat husband have any objections? No, he will be fine with it. Oh, I know him through and through, that peasant. I'll tell you exactly what will go through his mind. First of all, he'll see right through our stated reasons and understand right away that I am making this feast for my own honor. He'll consider me a fool, deserving of a husband whom people consider a fool. He will recognize that my ancestry is more ancient and illustrious than his, but he will dismiss it as deriving from an empire that no longer exists. In his mind, I am nothing without him. I am only queen because he is king. He is the one that counts."[4]

"Then you are saying he will object, your majesty?"

"Not at all. He will be happy to indulge me anyway. He knows that my feast will draw enticements and that is important to him.

---

3. *Esther Rabbah* 3:9, 3:3; *Me'am Loez.* See *Yefai Anaf,* who writes that they divided the clothing evenly; Achashverosh wore four of them, and Vashti wore the remaining four.
4. *Malbim; Alshich; Menos HaLevi.*

The more Jews drawn into his trap the better. He is just as much enamored of hedonistic pleasures as I am. At the same time, he wouldn't mind having his wife right where he can keep an eye on her, would he?"[5]

"I understand, your majesty."

"Wonderful. Now hurry up. There is no time to waste. Make sure everything is ready on time, or I will have you flogged."

Fortunately for the lady-in-waiting, everything was ready on time. Vashti drew hordes of people to her feast, and many of the women who at first came to Achashverosh's feast crossed over to the queen's.

Vashti also made good on her promise to display the vessels of the *Beis HaMikdash*. This was even more galling to the Jews than Achashverosh's display of the vessels. Achashverosh at least was not connected to the destruction itself. Vashti, on the other hand, was the direct descendant of Nevuchadnezzar, the man who had destroyed the *Beis HaMikdash*. She was a living link to that awful tragedy, and now, she was flaunting the spoils of the fallen Jewish kingdom. For many of the Jewish women, it was too much to bear, and they returned to their homes; they felt sure Hashem would cause Vashti's brazen activities to lead directly to her downfall. Unfortunately, others remained in spite of the humiliation and the salt rubbed in the national wounds.[6]

While this was going on, Mordechai and the members of the Sanhedrin fasted and prayed to Hashem. They pleaded with Him on behalf of the Jewish people trapped by their desires at the royal feast, and they also pleaded with Him to visit His divine wrath on the heads of the wicked king and queen, the sworn enemies of the Jewish people and their God. Their prayers were answered, and on the seventh day of the feast, the wheels of providence began to grind. Slowly but inexorably, the downfall of the wicked began on the day of their highest arrogance and conceit.[7]

For six days, the feast continued with wild merrymaking for Jew and pagan alike. On the sixth day, however, there was a change of mood among the Jews. The next day, the seventh and final day of the royal

5. See *Megillah* 12a; *Iyun Yaakov; Maharsha; HaKosev; Megillas Sesarim; Rambam; Maharal. Esther Rabbah* 3:10; *Yalkut Shimoni* 1049; *Malbim* to *Esther* 1:9. *See Rokeach;* see *Rashi* to *Sotah* 36b. Some suggest that unlike Achashverosh's feast which was outdoors and in public, Vashti showed modesty in making her feast indoors (*R' Yosef ibn Yachia*).
6. *Esther Rabbah* 3:5; *Rambam* to *Esther* 1:9; *Gra; Menos HaLevi; Me'am Loez.*
7. *Targum Sheni* 1:9.

feast, promised to be the crowning moment of the entire phenomenal experience, but for the Jews it also had other, more important significance. It was Shabbos, the holiest day of the week, a day celebrated by sober festivities infused with Torah and spirituality, unlike the pagan feasts that featured drunkenness and immorality. And it was also Yom Kippur, the holiest day of the year, a day of fasting, prayer and repentance. For the Jewish revelers, the spiritual tug of the day was too strong too resist, and with the grace of Heaven, they were able to escape the palace before the feast sank to the lowest levels of depravity.[8]

When the morning of the seventh day dawned, Achashverosh awoke with a feeling of unease. The one hundred and eighty days of the imperial feast had come to an end, and now the seven days of the Shushan feast were about to come to an end. And then it would all be over. Nothing more than a memory. He had accomplished everything he had set out to do. He had solidified his relations with the most important personages of every corner of his empire. He had impressed the entire civilized world with his seemingly limitless power and wealth. He had won the everlasting loyalty of the residents of Shushan, and he had set the Jews on a path that would lead to their destruction. And in the process, he had enjoyed the best time of his life. But what now? He felt the urge to do something to make this last day especially memorable, and his thoughts turned instinctively to wine.

Throughout the entire six months of festivities, Achashverosh had controlled his own drinking and that of his subjects. He did not let himself or anyone else step over the line of intoxication. Wine flowed freely as long as it brought people to the heights of alcohol-induced euphoria, but as soon as they seemed about to become drunk, the wine ceased to flow. On this day, the glorious final day of the festivities, Achashverosh decided to throw caution to the winds. There would be absolutely no restrictions. Everyone would be allowed to drink until they fell over senseless. The festivities would climax with a drunken bang to end all drunken bangs. It would be a day to remember.[9]

8. *Megillah* 12b; *Targum Sheni; Pirkei d'Rav Eliezer; Ya'aros Devash; Menos HaLevi.* R' Yonasan Eibeschutz comments that the fact that this spiritual triumph occurred on Yom HaKippurim is alluded to by our calling the holiday Purim.

9. *R' Yosef ibn Nachmiash; Midrash Lekach Tov; Rambam.* Some suggest that it took Achashverosh seven days to become inebriated. Others suggest that he never became drunk, only euphoric, from the wine. This would further point up his lowness, since then he could not use drunkenness to excuse his foolish actions at the party. See *R' Shmuel di Uzidah, Sha'ar bas Rabim; Sifsei Chachamim; Menos HaLevi.*

Achashverosh ordered that strong wines of very old vintage be brought from the royal wine cellars. In addition, he had designated a different personal attendant to serve him wine each day. Now, on the seventh day, he ordered all seven attendants to stand behind him at the ready with a full decanter of wine to make sure that he would never have to wait even one extra moment for a fresh drink of wine. Within a short time, the king and his cronies were thoroughly inebriated. They drank and laughed and drank some more.

"Look at my wife's party," Achashverosh said, his words slurred.

He pointed with his goblet in hand, and the wine in it sloshed over and stained his garments. He brushed at the stain with his sleeve and only succeeded in spilling more wine.

"Bah!" he shouted. "What does a stain matter? I am king!" He pointed again at Vashti's party, this time with his free hand. "Do you think they are having as good a time as we are?"

"Impossible, your majesty," declared a courtier. "Can there be a greater joy in this world than drinking the king's choicest wines in the company of the king himself?"

Not unexpectedly, the celebration quickly deteriorated into lewd dissipation. The ballroom reverberated with suggestive music, drunken laughter, song, and debauchery. Presently, an argument broke out between the Persian and Medean nobles of the imperial court defending their nationalities.

The insults flew back and forth as more and more men joined the argument on both sides. With the situation about to get out of control, Achashverosh called for silence.[10]

"Gentlemen, gentlemen," he declared, "your arguments are for the wind. You are both wrong. Neither the Persians nor the Medeans can compare to my own wife Vashti, the queen!"

"Your majesty, may I take the liberty of speaking boldly?" asked a young courtier with a sly grin.

"Speak!" said Achashverosh. "You have my permission."

"Your majesty, your wish is my command. We have all heard you sing the praises of the queen, but is it not possible that it is the product of her royal garments and jewels? You must admit, your majesty, that being a queen is an unfair advantage."

---

10. *Megillah* 12b; *Targum Sheni*; *Pirkei d'Rav Eliezer*; *Midrash Panim Acheirim*; *Esther Rabbah* 3:13; *Menos HaLevi*; *Yad HaMelech*.

Achashverosh, his eyes slightly out of focus, scowled at the young courtier. "You raise a good point, young fellow. I can see that royal garments might make anyone seem beautiful." "Yes, your majesty," said the young courtier.

"With your majesty's permission, may I speak my mind without fear of retribution? If I offend you, please attribute my bad manners to the wine, not to any disrespect I may harbor in my heart."

"Go ahead," said Achashverosh impatiently. "What's on your mind? Speak!"

"Well, your majesty, it seems to me the only way we can make a fair comparison is if the queen appears before us."

Achashverosh fixed the young courtier with a long stare and fell silent. The courtier trembled with fear, sure that he had overstepped his bounds and brought disgrace and death upon himself.

"You know something, young fellow?" said Achashverosh at last. "You are a brazen scoundrel to ask for something like that, but you are really on to something there. In fact I should have thought of it myself. Here I've been displaying all my treasures and wealth for six months, and I neglected to display my most prized trophy - my wife![11] I want everyone to know that I possess the most prized treasure in the empire. We will do as you say, young fellow. She will come before us."[12]

Events, clearly guided by the divine response to Mordechai's prayers, had now taken an exceedingly bizarre turn. Achashverosh had completely lost command of his senses in a torrent of strong wine. He was headed down the path to doom.[13]

Achashverosh snapped his fingers. "Attendants! Come here, all seven of you."

The seven attendants put down their wine bottles and ran to stand before the king.

"Listen to me carefully," said Achashverosh. "You heard what has been going on here. I want you to go as a group to Vashti and tell her to come here immediately by command of the king. One of

---

11. *Megillah* 12b; see *Ben Yehoyada*; *Esther Rabbah* 3:13; *Menos HaLevi*; *Rabbeinu Bachyei*; *R' Avigdor Kohen Tzedek*; *Chasam Sofer*; *Yishai Elokim*.

12. *Rabbenyu Bachei*; *R' Avigdor Kohen Tzedek*; *Malbim*. Achashverosh had not entertained thoughts of having the queen appear unclad at the first feast, where many rulers and generals who had also served under the Babylonian Empire were present. Had he humiliated the princess of their former emperor they would not have taken it well. Achashverosh's authority and stature might have been undermined (*Yad HaMelech*).

13. *Megillas Sesarim*.

you is to bring her crown along. After everyone has seen her, she may put the crown upon her head to prove that she is indeed the queen who is familiar to all, not some impostor. Also, when she puts on the crown in my presence, she will realize that her only claim to royalty is as my wife. Now go!"[14]

"Your majesty," said one of the attendants, "why are you sending seven simple men such as we are? Wouldn't it be more appropriate to send distinguished people to bring the queen to you?"

Achashverosh looked at him through narrowed eyes. "What is going on today? Everyone seems to feel free to question everything I say. First our clever young scoundrel and now you. It is not for you to second-guess my commands. Do you hear me?"

"Yes, your majesty. Oh, yes, your majesty. I meant no offense. A thousand pardons, your majesty. Please take pity on me. I am nothing but a miserable dog. It is as if I said nothing, your majesty."

"Indeed, it is. But I will answer your question nonetheless. I am sending you seven for that very reason. Because you are nothing but miserable dogs. I want Vashti to be humiliated. I want her to let go of her haughty airs and acknowledge that she is nothing without me. And when others see the haughty Vashti humble herself before me, they too will be subservient to me. Do you understand?"[15]

"Oh, yes, your majesty."

"Then begone with you. Go get the queen!"

Who were these seven attendants? The *Megillah* identifies them as Bizesa, Charbonah, Bigsa, Avagsa, Zesar and Carcas, men of no particular distinction (although some suggest Achashverosh sent Haman and Eliyahu *HaNavi*).[16] In fact, these weren't even their real names but rather words to recall different aspects of the incident. Vashti faced imminent humiliation (*bizesa*) before the people, making her a laughingstock even in the eyes of the lowly women who worked with the olive (*zesar*) and wine presses. The attendants were the messengers God sent to bring chaos and commotion to the feast. Vashti had caused her own destruction (*charbonah*) because of her

14. *Targum Sheni; R' Yosef ibn Yachia.* Some suggest that the king did not order Vashti to appear unclothed, merely dressed in plain garments instead of her royal ones. See the *Maharal* for further discussion regarding this view.

15. *Menos HaLevi; Yad HaMelech; Malbim; Alshich.*

16. See *Ibn Ezra.* Again, Achashverosh wished to compare himself to Hashem. Just as Hashem has seven constellations to serve the world, so he was served by seven attendants.

immoral lifestyle and because she had prevented the reconstruction of the destroyed *Beis HaMikdash*.[17]

In truth, Vashti had brought this retribution upon herself through her treatment of the Jewish girls who worked in the palace. She forced them to work on Shabbos, performing forbidden labors such as combing and beating wool and flax. She also insisted that they do their work immodestly attired. If the women refused to obey, she would have them executed. In the meantime, she would allow other maids on the palace staff to rest from work on Shabbos so that they could stand by and laugh and jeer at the Jewish girls forced to work on Shabbos.[18]

Vashti conducted a concerted campaign against Shabbos observance. She was convinced that the most effective way to prevent the reconstruction of the *Beis HaMikdash* was to promote Shabbos desecration, and she concentrated her efforts against the young Jewish girls directly under her thumb. She prevented them from wearing their fine Shabbos clothes and singing songs of praise to Hashem on Shabbos, and she deprived them of their physical and spiritual day of rest.

Because of her campaign against Shabbos observance, her efforts to prevent the reconstruction of the *Beis HaMikdash* and her profane use of the captured Temple vessels, it was decreed in Heaven that Vashti was to die; Achashverosh was spared so that he could marry Esther and sire a son who would rebuild the *Beis HaMikdash*. And because of the humiliation of the young Jewish girls in the palace, Vashti suffered immense humiliation and indignity before she finally died.[19]

When the seven attendants entered the queen's ballroom, they found her sitting amidst a large circle of admirers, drinking wine and laughing. The guests glanced curiously at the seven undistinguished attendants, then turned their backs disdainfully, as if they had seen nothing at all.

"Your majesty," one of them called out, "we bear a message from his majesty the king. He wants you to come to him."

---

17. See *Targum Rishon; Midrash Lekach Tov; Esther Rabbah* 3:12; see *Yefei Anaf* and *Rashash* there.

18. *Megillah* 12b; *Iyun Yaakov; Targum Rishon; Chida, Esther* ch. 2; *Rambam*

19. See *Esther Rabbah* 5:2; *Midrash Panim Acheirim; Rashi; Maharal; Sifsei Chachamim; Menos HaLevi.*

Vashti looked down her nose at them for an agonizingly long minute. Then she motioned them forward with an imperious flourish of her bejeweled fingers.

"Seven little men to carry a single message?" she sniffed. "How odd."

"Your majesty, could we speak with you in private?"

"Why do we need to speak? My husband wants me to come, and I shall. Eventually. Tell my husband to be patient. I will be along soon."[20]

"Your majesty, I beg of you," said the attendant, "let me speak to you in private. There is more to the message."

Vashti looked at the attendant with utter scorn. "I will certainly not speak with you in private, little man."

"Very well," the attendant groaned. "The king orders you to come to him immediately. He wants to show off your beauty to everyone there."

A shocked gasp greeted his words. The queen gawked at him in disbelief.

"Are you completely out of your mind?" she shrieked.

"I am so sorry, your majesty," he said. He gulped and turned to the other attendants. "Am I not telling the truth?"

They all nodded in assent.

Vashti grabbed her head with both hands. "I can't believe that fool would stoop so low. He must be drunk out of his head. Doesn't that fool know that my humiliation is also his humiliation? What an idiot! Go back and tell your foolish master that I'm not coming. The nerve!"[21]

The seven attendants brought Vashti's reply back to the king, all of it. They did not omit even one derogatory word.

Achashverosh was annoyed by Vashti's disrespect. His mellow, wine-soaked mood began to shift to anger.

"Listen to me," he shouted. "You go back to Vashti and tell her that if she does not comply with my wishes, I will have her executed. Then we will see how she looks when she is dead! Don't bother coming back without her."

The attendants scurried back to the queen with the king's reply. "You must come at once and present yourself before his guests."

A chill went through Vashti as it dawned on her that Achashverosh was deadly serious. She quickly discarded her haughty airs and became conciliatory.

---

20. *Rambam.*
21. *Targum Sheni; Ibn Ezra; Eshkol HaKofer; Maharal.*

"Look, gentlemen," she said, "the king is apparently determined that I do this . . . this . . . thing for him." She threw up her hands. "What can I do? I must submit to the will of the king. But surely there must be some room for compromise, for some consideration to my status as queen of the realm. Perhaps the king could bring his entourage here to see me. That would be more respectable for me. Perhaps he can come with some of the highest noblemen, men of distinction, unlike yourselves. Don't you see there are so many options? All we have to do is think a little. We can work it out."

The seven attendants returned to the king with Vashti's suggestions, but he remained adamant.[22]

"I'm sorry, your majesty," said the attendant when he returned to Vashti. "The king refuses to budge. It must be exactly as he originally demanded. You must come to him and show yourself to his guests. There are no ifs, ands or buts about it."

"My dear little man," said the queen, "there is always some room for compromise – but I guess the king doesn't agree." Vashti shrugged. "I thought it was reasonable, but what do I know?"[23]

Slowly it sunk into Vashti's consciousness that every avenue of escape from total humiliation was cut off, and she flew into a terrible rage, screaming and cursing in the strange Babylonian and Chaldean dialects of her youth, which the attendant happened to understand. She stormed back and forth, kicking at the precious vessels and smashing the delicate crystals under her shoe.

"Listen to me, you little, little men," she hissed when she had finally calmed down somewhat. "You go back to that drunken fool of a master, and tell him he is not even worthy of being my father's stable boy, let alone the husband of my father's daughter. With the morality of a horse, what kind of king can he possibly be? He is not even worthy of running in front of my father's steeds. Pah! I remember him spending time in my father's stable; now that he is king, he hasn't changed."

"Your majesty, please don't say these things to us," pleaded the attendant. "The king will ask us what you said, and we will be obliged to repeat every word."

---

22. *R' Shmuel di Uzidah; Maharal; Ben Yehoyada; Yishai Elokim.* The immoral Vashti wanted the king and all his male guests to join her and her friends at the feast. Achashverosh knew this and would not permit it.

23. See *Esther Rabbah* 3:13; *Targum Sheni; Midrash Panim Acheirim; Yalkut Shimoni;* and *D'na Pishra* for further insight into the ongoing debate and the compromises Vashti suggested.

"I don't care! Repeat what I say! I want you to tell him every single word. I want him to know what an idiot he is. Oh, he infuriates me. That drunken bum thinks he can compare to my father. What a joke! My father could drink a thousand men under the table without getting drunk. He could drink wine like an ox drinks water, with no ill effects. But this fool of a husband of mine gets drunk like a peasant. He is out of his mind. What sane person would treat a respected queen as he is treating me?"

"Your majesty, I plead with you, I implore you, do not say these things to us. Even if you think them, please don't say them aloud. It will only make it worse if we hear them and all your ladies hear them. Please, your majesty, can you please calm down?"[24]

"Calm down? Calm down?" she sputtered. "I see you are also out of your mind. How am I supposed to calm down when my husband has just told me to show myself unclothed to all his guests? Me, a respected queen, his own wife, the great-granddaughter of Nevuchadnezzar who ruled the world, me he tells to do this? Me he treats like some peasant or maidservant?"

"Your majesty, please come," said the attendant. "There really is no choice. Why work yourself up and keep sending these insulting messages back to the king? If you come, we won't have to repeat any of these things. Will you come?"

"But don't you realize how stupid it is for me to show myself to his guests? Does he think that every single one of his guests will have consenting opinions about my appearance? I think that is impossible. No matter how great things are, someone always has something negative to say. And where does that leave the king? With people who will call him a liar! Don't you see? The plan is not good. The logic is faulty. Do you understand what I am saying?"[25]

"Yes, your majesty."

Her eyes lit up, and she smiled graciously. "Perfect. Then go back and explain it to the king."

"We cannot, your majesty," the attendant replied. "The king has given us specific instruction not to come back without you. He is not interested in arguments, negotiations and compromises.

---

24. See *Megillah 12b* and *Tosafos HaRosh* there; *Ben Yehoyada*; *Esther Rabbah 3:14*; *Aggadas Esther*; *Yosef Lekach*.

25. *Esther Rabbah 3:4*; *Menos HaLevi*; *Alshich*; *Midrash Panim Acheirim*; *R' Yosef ibn Nachmiash*.

He wants you to come, exactly as he said, and that is the end of it. Period."

In an instant, the queen's rage was back in full force. "I am the queen. Such humiliation! Why can't that fool of a husband of mine send for me with more respectable messengers? Noblemen, officials, warriors. Not sniveling little wine stewards like you. How dare he treat me like a common criminal or a slave! Tell him to send better messengers, and I will come."[26]

The attendant drew himself to his full height. "Your majesty, you are wasting your time and putting yourself into great and unnecessary danger. The king specifically expressed his wish that we bring you and not more noble messengers. This is his wish, and there is nothing you can do to change it. You want options? Well, there are options from which you can choose. You can come peacefully with your head held high, or we can drag you there against your will. The choice is yours!"

Vashti sighed, like a punctured balloon. "I'll come with you," she said. "But I need a few minutes to prepare myself if I am to endure this terrible ordeal with dignity."[27]

The attendant bowed deferentially. "Of course, your majesty. That seems to be a very reasonable request, and I am sure the king would have no objections. We will wait here. When you are ready, we will escort you to the king."

As the queen walked off to her chambers to prepare herself the angel Gavriel came down and planted certain thoughts in her mind, thoughts that would ensure her ignominious downfall. The queen closed the door behind her, and everyone settled down to wait anxiously for the next development in the enfolding drama.

Everything was quiet for the first few minutes, and then a series of horrible screams rent the air. "What happened in there?" the attendant asked, ashen-faced. "Why was the queen screaming?"

"I'm not sure," said one of the ladies-in-waiting. "I think she was saying that something had happened to her. This may sound ridiculous, but she said something about a tail. She was crying out that a tail had materialized on her forehead. She had just finished making her preparations in front of the mirror when a long piece of skin

---

26. *Alshich; Menos HaLevi; Malbim, Melo HaOmer; R' Chaim Abalafia; Menos HaLevi;Yad HaMelech.*
27. See *Rambam; R' Elisha Galico; Maharal; Menos HaLevi; Alshich; Malbim.*

shaped like a tail just grew out of her forehead. So she started
screaming. What would you have done under the circumstances? A
tail on the forehead is something to scream about."

"I have to disagree with you," said a lady with blue hair. "I was
also there, right outside the room, and I'm quite sure I heard what
she said. She didn't mention anything about a tail."

"I heard her say something about lesions," said one lady. "She
was screaming that lesions had broken out all over herself, that she
couldn't go out in public all covered in lesions. People would think
she didn't keep herself clean. That was about all of it."

"Look, maybe this is all for the best," said the lady in green. "If she
has a tail on her face or lesions she won't be able to go to the king."

The king's attendants stood by without comment, listening to the
conversations of the ladies-in-waiting.

Many minutes passed, and still the queen remained barricaded in
the powder room by herself.[28]

The door opened a crack, and the queen's toe appeared. All eyes
strained forward to catch the first glimpse of her. Everyone stared in
dismay. There were no tails or lesions. Vashti was as normal looking as ever.

The king's attendants and the ladies-in-waiting exchanged puzzled glances. What was the queen talking about? Had she lost her
mind? Was she suffering from hallucinations? Perhaps it was all a
ruse to avoid the king's command.

"Your majesty, are you feeling well?" asked the lady in green.
"We see nothing on you. No tails, no lesions. You look as you
always do."

"Liar!" shouted the queen. "You just want me to go like this and
be humiliated!

"Your majesty, listen to me," said the king's attendant. "All of us
here see quite clearly that there is nothing wrong with you. Now,
some people might accuse you of play-acting in order to avoid the
king's command. I do not harbor such suspicions. You are clearly
under the delusion that you have become deformed. The royal
physicians tell us that stress sometimes plays tricks on the mind,

---

28. *Megillah* 12b; *Rambam; Yad HaMelech; D'na Pishra.* See *Sefer HaAruch* under letter
zayin, "*zanav*." The reference to a tail was symbolic. This showed that Vashti was the
"tail" end of Nevuchadnezzar's dynasty, and with her death it would be over (*Chida*
to *Esther* ch. 2). See *Ein Yaakov* and *Menos HaLevi* who discuss what the tail represented and why Vashti was punished in this way. Some suggest that she developed something similar to a camel's hump or a hunched back (*Midrash* in *Torah Sheleimah*).

and you are clearly under stress. Come with us to the king as he commanded. In an hour it will be over. Then you can retire to your apartments and lie down for a while. Your stress will pass, and you will come back to normal. You will see. Just come with us, and all will be well."

The queen hesitated. Apparently, everyone thought there was nothing wrong with her. Maybe it was a delusion caused by stress. Maybe she should go and just get it over with.[29]

Vashti squared her shoulders with renewed pride. "Thank you, ladies. That is exactly what I needed to hear. I appreciate your loyalty and your concern for my welfare. You are right, of course. In my family traditions, we never humiliated people like this. Even rebels on their way to execution were allowed to keep their dignity. And my foolish husband Achashverosh heaps this humiliation on me? On Vashti? Well! I simply won't stand for it. He can do whatever he pleases, but I am not coming to him, not under any circumstances. I've had enough!"

"We are behind you, your majesty," said her ladies. "We will stand by you no matter what happens."

"Thank you so much, ladies," said the queen. She turned to the king's attendants. "As for you, little men, get out of my sight right now. Go back and tell that big boorish husband of mine everything I said. Do not omit a single word, no matter how scathing."[30]

When the attendants returned to Achashverosh, they found him seething with impatience. Hashem had obviously kindled the coals of wrath in his heart, and they seemed about to explode into a raging fire.

"Where have you been so long?" demanded Achashverosh. "And where is the queen?"

"May we speak in private, your majesty?" they said.

Achashverosh sent away everyone within earshot, and the attendants reported to him in full, including everything Vashti had said in her native Babylonian dialects.

The news struck Achashverosh's heart like a spark on dry tinder. He exploded in a great conflagration of rage, bellowing at the top of

---

29. *Rambam.* Others suggest that Vashti was experiencing a particularly difficult monthly cycle. She became very ill and clearly could not appear in public in the manner that Achashverosh requested. This was in retribution for making Jewish women work under similar conditions (see *Midrash Megillah; Menos HaLevi*).

30. *Esther Rabbah* 3:14; *Midrash Aba Gorion; Gra; Yosef Lekach.*

his lungs. His face turned a bright crimson, and his eyes bulged in their sockets.[31]

"What an outrage!" he roared. "What disrespect! I've never seen anything like it. Has there ever been a person more ungrateful than Vashti? After all that my father did for her! He spared her life when he killed her father Belshazzar, and he gave her to me. She could have been dead, rotting in some grave, and instead she is queen of an empire. And she thinks it is all coming to her. How ungrateful! What a nerve this woman has."

The king's volcanic outburst brought guests running from all sides, stumbling over each other with their solicitous questions.

"What happened, your majesty?"

"What has Queen Vashti done, your majesty?"

"What can we do to be of help, your majesty?"

."Can I bring you a glass of water, your majesty?"

"Can I bring you another glass of wine?"

Achashverosh tried to reply, but he could only splutter with frustration. The violent storm aroused in his emotions by Vashti's words mixed with too much wine kept gaining in force. It swept away his ability to respond with any measure of calm. It swept away his ability to think clearly and rationally. Deep down, he knew he had acted like a fool, that his wine-induced command to his queen was inexcusable, but he was powerless to do anything about it. The violent storm of rage swept him inexorably to a climax of royal retribution. On the outside, he glowered, but on the inside, he cringed, wondering if he could do anything to save Vashti's life.[32]

---

31. *Melo HaOmer* to *Esther* 1:22; *Chasam Sofer*; *Esther Rabbah* 3:15.

32. See *Rambam*; *Gra*; *Melo HaOmer*; *R' Shmuel di Uzidah*; *Yosef Lekach*. See *Yoma* 75a regarding the benefits of verbal expression to rid oneself of anxiety.

Vashti on Trial

6

Even in his drunken stupor, Achashverosh knew he had gotten himself into serious trouble. Although Vashti had infuriated him by her refusal to respond to his summons, he did not want to lose her. She was a woman of royal stature, she was his wife, and he owed her the benefit of doubt. But he faced a serious dilemma. He wanted to spare her life, yet he could not allow himself to be humiliated in front of his nation.

Achashverosh knew he would have to bring Vashti to the bar of justice before he could do anything at all. If he wanted to save her life, he needed to appoint wise and experienced judges who would give her a fair trial. Ordinarily, the king himself presided over the courts in cases involving capital punishment. In this case, however, he had to recuse himself because of his anger and his personal involvement.[1]

His first choices for trial judges were the distinguished Jewish scholars of the Sanhedrin and the

1. *Gra; Menos HaLevi.*

tribe of Yissachar, known for their knowledge of Torah law, Persian and Medean law, general wisdom and familiarity with the astronomical and astrological charts. They were also conversant with legal precedent and able to cite voluminous case law for just about every legal situation. They were recognized and respected throughout the empire as fair and impartial arbiters of the law.[2]

Achashverosh pinned his hopes, to a large degree, on the astrological expertise of the judges. Perhaps they could find some vindication of Vashti's behavior in the pathways of the stars. Who knows? Perhaps it was written in the stars that the king was to suffer a violent death and only his embarrassment at Vashti's rejection had spared him. If that were the case, Vashti deserved to be rewarded, not punished. Or else, Vashti may have been under an adverse astrological influence caused by the confluence of incompatible signs. If that were the case, she would have been incapable of responding rationally and could not be held responsible for her actions.[3]

Of equal and perhaps greater importance was the issue of culpability and mitigating circumstances. Of course, on the face of it, *prima facie*, defiance of the king was a capital offense, punishable by death. But surely, the circumstances of the offense had to be taken into consideration. One, the king had been intoxicated with wine when he issued his command. Two, the queen was a high royal personage, descended from the illustrious imperial lineage of Babylon, and she deserved to be treated with respect, not ordered to appear in front of a multitude of drunken guests at the king's feast; she certainly should not have been summoned by lowly wine stewards instead of men of higher birth. Third, the queen had not actively defied the king's command; she had merely failed to comply through inaction.[4]

---

2. *Esther Rabbah* 4:1; see *Matnos Kehunah; Yefei Anaf; Megillah* 12b; *Targum Rishon; Rabbeinu Bachyei; Rokeach; Aggadas Esther*; see *R' Saadiah Gaon; R' Yosef ibn Nachmiash; Menos HaLevi; Ibn Ezra; Targum Rishon; Ya'aros Devash*. See *Ben Yehoyada* to *Megillah* 12b; who points out that if Vashti was twelve years old at the time Belshazzar was overthrown, she would have been nineteen in the third year of Achashverosh's reign. If Vashti was nineteen, then she would not yet have been liable for the punishment of *kareis* according to Jewish law. The critical issue was whether an additional month of Adar had been added, making it a leap year; if it was a leap year, she would be a month shy of her twentieth birthday. If not, she would already be twenty years old, and thus liable to the death penalty. The Jewish scholars were needed to resolve this question. Some commentators question this approach, considering that Vashti was not Jewish and she was not being tried by a Jewish court.

3. *Menos HaLevi.*

4. See *Gra; Menos HaLevi; Yosef Lekach; Alshich; Yad HaMelech.*

On the other hand, there were the broader ramifications to be taken into account. This was no ordinary private domestic squabble in the royal apartments. The queen had publicly humiliated the king who ruled half the world. Not only had she committed an offense against her husband, she had also done damage to the institution of the throne. Furthermore, if the queen escaped punishment, a dangerous precedent would be set for families throughout the empire. The status of men would fall in the eyes of women, and they would treat their husbands with disrespect.[5]

This was indeed not a simple case, and Achashverosh hoped the Jewish sages would be the best qualified to find their way through the legal and ethical maze and snatch his beloved Vashti from the jaws of death.

There was no time to waste. With the feast proceeding all around him, the king summoned the Jewish sages for an immediate consultation.

The sages were much perturbed; they felt they were walking into a snake pit. If they were to exonerate Vashti, the empire would be in an uproar. Accusations of undermining the throne would be hurled against the Jews. If, however, they were to have her executed, the king might have second thoughts and seek to pardon her, but it would be too late; then he would blame the Jews for killing his beloved queen. Furthermore, if they were to condemn Vashti to death, they would be accused of exacting vengeance for her halting the reconstruction of the *Beis HaMikdash*. There was no question about it. This was a trial to be avoided at all costs.[6]

One of the sages stepped forward to address the king. "Your majesty, my colleagues and I are deeply honored that you have chosen us to adjudicate at this landmark trial you will be conducting today. It is an immense honor that you have such confidence in our fairness, impartiality and skill. The reputation of Jewish jurisprudence was earned through centuries of outstanding performance, but I must inform you, your majesty, that conditions have changed."

Slouched in a chair, the king looked miserable. "How so?" he asked.

"Before the destruction of our Holy Temple, we would ask all our difficult questions of the *Urim VeTumim*, which the High Priest wore, and God would answer us directly. But those days are gone.

5. *Alshich; Chida; Megillas Sesarim; Yosef Lekach; Menos HaLevi; Melo HaOmer.*
6. *Yefei Anaf* to *Esther Rabbah* 4:1; *Megillah* 12b, Rambam.

We have no Temple, and we have no *Urim VeTumim*. We are reduced to the level of ordinary men. We have suffered exile and tragedy, and our scholarship has suffered as well."

"But surely your sages are men of towering stature, aren't they?"

"Some of them are indeed, your majesty," said the sage. "But our greatest sages left the palace when you brought out the sacred vessels of the Holy Temple and used them during the feast. They could not sit by and watch; it was much too painful for them. Who knows where they have gone? All you have available to you are the miserable few you see before you right now, the ones who did not have the courage to leave when the sacred vessels were displayed."[7]

Achashverosh scowled and grunted, but he said nothing.

"Perhaps you could call on the judges of Ammon and Moav," the sage added hastily. "They have had a rather peaceful history. I believe you have a close personal relationship with them. Moreover, intoxication will undoubtedly be a crucial issue in the deliberations of the trial judges, as the patriarchs of Ammon and Moav were born as a result of intoxication. They may have some additional insight into the issue that will help them penetrate to the core of the case."[8]

"So?" asked Achashverosh. "Will this incline them to exonerate Vashti?"

"I'm not sure, your majesty," said the sage. "But now that you mention it, there is another important point. The most famous woman of Moabite extraction is Ruth, a woman known for her extraordinary modesty. I think this would qualify the Moabite judges to consider a case in which Vashti's modesty caused her to decline the king's invitation. I think they would conduct a trial that was clearly fair, yet would seek to exonerate the queen if it were at all possible. After all, isn't this what you want, your majesty?"[9]

"Hmm," said the king, "Let me think." He leaned back and closed his eyes. Presently, his breathing settled into a regular pattern, his lips fluttering with each exhalation. The Jewish sages weren't sure if he was thinking or if he had fallen asleep.

At that very moment, the angels and the righteous Jewish people aware of the royal summons to the sages prayed to Hashem. "O Lord, in the merit of the many sacrifices we brought to You when

---

7. *Rambam.*

8. *Megillah* 12b; *Esther Rabbah* 4:1; *Me'am Loez.* This refers to the incident of Lot and his daughters.

9. *Ben Yehoyada* to *Megillah* 12b.

the *Beis HaMikdash* was still standing, please extract our people from this predicament. Please let Vashti be found guilty and executed for her obstruction of the reconstruction, but let it all happen without our involvement."[10]

Apparently, the prayers were accepted. The king opened his eyes and looked at the Jewish sages. He seemed preoccupied with other thoughts.

"You can go," he said, dismissing them with an imperious wave of his hand. He did not give them another thought. His mind was already focused on his next option — his elite officer corps.

Achashverosh's thoughts turned in the direction of his officers, seven of them in particular. Each of these officers attended to Achashverosh personally on a different day of the week. On this day, however, the grand finale of the seven-day Shushan feast, all seven were in attendance. They were available to serve as the trial judges.

Although they did not have a background in law, these seven held high office in the imperial administration as trusted advisors of the king. At the same time, people would accept the unanimous ruling of seven officers as impartial, especially since they were not natives of the imperial capital.[11] Achashverosh could count on them to do his bidding, and he knew he could communicate his wishes to them with the slightest twitch of his face.[12]

The seven officers are identified in the *Megillah*. Karshena, who was from Africa, supervised the maintenance of the royal livestock and the royal stables. Shesar, who was from India, supervised the wine cellars in the royal palace. Admasa, who was from Europe, was the royal surveyor and supervisor of crops. Tarshish, who was

---

10. See *R' Shmuel di Uzidah; Targum Rishon, Megillah* 12b. See *Alshich* to *Esther* 1:17, where he describes how the seven *korbanos* should atone for the seven transgressions committed at the feast.

11. *Targum Sheni; Esther Rabbah* 4:2,3; *Megillah* 12b; *Rokeach; R' Yosef ibn Nachmiash; Menos HaLevi; Yosef Lekach; Malbim; Me'am Loez.* Others suggest that these were highly decorated officers, who had served under Belshazzar, and had been spared by Darius when he assassinated the king. They merited this because they did not use the vessels of the *Beis HaMikdash.* Some suggest that these seven officers were former leaders of the first seven of the one hundred and twenty-seven nations Achashverosh ruled (*Me'am Loez*).

12. *Malbim, Me'am Loez; R' Shmuel di Uzidah.* Some suggest, as we will see, that only one of the seven was serving the king on this day, as each one was assigned one day a week to serve him. According to the view that these men were distinguished officers long before Achashverosh rose to power, it would be highly improbable that they would be biased in favor of the king; more likely they would do what they determined was right.

from Egypt, was the royal butler and the manager of the royal
household. Meress, who was from Yerushalayim, was the main
chef, the one who prepared and inspected the king's personal food.
Marsena, who was also from Yerushalayim, was the royal baker.
Memuchan was the royal caterer, the manager of the royal kitchens
and supervisor of all food preparation.[13]

There is some uncertainty regarding the names of the officers.
Were these their actual names or were they titles reflecting their
imperial duties? There are also a number of questions regarding the
identity of these men. According to some, they may have been from
Ammon and Moav.[14] According to others, they may have been Jews,
and Memuchan may have been the prophet Daniel, who sought to
remove Vashti for the spiritual benefit of the Jews. Furthermore,
Belshazzar had given Daniel a wealthy Persian wife who refused to
speak anything but Persian in their home. Abused himself, Daniel
sought to make an example of Vashti for the entire kingdom to
ensure that other men would not have to suffer similar abuse.[15]
According to this view, he was called Memuchan, because he was
always ready to perform miracles.[16]

There is a more widely held view that Memuchan was none other
than Haman, the Amalekite descendant. He was called Memuchan
either because he had been prepared to bring destruction to Vashti and
ultimately to himself or because he was always ready to speak out and
offer his unsolicited opinion and advice.[17] According to some, he was

---

13. *Esther Rabbah* 4:2; *Midrash Abba Gorion*; *Midrash Panim Acheirim*; *Me'am Loez*. Some
suggest that the names of these officers also referred to the impending suffering and
death which would befall them in the future.

14. See *Rashi* and *Maharsha* to *Megillah* 12b.

15. *Esther Rabbah* 4:6; *Pirkei d'Rav Eliezer* 49; *Targum Sheni*. See *Tosafos* to *Megillah* 12b;
Me'am Loez. Some suggest that Vashti's refusal to come merely stemmed from her
wish to avoid seeing Daniel whom she despised for prophesying the end of
Nevuchadnezzar's reign. She had not forgiven him for this, and would do anything
not to cross paths with this man whom she considered evil (*Midrash Megillas Esther*).

16. *Midrash Panim Acheirim*; *Targum Sheni*; *Midrash Chaseiros V'Yeseiros*.

17. See *Rashi* and *Maharsha* to *Megillah* 12b; *Aggadas Esther*; *Bava Basra* 19a; see *Yosef
Lekach*. Others suggest that Memuchan was the angel Gavriel who was sent as the inter-
mediary who would bring about Vashti's death and thus lay the groundwork for
Esther to eventually become Queen. Others point out that the letters of Memuchan can
be rearranged to spell *mum kan* (as in *Esther* 1:16); literally, *a blemish is here*. His words
would cause his own downfall in the future (*Rokeach; Chida*). The numerical value of
Memuchan is 156, the same as that of Yosef. Because Yosef's brothers had sold him,
their descendants would suffer at the hands of Memuchan. They would ultimately be
saved by Mordechai, a descendant of Binyamin who was not present at the sale (*Chida*).

the least knowledgeable and the most foolish among the king's advisors. According to others, he was the most knowledgeable.[18]

The king convened the trial with the seven officers presiding. The wine stewards and other witnesses were called to give testimony about all that had transpired. Once the facts of the case had been established, the officers began their deliberations in the presence of the king.

"Gentlemen, you have a grave duty to perform." said Achashverosh. "You must uphold the laws of the land with complete fairness and impartiality. What Vashti has done cannot be taken lightly. It is a very serious matter. At the same time, you must also take into consideration every mitigating circumstance and nuance of the law. You must also look at the technicalities. Did she really disobey me? Or did she actually disobey the people I sent to fetch her? You see what I mean? An arcane but crucial question of legal interpretation. Let me give you another example. The law states clearly that defying the king is punishable by death, but we have to divine the intent of the law rather than the superficial meaning of the words. Was the legislation formulated with citizens and commonfolk in mind or even members of the king's immediate family? Does it include the king's father or wife? Think about it, gentlemen. Not so simple, is it?" [19]

"Not simple at all, your majesty," said Memuchan. "But I have some thoughts on the matter."

It was obvious that Achashverosh wanted them to spare Vashti, but Memuchan did not want this to happen. He feared that unless Vashti were punished the humiliation she had caused the king would fester in his heart and result in a great deal of suppressed wrath. Eventually, that wrath would spill over and injure the king's advisors, Memuchan among them.[20] Memuchan also felt that the

---

18. *Esther Rabbah* 4:6; *Megillah* 12b; *Targum Sheni; Rambam; R' Yosef ibn Nachmiash;* see *Yerushalmi Sanhedrin* 4:7; *Eshkol HaKofer.* Some say that when Memuchan spoke, the other six officers remained quiet. They preferred to remain silent until they would determine it necessary to speak. Others suggest that each of the seven officers served the king one day a week. Since that day was Shabbos, it was the turn of the last one to officiate before the king, i.e., Memuchan. Due to the importance of the day's events, all seven officers were present. See *Midrash Panim Acheirim; Aggadas Esther; Tehillah L'David* in *Me'am Loez;* see *Ye'aros Devash;* see *Me'am Loez.* Some suggest that Memuchan was the highest-ranking of the seven, and most knowledgeable in astronomy and astrology. The zodiac of the seventh day of the week, Shabbos, is not one of prosperity, indicating that Haman would not succeed in his efforts to eventually bring his daughter to the throne, as he had hoped.

19. *Me'am Loez; Ibn Ezra; Alshich; Yosef Lekach.*

20. *Rishon LeTzion.*

death of the queen would weaken the established power structure in the palace and allow him more opportunities for advancement.[21]

In addition, Memuchan bore a personal grudge against Vashti, because she consistently treated him like dirt. She slapped and insulted him in public, and she snubbed his wife by not inviting her to the feast. This was not only a personal affront to him, it also caused a lot of friction with his wife who derided him for being inconsequential in the palace hierarchy.

Perhaps most important of all, Memuchan was concerned for his own safety. His astrologers had seen it written in the stars that Achashverosh's wife would have him killed. This frightened him, and he tried desperately to do something about it. He was hoping that if he could engineer Vashti's death and replace her with his own daughter as queen, he would be safe. After all, it was unlikely that a daughter would have her father killed.[22]

"With your permission, your majesty," said Memuchan, "may I offer my views on the accusations against Vashti?"

"Of course, you may offer your views," said Achashverosh. "Why do you think I called you here? Go ahead. Speak!"

"Your majesty, I am just your humble servant. How can I — or anyone else for that matter — compare with you in knowledge, wisdom and power? Yet I feel compelled to speak out in your presence and point out certain aspects of this case that may have escaped your notice because you are so emotionally involved. Please bear with me."

"Go ahead," said Achashverosh. "Get to the point already."

"Yes, your majesty. It appears to me that Vashti has humiliated you not only by refusing to comply with your express royal command but also in the insults she directed against you in the process. She called you a fool, unfit to clean her father's stables, unfit to rule. She challenged your authority, angered you and embarrassed you. Therefore, it seems to me that she has committed three capital crimes.[23] One, by her insubordination, she has behaved in a manner unacceptable in a queen. Two, she has flaunted the authority of the king. Three, she has done so in full view of the public, thereby seriously undermining the king's authority."[24]

---

21. *Maharal; Yosef Lekach.*
22. *Esther Rabbah* 4:6; *Matnos Kehunah; Pirkei d'Rav Eliezer; Gra; Iyun Yaakov; Me'am Loez.*
23. *Gra; Menos HaLevi.*
24. *Esther Rabbah* 4:7; *R' Shmuel di Uzidah; Eshkol HaKofer.*

"So far I haven't heard anything new from you, Memuchan," snapped Achashverosh. "Is this all you have?"

Memuchan shook his head. "Pardon me, your majesty, but I feel I must build up to my points. I have much to say. Much that is new."[25]

"Then say it. Get to the point."

"Certainly, your majesty. I would like to analyze Vashti's behavior. Why would a queen commit such heinous offenses? I can understand perfectly well that she might be a little resistant to appear in front of hundreds, if not thousands, of guests. But did she have to be so abusive? Did she have to heap insult on the king's head in front of all her ladies-in-waiting and the attendants the king had sent to fetch her? Did she have to tell them with such arrogance to repeat all her words to the king? How do we explain such behavior?"[26]

Achashverosh leaned forward. "Go ahead. I'm curious. How do you explain it, Memuchan?"

"It appears to me that Vashti has psychological problems. She cannot accept your superiority as the king, and therefore, she has to assert herself by flaunting your authority. She lives in denial; continually deluding herself that her position as queen derives from her royal Babylonian lineage, although all of us know this is nonsense. Should she succeed in this outright rejection of the king's command, she will brag about it for years and make herself out to be a sympathetic heroine."[27]

Achashverosh grunted. "Interesting analysis, Memuchan, but what's the point? Should we come down at her like a ton of bricks just because she has delusions of grandeur? If she is in denial, as you have so cleverly discerned, perhaps we should get her help. Instead of punishment we should get her some counseling."

"Oh, no, your majesty," said Memuchan hastily. "That was certainly not my main point. As you say, we could deal with psychological problems without resorting to . . . er . . . er . . . drastic measures. No, your majesty, there is a much deeper problem here, more serious issues that we must address. You see, if what Vashti did was no more

---

25. *R' Yosef ibn Yachia.*

26. *Maharal; Menos HaLevi; R' Shmuel di Uzidah; Alshich.* See *Yad HaMelech.* Many point out that Memuchan used great circumspection in detailing his next accusation, for if misunderstood, his words would seem disrespectful. He therefore took great care to use words which would not lend themselves to misinterpretation.

27. *Yosef Lekach; Maharal; R' Shmuel di Uzidah; Alshich; Menos HaLevi.*

than a personal affront to the king, there would indeed be a possibility of dealing with it magnanimously and discreetly. But the fact of the matter is, Vashti attacked and humiliated the entire empire. She threatens to undermine the very foundations of the throne."[28]

"Indeed? How so?"

"Vashti's rejection of your command is part of a greater pattern of outright disdain. It manifested itself in her humiliating response to you today, and it has manifested itself consistently in her treatment of your nobles and advisors. I can tell you this from personal experience. She has repeatedly harassed and abused me, as well as numerous others." Memuchan turned to the other officers. "Isn't that so, gentlemen?"

The six officers gulped and nodded.[29]

Memuchan continued. "Do you think for a moment, your majesty, that we care about ourselves? Not even a trifle. We are only concerned that this pathological behavior will have serious ramifications for the king and the empire. We believe Vashti has undermined your authority. She has attacked the king, his closest advisors and the vital institutions of government. Not just some peasants or city rabble. The best minds that now surround the throne will slip away one by one and seek other avenues to success.[30] If the king cannot control his own wife, they will think, how can he expect to control a vast empire? Before you know it, you will be left with fools for advisors, and you may even find yourself facing anarchy and rebellion in the empire. This is a crisis situation, your majesty.[31]

"What Vashti has done tears at the very fabric of Persian society. You will no doubt agree, your majesty, that the bedrock of society is the family unit. As long as the family is strong, there will be stability in the empire, and we will continue to produce the kind of citizen that makes the empire powerful and feared. But allow the family unit to weaken, and we will have problems!"

"Agreed," said Achashverosh, "but what has this to do with Vashti?"

"Everything, your majesty!" declared Memuchan. "Everything! Vashti's offense will not go unnoticed. Women throughout the empire will hear about what she has done, and they will follow suit.

---

28. *Eshter Rabbah* 4:7; see *Maharzu; Yefei Anaf; Malbim; Yad HaMelech.*

29. *Esther Rabbah* 4:7. *R' Yosef ibn Yachia.*

30. *Targum Rishon; R' Yosef ibn Yachia; Megillas Sesarim; D'na Pishra.*

31. *D'na Pishra; Melo HaOmer.*

No longer will the women of the empire respect and obey their husbands. They will laugh at them instead. I can just hear a typical conversation in a typical Persian home. The lady of the house will say to her husband, 'Don't you tell me what to do, you miserable oaf! Who do you think you are to give me orders? So what if you are my husband? I don't have to listen to you. Look at Vashti, brought to the palace as a slave captured in war and married off to the great Achashverosh. Does she listen to him? Hah! So why should I listen to you? Do you consider yourself better than the king?' And how is her husband to answer this lady? What can he say? Nothing! Multiply this scene by the hundreds, the thousands, the millions, and you have an empire teetering on the verge of collapse."[32]

"Now wait just a minute, my dear Memuchan. I see no need to push the panic button yet. Don't underestimate the women of the empire. They are wise and intelligent. You could not build an empire if the homes are guided by foolish women. These women will understand that there are unusual and mitigating circumstances involved. They will understand that I was under the influence of too much wine and that the request I made of the queen was simply outrageous. They will not assume they can ignore the wishes of their sober and reasonable husbands."

"True, your majesty, but only if they receive accurate information. The story will change countless times as it spreads through the empire. No one can know what fantastic details will be added and what important details subtracted. But we can be sure of one thing, your majesty.[33] The queen will come across as heroic and clever, and the king — please forgive me — will be a laughingstock. This affair will not blow over quickly; it will fester like a cancer in the bowels of Persian society. Women will laugh in their husbands' faces and do as they please. Men will be powerless in their homes. Children will grow up, for all intents and purposes, with overbearing mothers and no father figures. Anarchy and endless domestic strife will be the order of the day, and of course, the empire will be destabilized. Is that what you want, your majesty?"[34]

---

32. *Targum Sheni; Midrash Panim Acheirim; R' Elisha Galico; Rabbeinu Nesanel; Alshich; Malbim.*

33. *Yosef Lekach; Alshich; Menos HaLevi; R' Shmuel di Uzidah; Malbim.*

34. *Targum Rishon; Aggadas Esther; Ibn Ezra; R' Yosef ibn Nachmiash; R' Elisha Galico; R' Shmuel di Uzidah; Menos HaLevi; Malbim.*

Achashverosh shifted uncomfortably. "No," he replied.

"I don't think anyone does, except for Vashti, of course. You went to so much trouble to host an imperial feast for one hundred and eighty days and a special feast for Shushan for seven days, all to impress your subjects with your power and greatness. And it was all for nothing! With her arrogant defiance, Vashti has in one fell swoop made mockery of everything you've worked to accomplish over the last few months. Mark this day on your calendar, your majesty, as a day that will live in infamy, the day that the queen of Persia rose up against the king and pulled the carpet out from under his feet. How will this day be remembered, your majesty? How will this critical drama be brought to a happy resolution?"[35]

Achashverosh's eyes were still bloodshot from all the wine he had consumed, and his brow glistened with sweat. "You've convinced me," he said, "that I must take this very seriously. Much as it is distasteful to me, I have to do something about it. Very well, you are the judges. Judge! Pass a verdict!"

Memuchan and the other officers exchanged glances. This was the tricky part. They absolutely did not want to pass judgment on the queen. What if the king accepted their verdict and had the queen executed?[36] Would he then turn his wrath on them for causing her death? And what if he spared the queen? Wouldn't she turn around and avenge herself on the judges who had tried to have her executed? It was a no-win situation. It was up to Memuchan to extricate them from this terrible predicament.

"Your majesty, after careful consideration," said Memuchan, "we have come to the conclusion that it would be just about impossible to find any judges that can render an impartial ruling in this case. By flaunting the authority of the king and all he represents, the queen has in effect damaged and offended every single person of consequence in the empire. I fear that none of us can be objective on this matter. There is only one choice. The king himself must be the judge. Although you have also suffered a personal affront and attack on your authority, you are the only one who can rise above your personal considerations and make a determination that is purely for the good of the empire."[37]

---

35. *Esther Rabbah* 4:10; see *Yefei Anaf* there; *Midrash Lekach Tov; Menos HaLevi; D'na Pishra.*

36. *Menos HaLevi. R' Elisha Galico.* Others suggest that Memuchan discerned that the King wanted her to be punished. Therefore he was the first to speak, assuming that it would be to his great benefit to support the king.

37. *Yosef Lekach; Menos HaLevi; Megillas Sesarim; R' Yosef ibn Yachia; Gra.*

Achashverosh chewed on his knuckles and squirmed in his seat. "All right, Memuchan," he said at last. "All right. You've really left me no choice. I see I will have to judge my own wife. It will be difficult, but I will have to do it. In the meantime, do you have any suggestions for me? How should I rectify the situation?"

Memuchan stroked his mustache thoughtfully. "I think it is imperative that a new royal decree be issued to proclaim the power of the king to judge all cases and carry out his verdicts without the need to seek or consider anyone's advice or counsel. The decree must be recorded in the royal archives to ensure that it will remain in force in perpetuity without ever being revoked or annulled, and copies of the decree must be sent to every corner of the empire. Furthermore, your majesty, there must also be a second decree." Memuchan paused to gather his thoughts.[38]

Achashverosh drummed his fingers impatiently on his armrest. His wine-soaked skin was blotched, and his eyes were bleary and disoriented.

"Yes, your majesty," continued Memuchan. "The second decree is very important. There must be an immediate royal decree to nullify the pedigree and lineage of every woman at the moment she gets married. From that time on, her only claim to honor and stature is through her husband. No woman should pride herself on her own lineage, as Vashti did so arrogantly with Nevuchadnezzar. By royal decree, this will come to an end! Every woman traces her lineage only through her husband's bloodlines. Every woman bows to her husband's will. Every woman speaks her husband's language in the home; think of it, if your attendants had understood what Vashti was saying in Chaldean, or if Vashti had spoken in Persian, they might not have repeated her abusive tirade to you, and much grief would have been avoided. This decree must also be disseminated to every corner of the empire. Order must be restored!"[39]

"Yes, that is an excellent idea," said Achashverosh enthusiastically.

Memuchan lowered his voice. "And now, your majesty," he said, "these two decrees must be accompanied by a letter detailing Vashti's crime and her punishment. The decrees will restore order,

---

38. *Targum Rishon; R' Eliezer Ashkenazi; Yosef Lekach; Menos HaLevi; Alshich; Malbim.* Haman was destined to regret having said this. When the king ultimately turned against him, it was not necessary to take counsel, due to this law. He could merely have Haman put to death immediately.

39. *Melo HaOmer; Me'am Loez.*

and the letter will instill fear in every heart. As it should be. That is all I have to say, your majesty."[40]

Achashverosh reached for a bottle of wine but then thought better of it. He had had far more than enough to drink for one day. His hand shook as he laid it on his armrest.

"You have spoken with true honor and loyalty, Memuchan," he said. "But you have not spoken about what should be done with Vashti."

"No, I haven't, your majesty," said Memuchan. "As I said before, I believe you must judge the queen and issue the verdict."

"Yes, of course," said Achashverosh. "I have agreed to that. But you are my advisor. It seems she has brought a death penalty on herself, but politically, that is not an easy thing to do. Let's have some advice."

Memuchan stroked his mustache some more. "Hmm. A delicate situation. So what do we do? Aha! I have it! Yes, I think it will work perfectly. Your majesty must issue a decree. On pain of immediate death, no one is to enter the presence of the king unless summoned. Then your majesty must decree that Vashti should never again appear before you. Naturally, Vashti will not be able to restrain herself from coming to see you, and as soon as she walks in I will sever her head with my sword. I will have done my duty of safeguarding the royal decree, and you, your majesty, will remain above reproach.[41] Nonetheless, when word reaches all the provinces about the royal decree and its strict and swift enforcement, discipline will return to the empire. All thoughts of anarchy and rebellion will vanish."[42]

According to another version of this scene, Memuchan did not propose any sort of death penalty for Vashti, only that the king divorce her and banish her from his presence forever.[43] Others suggest that Memuchan counseled that Vashti was to be brought before the king by force and then executed, to demonstrate that the king's will could not

---

40. *Aggadas Esther; Menos HaLevi.*

41. *Targum Rishon; Matnos Kehunah* and *Yefei Anaf* to *Esther Rabbah* 4:9. See *Midrash Panim Acheirim; Megillas Sesarim; Gra; Malbim; Me'am Loez; Midrash Eliyahu.* Haman was careful not to suggest the death penalty on his own because he feared repercussions should the King later regret his decision. Haman masterfully created the background for a scenario in which the king himself would arrive at that conclusion, but never uttered the suggestion himself.

42. *Megillas Sesarim; Menos HaLevi.* The decree would teach every female, married or single, that if the great Queen Vashti, herself of royal blood, could be put to death, any disobedience among the commonfolk towards the man of the household would certainly not be tolerated. See *Aggadas Esther, R' Elisha Galico; R' Shmuel di Uzidah; Malbim.*

43. *Targum Sheni; Rokeach; R' Saadiah Gaon; Menos HaLevi.*

be thwarted; Vashti would not be allowed to act as a heroine who had defied the king's will, caused the king to be ridiculed and escaped retribution.[44] Still others suggest that Memuchan proposed that the queen be deposed and forced to stand by as another woman became queen, after which she would either commit suicide or be executed.[45]

In any case, Achashverosh was amenable to Memuchan's proposals, but he did express some reservations. "For all of her shortcomings," he said, "I have adjusted to living with Vashti. I know her already, and I've gotten used to her. But how am I supposed to live without her? Who will take her place? And how do I know that her replacement won't cause the same problems or even worse?

"I would not be concerned, your majesty," Memuchan said in his most reassuring tone of voice. "I have no doubt you will find a far better woman to take Vashti's place. First of all, I think you would be well advised to avoid anyone with a distinguished pedigree. A commoner with a sterling character and personality would be best. I'm sure your new wife will be so good that you will quickly forget Vashti."[46]

Achashverosh glanced at the other six officers and raised his eyebrows quizzically, as if to ask their opinion on the matter. The officers were not really in agreement with Memuchan. They were not pleased with the idea of executing the queen of the realm. They were also concerned that Memuchan was gathering a lot of influence for himself, thereby diminishing their influence at the court. Miraculously, however, they did not impart their misgivings to the king. They just nodded their heads in meek assent.[47]

"Good, good, I shall now pass judgment," said Achashverosh.

Although he was still intoxicated from all the wine he had drunk, he did not bother to wait until the next day when his mind would be clearer and more rational. Having reached a conclusion in his mind, he plunged ahead impulsively.[48]

---

44. *Menos HaLevi; R' Shmuel di Uzidah; D'na Pishra;* see *Aggadas Esther,* who says the counsel came from Daniel.

45. *Chasam Sofer al HaTorah, Parashas Tetzaveh; Menos HaLevi.*

46. *Alshich; R' Elisha Galico; Maharal;* see *Toras Moshe* to *Parashas Tetzaveh, s.v. bayom.* According to those who suggest that Memuchan was Daniel, he informed Achashverosh that his suggestion was based on the Torah, which requires that a woman honor her husband (*Pirkei d'Rav Eliezer* 49; *Radal; R' Avigdor Kohen Tzedek*). Of course, the Torah also requires a husband to honor his wife.

47. *R' Yosef ibn Yachia; Gra; Menos HaLevi; Malbim.*

48. *Esther Rabbah; Rashi* to *Megillah* 12b *Megillas Sesarim; Gra.*

"I hereby pronounce Vashti guilty as charged," he declared. "I hereby condemn her to death for her offenses against the crown. I hereby authorize my trusted advisor Memuchan to carry out the order of execution." He also ordered the proclamations and decrees prepared and distributed, exactly as Memuchan had proposed.[49]

Memuchan was delighted. He had gained a strong influence over a foolish king who was ready to sacrifice his wife to his popularity, and he felt sure he would be able to manipulate this king to his advantage.[50] Memuchan ordered Vashti to be brought unclad before the king, forcibly if need be. After she had suffered humiliation, she was beheaded. According to other versions, she was either burned at the stake or hanged from a gallows.[51]

With Vashti's death, the Babylonian royal line came to an end. This evil woman who had forced young Jewish girls to work unclad on Shabbos perished in humiliating fashion on the very day of the week she had desecrated. This vindictive enemy of the Jewish people, the last survivor of Nevuchadnezzar's bloodline, the prime cause in bringing the reconstruction of the *Beis HaMikdash* to a halt, was executed to make way for a Jewish girl who would wear her crown with more grace and distinction. Nevuchadnezzar's lineage had come to an end.[52]

After Vashti's execution, Achashverosh sent letters and proclamations to all the provinces of his empire. The letters, which told the story of Vashti, her insubordination and her comeuppance, were read as the introduction to the proclamations.[53]

"No longer will it be sufficient for a woman just to speak respectfully to her husband," the king decreed. "Every woman must also become subservient to her husband and accede to his every wish. The man is to be king in his home, just as the king rules over his empire. Any woman who goes against her husband's wishes will be put to death, as was Vashti.[54] Furthermore, the woman will no longer be allowed to speak her native language, only the language of her husband, as a sign of submission to his mastery. No longer will the

---

49. *Esther Rabbah* 4:11, and *Yefei Anaf* there; *Targum Rishon* to *Esther* 1:21; *Megillas Sesarim.* Achashverosh would thus feel blameless by having Memuchan take responsibility for Vashti's death (*Menos HaLevi*).

50. *Yalkut Shimoni* 1044.

51. *Esther Rabbah* 4:11; *R' Elisha Galico.* According to *Chasam Sofer* and others, Vashti was killed on 25 Nissan.

52. *Esther Rabbah* 5:2; *Yalkut Shimoni* 1051; *Midrash Abba Gorion.*

53. See *Rashi* to *Esther* 1:21; *Yosef Lekach; Menos HaLevi.*

54. *Targum Sheni; Rashi* to *Esther; Aggadas Esther; Ma'amar Mordechai; Malbim.*

entire empire be required to speak Persian. Instead, every province will speak its own native language, so that all the men will understand perfectly everything going on all around them, and no wife will speak in an strange language, as Vashti spoke in Chaldean."[55]

In an act of respect, the letters and proclamations to each of the provinces of the empire were written in its respective language.

The king hoped to accomplish many and varied goals with his missives. He hoped to promote domestic harmony and spousal obedience throughout the empire.[56] He also hoped that by giving all men full dominion in his own home they would accept the king's dominion over the empire.[57] At the same time, he hoped that reverting to the native language in each province would discourage any nascent rebellions, since the provinces would be separated from each other by language barriers.[58] The idea of each of his one hundred and twenty-seven lands speaking a different language also appealed to Achashverosh. It made the empire seem larger and more diverse and also gave it a sense of symmetry. Finally, the change of languages, coupled with Vashti's death, would also close the book on the Babylonian origins of the Persian Empire.[59]

Ironically, the king's letters and proclamations had the opposite effect from what he had intended. From the highest dignitaries to the lowest peasant, people laughed at the letters and proclamations, considering them the work of a fool. Why would he have to tell them the long story about Vashti's perfidy and execution? To impress on them that disobedience to the king was punishable by death?[60] Everyone already knew that. Why would the king have to issue proclamations that every man should be the master of his own home? Everyone already knew that; even weavers were the masters of their own homes. Apparently, the king himself couldn't control his own wife and, there-

---

55. *Esther* 1:21; *Yosef Lekach; Menos HaLevi; Malbim; Mishtei Yayin.*

56. *Rokeach; R' Elisha Galico; Alshich.*

57. *R' Elisha Galico.*

58. *Megillas Sesarim; Yosef Lekach; Alshich.*

59. *Menos HaLevi; Maharal; Yosef Lekach; R' Shmuel di Uzidah; Alshich.* Much of the shame which Achashverosh endured at Vashti's hands was due to the fact that he had agreed to speak in her native tongue of *Kasdis* (Chaldean), a Babylonian dialect, rather than the accepted *Sarsi* of Persia. Had Achashverosh's attendants understood Vashti's words, they may not have repeated them verbatim to the king, and the entire incident would have been avoided. The new decree ordering women to speak the language of their husbands – unlike Achashverosh's own practice – would prevent another such incident from occurring (*Yosef Lekach; Melo HaOmer; Chasam Sofer*).

60. *Yosef Lekach; Menos HaLevi; R' Shmuel di Uzidah.*

fore, was trying to teach everyone else how to do it. What a fool! As for teaching the women new languages they had not learned in their youth, that was certainly a silly idea. Women were needed at home; they did not have time to attend language classes. At least, they shouldn't have.[61]

Clearly, the hand of providence was guiding all these seemingly inexplicable events. Achashverosh's silly proclamation undermined his credibility in the provinces, so that the proclamations he sent later against the Jews were not given immediate credence and attacks on the Jews did not materialize.[62] The language barriers also prevented provinces from joining forces against the Jews.[63] The concentration of absolute autocratic power in the hands of the king would ultimately allow him to have Haman and his sons hanged on the spur of the moment, without having to go through a lengthy trial.[64] The king's absolute power also allowed him to follow Memuchan's advice to take a commoner for his second wife. By bypassing the court system and royal genealogical department, the king opened the way for Esther to become queen without having her ancestry checked and her nationality revealed. And irony upon ironies, Memuchan's devious machinations to bring about Vashti's downfall for his own benefit would pave the way for Esther's accession to the throne.[65]

Within a few short hours, a series of unexpected events had caused a huge empire to change course. A fabulously wealthy and immensely powerful king, who ruled over half the world, presided at the head of a structured imperial government with an elaborate judicial system. He had everything he could possibly want. Then a foolish, wine-induced command to his wife led to the abolition of the courts, the shift to autocracy and absolutism, the foolish execution of the queen over an insignificant slight, and the ultimate downfall of the enemies of the Jews.

It could only be divine providence.[66]

61. Rashi to Megillah 12b; Maharsha; Esther Rabbah 4:12 with Radal; Yosef Lekach; Yedei Moshe.
62. Yad HaMelech; Ma'amar Mordechai; Rashi to Megillah 12b; Maharsha; Yosef Lekach; Menos HaLevi.
63. Megillas Sesarim.
64. Commentaries.
65. Yosef Lekach; Chida; see Maharsha to Megillah 15. Achashverosh had thus far ruled for two years and 180 days, totalling 888 days. This sum includes 126 Shabbosos; this day was the 127th Shabbos that Vashti was queen. It was only fitting that this queen of the ruler of 127 provinces, who had forced Jewish women to desecrate Shabbos 126 times, should now die on the 127th Shabbos. Perhaps it was also in the merit of our mother Sarah who lived 127 years that Vashti was killed on her 127th Shabbos as Queen. Furthermore, she also deserved punishment for neglecting to show any gratitude for having been granted her reign.
66. Malbim; Yosef Lekach; Menos HaLevi; Chasam Sofer al Ha Torah to Parashas Tetzaveh.

The Search for a Queen

7

Achashverosh awoke the next morning with a hangover, but otherwise, he was well-rested and back to normal. His wine-induced stupor had dissipated, as had his monumental fury.[1] He also had no recollection whatsoever of what had transpired in his palace the previous day: not the command, not the trial, not the execution.

He got out of bed and stretched, eager to begin a new day of involvement in the intricate affairs of state. As was his custom, he went to join Vashti for breakfast in the flower-bedecked morning room. To his astonishment, she was not there. Moreover, breakfast had been laid out for only one person. How very odd. Perhaps, he thought, Vashti had risen early for breakfast and a stroll in the gardens, although this was quite out of character. Ordinarily, the queen stayed up late at night and slept late in the morning. Perhaps she had suffered ill effects from the wine and had gone out for some fresh air.[2]

---

1. *Targum Ris]hon; Targum Sheni; Esther Rabbah* 5:2; *Yad HaMelech*.
2. *Esther Rabbah* 5:2; *Pirkei d'Rav Eliezer* 49.

Achashverosh pulled a velvet bell cord, and the royal butler appeared almost immediately.

"Would you like something hot to drink, your majesty?" he asked.

"That sounds good," said Achashverosh. "I think I will, but first, tell me something. Do you know where Queen Vashti has gone?"

The butler, realizing that the king had forgotten all, trembled with fright.[3] "I am sorry, your majesty," he said. "I really couldn't say. I haven't seen her majesty all morning."

"Very strange," said Achashverosh. "Perhaps my officers will know. Send them to me right away."

A few minutes later, some of his officers stood in front of the king.

"Good morning, gentlemen," said the king. "I haven't seen Vashti all morning. Would any of you perhaps know where she has gone?"

The officers glanced at each other with consternation. This was the worst thing that could have happened.

"Your majesty, you have no recollection at all of last night?" asked one of the officers.

"What am I supposed to remember?" asked Achashverosh. "We were having a high time at the feast. We drank rivers of the finest wines. We ate delicious foods and told wonderful stories. And then I went to sleep. What else was there?"

The officer took a deep breath and let it out slowly. "Your majesty, yesterday you commanded that the queen appear before your guests unclad. She refused, and you had her executed."

"Executed! Executed?" screamed Achashverosh. "Are you out of your mind? Vashti has been executed? But why?"[4]

"She didn't simply refuse to come, your majesty. She humiliated and insulted you. Memuchan advised you to have her executed. You found his arguments persuasive, and you ordered it done."[5]

Achashverosh grabbed his head in his hands and rocked back and forth, tears of grief and frustration streamed from his eyes. "It is coming back to me," he groaned.[6] "Little wisps of memory. I recall the summons. And I recall being drunk and out of my mind. I vaguely recall banishing her from my presence, but I do not recall ordering

3. R' Elisha Galico.
4. Yalkut Shimoni 1051; Midrash Abba Gorion.
5. Yalkut Shimoni 1051; Midrash Abba Gorion; Rokeach.
6. Pirkei d'Rav Eliezer 49; Radal.

her executed.[7] Why would I want her dead? What did she do anyway, refuse an inappropriate summons? On the contrary, she showed herself to be a chaste and modest woman. For that she deserved to die? You are my best and finest, my elite officers. How could you let me do something like that? I am disappointed in you. Oh, what have you done? You've caused me to lose my queen, and I will never forgive you for it. Leave me at once, or I will have you killed on the spot."

The officers turned to go.

"But don't go too far," said Achashverosh. "Your days are numbered."

"Please spare us, your gracious majesty," said the officer. "We meant no harm. Memuchan did all the talking, and you seemed so convinced by what he said. You were furious with the queen. We saw no point in trying to dissuade you."

"No point in trying to dissuade me? Listen to yourself! You should have spoken up and tried to make me see reason. You had no right to remain silent. Don't worry. You erased Vashti from memory and caused her death, the same will now happen to you.[8] You will soon be swinging from the gallows. As for Memuchan, a quick trip to the gallows is too good for him. I will keep him alive for a while. I will lull him into a false sense of security, and then at the moment of his triumph, I will show him my true face. I will crush him like a bug and enjoy every moment of his horror. Do you understand?"

"Yes, your majesty."

"Good. Be happy that your end will come quickly. Now begone, all of you cowards!"[9]

---

7. *Targum Rishon.*

8. *Targum Sheni; Targum Rishon; Megillas Sesarim; Midrash Aba Gurion.* Although these advisors had not actually suggested that Vashti be killed, Achashverosh held them responsible for remaining silent when they should have spoken. Here, too, he demonstrated his utter foolishness. Following the mistake of killing his wife, he further blundered in debilitating his cabinet by killing his most important ministers.

9. *Me'am Loez.* Much of the difference of opinion among the commentators here depends on whether they understand Memuchan to have been Haman, or Daniel. Most commentators agree that Memuchan was Haman, and that he was left alive to later die at Achashverosh's command. Those who held that Memuchan was Daniel state that he was kept alive and reinstated to his position at a later time. Other suggest that Memuchan was left alive because his argument made sense to some extent, while the others could not defend themselves. See *R' Yosef ibn Nachmiash; R' Shmuel di Uzidah; R' Elisha Galico.* Achashverosh's opinion of Haman was to be drastically altered after a plot to assassinate the king would be uncovered. Achashverosh was led to think that Haman was indirectly responsible for saving the King. The King's affection for Haman rose greatly at that time. The seven officers who were killed were punished by Hashem because they had been involved in the prevention of the construction of the *Beis HaMikdash*; see prologue (*Yalkut Shimoni; Midrash Panim Acheirim*).

After the officers left, Achashverosh called for his scribes. Only the day before they had been called upon to record the new royal decrees. Now the king called for them again. He commanded them to record the entire episode from his new perspective so that Vashti's memory would be preserved in a better light, so that her death would be viewed as something of an unfortunate accident.[10]

Time passed, and Achashverosh could not stop thinking about Vashti and all that had transpired. It occurred to him that her attitude to the Jews might have angered their God and brought His wrath down upon her head. She had been instrumental in halting the reconstruction of the Temple. She had forced Jewish girls to work unclad on Shabbos, and now she had been killed on a Shabbos. Could it be just a coincidence? Achashverosh had given his overt or tacit approval to everything she had done, and now he blamed himself for her death.[11]

For days, he roamed through the palace like a wraith, howling in anguish, "Vashti! Where are you, Queen Vashti?"[12] He would often sit in the gardens, sobbing with grief, and the servants who hung back nearby could hear him berating himself, "Oh, Vashti. She was such a good queen, the best queen in the world. Oh, how could I have mistreated her so? How could I have commanded her, a modest queen, to do something inappropriate? How could I have demeaned her by sending wine stewards instead of princes to fetch her? If only I had shown a little more patience. If only I had waited a day for the wine to dissipate. If only I hadn't been such a fool. If only . . ."[13]

Constant self-recrimination drove Achashverosh into deep depression. He found it hard to go to sleep at night. He kept an engraving of Vashti beside him and looked at it ceaselessly, that being his only connection to the dead queen.[14] He lost his appetite, and when he did eat, he kept remarking obsessively on Vashti's food preferences. This she liked, this she didn't like. This is how she used to eat this or drink that.[15]

---

10. *R' Shmuel di Uzidah*. This proves once again Achasverosh's foolishness. After declaring a new law in his empire designed to support his having killed Vashti, he killed these officers for not trying to prevent her execution, which showed his regret for the act. This served to contribute to the skepticism of the citizens, further substantiating their opinion of his stupidity.

11. *Esther Rabbah* 5:12, *Menos HaLevi*.

12. *Ibn Ezra; Yosef Lekach; Yedei Moshe; D'na Pishra*.

13. *Esther Rabbah* 5:2; *R' Yosef ibn Yachia; Rashi; Alshich; Chida*.

14. *Esther Rabbah* 6:11; *Menos HaLevi; R' Shmuel di Uzidah; R' Yosef ibn Yachia; Rashi; Yosef Lekach*.

15. *Yosef Lekach*.

He also suffered from extreme anxiety. He worried that he would never find a queen to replace Vashti. He did not believe there was anyone in Shushan who remotely compared with her in stature, nobility, and any of her other qualities.[16]

As Achashverosh's condition worsened, the palace staff became concerned for his mental health and even his life. They saw the king edging closer and closer to the edge, and they feared he would go over.[17]

No one knew what to do. The king's elite officers had already been disgraced and executed because of their involvement in Vashti's downfall. The remaining advisors were so intimidated that even those who had ideas remained silent. Why risk offering an opinion that might bring down the royal wrath on the head of the advisor?[18]

Presently, a group of bright young officers came to the fore. The king had commissioned them for his armies and shown favor to them, and now, they wanted to preserve their prerogatives in the palace.[19] They feared that should the king die or go mad, his successor might be someone who didn't know or care for them. Although they had climbed only a few rungs on the ladder of influence and privilege, they feared that a new king might cause them to lose even that, leaving them at the very bottom of the ladder.[20] Moreover, with all the usual advisors either dead or paralyzed by fear, here was a chance for truly rapid advancement. All that was needed was a little imagination and a little boldness.[21]

The young officers sought an audience with the king and designated one of their number to serve as the spokesman for the group. The king received them with a distracted air, as if he were just going through the motions.

"Your majesty, pardon me if I speak a little directly," said the officer. "As you know, I am a soldier, not a diplomat. I fight for your majesty on the battlefield, and unfortunately, I am not sufficiently schooled in the niceties of palace etiquette."

16. *Yedei Moshe; R' Shmuel di Uzidah.*

17. *Ma'amar Mordechai.*

18. *R' Yosef ibn Nachmiash; Eshkol HaKofer.*

19. *Menos HaLevi; Midrash Lekach Tov.* R' Shlomo Brevda (*Sefer Kimu V'Kiblu*) writes that they were common workmen such as barbers, bath attendants and stewards.

20. *Midrash Lekach Tov; Menos HaLevi;* see *Esther Rabbh* 6:11.

21. *Yosef Lekach.* Others suggest that this was Haman. The initial letters of the words *vayomru na'arei hamelech mesharsav* can be rearranged to spell *v'Haman,* and Haman (*Sefas HaYam*).

Achashverosh replied, "Never apologize for being a soldier. You are doing just fine. Speak honestly, and you have nothing to fear."

"Well, we feel we do have something to fear, your majesty. We fear for your well-being and safety. We feel your pain, and we would do anything to alleviate it. You have grieved long enough, your majesty. You can't let this go on forever. Your empire needs you. Your people need you. It is time to look to the future. It is time to find a new queen. Let us help you do it."[22]

"You think it is such an easy thing?" asked Achashverosh. "Where would I find someone as high-born and superior as Vashti? And how do I know I will not have similar problems with a new wife?" He sighed and lowered his voice; it seemed he was almost speaking to himself.

"With all due respect, your majesty," said the officer, "I believe there are countless citizens who would jump at the chance to be your queen. Let us find them. Let us send out a call in Shushan for all who want to be considered as prospective brides for the king. We will have responses, and there will be choices. You will find the one you seek."[23]

"Very well," said Achashverosh. "We will see."

As the officers had predicted, a number of eligible candidates did indeed come forward, but Achashverosh did not treat them with gentlemanly respect. Before long, there were no longer any prospects. In fact, anyone with an eligible daughter sent her into hiding to escape the attentions of the king.[24]

"Look what is happening," said Achashverosh to the young officer. "Your plan has not worked out as you expected. There are no candidates. How embarrassing this is for me!"[25]

"All is not lost, your majesty," said the officer. "We have been searching among the high-born families. Perhaps this is not such a good idea. I think we should concentrate only on the commonfolk. We should issue a call for prospective brides for the king with qualifications being appearance, personality and good character. She must be young, never married, well-spoken and tall.[26] Furthermore,

---

22. *R' Yosef ibn Nachmiash; Menos HaLevi; Megillas Sesarim.*

23. *Akeidah; Malbim;* see *Menos HaLevi; Yedei Moshe.*

24. *Malbim; Megillah* 12b.

25. *Malbim.*

26. *Megillah* 12b; *Targum Rishon; Targum Sheni; Yosef Lekach; R' Yosef ibn Yachia; Rokeach; Menos HaLevi; Gra; D'na Pishra; Eshkol HaKofer;* see *Ramban* to *Shemos* 12:30.

you should not give her Vashti's crown with all its powers and privileges. Rather, she should have a lower title as the royal consort. That is what we think, your majesty. We think it can be done."

"And how would you accomplish this search?"

"It would have to be a concerted effort by imperial and provincial agencies. The local constabulary in each province will organize a search. When they have enough candidates, they will conduct a regional contest. All one hundred and twenty-seven provinces will have such a contest and send the winners to Shushan. The result will be a gathering of the most eligible candidates in the world.[27] They will be brought to the royal harem and entrusted to the care of the eunuch Haggai, the chief royal beautician, where they will be conditioned from the beginning to be in awe of the king and always have the proper respect. They will also be carefully screened to ensure that none of them has any secret intent to avenge the death of Vashti. The king will eventually meet each of them and choose the one most fitting."[28]

"Sounds good so far," said Achashverosh. "Let me hear more."

"Each of these finalists will remain in the harem under Haggai's supervision for twelve full months, during which she will use the royal facilities and prepare herself."[29]

Achashverosh leaned back and grinned ear to ear. "Young man, I like it. This sounds like an excellent plan, and I believe you and your friends are capable of bringing it to a successful conclusion. At your ages, you're all looking for wives yourselves, so you are perfectly attuned to this project. You understand modern culture, what's trendy and what's passé. Yes, I think it will work. And with my new powers, I don't have to consult with any cabinet members or other officials in order to implement it. I am very impressed with you and your friends, young man. You have a bright future in the empire. I feel better already. Let's do it!"[30]

---

27. *Yosef Lekach; Yad HaMelech.*

28. *Aggadas Esther; Esther Rabbah* 5:3; *R' Yosef ibn Yachia; R' Elisha Galico; Gra; Yosef Lekach; Megillas Sesarim; Malbim; Yedei Moshe.* See *Sefer Pirush Achashverosh;* until now Haggai's position was of little importance. See *Menos HaLevi,* who remarks that many of the King's other officers would have suggested the idea, but they had grown daughters of their own and would not want them to be included in the contest, knowing Achashverosh as they did. See *Esther Rabbah* with *Matnos Kehunah* and *Yefei Anaf.*

29. *Rokeach; R' Avigdor Kohen Tzedek; Alshich, Gra; Yosef Lekach.*

30. *Aggadas Esther; Menos HaLevi.*

The call went out in confidential diplomatic dispatches to the local governments of all the provinces of the empire. They were told to act with discretion in order to avert any bad publicity, but the inevitable happened. When the first contestants were taken from their homes by the imperial agents, word spread quickly, and virtually all eligible contestants went into hiding.[31] Moreover, the families of those already taken paid heavy bribes to affect their release, and before long, there were practically no candidates in imperial custody.[32] What a sharp contrast this was to David *HaMelech*. When he had sought a wife, families brought their daughters and pleaded to have them considered. People knew that David sought a spiritual, intellectual and emotional companion. But Achashverosh sought only to satisfy his lust.[33]

Achashverosh was undaunted. He ordered that the local constabularies be continually shuffled in the hope that new officials would require new bribes and the families would eventually be drained financially. Besides, incorruptible, bribe-resistant officials might emerge here and there. With much perseverance, the royal effort continued, and presently, a number of candidates were assembled.[34]

In Shushan itself, the search created pandemonium. Divine providence was setting the stage for the dramatic events that would follow. First of all, it could be none other than the divine hand that prevented a revolt against Achashverosh in light of what he was attempting to do.[35] Furthermore, the divine hand exacted retribution from the haughty families that had oppressed, persecuted and humiliated the Jews. They now saw their daughters rounded up like cattle in stalls. These people treated all Jews with revulsion. If food fell on the floor or was touched by another person or even an insect, the food was still considered clean. But if a Jew touched it, they would cast the food away. Now the tables were turned as they watched their daughters dragged away.[36]

---

31. *Megillah* 12b; *Menos HaLevi.*

32. *Menos HaLevi; R' Shmuel di Uzidah; Malbim.*

33. *Megillah* 12b with *Ben Yehoyada; Yad HaMelech.*

34. See *Yalkut Shimoni* 1051; see *Baal HaTurim* to *Bereishis* 41:34. Some suggest that the officers entered the storage areas of homes on the pretext of seeking produce, and found potential contestants in hiding. Others suggest that a food shortage was engineered in the cities, and contestants were caught when they came out of hiding in search of food (*Einei HaEidah*).

35. *R' Shmuel di Uzidah.*

36. See *Esther Rabbah* 5:3 with *Matnos Kehunah* and *Yefei Anaf; R' Shmuel di Uzidah.*

The search dragged on for four years. Thousands of prospects passed through the imperial agencies, but none even came close to finding favor in the eyes of the king. Bribery and hiding still kept the numbers exceedingly low. The king grew frustrated and angry. Demographic studies using statistics had shown that candidates produced by the search represented only a small fraction of the potentially suitable candidates in the realm.[37]

Achashverosh ran out of patience. He issued a decree that anyone caught withholding an eligible candidate from the imperial agents would be put to death. All eligible candidates were to be brought to the appropriate offices immediately![38]

This decree finally had the desired effect. The people realized they would not be able to hold back their daughters, and their attitudes turned completely around. Bowing to the inevitable, they now contended as hard as they could to give them the best chances to succeed in the contest. Many of them brought their daughters directly to the palace in Shushan.[39]

One potential Jewish candidate did not quite fit the criteria established by the king, but her extraordinary grace virtually guaranteed her being taken to the palace along with the rest of the candidates. Her name was Esther, and she was Mordechai's first cousin and wife.

Avichayil, Esther's father, was Mordechai's uncle. He died before Esther was born. Her mother died right after childbirth, leaving the infant Esther without parents. Mordechai took the little orphan into his home and raised her with great love and care. Mordechai was both guiding father and nurturing mother to Esther as he brought her up in seclusion.[40] He taught her Torah and *mitzvos*, and he made sure

---

37. *Aggadas Esther; Seder Olam* 29; *Seder HaDoros; Yalkut Shimoni* 1053; *Midrash Panim Acheirim; R' Yosef ibn Nachmiash.*
38. *Targum Sheni; Yalkut Shimoni.*
39. *Targum Sheni; Midrash Panim Acheirim; Yalkut Shimoni* 1053; *Midrash HaGadol; Aggadas Esther; Akeidah.* Some suggest that Iyov was able to hide his daughters. Others say that his daughters were potential finalists, but Hashem wanted Esther to be chosen instead. See *Bava Basra* 16b with *Maharsha; Yerushalmi Sotah* 5:6; *Esther Rabbah* with *Etz Yosef; Bereishis Rabbah* 57:4; *Yalkut Shimoni* 891.
40. *Malbim; Yishai Elokim; Rambam; Yad HaMelech; Rokeach; Sefas HaYam; Me'am Loez* to *Esther* 2:8; *Megillah* 13a with *Rashi; Midrash Tehillim* 22:23; *R' Yosef ibn Yachia; Targum Rishon; Targum Sheni* to *Esther* 2:8. See *Targum Rishon* to *Esther* 2:7, where he writes that Mordechai was Esther's uncle, her father's brother. Some suggest that an angel raised her (*Rokeach*). Others suggest that Mordechai then had a wife, who nursed her. Years later, Mordechai would marry Esther (*Midrash Tehillim* 22). Mordechai was so devoted to caring for Esther that once, when she was an infant and no nursemaid was available, he miraculously found himself able to nurse her himself (*Bereishis Rabbah* 30:8; *Yalkut Shimoni* 1053; *Tosafos Yeshanim* to *Shabbos* 53b; *Rokeach; R' Chaim Abulafia* to *Esther* 5:8).

she had everything she needed and was always dressed beautifully. She grew up to be a beautiful girl, both outwardly and inwardly, and she did not exhibit any of the depression and complexes so common among orphaned children. Because of the excellent upbringing she received from Mordechai, Esther was worthy of becoming a queen and redeeming the Jewish people from exile.[41] When the *Beis HaMikdash* was destroyed, people felt as if they had become abandoned orphans. Now Hashem would make an orphan the agent of their redemption and the reconstruction of the *Beis HaMikdash*.[42]

At the time of Achashverosh's search, many suggest that Esther was already about seventy-five years old, far past the age limit for the candidates, she was mentioned as one of the four most striking women in history.[43] Her complexion had a certain greenish yellow tinge, but remarkably, this did not detract from her beauty. Hashem had anointed her with a special grace that perpetually gave her a welcome appearance. Together with her grace, it was a phenomenal combination.[44]

There is some question about her name, which appears in the *Megillah* as both Esther and Hadassah. According to some, her name was really Esther, but she was called Hadassah because she was compared to a *hadassah*, a myrtle twig. Just as a myrtle is fragrant but bitter to the taste, so would Esther, fragrant in character and deeds, be a bitter pill for Haman. Just as a myrtle retains is freshness in all seasons, so would Esther and all the righteous merit both this world and the next; she would remain righteous even after her marriage to Achashverosh, never forgetting her exalted Jewish heritage.

---

41. *Esther Rabbah; Yefei Anaf; R' Elisha Galico; Megillas Sesarim* to *Esther* 5:8; *Me'am Loez; Yad HaMelech.*

42. *Esther Rabbah* 6:7. Amalek was a grandson of Eisav, who had great merit for having greatly honored his father, and thus his descendants were very successful. In order to counter the evil decree of Haman, Eisav's descendant, the Jews needed a corresponding merit in this area. Esther had no father or mother, and thus had never disobeyed her parents. See *Ya'aros Devash; Kiddushin* 31b. Although Esther was of royal lineage and was worthy to become queen, the Jews perceived her as a mere orphan who would not be able to exert much influence on their behalf. Hashem wanted them to place their trust in Him rather than Esther (*R' Chaim Abulafia; Me'am Loez* to *Esther* 2:8).

43. *Bereishis Rabbah* 39:23; *Maharzu; Midrash Panim Acheirim; Targum Rishon; Rokeach.* There are many opinions regarding Esther's age at the time, including 40, 75 and 80.

44. *Megillah* 13a with *Etz Yosef; Ben Yehoyada; R' Shmuel di Uzidah;* see *Chagigah* 12b with *Maharsha.* Some suggest that she was as green as an *esrog;* others that she had a teal color. There is an opinion that her complexion had a golden yellow tinge, like the yolk of an egg. See *Tikunei Zohar* 421, pg. 56b; *Be'er LaChai Ro'i* and *Gra;* also *Tosafos* to *Succah* 31b.

Just as the myrtle is not too tall nor too short, and its fragrance a pleasant one, so was Esther.[45]

According to others, her name was really Hadassah, but she was known as Esther for two reasons. The name Esther is related to the word *seser*, which means hidden; Esther's identity was concealed to the point that all nations claimed her for their own, and she herself always remained secluded from public view even after she became queen.[46] The name Esther is also related to the word *sahar*, which refers to radiance, especially of celestial bodies; Esther was as luminous as the moon or Venus, and she brought light into Jewish lives darkened by Haman's persecution.[47]

In either case, the name Esther itself is of Aramaic or Persian origin. Mordechai knew prophetically that Esther would become queen, and he provided her with a name that would conceal her identity.[48]

There is also some question regarding the relationship between Mordechai and Esther. According to some, he married her.[49] According to others, he married her but did not live with her. According to yet others, they never married. She was his ward, and he cared for her as such all through the years.[50]

When the search in Shushan got under way seriously, Mordechai was prepared to risk his life to prevent her from being taken to the palace. He concealed her in a secret room, where

---

45. *Megillah* 13a with *Sifsei Chachamim* and *Ben Yehoyada*. See *Maharal; Targum Sheni; Midrash Panim Acheirim*. See *Esther Rabbah* 6:5; *Yalkut Shimoni*. See *Rokeach* who writes that she looked like the blossom (or flower) of a myrtle tree. See *Rashbam* to *Bava Basra* 78b; also *Targum Sheni; Yalkut Shimoni* 1053; *Midrash Panim Acheirim* to *Esther* 2:8. See *Sefer HaAruch* under letter *samech*, "*sachan*."

46. *Megillah* 13a, with *Maharsha*; see *Midrash Tehillim* 22:23; *Ya'aros Devash, derush* 15; *R' Avigdor Kohen Tzedek*.

47. *Megillah* 13a with *Rashi; Targum Sheni; Me'am Loez; Shemos Rabbah* 15:6.

48. *Yosef Lekach; Menos HaLevi; Akeidah*.

49. *Megillah* 13a; *R' Elisha Galico; R' Shmuel di Uzidah; Yishai Elokim; Menos HaLevi*. The *Megillah* implies only through a play on words that Mordechai married Esther, saying he took her *l'bas*, as a daughter, which is interpreted as *l'bayis*, to his house, as a wife. According to some, Achashverosh never found out that Mordechai and Esther had been married. Since the *Megillah* was written during the King's lifetime, the information was only given through a hint (*Etz Yosef* to *Megillah* 13a).

50. See *R' Elisha Galico; Yedei Moshe; Me'am Loez. Ya'aros Devash* writes that Mordechai was a *gilgul* (reincarnation) of the soul of Moshe, and Esther, that of Basya, Pharaoh's daughter. Haman was a *gilgul* of the Egyptian whom Moshe had killed, and was now bent on revenge. Events would conclude the same way this time: Mordechai would prevail over Haman just as Moshe had killed the Egyptian.

she remained hidden right under the noses of the imperial agents. But Hashem had other plans.[51]

Word reached the imperial agents that she had been spotted near the house of a Jew, and they sent squads to seek her out.

Mordechai, realizing it was Hashem's will that Esther be taken to the palace, ceased to resist. To conceal Esther's identity and his own violation of the king's decree, he brought Esther to another part of the city and told her to mingle with a group of girls where she would be easily spotted.[52]

Within minutes, Esther was approached by imperial agents and ordered to accompany them to the palace. Although she knew this was her destiny, she refused. She wanted to go on record that she was acting against her will and better judgment. Without further ado, the imperial agents took her forcibly and brought her to the palace.[53] She had been caught in the net, but she told no one who she was, not her parentage, not her nationality. She remained the mystery woman.[54]

Esther's arrival at the palace caused a great stir. The ministers and courtiers whispered to each other that this mysterious lady would surely be the new queen. No one had ever seen a woman who combined within herself such grace, charm, personality and character. Vashti was nothing compared to her. It seemed too good to be true, but the search had apparently come to a successful end. Of course, it all depended on Achashverosh, but how could he not choose her?[55]

---

51. *Targum Sheni; Malbim.*

52. *Yalkut Shimoni; Targum Sheni; Rambam to Esther; Yosef Lekach; Ma'amar Mordechai.* Some suggest that the angel *Gavriel* exposed Esther's hiding place so that she would be taken to Achashverosh. See *Zohar* 271 and *Rokeach.* Some say that the prevailing laws made it possible for Esther to escape her home to flee from capture. Since all men were to be masters in their homes, Mordechai could not excuse himself by telling the police that Esther had left without permission. This would have been in clear violation of the first letter (*Chasam Sofer*). Some suggest that Mordechai tried to hide Esther until the very last moment. While he was on duty at the palace gate, and unable to prevent it, Esther was taken forcibly to the palace (*Eshkol HaKofer*).

53. *Targum Rishon; R' Elisha Galico; R' Shmuel di Uzidah.* Some suggest that amid the chaos, no one knew from what home she came and thus they did not know who she was (*Tzuf Devash*).

54. *R' Yosef ibn Nachmiash.* Some suggest that those who found her mysteriously died, and her true identity was not known (*R' Elisha Galico*).

55. *Ma'amar Mordechai; Pirush Megillas Achashverosh.*

Esther Is Chosen

8

Haggai was shouting instructions to his assistants over the hustle and bustle of the royal harem lobby when Esther and her escort of imperial agents arrived.

One of the imperial agents approached Haggai. "Sir, we have brought you a new candidate. Direct us to her quarters, and we will escort her there."

"Tell me her name and nationality," said Haggai.

"Her name is Esther," said the agent. "As for her nationality, she refuses to disclose it. We saw her on the street and took her. The name sounds Persian or perhaps Aramaic to me, but your guess is as good as mine. If you tell me where to bring her, I can return to continue the search."

Haggai pulled at his left earlobe. "Very interesting. A mystery woman no less. You and your friends can go, my good man. She seems too unique to be quartered with the others in the harem. I will have to find better accommodations. Thank you and good day."

After the agents left, Haggai slowly walked over to Esther.

"Good afternoon," he said and bowed from the waist. "I am Haggai, royal beautician and keeper of the harem."

"And I am Esther. Reluctant visitor to the palace."

"Well, perhaps we can make you forget your reluctance. I will give you a personal tour of the palace."

"Thank you, kind sir, but it is really not necessary. I am not sad. This is where my destiny has brought me, and I accept it."

They stepped out into the perfumed air of the royal gardens. The afternoon sun glowed crimson in the western sky.

"By the way," said Haggai, "the gentlemen who escorted you here neglected to mention your nationality. What is it? Who are your people?"

"It would please me if you would not ask me such questions. I have resolved not to disclose my background."

"Indeed? And why is that?"

"I have resolved not to disclose that either. If you really are concerned about my state of mind, you must respect my privacy."

For the rest of the afternoon, Haggai showed her through the royal gardens, halls, chambers, wardrobe rooms and treasure house, giving her a running commentary and attending gallantly to Esther's every need. He was convinced beyond the shadow of a doubt that the lady he was escorting would be the next queen, and he went out of his way to please her.[1]

After the grand tour, he brought Esther to a lavishly appointed apartment. Then he hurried off and returned a few minutes later with jewelry far more expensive than any he had given to the other contestants. He also gave her a glittering necklace from the royal treasure house.

The next morning, he brought armloads of exquisite clothing fit for a queen. But when he returned bearing even more gifts, he was disappointed. He had expected her to be royally dressed, made up and bejeweled, but instead, he found her in her customary modest attire.[2]

---

1. *Yedei Moshe; R' Yosef ibn Yachia; Alshich; R' Shmuel di Uzidah; Gra; R' Elisha Galico; Menos HaLevi; R' Yosef ibn Yachia.* Some suggest that those who were forced to come were taken to the women's chambers, and the ones who volunteered were under Haggai's charge, but only Esther remained in the King's Quarters (*Menos HaLevi*).
2. *Targum Rishon; Aggadas Esther; Rashi; R' Yosef ibn Yachia;* see *Sechel Tov* to *Shemos* 15:15; *Midrash Lekach Tov; Menos HaLevi; Targum Rishon.* See *R' Shmuel di Uzidah; R' Elisha Galico; Menos HaLevi; Yalkut Shimoni; Krovetz L'Purim.*

Haggai arranged for seven maidens to come and serve Esther's every need.[3] These girls were Queen Vashti's personal attendants, and now they were Esther's.

Esther knew about Vashti's servant girls, how they had helped in persecuting the Jewish servant girls, but she hoped they had only done so out of loyalty and that their loyalty would now be to her. Nonetheless, she would have to be careful and clever.

The seven servant girls arrived, and Esther was pleased to see that they appeared uncomplicated and eager to please.

"There are seven days of the week," Esther began, "so each girl will come to me for only one day. The rest of the time is your own. Sleep. Eat. Talk to your friends. Whatever you want to do. Understood?"

"Yes, thank you, milady."

"Good. Now listen, I need your absolute loyalty, and Haggai tells me that you are all loyal girls."

They all nodded.

"My privacy is very important to me," Esther continued. "I have certain habits and practices that I do not want to share with the public, but it will be impossible to hide them from you. I have a liking for certain types of foods prepared in certain special ways, and there are certain things I do and certain things I don't do. I want your solemn promise that you will not talk to anyone about my practices, my diet, my health care, my lifestyle, or anything else about me, not even among yourselves. Do you promise?"

They all nodded.

"One by one," said Esther. "Declare your promise."

They did.

"Good," said Esther. "If you keep your promise, you will be rewarded.

"Here is another of my little wishes," continued Esther. I don't want you to use your names. I will give you special names, and I will call you by those names only. I don't even want to know your given names. Understood?" [4]

The girls shrugged and nodded. Who could account for the tastes and idiosyncrasies of the aristocracy? Who were they to argue or even question?

---

3. *R' Shmuel di Uzidah; Yosef Lekach; Gra; Menos HaLevi.*
Many suggest that the candidates had maidens of their own ethnic groups attending them. See *Rashi* and *Sifsei Chachamim* to *Megillah.*
4. *Megillah* 13a and *Ben Yehoyada; see Rif* to *Ein Yaakov; Targum Rishon; Ya'aros Devash.*

Esther assigned names to each of the girls and told her which day
of the week she was expected to come. The last girl, the one who
would serve her on Shabbos, she named Regoitha, which reminded
her of the Hebrew word for rest. She would be Esther's special sign
of Shabbos in her apartment.

With her clever plan, Esther had arranged her life so that she
could remain fully observant of all the laws of the Torah without
anyone suspecting she was Jewish. On Shabbos, Regoitha would
see Esther refrain from touching certain objects or performing certain actions, like lighting a fire, but she assumed Esther behaved
similarly every other day of the week as well. She had no idea
Esther was keeping Shabbos as the Jews did.[5] Esther also had a private kosher kitchen in her apartment, which she allowed no one
else to use. She also restricted her diet to only certain foods. The
girls assumed she had strange eating customs, but once again, it
never occurred to them that she was following Jewish dietary
laws. And because everything about Esther was so secretive no
one on the outside knew about her lifestyle. No one suspected she
was a Jew.[6]

What did she actually eat? Some say she ate only from her own
kitchen, adamantly refusing the delicious dishes prepared by the royal
chefs on the pretext that they would be bad for her health. For the
same ostensible reason, she maintained a vegetarian diet.[7] Others say
that she did accept some foods from the royal kitchen. Taking her cue
from Chananiah, Mishael and Azariah in the court of
Nevuchadnezzar, she ate only beans, peas, lentils, rice, seeds, citrons
and lettuce brought to her by her trusted maidservants. These foods
were good for her complexion, giving her face an added healthy glow.[8]

Some suggest that Esther could not avoid the meat meals prepared in the royal kitchen. Some say she ate the meat under duress.
Others say while she ate foods prepared with meat, she made sure

---

5. *R' Shmuel di Uzidah; Midrash Megillas Esther; Midrash Lekach Tov.* Some suggest that
she told them she was Jewish and had them convert to Judaism (*Midrash Megillas
Esther;* see *Menos HaLevi*).
6. *Yalkut Shimoni; R' Yosef ibn Yachia;* see *Megillah 13a; Targum Rishon; Eshkol HaKofer;
Ben Yehoyada;* see *Midrash Lekach Tov.*
7. *Midrash HaGadol; R' Yosef ibn Yachia; Malbim.*
8. See *Megillah 13a* with *Tosafos; Ben Yehoyada; Anaf Yosef; Sefer HaAruch* under letter ק,
"*k'tal*"; *Me'am Loez.* See *Daniel 1:16* with *Ibn Ezra; R' Saadiah Gaon.* Some suggest that
they ate foods that caused their mouths to emit an unpleasant odor so that
Nevuchadnezzar would not want them as his stewards, and Esther did the same here.

to avoid the meat itself. Yet others say that she never took a morsel of non-kosher food into her mouth but gave it all to the dogs.[9]

As time went on, Haggai continued to give Esther ever more preferential treatment. He overwhelmed her with jewelry and all sorts of gifts, which she politely declined, and went out of his way to make life as pleasant as possible for her.[10] Esther took advantage of her privileged position to organize her life in as discreet and Jewish a way as possible. She spent her days either in the privacy of her apartment or in secluded parts of the palace where she did not have to see idols or idol worship and where she found pleasant surroundings suited to the different seasons of the year.[11]

Meanwhile, the contest progressed apace. The search in all the provinces was completed. Each of the hundred and twenty-seven provinces sent several contestants to Shushan. Every contestant was given twelve months during which to prepare themselves. During the winter and summer months, they were given specific remedies to protect them from changing weather.[12] The treatments enhanced the appearance of all the contestants — except for one. On the day she was to see the king, the daughter of Haman, otherwise known as Memuchan, found herself erupting with wastes, and her mouth emitted a vile odor. Mortified, she fled from the contest in embarrassment.[13]

For the protection of the king, Haggai also kept close watch over the health of each contestant, keeping a sharp eye open for any signs of infectious disease. Only after a full year under his supervision, having observed her during all seasons and under all conditions, was Haggai prepared to give her a clean bill of health.[14]

After completing the full year of preparations, the contestants were ready to be introduced to the king. Afterwards each would be sent to the royal harem, under the supervision of Shashgaz. Any contestant not chosen as Queen by the King would remain in the

---

9. See *Megillah* 13a with *Rashi*; *Ben Yehoyada*; *Midrash Eliyahu*. Others suggest that she gave the meat to a demon, and that it was assumed that she had eaten it. Others suggest she ate fish.
10. *Yosef Lekach; R' Elisha Galico.*
11. *Midrash Abba Gorion; Pirush Megillas Achashverosh; Malbim.*
12. See *Shabbos* 80b; *Megillah* 13a with *Rashi*; *Targum Rishon; Midrash Lekach Tov; Menos HaLevi; Pirush Megillas Achashverosh; R' Yosef ibn Yachia*; see *Ramban* to *Shemos* 23:30.
13. *Targum Rishon* to *Esther* 5:1.
14. *Targum Sheni; Menos HaLevi; Eshkol HaKofer; Malbim.* In reality this, like everything else, was done for the benefit of the Jews. The Jews were being judged by Hashem to determine whether they were worthy of having Esther deliver them. If the Jews would be found favorable, Esther would be chosen Queen (*Megillas Sesarim*).

harem for the rest of her life. She would not be allowed to return
to civilian life, since it would be unseemly for a woman who met
the king to marry a commoner. It was an awful prospect — either
the heights of glory as queen or the pit of despair, condemned to a
life of rejection, loneliness and boredom in the harem.[15] Haggai
was sensitive to the turmoil in the hearts and minds of the contestants. It was important that their minds be set at ease.
Furthermore, he feared that the concentration of hundreds of anx-
ious women in the harem might generate a spirit of discontent and
even rebellion.[16]

The solution, Haggai decided, lay in extravagant indulgence.
Each contestant was allowed to request anything she desired, no
matter how lavish or expensive; many chose jewelry and exquisite
garments. In this way, Haggai really made them feel like a queen, at
least once, a feeling very few people in the world ever experience.
He hoped that this would calm them and make them excited about
being presented to the king.[17]

For twelve months, Esther lived in her apartment awaiting her call.
She led a simple and modest life, speaking kindly to all she met, including the other contestants, keeping to seclusion, eating her own food
and keeping her own company. Haggai visited her often. He inquired
after her welfare and brought her gifts. He also pressed her about her
identity and background. Her responses were always the same; she
spoke politely, declined his gifts and never revealed who she was.[18]

Why was it so important for Esther to keep her identity secret?
There were many reasons.

First of all, she felt it would be immodest to present herself as a
descendant of Jewish royalty. Modesty was a characteristic deeply
ingrained in her lineage. The Jewish matriarch Rachel had modest-
ly remained silent when her father replaced her under the wedding
canopy with her sister Leah. By this act, she merited that her grandson Shaul be chosen the first king of Israel. Shaul himself was mod-

---

15. *Alshich; Ibn Ezra; R' Yosef ibn Yachia; Gra.*

16. *Ibn Ezra; Midrash Lekach Tov; R' Yosef ibn Nachmiash; Aggadas Esther; Yosef Lekach;
Yishai Elokim, Yalkut Shimoni.*

17. See *R' Yosef ibn Nachmiash; R' Elisha Galico; Targum Rishon; Targum Sheini; Rashi;
Menos HaLevi; Maharal; Midrash Lekach Tov; Yedei Moshe; D'na Pishra; Midrash Lekach
Tov.* See *R' Shmuel di Uzidah,* who explains this system in great detail; *Yalkut Shimoni*
1053; *Midrash Panim Acheirim.* This was orchestrated from above so that Esther would
gain the attention of the public through her unique behavior.

18. *Yalkut Shimoni; Yosef Lekach; Yedei Moshe; Iggeres Purim.*

est about his appointment to the throne, and in his merit, his grand-daughter Esther would be blessed with *ruach hakodesh,* divine inspi-ration, and the honor of being the redeemer of the Jewish people.

Furthermore, Mordechai had instructed her to remain silent, and she was glad to comply with anything he told her, even if she did not understand his motivation.[19] Mordechai had many good reasons for instructing Esther to remain silent. He knew that divine providence was guiding Esther toward the throne, and he felt it was their respon-sibility, Mordechai's and Esther's, to act in a way that would facilitate the divine plan. Because of the anti-Jewish sentiment in the nation, and especially in the palace, he thought Esther would not be considered as a serious contestant for queen.[20] Besides, if her identity was discovered, her age would likely be discovered as well, and Achashverosh would not knowingly marry a seventy-five-year-old woman.[21]

In addition, since Achashverosh had decide to seek a wife among the commoners it would be better to conceal her Jewish lineage which traced back to the royal house of Shaul. Moreover, Mordechai feared she would become the target of malicious slan-der and rumors designed to provoke Achashverosh's anger against her and cause her to be executed, just like Vashti. By hiding her Jewishness, Esther was less likely to be exposed to danger and more likely to be chosen queen and to serve effectively. It would certainly be easier for her to advocate for the Jews if no one knew that she herself was Jewish.

There were also other safety considerations involved. First of all, since Esther had not come forward to the call of the royal decree but had remained hidden for a while, there was a danger that the king would avenge himself on her accomplices. He might even exact retribution by punishing the entire Jewish nation. And if he discovered Esther was descended from Shaul, he might think she had tried to avoid the contest because he was not good enough for her, and then he would become even more incensed. Finally, if Esther were to be chosen queen, she would run the risk of being treated as Vashti had been, and forced to display which nationali-

---

19. *D'na Pishra; Alshich.* Another reason for Esther's silence was that it was a trait of her ancestor. Binyamin's stone on the *Choshen* (Breastplate) of the *Kohen Gadol* was the *yashfeh,* which also spells *yesh peh,* has a mouth. This was appropriate for the tribe of Binyamin, for he knew that his brother Yosef was alive in *Mitzrayim,* yet he honored his request to keep it hidden from Yaakov and remained silent.

20. *Midrash R'Zechariah HaRofei.*

21. See *Melo HaOmer.*

ty produced such a queen. But if she did not reveal her nationality, this could not happen.[22]

There was also an element of spiritual protection in keeping her identity concealed. According to the Torah, Esther did not have to risk her life to avoid complying with Achashverosh. If Achashverosh knew she was Jewish, his intention and actions might also be directed at inducing her to violate the Torah. In this case, *chillul Hashem*, desecration of the Name, would be involved, and she would have to give her life before she did anything to violate the Torah.

Mordechai may also have been concerned that Esther's accession to the throne might effect radical changes on his own life. If the king were so smitten with Esther, he might decide to extend his favors to members of her family. Mordechai wanted to live the low-profile life of a Jew in exile. He did not want royal favors and honors, and the most effective way of avoiding them was by concealing his connection to Esther.[23] If Esther admitted she was Jewish, it would no longer be possible to conceal the connection. Mordechai may also have been worried that if the king was taken with Esther, a Jewish woman, the noblemen of his court might also become inclined to seek wives among the Jewish people. That would be a disaster to avoid at all costs.[24]

Others see the concealment of Esther's Jewish identity not as a means of helping her become queen but as a means of avoiding it. Mordechai hoped that Esther's refusal to give information about herself would result in her rejection as a candidate. He also feared that if Achashverosh knew she was Jewish and checked her lineage he would discover that she was descended from Shaul. This would delight him to such an extent that he would never let her go.[25]

22. *Mechilta Beshalach; Yalkut Shimoni; Targum Rishon; Midrash HaGadol; Maharal; Yosef Lekach; Gra; R' Avigdor Kohen Tzedek; Binyan Ariel. Menos HaLevi; Yedei Moshe; R' Yosef ibn Nachmiash;* see *Sanhedrin* 74b. When she later told Achashverosh who she was, it was no longer a problem. By that time their relationship had developed to the point that her lineage was not taken into account.
23. *Yalkut Esther; Menos HaLevi.*
24. *Nachal Eshkol.*
25. *Menos HaLevi; Yosef Lekach; R' Avigdor Kohen Tzedek; Binyan Ariel, Rashi; Etz Yosef; Yefei Anaf; Menos HaLevi; Yosef Lekach.* Others suggest the opposite; Mordechai wished to do everything possible to fulfill the will of Hashem, which was that Esther become Queen. He knew prophetically that Esther would be her people's savior, and he felt that hiding her Jewishness would ensure her being chosen. Though she would have to marry Achashverosh, she would thus accomplish her mission (*Ibn Ezra; R' Shmuel di Uzidah; R' Elisha Galico*). Others point out that it was to the benefit of the Jewish nation that no one knew Esther was Jewish. Otherwise, whenever she would do something on behalf of the Jews, even when justified, people would accuse her of being biased and acting for her personal interest instead of the good of

In any case, regardless of whether or not he wanted her to become queen, Mordechai was worried about her. He knew she was in danger in the palace, that Achashverosh might discover her secrets and kill her in a fit of anger, that jealous rival contestants might plot against her or try to harm her with magic spells.[26]

As a high-ranking Jewish nobleman, Mordechai had access to the palace, and he took full advantage of this privilege.[27] Every day, he strolled slowly past the courtyard of the royal harem, his eyes and ears wide open. Since Esther kept her identity concealed, no one dreamed of connecting her with the Jewish sage, and they did not refrain from discussing her in his presence.[28] By gathering information, he would be able to protect her better. In addition, Mordechai knew full well that Esther's presence in the palace was an important part of the divine plan, and that Hashem would soon perform miracles for her. He wanted to witness them.[29]

From time to time, Mordechai would catch a glimpse of Esther, and this was reassuring to both of them. For Esther, just the sight of him gave her strength and comfort in her trying circumstances.[30] Sometimes, when they were even able to exchange a few surreptitious words, Esther would ask him for guidance on ritual laws, dietary laws or the laws of Shabbos. She was determined to violate as few laws as possible in her enforced isolation.

Mordechai's kindness and solicitousness toward Esther while she was in the palace deemed him worthy of one day becoming the leader of the entire Jewish nation.[31]

The months flew by, and Esther still remained silent. She also continued to decline the jewelry Haggai offered her, preferring her simple, modest and unadorned appearance. Inwardly, she hoped that Achashverosh would reject her if she did not beautify herself for him.

One day, Haggai appeared at her apartment.

"You know that I am devoted to you."

Achashverosh's empire. In such a position Esther would be unable to help her coreligionists (*R' Yosef ibn Yachia; Alshich*).

26. *R'Elisha Galico; Eshkol HaKofer; Esther Rabbah 6:8; Maharzu.* Some suggest that some magic did affect Esther. When she came before Achashverosh, her legs buckled under her (*Yalkut Shimoni*).

27. *Ibn Ezra; D'na Pishra.*

28. *Yedei Moshe; Menos HaLevi; R' Shmuel di Uzidah; Rishon LeTzion.*

29. *Targum Sheni; R' Yosef ibn Yachia; Menos HaLevi.*

30. *Targum Rishon; Eshkol HaKofer; Yosef Lekach; Gra.*

31. *Esther Rabbah 6:8; Pirkai D'Rav Eliezer; Midrash lEkach Tov; Ibn Ezra, Menos Levi, Maharal.*

"Yes, Haggai. You are very kind."

"Can I then ask for a kindness in return?"

"Of course, Haggai."

"In a short time you will be called to the king, and that worries me immensely. You have rejected all gifts and enhancements to help you prepare to meet the king. Instead of eating the excellent food from the royal kitchen you subsist on nuts and vegetables. Don't you think all this shows disrespect to the king? All right, I understand that you are worried for your own safety. Perhaps you think your gods, whoever they are, will protect you. But how about me? Will your gods protect me as well? Why aren't you concerned that the king will banish or even kill me for not seeing to it that you are properly prepared for him? I tell you, both of us may end up swinging from the gallows together."[32]

As a Jewish married woman, Esther had been concerned that an encounter with the king would involve violating the Torah's prohibitions. But now that she was being told outright that she would be killed if she resisted, she was clearly acting under duress and exonerated from sin.

"Very well," said Esther. "I'll do it."[33]

"Oh, and one more thing, if I may."

"Yes, Haggai?"

"What is your nationality? It would be a big help if I knew."

Esther responded. "Enough is enough. You ask too much. My privacy remains mine."

After Haggai left, Esther sat down, depressed. It seemed there would be no escaping Achashverosh and she grew pale thinking about the fate that awaited her. But somehow, her pallor did not detract from her. The special grace with which Hashem anointed her remained with her.[34]

As her turn to be brought to the king drew near, all eyes turned in her direction. Everyone expected the king to choose this extraordinarily graceful woman as his new queen. People were also impressed with her modesty and simplicity. Who had ever heard of a woman who wanted nothing for herself, no fancy clothing, no jewelry, no furs? Furthermore, no one knew who she was and from where she

---

32. *Midrash Lekach Tov; Yalkut Shimoni; Menos HaLevi.* Some suggest that Esther only refused to put on make-up on Shabbos since it is prohibited (*Einei HaEidah*)
33. See *Sanhedrin* 74b; *Menos HaLevi.*
34. *Gra.*

had come. The aura of mystery was alluring, and before long, Esther became a topic of conversation in every part of the palace.[35]

Every nationality claimed her for their own.

"She is Persian," declared the Persians.

"Ridiculous," said the Africans. "Can't you see she is African? She even speaks our language."

"What does that prove?" said the Indians. "She speaks our language as well."

And so went the arguments. The people did not know that Esther actually spoke seventy languages, which she had learned from Mordechai.

Whenever she passed by in the palace, noblemen stopped to watch her.[36]

On the day she was called to the king, it was already a foregone conclusion in the palace that Esther would be the new queen, that the visit to the king was just a formality to make it official. People vied with each other for the assignment of escorting her to the king, offering exorbitant sums for the honor and privilege. Maidservants fought with each other, everyone wanted to forge some kind of personal connection with the future queen.[37]

The day for Esther to meet the king had arrived. The angel Gabriel protected her, and she was comforted by his presence. Esther however was desolate. She felt as if she were going to her execution. She bowed to her fate, knowing it was the will of Hashem.

Esther had never seen Achashverosh, but she immediately recognized his bearish hulk, his bushy eyebrows and his glowering eyes.[38]

"I have an important question to ask you," Achashverosh asked. "The report on you was quite skimpy. It was missing important background information. Who are you? Where are you from? What is your nationality? I need to know these things, Esther."

"Your majesty, you are a mighty king," Esther replied, "the mightiest in all the world. You have the power of life and death over

---

35. *Esther Rabbah 6:9; see Radal; Yefei Anaf.*

36. *Megillah 13a; Esther Rabbah 6:9; Rokeach.*

37. *Esther Rabbah 6:10; see Matnos Kehunah and Yefai Anaf.*

38. See *Sanhedrin* 74b and commentaries, which discuss this matter in detail. Many suggest that Esther never actually had relations with Achashverosh. She had a demon with her which assumed her form and took her place. Some suggest the name of the demon was *Moch*. See *Tikunei Zohar* 421, page 58 and *Nitzutzei Zohar*. See *Megillas Sesarim; Ben Yehoyada* to *Megillah* 13a; and *Nachal Eshkol; Ta'amei HaMinhagim.*

millions of people. If you wanted to, you could force me to do any-thing at all, say anything at all. All you would have to do is torture me or threaten to kill me, and I would certainly tell you anything you want to know. But then would I be a fitting queen for you, your majesty, or just another servant girl?"

Achashverosh beamed. "You impress me with your wisdom and intelligence, Esther. You are right, of course. If I force you to tell me, then you are useless to me. You must tell me of your own free will."

"Then I choose not to say. Please do not be offended, your majesty. No offense is intended. But my privacy is important to me, and I would be ever so grateful if you would respect it."

Achashverosh knit his brows and thought for a moment or two. "Very well, I will respect your privacy. Perhaps someday you will tell on your own."

"Perhaps, your majesty," said Esther. "But I do not promise."

The next day, the king summoned Haggai to his chambers and greeted him excitedly at the door.

"You were right, Haggai, this is the one. You will be rewarded, my fine fellow. Good job!"

"I have an important announcement to make," Achashverosh declared when everyone was assembled. "I will address myself to Esther, but I want everyone to hear what I have to say.

"I have discovered that behind the fine exterior is an even finer interior. You are kind, courteous, gracious, mature, intelligent, wise. And oh, so modest. You want nothing for yourself. What a splendid person you are! I am fortunate to find you."

Achashverosh bent down to a small table behind his chair and brought forth a crown. He walked over to Esther.

"Esther, I make you my queen!" he declared.[39]

He placed the crown upon her head, and miraculously, it fit perfectly.

"Look, everyone!" shouted Achashverosh. "It was never adjusted to her head, and yet it fits perfectly. There is no doubt about it. This was meant to be. Esther is my predestined queen!"[40]

---

39. *Ya'aros Devash; Yad HaMelech; Eshkol HaKofer.* See *Chasam Sofer; Yevamos 60b; Alshich.* Some suggest that after Achashverosh had Vashti killed, there was a rebellion, and much of his empire was lost. When he married Esther he got part of it back, and when Mordechai would become viceroy to the King, he would get the rest of his empire back. See *Midrash Tehillim 22.*

40. *Alshich; Ya'avetz to Krovetz L'Purim.*

While everyone applauded and cheered, Achashverosh whispered to one of the servants to collect all the engravings of Vashti from the royal apartment and whisk them away. And so the last vestiges of the former queen were removed. A new queen had come to take her place.[41]

The hand of Heaven was clear. Of all the thousands of contestants who competed ambitiously for the prize of the royal crown, the only contestant who had declined to compete, who had eaten simple foods and worn simple garments, was the one chosen.[42]

In the month of Teves, the tenth month of the seventh year, Achashverosh felt that his monarchy was finally complete. He had not completed the subjugation of his empire until three years into his reign, and by then, he no longer had a queen beside him. Now, in his seventh year, Achashverosh had an empire and a queen. It was cause for celebration.[43]

---

41. *Esther Rabbah* 6:11.
42. See *Eshkol HaKofer*.
43. See *Esther* 2:14.

A Queen of Mystery

9

For the first time in his life, Achashverosh was truly happy. His empire was secure, and his queen was more beloved to him than anything else in the world. In fact, he was so happy that he decided to make a feast in honor of the new queen. The feast would be the queen's official inauguration and the king's demonstration of his undying love.[1]

Unlike the feast he had hosted four years earlier, the feast of Esther was a more modest affair, but it was more pleasing to Achashverosh than the first. It did not celebrate Achashverosh's victory, nor his throne nor the impending destruction of his hated Jews.[2] It was just for his beloved Esther, and the guest list was limited to his loyal courtiers, eminent noblemen, dignitaries, scholars and the local populace. He also invited all the agents and officials who had worked so hard to assemble contestants for the

---

1. *Megillah* 13a; *Midrash Lekach Tov; R' Yosef ibn Yachia; R' Elisha Galico, Yedei Moshe.*
2. *R' Elisha Galico; Gra;* see *Yosef Lekach.*

beauty pageant. This feast would also serve as a show of royal gratitude to them.[3]

Achashverosh also remembered the fiasco of the earlier feast, and he was determined not to repeat the same mistakes. He did not invite foreigners or soldiers, and there was no debauchery or immoral behavior. He also kept Esther beside him throughout the feast, since it was in her honor.[4] Also unlike the first time, the food at the feast was kosher to accommodate the Jewish guests, but at Mordechai's behest, none of the Jews of Shushan attended.[5]

In fact, most of the people of Shushan did not attend the feast. They simply couldn't afford it. Attendance would involve a gift for the king, new outfits fit for a visit to the palace and all sorts of other expenses far beyond the capabilities of the local citizenry. Nonetheless, Achashverosh wanted them to share in the celebration, and he declared a national holiday on which people would feast in their homes in honor of the Queen. He also gave gifts to his subjects to help them pay for the feast and to compensate them for wages or earnings they would lose by not working on the day of the feast.[6]

In his own mind, Achashverosh hoped to gain one more thing from the feast. He was obsessed with the mystery of Esther's origin. Although he could not press Esther to tell him, as she had so aptly pointed out, he was consumed with curiosity. Haggai had tried to find out and failed, as had others in the palace, but Achashverosh was not discouraged. One way or another, he would find out. The feast, he thought, would present him with many opportunities for discovering her secret. Perhaps someone who knew her would attend and casually reveal her identity in the course of conversation. Perhaps he might even persuade Esther to drink a little wine and let down her guard. Perhaps the honor he was showing her might even cause her to feel obligated to divulge her secret.[7]

In a further show of good faith, Achashverosh ordered Haggai to release all the original candidates from the harem and send them home, a radical departure from royal custom. Perhaps now she

---

3. *Menos HaLevi.*

4. *Gra; Menos HaLevi; R' Shmuel di Uzidah; Ma'amar Mordechai.* See *Bereishis Rabbah* 53:10; *Rokeach.* See *Bereishis* 2:18 with *Rashi* and *Sifsei Chachamim.* See *R' Yosef ibn Yachia* who posits that this feast had as many people as the first one.

5. *Menos HaLevi.*

6. *Menos HaLevi; R' Elisha Galico; R' Shmuel di Uzidah.*

7. *Sifsei Chachamim* to *Megillah* 13a; *Yishai Elokim; Malbim.*

would be convinced of the depth and sincerity of his love for her, and she would tell him her secret.[8]

However, things did not work out quite as Achashverosh had expected. Esther was so immensely popular that every group and nationality claimed her for their own, speaking as if they knew Esther from before. It was thus impossible to determine who she really was. Even if guests who knew had been present, as the king had hoped, there was no way of identifying them among all the others who claimed her for their own.[9]

But Achashverosh did not give up. After the feast, he tried different stratagems. He declared the abolition of taxes in his empire for seven years in Esther's honor. He hoped this would induce Esther to reveal her nationality so that her people could take credit for the tax relief throughout the empire. Ironically, the only people not exempt from taxes were the despised Jews, Esther's true people.[10]

Achashverosh also gave generous gifts to local and foreign officials, to dignitaries and noblemen — all in Esther's honor.[11] He declared a general amnesty and pardoned all prisoners — all in Esther's honor.[12] He hoped that Esther would be so grateful for the honors he was showing her that she would tell him that which he wanted most to know. Otherwise, perhaps some grateful subject from somewhere in his far-flung empire would come forward and identify the Queen.

All the King's acts of kindness made an enormous impression on the empire. The King's prestige rose dramatically, as did the fame and glory of the Queen who had inspired all this magnanimity. But the Queen herself remained unmoved; she continued to guard her secret.[13] As for someone coming forward with information, hundreds of people did, all claiming Esther as their own. It was almost comical, but the king was not amused.[14]

Strangely, the King never noticed that the only people who did not come forward to claim Esther as their own were the Jews,

8. *Rokeach; Rambam; Yosef Lekach; Malbim.*

9. *Rashi to Ein Yaakov, Megillah* 13a.

10. *Megillah* 13a; *Rashi; Yosef Lekach; Sifsei Chachamim* to *Megillah* 13a; *R' Shmuel di Uzidah; Melo HaOmer; Malbim; Yishai Elokim.*

11. *Megillah* 13a with *Rashi* and *Sifsei Chachamim; Midrash Lekach Tov.*

12. *Pesikta Rabbasi.*

13. *Targum Rishon; Rashi* and *Sifsei Chachamim* to *Megillah* 13a.

14. *Rashi* to *Ein Yaakov, Megillah* 13a.

although they would not have been believed if they did. Perhaps he thought it was because they had not been given tax relief. In any case, many Jews knew full well who Esther was, but as Mordechai remained silent, so did they. In the merit of this silence, they were deemed worthy of redemption from their exile.[15]

One morning, Achashverosh took stock of all his plans and actions. Admittedly, they had earned him tremendous goodwill with his subjects, but they had failed to elicit the information he sought. It was driving him so mad that he decided to swallow his pride and make another plea directly to Esther over breakfast.[16]

He sought her out in the sunny morning room, where she was dining.

"Good morning, Esther my queen," he said.

Esther's eyes narrowed. "Good morning to you, your majesty."

"This is not an easy thing for me, Esther. It is beneath me to press you for the answer, but I really must know. Look, if you tell me, what do you think I will do? Why, I will shower your people and your family with gifts and honors for producing a heavenly queen such as you. There really is no reason for you to keep your nationality hidden from me."[17]

Esther took another sip of her tea. "Milord, I am not trying to make things difficult for you, but I have my reasons for keeping my background secret. You must trust me. Perhaps things will change one day, and I will be free to tell you. Right now, however, I must remain silent."

"I understand how you feel," said Achashverosh, "but you must also understand how I feel."

"I do, I really do." Esther drew a deep breath. "Just to show you my good faith, I will tell you a little bit, but first you tell me about yourself, your own background. What is the first thing that comes to your mind?"

"Why, that I am a king, of course," said Achashverosh. "That royal blood flows in my veins."

"Then I will tell you the same about me. Royal blood flows in my veins, too." She smiled. "And because of you, I, too, am a queen."[18]

---

15. *Rambam to Esther; Ya'aros Devash.*

16. *Menos HaLevi.*

17. *Rambam to Esther.*

18. *Targum Rishon; Midrash Lekach Tov; Midrash Abba Gorion; Yalkut Shimoni.*

Achashverosh frowned. "I appreciate your telling me this, Esther. But I must know some more. Tell me your nationality. It will cause no harm. I promise you this."

"Milord, you are pressuring me, and you agreed that you wouldn't. Besides, if you press me to the wall I may say the wrong thing, and then we will have trouble. Do you want me to end up like Vashti did? Do you want to kill me?"

"Heaven forbid!" cried Achashverosh. "I would never do anything to hurt you. You know that. And I don't mean to pressure you. It's just that this curiosity is too much for me. We are close, you and I, Esther. I can tell you how I feel, can't I?"

"Of course you can, milord."

"Then is there anything you can tell me? Any morsel of real information that will still my curiosity, at least for a while?"

Esther sighed. "All right," she said. "But only if you give me your word that you won't pressure me further. And if you will not reveal what I tell you to anyone else."

"I give you my word. On both counts."

"And I accept it," said Esther. "It is really a sad story. My father died before I was born, and my mother when I was but a young child. A Jewish scholar found me in the street and took pity on a lost orphan. He raised me in his home until I was old enough to fend for myself. I shall be forever grateful to him."[19]

Achashverosh's eyes opened wide. "A Jew? Well, I suppose a Jew can do something good once in a while. I am happy that this Jew found you, although I would have preferred that a Persian had found you. Or a Mede. Or even an Indian."

Esther shrugged. "This is what was fated. He was very kind to me, this Jew. He took very good care of me all the years I was growing up. I have no complaints. Nothing but gratitude."

"Then I suppose I am grateful to him as well for taking care of my future wife and queen. Who is this Jew? Does he live here in Shushan? Have I ever heard of him?"

"Actually, he does, and you have. His name is Mordechai."

"Mordechai! Of course, I know him. He is one the leaders of the Jews, a wise man, I must admit. I have called on his services

---

19. *Targum Sheni; Midrash Panim Acheirim.* Some suggest that Esther told Achashverosh that she was raised by Hashem, Who cares for orphans. Perhaps she told him that Mordechai was Hashem's emissary to care for her (*Aggadas Esther*).

from time to time. By the way, Esther, do you yourself know your nationality?"

Esther fixed him with a stern look. "Your Majesty."

Achashverosh threw up his hand in mock defense. "Wait a minute, Esther. I was not pressuring you. I gave you my word, and I will keep it. I was only wondering if you are a mystery even to yourself."

"I know my nationality. But I want no more questions."

"You will get none." Achashverosh cleared his throat. "A little earlier, you made a remark that disturbed me. You asked if I wanted to kill you as I had killed Vashti. I want you to know, Esther, that killing Vashti was not my idea. It was my counselors who pressed me to do it. I was drunk at the time and wasn't thinking clearly, and my counselors persuaded me that I had no other choice. The next morning, I regretted my actions. Oh, did I regret what I had done under the influence of wine. Believe me, Esther, I am not the guilty one. My counselors bear the guilt."

"I understand, milord. But isn't a king responsible for his counselors? Shouldn't a king make sure he chooses good counselors?"

"Of course, of course. But how can you peer into someone else's soul and heart and know what evil lurks there? Do you have any suggestions?"

"Well, I would suggest you see what your predecessors did and follow their example. Actually, I recommend that you get a good Jewish advisor. They are wise and sober men. Nevuchadnezzar relied on a Jewish sage and prophet named Daniel. Cyrus had as his advisor a Jewish prince named Zerubavel. Why don't you call on Mordechai to advise you in the grand tradition of imperial monarchs? I can vouch for his character. You, of course, would have to be the judge of his wisdom and knowledge."

Achashverosh leaned back and smiled. "You are a brilliant woman, Esther. Absolutely brilliant. And I have no doubt you are a good judge of wisdom and knowledge as well. Mordechai it will be. Besides, I have an ulterior motive in choosing Mordechai as my advisor."

"Oh?"

"Wouldn't it make you happy to see him regularly in the palace?"

Esther smiled. "It certainly would."

"Then that is also a reason to choose him. Anything that makes you happy makes me happy, too."[20]

---

20. *Targum Rishon; Midrash Lekach Tov, Yalkut Shimoni; Malbim.*

Achashverosh had another ulterior motive as well. Although he had given his word to Esther to stop asking her questions, his curiosity still burned within him, and he hoped that Mordechai might provide some of the information he sought. Moreover, he hoped that Esther would feel more secure with Mordechai close by. Perhaps then she would at last volunteer to divulge her secret to him.

The next day, Achashverosh summoned Mordechai to the palace.

"I want to offer you a position in my government," Achashverosh said to the Jewish sage. "Queen Esther has recommended I appoint you chief royal advisor, and I concur. I know you personally and by reputation, and I am confident you will serve me well. I also know that you shy away from publicity and honors. You were conspicuously missing at the royal feasts. But it is important for the good of the empire that you accept this position."

"I am honored, your majesty," said Mordechai. "And of course, I accept." Especially, he thought, since this will allow me to be closer to Esther and take care of her.

"Excellent!" said Achashverosh. "Now then, here is your first assignment. As you know, Esther refuses to reveal her nationality. She is quite the mystery woman. Do you know anything about her background?"[21]

Mordechai did some quick thinking. If Esther had recommended him for the post of royal advisor, she must have divulged something about their relationship, but obviously not everything. "Your majesty, if you do not already know this, I raised Esther in my home. I found her as a little orphan, and I took her in. That is all I know."[22]

A sudden suspicion bloomed in Achashverosh's mind. Esther had spoken highly of Mordechai and recommended him for the position of advisor. They told the exact same story. Could it be that they were in collusion? Could it be that Esther was really Jewish and somehow related to Mordechai and that they had plotted together to gain power in the palace for the Jews? Oh, what a horrible thought, but what if it were true? There was only one way to find out. He had to put Mordechai to the test.[23]

"I am sorry to hear that, Mordechai," said Achashverosh. "I had hoped you could give me more information. But now I ask you as my advisor. How should I go about discovering Esther's secret?"

---

21. *See Gra; Ben Yehoyada.*
22. *Midrash Panim Acheirim; Ben Yehoyada,* see *Yosef Lekach.*
23. *Ben Yehoyada.*

Mordechai closed his eyes and placed his hand on his forehead. For several long moments, he stood lost in thought. Then he looked up and smiled. "Your majesty," he said, "I have a plan. It is a little radical, but it may just work."

"Go ahead. I am all ears."

"Esther is a strong woman. She is not swayed by gifts and material things, and she holds strongly to her beliefs. How can you crack through her defenses? By making her jealous, of course! I suggest that you organize a new contest. Assemble new contestants from all over the empire and let them compete against Esther. She may not want to give up her crown so easily, and who knows? She may actually volunteer to reveal her secret to you. What's more, it's always possible that you will find another woman who is even better than Esther. Then you will surely have the best woman in the world."[24]

Achashverosh clapped his hands with delight. "What a phenomenal idea! What excellent advice! Mordechai, you are my man. You have a scholarly, cunning mind. And I have a confession to make. For a moment back there I had this suspicion that Esther was a Jewish relative of yours and that you two were in cahoots, trying to help each other out. But this advice doesn't help her, only me. Clearly, my suspicions were unfounded, and you both have only my best interests at heart. I am pleased. See to it that your plan is put into action right away."[25]

Mordechai was delighted his plan had worked perfectly. He had deflected suspicion from Esther and from himself, and he had even engineered the possibility, albeit a remote one, that Esther would be sent away from the palace. He prayed that Hashem would lead them in the right direction, and that His will should be done.[26]

The machinery of the pageant was once again set into motion. The imperial agents reassembled all the contestants who had been sent home without seeing the king when Esther was chosen.[27] They also invited back a number of the rejected contestants for a second look. Contestants came from every corner of the empire, ambitious

24. *Megillah* 13a *with Maharsha; Pirush Megillas Achashverosh.* Some suggest that the ministers and other advisors themselves suggested making the second contest (*Targum Sheni*).

25. *Ben Yehoyada.*

26. See *Targum Rishon, Akeidah* and *Maharal* for further discussion of *u'vehikabetz besulos sheinis* (*Esther* 2:19).

27. *R' Elisha Galico; Gra.*

women hoping to replace the mystery queen, daughters of some of the highest ministers and noblemen in the empire. Even Haman persuaded his daughter to try a second time.[28]

To Achashverosh's chagrin, Esther did not react to the contest with jealousy. She accepted it calmly, and when the contest was held, she won again with great ease.[29]

Achashverosh threw up his hands in defeat and accepted Esther as she was, and he settled down to enjoy life with his new queen. According to most accounts, Esther lived under duress, as Achashverosh's wife. But at the same time, she was also Mordechai's wife; miraculously, she managed to slip away every once in a while to purify herself and return to Mordechai.[30]

And so Esther continued to live a dangerous double life — as a good Jewish wife who happened to be Queen of Persia.

---

28. *Pirush Megillas Achashverosh; Midrash Lekach Tov; R' Shmuel di Uzidah.*

29. *Rashi; Pirkei d'Rav Eliezer 50; see R' Elisha Galico.*

30. See *Megillah* 13a with *Rashi; Tosafos* and *Maharsha* to *Rashi.* See *Sanhedrin* 74b with *Tosafos.* The *Megillas Sesarim* suggests that Achashverosh refused to be with Esther until he knew her identity, lest she was of low class and lineage. Esther's forced marriage to Achashverosh did not invalidate her marriage to Mordechai. As seen earlier (ch. 8, footnote 38), many authorities believe that Esther had a demon which substituted for her with Achashverosh. When the demon presented itself to Achashverosh, Esther said a name of Hashem and disappeared. She was thus able to slip away to Mordechai undetected. Additionally, although most authorities believe that Esther gave birth to Darius, some believe he was born from the demon. He is still considered Esther's son since the demon took her image and was under her control. See *Ben Yehoyada* to *Megillah* 13a; *Ya'aros Devash, drush* 13; *Midrash Talpios.*

The Assassination Plot

10

Peace and tranquility returned to the palace, at least on the surface, after years of turmoil. Having at long last found the perfect queen, Achashverosh was happy, and he ruled his empire with a firm but generous hand. The mood in the palace was more relaxed than it had been for a long time; no longer did the courtiers labor under the shadow of a depressed monarch and the pressure of finding him a new queen.

Under the surface, however, anger and resentment festered in the palace, especially among the courtiers who were friends and relatives of Vashti, the former queen. They had pinned their hopes for advancement in the palace hierarchy on Vashti's favor, and now their future was in doubt.

Among the disgruntled courtiers were two men named Bigsan and Seresh, both of them cousins of the former queen. They had once been rising stars in the palace firmament, but now their careers were in decline. Bigsan was caretaker of the palace gate, and

Seresh was the king's cupbearer.[1] Although the two men were fast friends, having grown up together in the distant province of Tarshish, their conflicting schedules did not give them many opportunities to spend time together in the palace.

One day, the two men happened to meet in the crowded palace courtyard near the palace gate. They delightedly slapped each other on the back and sat down together on a bench under the shade of an oak tree.

"Seresh, my brother," said Bigsan in their familiar Tarsi dialect, "how have you been?"[2]

"Don't ask, Bigsan. Ever since that foul Mordechai became advisor, I've had nothing but heartache."[3]

"Watch your tongue, Seresh. There are many people around." Bigsan peered back at the palace gate and froze. "Aha! My good friend, take a look behind you. Mordechai himself is sitting on a bench not more than twenty paces away, looking into one of those books he always carries with him."

Seresh shrugged. "Just make sure we talk only in Tarsi, and no one will understand us. We're a long way from Tarshish. In fact, I'd wager we're the only two people in Shushan who speak Tarsi. As long as we speak our own private language, we are as private here in the crowded palace courtyard as we would be if we were alone on a mountaintop."[4]

"No problem, Tarsi it is." Bigsan chuckled. "Actually, I think I'll get a kick out of talking about Mordechai behind his back right in front of his face, if you know what I mean."

"Yeah, I'll get a kick out of it, too."

---

1. See *Rashi* to *Megillah 13b, Maharsha; Ben Yehoyada; Ma'amar Mordechai.*

2. *Megillah 13b; Midrash Lekach Tov.* See *D'na Pishra; Pirush Megillas Achashverosh; Ma'amar Mordechai.* Some suggest that they spoke the *Kasdi* language, which was the language in which Vashti had spoken to Achashverosh (see *Aggadas Esther* and *Pirkei d'Rav Eliezer*). Others say they spoke Persian (*Pirush Megillas Achashverosh*). Some suggest that he was furious at having been appointed to the undignified post of Gatekeeper, instead of a more prestigious position (*Yad HaMelech*).

3. *Esther Rabbah* 6:13; *Matnos Kehunah; Radal; Pirush Megillas Achashverosh; Tzuf Devash.*

4. See *R' Shmuel di Uzidah; Melo HaOmer.* Some posit that they knew that Mordechai understood what they were saying, but did not care. They assumed that as a Jew, Mordechai was not concerned about the King's life. They were unaware that he was related to Esther and that he would denounce them. Others suggest further that it was understood that the Jews would condone a plot to kill the King who had prevented the rebuilding of the *Beis HaMikdash* (*Yedei Moshe*). Some say even further that they wanted Mordechai to join in the plot; they were angry with Achashverosh but not Mordechai (*Ma'amar Mordechai*).

"I think it's disgusting," said Bigsan, "that Achashverosh appointed a dirty Jew like Mordechai his chief advisor. Ever since Vashti was . . . er . . . died —"

"You can be blunt, Bigsan. We're speaking Tarsi, remember? 'Ever since Vashti was murdered' is what you wanted to say, isn't it?"

"It sure is, Seresh. That's what it was. Just plain murder by her drunken husband. Ever since that gorilla that calls himself king brutally murdered our sweet cousin, the palace has been out of control. It would have been only fair that a loyal public servant such as I, who has been working in the palace for many years, should have at least been considered for the position of chief advisor. And I'm willing to wager that if Vashti had been alive, I would have been appointed."[5]

"Unless I would have been," Seresh interjected.

"All right," said Bigsan. "Unless you would have been. I wouldn't have minded so much if my friend were chosen over me, but a Jew? What is going on here? Where is a little respect for seniority?"

Seresh shook his head sadly. "You think you have problems, Bigsan? Be happy you're not in my shoes. Ever since that gorilla, as you call him — perhaps a bear would be more appropriate? — ever since he married that Esther he spends his evenings in her company, and I have to be available at all times to bring him drinks. And after he's full of drinks, what do you think he has to do?"

"Relieve himself?"

"Exactly. And I am the one who has the high honor of attending him while he relieves himself. Can you imagine? Oh, how the mighty have fallen.[6] Or rather, been pushed down. This never would have happened under Vashti.[7] But now, I have to serve him hand and foot late into the night. When I should be asleep in bed, I'm standing in the hallway outside his chamber, waiting to bring him a cup of wine or to escort him to his privy. Because of him, I'm tired all the time. I walk around in a daze. I never had to work so hard when Vashti was alive."

"Those are problems, Seresh, but mine are even worse. I have to take care of the offices at the palace gate, and believe me, it is a ton of work. Very often, I have to work very late into the night, and just

---

5. *Esther Rabbah* 6:13; *Matnos Kehunah; Radal; Pirush Megillas Achashverosh; Tzuf Devash; Yalkut Shimoni* 1053; *Midrash Panim Acheirim.*

6. *Megillah* 13b with *Rashi; Ben Yehoyada; R' Yosef ibn Yachia; Alshich.*

7. *Yishai Elokim.*

like you, I am deprived of sleep. Sometimes I even stick my feet into cold water just to revive myself and keep from falling asleep. But you know what the worst part of my job is?"[8]

"I give up. Tell me."

"I have to see that Mordechai every day," said Bigsan, "and it makes my blood boil. Do you know what else he's done?"

"I give up," said Seresh. "Tell me."

"He's installed the Jewish court, called the Sanhedrin, right here in the palace gates. He could have stayed near the gate to the harem, where he used to sit. Why did he and his Jews have to set themselves up in the palace gate of all places?"[9]

"What! Such colossal nerve! Did you tell Achashverosh?"

"Hah! What good would that do?" Bigsan sneered. "Esther has him wrapped around her little finger. I even heard that it was her idea to appoint Mordechai chief advisor. It seems he found her on the street as a little orphan and brought her up in his home."

Seresh's eyes opened wide. "Really? Well, no wonder then that Mordechai got the job. If she grew up in his house, he must have filled her head with all sort of Jewish nonsense. Why, she's probably no better than a Jew herself now."

"Exactly," said Bigsan. "Ach, if only Achashverosh had chosen my beautiful daughter as his wife, but he never even looked at her. He was completely under that Esther's spell. And how could he even compare the two? My daughter is a noblewoman and Esther is a homeless orphan brought up by a Jew.[10] But no, all he wanted was Esther. Well, serves him right. Now the two of them, Esther and her Jew, are probably conspiring to take over the palace. And I won't be surprised if they succeed."[11]

"Neither will I," said Seresh. "Someone should do something about the situation before it is too late."

"Yes, I agree," said Bigsan. He chewed on his lower lip. "But who?"

"Are you thinking what I'm thinking?"

"I think so, Seresh. You and I have to step forward to save the kingdom. The future of all Persia is in our hands."

"A very thrilling thought, Bigsan. But also very disturbing. What should we do? And how would we do it?"

---

8. *Targum Rishon; Yosef Lekach; Ma'amar Mordechai; R' Elisha Galico; Malbim.*
9. *Midrash Lekach Tov.*
10. *Yishai Elokim; Pirush Megillas Achashverosh.*
11. *Targum Rishon; Midrash Lekach Tov.*

"You ask solid questions, Seresh. Perhaps we should . . . er . . . do away with Mordechai. What do you think?"

"Not a bad idea. But there's a problem. What if suspicion falls on us?"[12]

"True," said Bigsan. "Perhaps we should try a bolder plan. We should kill Achashverosh and Esther. With them gone, Mordechai will fall by the wayside, and it may even happen that my daughter will chosen queen by the new king, wouldn't that be wonderful? We would recover our former status, and most important of all, we could catch up on some of that sleep we've been missing.[13] And if we are caught, we can always blame Mordechai for everything by claiming he ordered us to do it."[14]

"Bigsan! I never knew you were such a brilliant man."

"I have to admit I discussed all this with Haman. But wait, Seresh, there's more. The tensions between Persia and Greece in Asia are rising. Think of the reward we could ask from the Greeks if we presented them with Achashverosh's head."[15]

"You've convinced me, Bigsan. But how are we going to pull this off? Do you think it's so easy to take out a king and queen?"

"Who said it was easy? But we're in a great position. We have the assistance of the king's personal cup bearer!"

"Really? Oh, I mean, uh, yes, we do, don't we? All right, let's talk details."

"Fine," said Bigsan. "I was sort of thinking about a staged murder-suicide. We bring a dagger concealed in a shoe and poison concealed in one of your cups. We poison Esther and stab Achashverosh, making it look as if she stabbed him to death and then took poison.[16] Otherwise, I suggest we use extracted snake venom on both of them. It works very quickly and is hard to detect, because it floats on top of the wine and leaves no residue in the cup."[17]

---

12. *Akeideh.*

13. *Yalkut Shimoni* 1053; *Midrash Panim Acheirim; Menos HaLevi.* See *Alshich,* who says that one initiated the conversation and the other followed his lead.

14. *Me'am Loez.*

15. *Yosifun.*

16. *Targum Rishon; Menos HaLevi.* Some suggest that they planned to deal Achashverosh a double blow: first the venom would weaken him and make ill, and then they would crucify him (*D'na Pishra*).

17. *Megillah* 13b; *Targum Sheni; Bereishis Rabbah* 88:3; *Matnos Kehunah; Menos HaLevi; Me'am Loez.*

"Yes, I think snake venom is a good idea," said Seresh. "It will kill him before he has a chance to call for help. But how would I prepare the poisoned drink? It would be too risky to activate the poison beforehand, and once he calls me I will not have enough time to get the drink and prepare the poison."[18]

"Don't worry, Seresh. That is where I come in. I will join you on the night we choose. When Achashverosh calls for a drink, I will take your place and go off to fetch his drink, while you will go into your laboratory and prepare the venom. We'll use a gold cup for the water, because gold will better conceal the smell of the venom. When I come back, you will drop the venom into the drink and hand it to Achashverosh. Then we'll go back to our posts, and act as surprised as everyone else when the good news is discovered."[19]

"Terrific, Bigsan. I think we have a plan. Let's just decide which night is best for us, and then make sure we get a night's sleep the night before."

They decided on a tentative date for the assassination, wished each other a good day and went off in different directions.

After they left, Mordechai rose slowly from his seat just twenty paces away. His face was somber, and his brow was knitted in deep thought. He had understood every word the plotters had spoken in Tarsi. As head of the Sanhedrin, he was required to know all seventy families of languages, and Tarsi was among them.[20] According to some, he divined their plan with great wisdom by reading their body language and the expressions on their faces.[21] According to others, he learned of their thoughts and words through *ruach hakodesh*, divine inspiration.[22]

---

18. *Rashi* to *Megillah* 13b; see also *Maharsha* there; *Einei HaEidah*. The positions of these courtiers is a matter of debate among the commentators. Some say that one of them was a palace gatekeeper and the other was in charge of the King's basins. Some hold that they were both palace gatekeepers, others hold they were both in charge of the King's basins.

19. See *Maharsha* and *Rif* to *Ein Yaakov, Megillah* 13b; see also *Rambam; Targum Sheni.* According to the *Maharsha,* one of the plotters would take the other's shift in addition to his own, while the latter would prepare the poison. Others suggest that one would leave his post at the gate to assist his fellow in preparing the poison (*Rif* to *Ein Yaakov*). Some posit that they planned to carry out the deed in the afternoon following the King's midday rest. When he would request his afternoon drink from his golden vessel, they would insert the poison (*Pirkei d'Rav Eliezer; Aggadas Esther*).

20. *Megillah* 13b.

21. *Yad HaMelech.*

22. *Targum Sheni; Megillah* 16a. *Chasam Sofer* explains that while Mordechai did overhear the plot, *ruach hakodesh* told him that it was not mere idle chatter born of frustration, but serious plans to carry out an assassination.

At first, Mordechai did not take any action. After all, it was quite possible that it had all been idle talk for an idle afternoon, and that it would never even be attempted. He did keep an eye on them, however, and their activities convince him that they were serious about the assassination plot. He realized he could wait no longer if he wanted to foil the plot.[23]

Mordechai could, of course, have pretended he had never heard the plotters, allowing them to carry out their plot and kill Achashverosh. Esther would then have been free to return home. But he decided to thwart the plot. If the plotters succeeded, he reasoned, the Jewish chief advisor would be blamed for the lax security. If it were discovered that Esther was Jewish, there would be suspicions of a conspiracy between her and Mordechai. In either case, a *chillul Hashem*, a desecration of the Name, would result. On the other hand, by speaking up he would make a *kiddush Hashem*, sanctifying the Name. He would bring honor to the Jewish people and gain royal favor for the reconstruction of the *Beis HaMikdash*.[24] Furthermore, he believed in his heart that Hashem had let him learn about the plot so that he should expose it.

Instead of going directly to Achashverosh with the information, Mordechai chose to tell Esther and have her inform Achashverosh.[25] First of all, she had better access to the king than he did. Second, he didn't want to take the credit for himself but preferred it go to Esther, the divinely chosen savior of the Jews. If the king found out that her information had come from him, it would only add to her stature for recommending him for the position. But he really didn't want the king or anyone else to find out about his involvement.[26] In fact, he specifically instructed Esther not to tell Achashverosh. He feared that if the plot never materialized he would be called a liar and if it somehow succeeded despite the foreknowledge he would be blamed and put to death.[27]

Esther repeated to Achashverosh everything exactly as Mordechai had told it to her. On her own initiative, she also told

23. *Menos HaLevi.* See *Alshich.*

24. *Yalkut Shimoni; Midrash Panim Acheirim; Me'am Loez.*

25. *Midrash Lekach Tov.*

26. *Nachal Eshkol; Menos HaLevi.*

27. *Yosef Lekach; Yalkut Shimoni; Midrash Panim Acheirim.*

him that Mordechai was the source of her information. She was confident that everything would work out well, and she wanted Mordechai to be rewarded.[28]

At first, Achashverosh was doubtful about the plot, but he decided to be extremely cautious, just in case it was true.

On the designated night, Achashverosh summoned Seresh to his chamber. The cupbearer seemed excited and even agitated. He eyes shone, and his hand trembled slightly.

"Seresh, are you feeling well?" asked Achashverosh. "You seem slightly feverish."

"Oh, I'm perfectly fine, your majesty. It must be the lighting."

"I see. Perhaps you are right. Anyway, I'm thirsty. Bring me a drink of cool water."

"Yes, your majesty. Right away, your majesty."

Seresh bowed and backed out of the chamber. As planned, Bigsan was waiting. He immediately ran off to get the water, while Seresh prepared the venom. Minutes later, Bigsan was back with a cup of water. The cup was made of gold. Seresh dropped the venom into the water, where it floated on the surface. Bigsan handed the cup to Seresh and patted him on the shoulder, "Good luck, my friend. Our new life begins tomorrow." Then he stepped behind the door, where he would be concealed when Seresh opened it.[29]

Seresh stepped into the chamber. Achashverosh was sitting on the edge of his chair, leaning forward, an unusual position for the usually imperious king.

"Your majesty, I have brought your water," he said.

"Very good," said Achashverosh. "I am thirsty. Here, come closer. Let me have a look at that water."

Seresh was gripped by fear, and his hand trembled, sloshing a few drops of water over onto the ground. Could Achashverosh suspect the plot?

"Be careful, Seresh," Achashverosh said sharply. "For someone who doesn't have a fever your hand sure shakes a lot. If you're not

---

28. *Ya'aros Devash.* Some suggest she did not initially tell Achashverosh that it was Mordechai who informed her of the plot.

29. See *Maharsha, Rif* to *Ein Yaakov* on *Megillas* 13b. See *Rambam, Targum Sheni; R' Shmuel di Uzidah; Toras Moshe; Pirkei d'Rav Eliezer* 50.

careful, you'll spill all my water before I get a chance to drink. Come here, let me take a look."

Seresh extended the cup gingerly, and Achashverosh peered into it.

"Hmm, looks a little dark on the surface to me," he said. "It must the lighting again, eh, Seresh?"

"I-I'm sure it is," Seresh managed to stammer.

"Well, I wouldn't doubt that it's the lighting, as you say. But I think I'll spill it out. Go and get me another cup of water."

"But your majesty," Seresh protested, "this is the finest water on earth. It is clear, cool and tasty. No bitter or salty aftertastes, just pure, fresh water. Water fit for a king."

"You've persuaded me, Seresh. But just to make sure that it's not contaminated or anything, let's have one of the guards take a drink first. Guards! Guards! One of you come in here."

Seresh realized that something had gone terribly wrong. If the guard drank the water and died, it was all over. He had to abort the plan immediately. As he walked to the guard with the cup in his left hand, he reached into it with the fingers of his right and scooped out the venom floating on the surface. But miraculously, it slipped back over his hand and fell into the water again just as he handed the cup to the guard.

As Achashverosh looked on intently, the guard took a deep swallow of the water. Almost instantaneously, he gagged and clutched at his throat. He gasped for air, and his eyes rolled wildly in their sockets. He trembled once, very violently, and then he stood stockstill. The cup fell from his hands, and he pitched face forward, dead before he hit the ground.

"Guards!" shouted Achashverosh. "Seize this blackguard who tried to kill me. He will hang for his crime."

The guards sprang forward and grabbed Seresh roughly by the arms.

"Guards, take him away!" said Achashverosh. "Get him out of my sight. And some of you look around in the halls and the nearby chambers. He may have had an accomplice. If he did, I want you to find him!"

The guards spread out through the vicinity, and in no time at all, they discovered Bigsan hiding behind the door. They dragged him before Achashverosh.

"You too, Bigsan?" he asked accusingly. "I thought I could trust you. Now you will swing from the gallows alongside your good friend Seresh."[30]

Some of the palace officials, including Haman, pleaded with Achashverosh for clemency for the plotters in light of their long and loyal service to the king. The plot was surely an unfortunate aberration, not a true indication of what these men represented.[31] Achashverosh would not be budged, but he did agree to execute only the mastermind of the plot and spare the accomplice. There was, however, no way of proving who was the mastermind, since each of them claimed to be the poor accomplice. Both of them were condemned to die.[32] They were impaled on sharp wooden stakes, and their bodies were hung from the gallows to twist together in the wind as a lesson and warning to anyone who might consider doing harm to the king.

As Haman watched them swing from the gallows, he was overcome by fury and frustration. How had the plot been exposed? Someone must have overheard them and reported their conversation. For some reason, he felt sure Mordechai was responsible, and he vowed to take revenge.[33]

The next day, Achashverosh took the matter of reward under consideration and decided against rewarding Mordechai, since he had not informed the king directly. But he did order that Mordechai's actions be recorded in the royal chronicles.[34]

Esther took this decision in stride. In fact, she was quite satisfied with it, since she believed a royal parade in Mordechai's honor would only inflame the vengeful passions of his enemies. Besides,

---

30. *Yalkut Shimoni; Midrash Panim Acheirim; Pirkei d'Rav Eliezer; Rambam.* Some suggest that one of the plotters was discovered at the other's post, while he was missing, a clear indication of conspiracy. Others posit that one of the two was assigned to serve the King drinks at night, while the other was in charge of the basin in which the King relieved himself. On the night of the plot one of the two carried out both tasks, and this led to their unmasking (*Ben Yehoyada*). Some are of the opinion that they attempted to strangle the King. One of the two was missing from his post, and when security guards investigated, the would-be assassins were caught in the act. Others suggest that the King gave his drink to an animal, which died upon drinking it.

31. *Yosifun.*

32. *Midrash Talpiyos.*

33. *Yad HaMelech; Yosifun; D'na Pishra.*

34. *Alshich; Rambam.* Some suggest that Achashverosh himself never knew that it was Mordechai who was behind the revelation of the plot. He only knew that his queen Esther had been made aware of it.

she had disobeyed his explicit instructions by revealing his involvement. If he were not rewarded, he might never find out that she had done so.[35] But she was determined to make sure that his actions were properly inscribed in the royal chronicles for future reference, and she undertook to supervise the inscription herself.

The royal scribe was Shimshai, the son of Haman. He tried many different stratagems to abort the inscription, but they were all to no avail. With Esther standing over him, he had no choice but to do as she instructed, and thus, all the details of the plot against the King were inscribed in the royal chronicles.[36]

In retrospect, strong parallels could be seen between this episode and the imprisonment of Pharaoh's wine steward. Just as Pharaoh's anger with his steward led indirectly to Yosef's rise to power, so did the anger of the royal servants against their king lead to Mordechai's rise to power.[37] Just as Pharaoh grew angry with his wine steward over the trivial discovery of a fly in the wine, so did Bigsan and Seresh grow angry with Achashverosh over a trivial thing such as sleep deprivation. Clearly, the divine hand could be seen guiding events to their ultimate favorable resolution.[38] As for Esther's insistence on giving the report in the name of its originator, it was a righteous act that led to the redemption of the Jewish people.

Five years would pass before the royal chronicles would be opened and the story of Mordechai's loyalty to the king read. One year after this episode, Esther would present Achashverosh with a son, who would eventually ascend the throne as Darius II; because his mother was Jewish, the boy was considered Jewish as well. Four years after that, in 3404, a great crisis would threaten the Jews of the Persian Empire. Who would have thought that an obscure and almost-forgotten entry in the royal chronicles five years earlier would hold the key to their salvation? Such is the way of divine providence, preparing the remedy before the affliction.[39]

35. *Alshich; Ya'aros Devash.*

36. *Menos HaLevi; R' Elisha Galico.*

37. *Megillah* 13a; *Bereishis Rabbah* 88.

38. *Ben Yehoyada.*

39. *Me'am Loez;* see *Ibn Ezra; Megillah* 13b.

Haman's Rise to Power

11

F ive years after the discovery of the assassination plot, Haman began his meteoric rise to power. As a descendant of Amalek and one of those responsible for the interruption of the reconstruction of the *Beis HaMikdash,* Haman deserved to die, not to rise to fame and glory as he was about to do. But in actuality, the divine hand was preparing him for a tremendous, crashing fall that would make a deep impression of Hashem's miraculous rescue of the Jewish people from the brink of disaster. Moreover, the frightening rise of the evil Haman would inspire the Jewish people to repent and return to their Father in Heaven.

The rise and fall of Haman is best described by the parable of the mother donkey, the baby donkey and the pig that lived on one farm. The donkey and its young offspring toiled faithfully for the farmer, for which they were rewarded with rations of barley. At the same time, the pig did absolutely no useful work, spending his days wallowing in the mud, yet the owner treated his pig far better than he did his donkeys. He fed the pig all manner of rich foods, and lots of it.

The mother donkey was very upset. "The farmer is a fool," she complained to the other animals. "Look what he's doing. He gives meager rations to the loyal, hard-working animals, but he indulges the pig who does nothing."

"Don't worry," the other animals reassured the mother donkey. "The farmer is fattening him up, because he intends to eat him since he doesn't do any work anyway. The laziness of the pig will lead to his downfall."

Sure enough, the farmer celebrated his next holiday by slaughtering the pig and roasting him on a spit over an open fire. The pig was gone, while the donkeys were still alive. The young donkey, however, did not understand exactly what had happened. He saw that the farmer had fattened up his pig and then eaten him. Therefore, the young donkey refused to eat his rations, afraid that he would soon find himself roasting on a spit just like the pig.

"You needn't worry," the mother donkey told her young offspring. "The eating did not lead to the pig's untimely death. It was his lazy lifestyle. If he had worked as hard as we do, he would still be alive today."

By granting Haman fame and glory, Hashem was just fattening him up for his eventual demise. Hashem was raising him up for a great fall, during which he would be literally raised up on a gallows fifty cubits high.[1]

Haman had been the one who had recommended that Achashverosh execute Vashti, and when that affair ended in a fiasco, Haman was demoted to a lowly position at the court. But time changes perspectives. At the time of Vashti's death, Achashverosh was sure that Haman had done him a great disservice. As time went on, however, Achashverosh found Esther, and she made him so happy that he completely forgot Vashti. In retrospect, Haman had actually done Achashverosh a great service by ridding him of Vashti and opening the door to the arrival of Esther.

Haman felt sure the time had come for him not only to recover his earlier honors but also to rise higher than he had ever risen before. He felt especially driven by a desire for revenge for the deaths of his

---

1. *Esther Rabbah* 7:1,5; *Targum Rishon; Rambam; Midrash Panim Acheirim; Me'am Loez; Ibn Ezra.*

friends Bigsan and Seresh, whom he had secretly encouraged and advised on the details of their plot to assassinate Achashverosh.[2] He had also enlisted the help of his son, who was a royal scribe, to suppress the reports of Mordechai's heroic involvement even though it was recorded in the royal records.

Although he did not know Esther personally, he thought he might find an ally in her. After all, how could she not favor such a clever and charming fellow as he? It did occur to him that she might be Jewish, but he didn't see this as a particular problem. In fact, that actually made them cousins, as she was descended from Yaakov and he from the older brother Eisav; he would quickly forget this familial connection with the Jews when he tried to have them exterminated. And if she wasn't Jewish, they had even more in common —customs, foods and idol worship. But in any case, the key to Haman's plan was not an alliance with Esther. It was money.[3]

When Nevuchadnezzar had destroyed the *Beis HaMikdash*, he had discovered fabulous treasures concealed in hidden storerooms. Some of these treasures were accumulated by the kings of Yehudah, and some dated all the way back to Moshe and Yosef. Nevuchadnezzar had appropriated this vast treasure and transported it back to Babylon, where he concealed it in hidden storerooms of his own.

Somehow or another, Haman had gained access to this fabulous treasure, and he spent the five years of his demotion filling his pockets and scheming his return to the halls of power.[4] Finally, when he felt he was ready to make his move, he asked for an audience with Achashverosh.

Haman appeared before the king with a sack full of riches, escorted by his numerous children as well as high-ranking ministers.

Haman bowed from the waist. "A small gift for your majesty," he said as he emptied the contents of the sack on the table and arranged them to their best effect. "A small token of my esteem."

Achashverosh was impressed. "Fortune seems to have smiled on you, my dear Haman. You are so kind to bring me these gifts. I gather you would like a small favor from me as well?"

2. *Yosifun.*

3. *Midrash Abba Gorion; Esther Rabbah* 7:4 with *Yefei Anaf* and *Radal.*

4. *Esther Rabbah* 7:5 with *Yefei Anaf; Pirkei d'Rav Eliezer* 50; *Radal;* see *Esther Rabbah* 10:13. *Targum Rishon; Midrash Lekach Tov* to *Esther* 3:6. See *Midrash Tehillim* 22:2, which says that one-third of his wealth would ultimately be used to rebuild the *Beis HaMikdash.* Hashem would ensure that the very money which Haman took from the first *Beis HaMikdash* would be used in the rebuilding of the second one (*Menos HaLevi*).

"Your majesty, the gifts come with absolutely no strings attached. But your majesty has sharp insight to see into my heart and read my inner thoughts. It is true. I do seek your majesty's favor. I once held a high position in the court, but unfortunately, I fell out of favor. I would like your majesty to reconsider my loyalty and my talents. Surely, they can be put to better use in your majesty's service than in the position I now occupy."

"Go on," said Achashverosh. "I am listening."

"Thank you, your majesty. The main reason I fell from favor is that I defended your majesty's honor and advised against leniency with Vashti. This was a painful piece of advice to offer, and I only did so out of extreme loyalty. Not surprisingly, it backfired on me, and I was demoted. But events have borne me out. Vashti has been replaced by Esther, who is a far superior queen, I believe."

"Indeed, she is," said Achashverosh. "Your point is well taken. It certainly took a lot of courage to advise that I condemn Vashti, and in retrospect, it was certainly good advice."

One of the ministers who had escorted Haman, a very old man with a white mustache, stepped forward and bowed ceremoniously. "With your majesty's permission," he said, "I would like to speak a few words in favor of my good friend Haman. He brings wealth and wisdom to the service of the king. And look at his beautiful family, all his noble sons. Why, one of them is already the king's scribe! And what about his distinguished lineage? A direct descendant of the great warrior Amalek, no less! And speaking about Amalek, Haman is also in possession of the secret Amalekite rites of sorcery and wizardry. I think that alone should qualify him for a high ministerial position, wouldn't you agree, your majesty?"[5]

"You make a good point," said Achashverosh. "Several good points. And I also have not forgotten, Haman, how you quelled the rebellion in India years ago. Do you recall that campaign?"[6]

Haman fidgeted. "Certainly I remember, your majesty. And I thank you for remembering as well. And there is yet another point I would like to make." He did not want to dwell on that campaign, since Mordechai's name was bound to come up as well. "I think ele-

---

5. *Yedei Moshe; R' Elisha Galico; Yishai Elokim; Gra; Yosef Lekach; R' Yosef ibn Yachia; Esther Rabbah 7:5 with Yefei Anaf; Menos HaLevi; Yad HaMelech.* It is hardly surprising that the same Achashverosh who had bought his way to power would be influenced by a large bribe.

6. *Targum.*

vating me would be a nice gesture to Queen Esther, since I was responsible for her accession to the throne. I think she would appreciate the gesture."

"Hmmmm," said the old minister, tugging fiercely at his mustache. "May I also add, your majesty, that we are a little undermanned since Bigsan and Seresh, ahem, departed the scene?"[7]

Achashverosh leaned back, pursed his lips and closed his eyes. Everyone in the room remained still and silent while the king pondered the complex issues that had been presented to him.

After a few long minutes, Achashverosh opened his eyes. "Gentlemen, you have made me aware of an old injustice, and I agree that it must be corrected as soon as possible. I also agree that Haman is a man of exceptional talents and qualities. And I also agree that I owe him a debt of gratitude, which I most certainly intend to repay." He paused for effect. "Gentlemen, I have decided to make Haman my new prime minister. No one but me shall rank higher in the palace. He will have authority over all my ministers, noblemen and officials, and over all the lands of my empire."[8]

There was a gasp among the audience, following by loud cheers and wild applause. Haman grinned from ear to ear.

"I will phase him in to the position," Achashverosh continued. "At the same time, I will elevate his colleagues so that he will have a ministerial team with which he is familiar and on which he can rely. When the transition is complete I will invest him with full powers as second in command to me."[9]

It never occurred to Achashverosh that Mordechai deserved this high position more than Haman did. It was ironic that Achashverosh should think he owed a debt of gratitude to Haman, who had actually conspired with Bigsan and Seresh to assassinate him, and that he should ignore the debt of gratitude to Mordechai that was duly documented in the royal chronicles. But all this was part of the divine plan, that the turning of the tables at the end should be as dramatic as possible.[10]

---

7. *Ma'amar Mordechai; Yad HaMelech; Malbim.* Some suggest that Achashverosh also sympathized with Haman, seeing him as being, like the king himself, a marked man for having counseled the death of Vashti. He therefore promoted Haman to this position.

8. *Yad HaMelech; Yishai Elokim; Menos HaLevi; R' Yosef ibn Yachia; D'na Pishra; R' Elisha Galico; Gra; Yosef Lekach.*

9. *Yad HaMelech; Alshich; R' Shmuel di Uzidah; Malbim.*

10. *Yosef Lekach; Me'am Loez.*

"Well, Haman," said Achashverosh, "are you satisfied?"

Haman rubbed his hands together with relish and squinted. "Your majesty! You do me great honor, and I hope that you will be pleased with my service, that you will feel that all I do brings honor to your name. After all, what am I but an extension of the king? Everything I do and say is all for the honor of the king, even when it means I will suffer for it, as in the Vashti affair. I pledge to serve you faithfully and loyally as prime minister. And in order to be effective, I have one small request to add."

"Speak, my good Haman."

"I think it would be appropriate for all the king's servants to bow to me when I enter and leave the palace courtyard and the palace gates. I think this will enhance the king's honor. I also think the noblemen and courtiers owe me a debt of gratitude for defending their honor and dignity from Vashti's assaults. It would only be fair that they show their gratitude to me."[11]

This request was exceedingly bizarre. Who had ever heard of bowing down to a minister or anyone other than the king? But Achashverosh did not seem to consider it strange. He agreed to it, and issued an order that everyone do as Haman wished. If he demanded that people bow down to him then that is what they were to do. Anyone disobeying Haman would be considered to have disobeyed the king himself.

Achashverosh also ordered that his personal chariot be made available to transport Haman through Shushan, with criers running before him and proclaiming his high position and royal favor.[12] Achashverosh also ordered that a special chair, as high as the king's throne, be set for Haman in the imperial chamber. Moreover, he prohibited anyone from sitting in Haman's chair when he was away, an honor ordinarily reserved for the king alone.

By having his chair elevated above the chairs of all the ministers, Haman was assured the honor and respect he felt he deserved, and he was satisfied — for the time being.[13]

For a few days, Haman strode arrogantly through the palace courtyard, enjoying the new honors Achashverosh had bestowed on him. Wherever he went, people stopped whatever they were doing

---

11. *Yedei Moshe; Malbim.*

12. *Megillas Sefer.*

13. *R' Shmuel di Uzidah; R' Elisha Galico; Gra; Yad HaMelech.*

and bowed down to him. It was a wonderful feeling, but somehow, it was not enough. He wanted people not only to bow to him but also to prostrate themselves before him as they would before a god.

In fact, that was exactly what he wanted — to be treated as a god! He felt it was only fitting, since he really was a god. With his immense wealth, his proficient sorcery and his vast political power, how was he different from any god?[14] He had controlled the fortunes of Achashverosh. He held the power of life and death, of success and ruin. Everything and everyone depended on him. He could see it in people's eyes. When they looked at him it was as if they were looking at a god. So why shouldn't he be treated as a god officially? But Haman was a crafty fellow, and he knew people would not easily accept him as an official god. Therefore, he had to maneuver them into recognizing his divine nature.

Cleverly, he had an idol sewn onto his coat just over his heart and another one in the middle of his back. He also wore a hat in the shape of a popular idol. Thus, people would prostrate themselves before him whenever he passed.[15] Hopefully, they would become accustomed to doing so and would not stop even when he no longer wore idols on his clothing. By his order, no one was to bow down to any god other than himself or Achashverosh.[16] He also had a large statue of himself erected in the palace courtyard and decreed that all that passed were obliged to bow down to it. In this way, Haman built a cult following around him. His popularity as the champion of the palace staff against Vashti's persecutions helped him along, as did the patronage and promotions he controlled in his new position as the rising prime minister.[17]

Strangely, Achashverosh himself was also caught up in the Haman cult and bowed down to him as if to a god. He further deluded himself into thinking that Haman had rescued him from the assassination attempt by Bigsan and Seresh. Since Haman had advised that Vashti be executed, and since that had resulted in the choice of Esther as the new queen, and since Esther had told

---

14. *R' Yosef ibn Nachmiash;* see *Malbim.*

15. *Midrash Megillah; Pirkei d'Rav Eliezer* 50; *Radal; Esther Rabbah* 6:2, 7:5; see *Megillah* 10b; *Tosafos* to *Sanhedrin* 61b; *Targum Rishon* 6:1; *Rabbeinu Bachyei; Ibn Ezra; Pirush Megillas Achashverosh.*

16. *R' Elisha Galico; R' Shmuel di Uzidah.*

17. *Targum Rishon; Chomas Anach.* Some suggest that it was an image of Achashverosh (*Pirush Megillas Esther*).

Achashverosh about the assassination plot and saved his life, it followed that Haman had saved his life. Despite the sheer stupidity of such reasoning, Achashverosh could not be convinced otherwise, and he showed his gratitude by bowing to him as a god.[18]

Most people, however, including the Jews, bowed to Haman and his statue only because the king had ordered that they do so. They bowed out of obligatory respect, not as an expression of divine worship.[19]

Even so, some of the palace staff, mostly lower level officials, were offended by the new regulations. They still remembered and revered the mighty Babylonian dynasty of Nevuchadnezzar, and they resented that Achashverosh, with Haman's advice, had killed Vashti, the last link to that glorious past. They were not at all pleased that they had to bow to Haman. But they did it nonetheless.[20]

Slowly but surely, Haman was succeeding in his designs, but he was still nervous about it. He had been a barber and a bath attendant in the province of Kartzoum for twenty-two years, and he could never live it down. The thought that people would still think of him that way gave him complexes and feelings of insecurity and inadequacy.[21] With this in mind, he was determined not only to elevate himself but also to subjugate everyone around him so that they would never dare to look down at him. That is why it was so critical that they bow down to him. And they really had no choice. After all, who would dare disobey the explicit orders of the king?[22]

Only one man dared stand up to Haman — Mordechai the Jew, his old nemesis. The hatred between the two men dated back to when Agag, Haman's grandfather, was killed during the reign of King Shaul, Mordechai's grandfather. Mordechai would not prostrate himself before Haman or his statue, nor would he even bow to him as a sign of respect.[23] He could have made it his business to

---

18. *Yad HaMelech.*

19. *Aggadas Esther; Midrash HaGadol; Rokeach; R' Avigdor Kohen Tzedek; Eshkol HaKofer;* see *Tosafos* to *Pesachim* 53b.

20. *Yad HaMelech.*

21. *D'na Pishra.*

22. *R' Elisha Galico; Yad HaMelech.* See *Yosef Lekach,* who holds that only servants of the king were required to bow to Haman.

23. *Midrash Megillas Esther; Sha'arei Binah; Midrash Lekach Tov;* see *Tosafos* to *Pesachim* 53b; *Alshich; Rokeach.* The numerical value of the names *Shaul* and *Agag* is equivalent to that of *shmad,*destruction. Shaul *HaMelech's* transgression allowing Agag to live made it possible for Haman to now prepare to eliminate the Jewish people (*Chasam Sofer, Parashas Zachor*).

avoid Haman altogether, but he didn't want to do so. As advisor to the king, it was Mordechai's duty to be in the palace.[24] While Esther could have gotten him permission to stay away, he didn't want her arousing suspicion by advocating for him.[25] Furthermore, Mordechai thought to himself, why should he bow to a man who was technically his slave, a man who had spent a good portion of his life as a barber and a bath attendant?[26]

But there was an even more important reason for his refusal to bow. He wanted to demonstrate to all the other Jews that Haman was not worthy of worship, that he was nothing more than a mere mortal of flesh and blood who would rot in his grave when his life came to an end. A Jew should bow only to Hashem. And since Haman was representing himself as a god, the Jews should not even bow to him out of respect. Mordechai knew that the Jews looked to him for leadership, and he was ready to risk his life to make sure they did the right thing. He had to set the example for others to follow.[27]

Mordechai greeted the new Haman with defiance. He refused to greet him or say any words of welcome when he saw him approaching, and of course, he refused to bow down to him. Moreover, even if Mordechai was crouching down to pick something up from the ground, if he saw Haman coming he would immediately jump to his feet and stand perfectly erect — just to make it clear that he would not bow down to him.[28] And while he stood erect, he would think in his mind that these actions should be an atonement for his ancestor Shaul, the Jewish king who had failed to kill Agag, Haman's ancestor, and also for the sins of idol worship in the time of Nevuchadnezzar.[29]

For his part, Haman had not expected Mordechai to bow down to him. And he didn't really mind. Actually, it would work to his advantage, and he would one day use Mordechai's refusal to justify his plan to exterminate the Jews. If Mordechai and the Jews capitu-

---

24. *R' Yosef ibn Nachmiash; Rabbeinu Bachyei.*

25. *R' Chaim Abulafia; R' Elisha Galico; R' Shmuel di Uzidah.*

26. *Yalkut Shimoni; Sha'arei Binah; Rokeach; Pirush Megillas Achashverosh.* See *Megillah* 16a; *Targum Rishon; Iggeres Purim.*

27. *Tosafos* to *Sanhedrin* 61b; *R' Avigdor Kohen Tzedek;* see *Tosafos* to *Pesachim* 53b; *Sefer Chassidim.*

28. *Targum Sheni, Rishon Letzion.*

29. *R' Elisha Galico; Eshkol HaKofer.* Some suggest that the by-laws of Persia protected Mordechai as a Jew, and he could not be forced to bow or enslave himself to anything. As far as he was concerned, he had the legal right not to bow (*Yosef Lekach*).

lated and did bow down to him, that would also work out well. This
would anger the Jewish God, and He would abandon them, leaving
them defenseless against their enemies.[30]

In the meantime, Haman had no intention of forcing a confrontation with Mordechai. He would just walk through the crowded
courtyard and pretend he hadn't even seen Mordechai. After all, if
he challenged Mordechai, the devious Jew might just announce
what had happened years ago. He did not want to risk having
Mordechai reveal that he had bought him as his slave.[31]

Haman's followers on the palace staff, however, would not let
Mordechai's intransigence pass without an argument.

"Who do you think you are, Mordechai," said one minister,
"that you so cavalierly disobey the king's instructions? Why don't
you bow down to Haman just like the rest of us are doing? Aren't
you grateful to him for saving the king's life from Bigsan and
Seresh? Besides, you know that all the palace staff are responsible
for each other.[32] Are you some kind of barbarian that cares nothing for his colleagues? You are a distinguished advisor to the
king, and if you don't bow down, others may follow suit. Doesn't
it mean anything to you that your arrogant actions are putting us
all in danger?"[33]

Many thoughts went through Mordechai's head. He could tell
them that Haman had really had nothing to do with saving the king
from Bigsan and Seresh. He could tell them that the king's edict was
not universal, applying only to people in the courtyard and the
palace gate, and that he was an exception to the rule. He could have
made other excuses, but he did not.[34]

"I'm very sorry," said Mordechai, "but I really have no choice in
the matter. I am a Jew, and Jews bow to no man."[35]

"Oh, really? And what about the children of your ancestor
Yaakov? Didn't they bow down to their uncle Eisav when they came
back to Israel from Aram?"

Mordechai smiled. "I see you know your Jewish history. If you
remember correctly, though, at the time one of the tribes had not yet

---

30. *Esther Rabbah* 7:6 with *Yefei Anaf; Yalkut Shimoni*

31. *Rambam; Yad Hamelech; Iggeres Purim.*

32. *Menos HaLevi; Malbim.*

33. *Melo HaOmer; Targum Rishon; R' Saadiah Gaon; Yad HaMelech.*

34. *Yad HaMelech.*

35. *Esther Rabbah* 7:8 with *Yefei Anaf.*

been born, namely Binyamin. I am descended from Binyamin. My ancestor never bowed to a man."[36]

"Very clever, Mordechai," said the minister, "but not convincing. Rachel was already expecting Binyamin at the time, and when she bowed, Binyamin bowed along with her."[37]

"Fool!" Mordechai argued. "When a mother bows, is that like the fetus bows as well? Nonsense! Look, I'm not trying to be difficult, but your comparison to Yaakov's children bowing to Eisav simply doesn't hold water anyway. You know that our Torah absolutely forbids idol worship. I can't do anything that even smacks of idol worship. When Yaakov's children bowed to Eisav, it was purely out of respect. There was no angle of idol worship whatsoever. Eisav never claimed to be a god, but his illustrious descendant Haman does. Therefore, I can't bow down to him, even as a gesture of respect."[38]

"I understand what you are saying," said the minister. "But this is a different situation. The king has ordered that we bow down to Haman. You must obey the command of the king. You can't refuse the king's command."

"Exactly!" Mordechai replied. "That is exactly my point. First and foremost, I am the servant of the King of Kings, the Master of the Universe, and I cannot disobey His command."[39]

As much as the ministers and courtiers pressed him to relent, Mordechai stood fast in his principles. Just as the righteous Yosef had resisted the sinful advances of Potiphar's wife, so did Mordechai, the descendant of his brother Binyamin, resist the pressure of his colleagues in the palace.[40]

The palace staff was frustrated by Mordechai's adamant refusal to bow to Haman, but they were not quite sure what to do about it. After much debate, they decided to complain about Mordechai to Haman. Although it would have seemed logical to complain directly to Achashverosh, there were a number of reasons for going to Haman instead.

---

36. *Midrash Panim Acheirim; Rambam; Menos HaLevi; Bereishis Rabbah.* Some suggest that Mordechai was a *gilgul*, reincarnation, of Yaakov, while Haman was a *gilgul* of Eisav. Yaakov had bowed to his brother Eisav but now Mordechai would correct that misdeed and not bow to Haman (*Shaar HaGigulim*).

37. *Rokeach* to *Parashas Beshalach.*

38. *Rambam.*

39. See *Alshich.*

40. *Esther Rabbah* 7:7 with *Anaf Yosef.*

Some of the courtiers were only interested in their own safety, which they felt was endangered by Mordechai's rash refusal to bow to Haman. They felt that to approach the king they would need an iron-clad proof of Mordechai refusing to bow, when in fact Haman and Mordechai had not had a direct face-to-face confrontation in the palace courtyard after the king's edict had been issued.[41] Besides, they didn't really want Mordechai to be put to death for his defiance, as would likely happen if the king were aware of the situation. They just wanted Mordechai cut down to size a bit so that he would no longer refuse to bow down. They would probably, they assumed, be able to accomplish that better by going to the talented and persuasive Haman, who would threaten to tell the king if Mordechai did not comply with the edict.[42]

Those of the courtiers who hated Mordechai and the Jews may have had their own motives for going to Haman instead of Achashverosh. First of all, they may have wanted to instigate a blood feud between the two ministers. Moreover, they felt Achashverosh would judge only Mordechai, while Haman would exact vengeance from all the Jewish people.[43]

There may also have been courtiers who were jealous of Haman for his rise in the palace hierarchy and whom Haman had belittled or insulted. They hated Haman passionately and wanted to cause his downfall. By complaining about Mordechai directly to Haman, they would precipitate a confrontation between the two men, and history had shown that the Jews always emerged victorious over Amalek. Haman would ultimately fall. In the interim, if Mordechai were exempted from bowing to Haman, perhaps they would also be excused.[44]

It is also possible that the ministers may simply have been insufficiently sure of their case to take it to the king. The fact was that Achashverosh allowed the Jews to practice their religion freely. He even allowed the Sanhedrin to hold its sessions in the palace gate. Maybe then the Jews were exempt from the edict to bow to Haman, even if only out of respect.[45]

They also weren't sure if Mordechai was genuinely concerned with the Jewish legalities or if he was conducting a personal vendet-

---

41. *R' Elisha Galico; R' Shmuel di Uzidah; Sha'arei Binah; Rokeach; Malbim.*
42. *Alshich.*
43. *R' Elisha Galico.*
44. *Yedei Moshe; R' Shmuel di Uzidah; R' Elisha Galico.*
45. *Megillas Sesarim; Yishai Elokim; Alshich.*

ta against Haman. He refused to bow, yet other Jews did bow.[46] He claimed descent from Binyamin, yet he called himself a Yehudi, indicating that he was descended from Yehudah. Was Mordechai really sincere or did he consider himself better than everyone else? And if Mordechai could discover a loophole for himself, could there be a loophole for the others as well? The ministers were confused. Better then to take their grievance to Haman and let him deal with it.[47]

Before the ministers approached him, Haman had studiously avoided confrontation with Mordechai. It was simply too risky. He also knew that the case against Mordechai was not open and shut by any means. As for the implicit disrespect in Mordechai's refusal to bow down, he did not have to deal with it unless he actually saw it.[48] Until then, he could make believe it didn't exist. But now that the ministers had lodged their complaint with him, Haman had no choice but to bring matters to a head.[49]

He had to see for himself. Although this fateful confrontation would lead to great danger for the Jewish people, they would persevere in the end. The eyes of the wicked are their worst enemy. Just as Cham had looked at Noach and been condemned to slavery, so did Haman's need to see for himself lead to his ultimate downfall.[50]

Haman removed the idols he had sewn onto his clothing so that Mordechai could not use those as a pretext for refusing to bow down. From afar, he saw Mordechai praying, bowing periodically in the direction of the wall. After he finished praying, he nodded and bowed in greeting to many passersby. Aha, thought Haman, so he does bow when he wants to.[51]

Slowly, he approached Mordechai and stopped a good distance away, waiting for the Jewish minister to take note of him and show his respect by bowing. Mordechai, however, ignored him completely.[52]

---

46. *R' Elisha Galico.*

47. See *Yafei Anaf; Malbim; Me'am Loez; R' Shmuel di Uzidah.*

48. *R' Yosef ibn Yachia; Rambam; Menos HaLevi; Gra; Yosef Lekach.* See *Gra* to *Mishlei* 15:25.

49. *Eshkol HaKofer.*

50. *Eshkol HaKofer; Ma'amar Mordechai; Alshich; Marahal; Aggadas Esther.*

51. *Ya'aros Devash; Ma'amar Mordechai ; Yad HaMelech.*
Technically, Mordechai should have bowed to Haman. Haman was clearly on the ascendance, and Mordechai endangered the Jewish people by his defiance. Nevertheless, Mordechai determined that he had to go beyond the letter of the law to atone for the Jews' earlier transgression. In addition, Haman sometimes had his idol with him, and this would have given the impression that Mordechai was bowing to the idol. To dispel this notion, Mordechai refused to bow.

52. *Targum Rishon; Midrash Abba Gorion; R' Chaim Abulafia.*

Haman drew closer and made eye contact with Mordechai. Surely now the Jewish minister would show his respect by bowing. But Mordechai looked right through him, as if he wasn't even there.[53]

Anger boiled and bubbled in Haman's heart. He stepped forward and said, "Hello, Mordechai."

"Hashem says that the wicked deserve no greeting," Mordechai replied.

A crowd had gathered around the two men, eagerly hanging on every word, every nuance. Haman was infuriated. What effrontery! What humiliation! He could no longer contain himself.[54]

"How dare you be so disrespectful to me?" he shouted. "Everyone bows down but you. What makes you better than everyone else?"

Mordechai fixed the seething Haman with a cool stare. "I am a dignitary of my people, the representative of Hashem. Furthermore, I am descended from Binyamin, the only one of the tribes born in the land of Israel. Because of my position and my lineage, I bear a special responsibility to Hashem, and I cannot bow down to a simple mortal.[55] It is my right to refuse according to Persian law. And besides, my dear friend, I have another right to refuse. Why should a master bow down to his slave?" He extended his foot to expose his boot. "Look! What does it say on my boot?"[56]

Some of the people in the crowd pushed forward to gaze at the writing on the boot. "Sold for a loaf of bread," they read aloud. "What does that mean?"

"Get away from here, you rabble!" screamed Haman, and the people immediately scurried away in fear.

Haman, burning with rage, was like a venomous snake ready to strike.[57] This was the last straw. Mordechai was clearly not motivat-

---

53. *Gra; Yosef Lekach;* see *Malbim.*

54. *Midrash Panim Acheirim; Midrash Abba Gorion;* see *Yeshayahu* 57a; *Menos HaLevi; Yosef Lekach; Me'am Loez; R' Chaim Abulafiah.* If Mordechai, as Haman's master, would have bowed to him, Haman would have been considered freed by Jewish law. Mordechai felt bound to validate the fact that Haman was still his slave (*R' Chaim Abulafia*).

55. *Esther Rabbah* 7; *Midrash Abba Gorion; Midrash Panim Acheirim; R' Yosef ibn Yachia.*

56. *R' Chaim Abulafia; Targum Rishon* 5:9; see *Megillah* 15b.

Some suggest that Haman believed that since on that day he was not a slave, Mordechai was required to bow to him. Mordechai believed that Haman was his slave for every day of the week, and he was thus not required to bow at any time (*Chida*). It was only fitting that Haman, Eisav's descendant, should have sold himself to Mordechai, a descendant of Yaakov. Just as Eisav had sold his birthright to Yaakov for some lentils, Haman sold himself for a loaf of bread (see *Baal HaTurim, Bereishis* 25:30).

57. *Rokeach.*

ed by religious considerations or any other of his many excuses. He only wanted to cause him humiliation. It was the old vendetta, Jew against Amalekite, carried on by the descendant of Shaul, the Binyaminite king of Israel who had wiped out the Amalekite cities. And it was also a personal vendetta between the two of them.

Well, this time it will be different, thought Haman. I will succeed where my ancestors have failed. Once and for all, these Jews will be exterminated from the face of the earth. I will go to Achashverosh and make it happen.[58]

But there was one problem with going to Achashverosh that Haman had not quite solved yet. If Achashverosh should learn that Haman was actually Mordechai's slave and the circumstances that had led up to it, Haman's newfound status in the palace would disintegrate.[59]

---

58. *Aggados Esther; Minchas Yehudah; R' Shmuel di Uzidah; R' Elisha Galico; Yishai Elokim.*
59. *Me'am Loez.*

Haman Casts Lots

12

Smarting with humiliation and anger, Haman wanted desperately to avenge himself. He wanted Mordechai dead. In his fury, he dredged numerous justifications for killing Mordechai. Not only had he humiliated Haman, not only was he arrogant and disrespectful, not only was he a Jew, not only had his ancestor Yaakov stolen the blessings from Haman's ancestor Eisav, he was also the descendant of the Binyaminite king who had almost entirely exterminated Haman's Amalekite nation.[1]

With his new power and influence in the palace, Haman felt confident he could satisfy his thirst for vengeance, but it would require clever planning. True, Mordechai's favor had waned in the five years since his almost-forgotten exposure of the assassination plot of Bigsan and Seresh, and Achashverosh would most probably side with Haman.[2] Nevertheless, it was not exactly feasible

---

1. *Targum Rishon.*
2. *Melo HaOmer.*

for Haman to come running to Achashverosh with complaints about the disrespect of another minister, like a little child complaining to its mother. Instead, Haman was already concocting a clever and diabolical plan.[3]

Haman's hatred was so intense that simply to kill Mordechai would not satisfy his bloodlust. He wanted to eradicate Mordechai's name from the world as if it had never existed. Killing Mordechai alone would not accomplish this goal. No, he would also have to kill all the Jewish sages and scholars that were Mordechai's colleagues; besides, they were responsible for Mordechai's disrespect by instituting ridiculous laws against bowing down to idols.[4] But then again, Mordechai was such a prominent figure that his contemporaries, who would identify themselves as Mordechai's people even after his death, would remember him. No, he would have to wipe out at least the tribe of Binyamin. But then again, Mordechai had been the leader of the Jews of Shushan, who would surely remember him after his death.[5] No, the Jews of Shushan could also not be allowed to live. But what about the Jews in the rest of the Persian Empire? Mordechai was surely well known among them as well. No, all the Jews in the Persian Empire would have to be killed, every single one of them, man, woman and child.[6]

Haman rubbed his hand together with relish. He would turn the tables on the Jews. He would make them pay for Yaakov's theft of Eisav's blessing. He would wipe them out, just as they wanted to wipe out the nation of Amalek.[7] Pharaoh had condemned Jewish males to death, but he would kill them all. Pharaoh had spared Jews who could work, but he would kill them all. He would not leave a single one alive, not even a convert.[8]

---

3. *Targum Rishon.*

4. *Alshich.*

5. *Megillah* 13b; *Rif* to *Ein Yaakov.* Haman attacked the Torah itself in an effort to still the "voice of Yaakov," thereby strengthening the "hand of Eisav" (*Bereishis* 27:22; see R' *Chaim Abulafia*).

6. See *Gra; Yosef Lekach; Kav HaYashar; Yedei Moshe; Alshich; Malbim; Esther Rabbah; R' Chaim Abulafia; Yad HaMelech; Midrash Eliyahu;* see *Pesikta Rabbasi* 13. Some suggest that since Mordechai was descended from both the tribes of Binyamin and Yehudah, there would be so many Jews seeking vengeance on Haman for Mordechai's death, the only solution was to kill all of them (*D'na Pishra*).

7. *Ma'amar Mordechai.*

8. *Rokeach; Midrash Tehillim* 22.

As for the Jews outside the Persian Empire, Haman was not concerned about them. Their numbers were negligible, and they would soon disappear of themselves.[9]

Haman rubbed his hand together in relish, delighted with his plan. Even in the worst case scenario, even if he could not carry out the decree of death, at least Mordechai would be killed, since the Jews would surely blame his intransigence for their predicament and kill him themselves. And in the best case scenario, he would rid the empire of all its Jews.[10]

Haman knew full well that Hashem punished the Jews when they were lax in Torah and *mitzvos*. He also knew that the Jews of Shushan had sinned by attending Achashverosh's feast. This time of vulnerability, therefore, would be a propitious time to attack the Jewish people.[11]

Based on this, Haman sent word that all practice of the Jewish religion should cease immediately. No one would be allowed to keep Shabbos, perform *bris milah* or learn Torah. Haman knew that stopping the Jews from serving Hashem would guarantee the success of his decree.[12]

Looking back into history, Haman compared two major encounters between the Jews and the Amalekites. In the most recent, Shaul had attacked the Amalekites and virtually wiped them out, with King Agag as the sole survivor. Centuries earlier, however, when the Amalekites had attacked the Jewish people coming out of Egypt at Refidim, they had been defeated by Yehoshua but not exterminated.[13] Furthermore, since their primary purpose had been to dispel the aura of Jewish invincibility, they had in one sense actually been victorious; henceforth, other nations were no longer reluctant to go to war with the Jewish people.[14]

How did these two encounters differ? wondered Haman. Why were they reasonably successful in the first encounter against

---

9. See *Yosef Lekach; R' Shmuel di Uzidah; R' Chaim Abulafia; Menos HaLevi.*

10. *Yad HaMelech.*

11. *Yishai Elokim.*

12. *Chasam Sofer; Megillah* 16b with *Rashi.*

13. *R' Yosef ibn Yachia; Midrash Lekach Tov.* Some suggest that Yehoshua had cast lots on Amalek to see who would live and who would die (*Pirkei d'Rav Kahanah* 3:9). Others suggest that Yehoshua killed many of the leaders, but Amalek still survived due to the fact that Yehoshua had not been commanded to kill them all, as Shaul was. That is the meaning of *Vayachalosh* (*Shemos* 17:13). See *Menos HaLevi.*

14. *Menos HaLevi;* see *Yalkut Beshalach* 265 and end of *Ki Seitzei.*

Yehoshua when they were nearly wiped out in the second against Shaul? There could be only one reason. Sorcery! In preparation for the battle at Refidim, they had used traditional Amalekite magic spells. They had also taken into account the celestial powers of the zodiac and sent into battle only those warriors protected by the astrological signs. Against Shaul, however, they had been taken by surprise and had not had time to prepare properly.[15]

Following this line of reasoning, Haman felt sure that if he harnessed the powers of magic and astrology, he would be successful against the Jews. In reality, however, the failure of Yehoshua to exterminate them was not due to any sorcery the Amalekites had used. Rather, it was because at that time Hashem had not yet commanded them to exterminate Amalek. Haman's misreading of history blinded him to reality and led him to blunder into his own downfall.[16]

Before putting any plan into action, Haman was determined to ascertain if he was destined to triumph over the Jewish people. Although he was a wizard of note in his own right, he consulted Bilam's works and sought advice from many respected wizards, magicians and astrologers.[17] The consensus was that he should cast lots to discover if the Jewish people were ripe for the taking.[18] If they were, he should have his son Shimshai cast additional lots to determine which day was most auspicious for their ruin.[19]

Haman took a pair of dice made out of bone and inscribed the first six letters on the six faces of each dye. He then rolled the dice three times. The results were the letters *aleph, gimmel, gimmel.* He was very excited. The numerical value of these three letters was seven, considered a lucky number. Moreover, these letters spelled out the name Agag, Haman's ancestor. Haman then checked the opposite faces of these three letters. They were *vav, daled, daled.* The numerical value of these three letters was fourteen, identical to the numerical value of the name Haman if all the letters are valued as units rather than tens. Moreover, the letters together spelled out

---

15. *Ya'aros Devash.*

16. *Rambam; Gra.*

17. See *Targum Sheni; Esther Rabbah* 7:11; *Midrash Talpios.*

18. See *Yefei Anaf* to *Esther Rabbah* 7:11.

19. *Targum Rishon;* see *Krovetz L'Purim.* Some suggest that Achashverosh conducted one of the two lotteries. Others suggest that Haman gave the task to professional astrologers who specialized in lotteries. (See *Pirkei d'Rav Eliezer* 50; *Radal; Midrash Lekach Tov; Nachal Eshkol; Menos HaLevi.*)

David, the king of Israel. The sign was clear. Agag would overpower David; Amalek would be victorious over the Jewish people.
Haman was ecstatic.[20]

Now came the tricky part. He had to find a day that would be
auspicious for the ruin of the Jews. He first cast for Sunday, but its
angel protested, "Master of the Universe, you created the heavens
and the earth for Torah and the *mitzvah* of *milah*, the covenants that
the Jewish people hold fast. If You destroy them you might as well
destroy the whole world."

Monday's angel protested that the Jewish people who keep themselves separate from the gentile nations represent the separation of
the waters above and below. Tuesday's angel protested that the day
on which trees, grass and Gan Eden were created was not an appropriate day to destroy the Jews who tithed their fruits and performed
the *mitzvah* of *lulav*. Wednesday's angel compared the Jewish nation
to the sun, the moon and the stars, which were created on that day.
Thursday's angel protested that birds and animals, which were created for the Jews to sacrifice, would have no meaning if the Jewish
people were destroyed. Friday's angel protested that the Jews are
called Adam, as was the first man created, and therefore they could
not be exterminated. Finally, Shabbos' angel protested that without
the Jewish people who rest on Shabbos there would be no purpose
to that day.[21]

Having failed to find an appropriate day of the week, Haman
sought a day of the month favored by the astrological signs, hoping
that the collective power of the month would override the individual power of the day. He used a double lottery system to determine
the auspicious date.[22]

He took two lottery boxes. In the left box, he placed lots for every
single date of the year, while in the right box, he placed lots showing the months only. He would reach into the left box with his left
hand and the right box with his right hand and simultaneous draw
lots from both of them. If the individual date on the lot drawn in his
left hand fell in the month on the lot drawn with his right hand, the

---

20. *Midrash Talpios; D'na Pishra.*

21. See *Esther Rabbah* 7:11; *Menos HaLevi; Midrash Abba Gorion; Midrash Lekach Tov;
Midrash Panim Acheirim.*

22. See *Rashi* to *Megillah* 13b; *R' Elisha Galico; Menos HaLevi.* This can be compared to a
man destined to live long who travels on a ship which is fated to sink. The individual
man (*perat*) will succumb to the collective ship (*klal*).

sign was accepted. He drew and drew until he came up with 13 Adar in his left hand and Adar in his right hand. A match![23]

Others suggest that the double lottery system combined days of the lunar year with the months. The left box contained lots numbered consecutively from 1 to 354, representing the days of the year, while the right contained lots listing the months of the year. He was to draw a number in his left hand and a month in his right hand. If that particular day of the year fell in that particular month it was a match. He drew and drew until he came up with 337 in his left hand and Adar in his right. The 337th day of the year did indeed fall in Adar, on the 13th day. It was a match![24]

The day of the drawing was 13 Nissan, the day that Pharaoh had foretold *ra*, an evil fate, for the Jewish people; the miracles of the Exodus that also took place in Nissan did not impress Haman. Tuesday, 13 Adar was exactly eleven months away. Haman exulted. The end was in sight. Eleven months, and the Jews would be no more.[25]

Haman now took a closer look at the month of Adar. Was this month auspicious for his designs or would another month perhaps be more suited? He scrutinized every other month of the year and discovered that each had some factor that militated against Jewish destruction. Some were months of Jewish celebration, some already had a surfeit of tragedy, and some were protected by the astrological influence of great Jewish sages.[26]

Now he turned his attention to Adar, specifically to Adar Sheini, the second month of Adar of a Jewish leap year. Incredible! Of all

---

23. *R' Shmuel di Uzidah*. Some suggest that Haman knew from the outset that Adar was an auspicious month; he merely went through the procedure to confirm his suspicions (*Eshkol HaKofer*).

24. *Ya'aros Devash*. Some suggest that first Haman cast lots for the day; since this took place on the 13th of Nissan, he began with the number 14. For whatever reason, Haman was not satisfied with any number but 13, bringing him to the 13th of Iyar. Then he searched for the right month. He took two boxes; in one he placed 12 tickets, each with the name of a month, and in the other he put 11 blank tickets and one with the word "lottery." He would then pick one ticket from each box. Picking a blank ticket with one hand would invalidate whichever month he had drawn with the other hand; when he picked the "lottery" ticket, that would determine which month was the correct draw. When Haman pulled out Adar, he also drew the ticket that said "lottery," and this was how he chose the month (See *Maharal; Malbim*).

25. *Malbim; Yalkut Shimoni* 1059; *Pirkei d'Rav Eliezer* 50; *Radal; Ya'aros Devash; Yad HaMelech*.

26. *Menos HaLevi; Alshich*. The month in which Haman drew his lots augured well for the Jews. Nissan was already a month that was good for them, and any evil plans initiated in this month would be to their benefit.

the months, this one alone had no celebrations, no terrible tragedies, no special astrological protections. Further investigation revealed that Moshe, the leader of the Jews who as an infant had been drawn from the water like a fish, died during the second month of Adar, whose astrological sign was a fish; it was clearly a time when big fish would swallow little fish.[27] Surely the Jews could have prevented his death if this were an auspicious month for them. And lo and behold, 13 Adar was still within the seven-day mourning period for Moshe, obviously an evil time for the Jews — and for Mordechai, who was compared to Moshe.[28] Moreover, 13 Adar was just over thirty days before the festival of Pesach, thereby being outside of its positive influence; it also fell during the time when innumerable Jews died during the plague of darkness.[29]

Haman smiled. Adar! There was poetic justice to it. The twelfth month of the twelfth year of Achashverosh's reign, an auspicious month for him and an inauspicious one for the Jews, whose leader Moshe had died at the age of one hundred and twenty, a variant of the number 12. Adar, the last month of the year, the perfect month to erase the last memory of the Jews![30]

There was only one drawback to Adar from Haman's perspective. He would have to wait nearly an entire year to carry through his evil decree, but at least, he could begin his preparations right away. He would have to convince Achashverosh to issue the decree, and he would have to make the arrangements for its distribution to all the provinces and its implementation. In the meantime, he would wait.[31]

A diabolical grin spread across Haman's face as he rubbed his hands together. He would relish every moment of anticipation for the next eleven months, but for the Jews the waiting would be long months of sheer torture. It couldn't be better![32]

---

27. See *Iyun Yaakov* to *Megillah* 13b; *Ya'aros Devash*.

28. *Maharsha* to *Megillah* 13b; see *Avudraham* to the *Al HaNissim* prayer. Some suggest the opposite: the *aveilus* (mourning) served as a source of merit for the Jewish people. (Similarly, the *hesped* (eulogy) for the righteous Meshuselach could have been a merit for the generation of the Flood; see *Yefei To'ar* to *Bereishis Rabbah* 32:7.) When the mourning was over on the 13th, the Jews had no further merit to protect them. See *Eliyahu Rabbah, Ohr HaChaim* 693.

29. *Sha'arei Binah; Rokeach; Maharal;* see *Eliyahu Rabbah, OhrHaChaim* 693.

30. *Yosef Lekach; R' Shmuel di Uzidah; Maharal; Torah Ohr.*

31. *Yedei Moshe.*

32. *Eshkol HaKofer; Ma'amar Mordechai.*

In reality, however, Haman had made some serious miscalcula-
tions. He had considered himself the big fish that would swallow
the Jews, whom he considered the little fish. But there were fish big-
ger than he in the sea.[33] He had considered Adar, the end of the year,
inauspicious for the Jews. But he did not realize that the end of the
word Israel was one of Hashem's Names. In the month at the end of
the year he would have to come up against Hashem and would certainly lose.[34]

Haman had considered the number 12 inauspicious for the Jews
because of Moshe's tragic death at the age of 120, a variant of 12. But
Moshe's death had not been tragic at all. Contrary to Haman's mis-
conception, Moshe had not been born in Nissan but on the very
same day of Adar on which he died, and thus as a perfectly righteous man, he had completed the full cycle of his life; furthermore,
since he was not permitted to enter Israel, he had to die in order to
allow the rest of the people to enter.[35]

Adar was actually auspicious for the Jews, because Moshe was
born during that month. Although he had also died then, his birth
was more significant than his death.[36] Furthermore, the Hebrew
word for lot is *pur*, which is cognate to *pru*, as in *pru urvu*, be fruit-
ful and multiply. The sign of Adar is a fish, which is also a sign of
proliferation, since fish multiply quickly. The month of proliferation
was not quite an auspicious time for death and destruction.[37]

Also, the tribe associated with Adar was Binyamin, the twelfth
tribe of Israel, whose merits controlled the fortunes of the month.
How then could Haman expect to prevail over Mordechai and
Esther of the tribe of Binyamin during the month of Adar?[38]

Finally, the length of time between the casting of the lots and the
date of the decree should have signaled to Haman that something
was amiss. In fact, the eleven-month wait was a huge benefit to the
Jewish people, because it gave them the opportunity for introspec-
tion, repentance and prayer. As a child mourns for his deceased par-

---

33. *Esther Rabbah* 7:11; *Melo HaOmer*; see *Pirkei d'Rav Eliezer* 50 with *Radal*; *Yalkut Shimoni* 1059.
34. *Maharal*.
35. *Sifsei Chachamim* to *Megillah* 13b; *Ya'aros Devash*; *Maharal*.
36. See *Megillah* 13b with *Rashi*; *Midrash*.
37. *Midrash Talpios*. Some suggest that *pur* comes from the word *pirurin* (crumbs). Haman used small stone chips or clusters of sand to make the *pur* (*Eshkol HaKofer*).
38. *Rokeach*.

ent for eleven months, so would the Jewish people bewail their fate, make amends and rescind the evil decree. For when the Jewish people follow the Torah faithfully, they are beyond the reach of the astrological signs.[39]

A parable about an angry bird describes Haman's attempt to avenge himself on the Jews for their victories over Amalek. The bird had built a nest by the seashore. Just as he finished, a large wave broke over the nest and washed it away. Furious, the bird decided to avenge himself on the sea. She filled her little mouth with sand and dumped it into the sea, and then she took a mouthful of seawater and carried it inland. In this way she hoped to destroy the sea by replacing it with sand.

Another bird came by and saw what the vengeful bird was doing. "You silly fool," she said. "What do you expect to accomplish? You will never destroy the sea, but you yourself will drown in the water you carry in your mouth." The vengeful bird did not pay heed to her friend's advice, and presently, she drowned.

As Haman planned and plotted to kill the Jews, a Heavenly Voice called out, "Fool that you are! Do you think you can destroy the Jews? Even when I wanted to kill them after they sinned with the Golden Calf, Moshe's prayer won Me over. Are you more powerful than I am? If you persist in your foolish ways, you will hang yourself by your own lots."[40]

Haman, however, refused to face the truth. Rather, he continued in his self-serving delusions, thinking that he could use his Amalekite sorcery and astrological manipulations to overcome the Jews. But the Jews, with faith and trust in Hashem, were beyond his reach, and in the end, all his machinations precipitated his own ultimate doom.[41]

---

39. *Targum Rishon; Ibn Ezra; Yedei Moshe; Eshkol HaKofer; Malbim.* See *Midrash HaGadol Bamidbar* 4:11.

40. See *Esther Rabbah* 7:10 with *Yefei Anaf; Midrash Abba Gorion; Yalkut Shimoni.*

41. *Esther Rabbah* 7:11; *Yalkut Beshalach* 265; *Ya'aros Devash; Shabbos* 156; *Rambam; Gra. Rashi* points out that Bilam realized that the Jewish nation is above magic and astrology, under Hashem's protection instead (*Bamidbar* 28:23).

THE REASON HAMAN CHOSE ADAR

	Targum Sheni	Esther Rabbah	Aggadas Esther	Midrash Abba Gorion	Midrash LekachTov	Yalkut Shimoni
Nissan	Pesach	Pesach	Exodus from Egypt	Pesach	Pesach	Korban Pesach
Iyar	Manna	Pesach Sheni	Amalek's Victory	Manna	Manna	Manna
Sivan	Giving of the Torah	Giving of the Torah	Giving of the Torah	Giving of the Torah	Giving of the Torah	Giving of the Torah
Tammuz	Yerushalayim's walls breached	Entrance into Eretz Yisrael	Yehoshua holds up the sun and is victorious in battle	Entrance into Eretz Yisrael	Entrance into Eretz Yisrael	Month of tragedy
Av	Dying stopped in desert	Full of Tragedies	King of Arad subdued	Month destined for Joy	Month destined for Joy	Full of Tragedies
Elul	Second Luchos are given	Tithe of cattle	Saved from Amalek (in days of Gideon)	Wall completed (in days of Nechemiah)	Wall completed (in days of Nechemiah)	Tithe of cattle
Tishrei	Sins are forgiven	Festivals	Inauguration of Beis HaMikdash	Festivals	Festivals	Festivals
Cheshvan	Noach saved by flood	Sarah died (Akeidah)	Beis HaMikdash completed	Sarah[1] (Akeidah)	Sarah	Beis HaMikdash completed
Kislev	Beis HaMikdash	Mishkan completed[2]	Sichon and Og captured	Mishkan (Tabernacle) completed[2]	Mishkan (Tabernacle) completed[2]	Mishkan completed[2]
Teves	Nevuchadnezzar oppressed Jews	Ezra	Sichon and Og captured	Miracle of Chanukah	Miracle of Chanukah	Sign of the Goat
Shevat	Bikurim, new year for trees	Men of Great Assembly	Taught and reviewed the Torah	Men of Great Assembly	Men of Great Assembly	Sign of the Bucket
Adar			Moshe died			Sign of Fish

1. Sarah's death was a *zechus*. After she died, the torch of the *Imahos*, the Matriarchs, was passed to Rivkah. Also, Sarah's death occurred upon finding out about the *Akeidah*. The merit of Cheshvan was thus the *Akeidah* itself; see *Iyun Yaakov* to *Megillah* 13b.)

2. The general text of the *Midrash* reads *Chanukah*. While this may refer to Haman's having sensed that this miracle would occur several hundred years later, several commentators suggest that the text should read *Chanukas HaMishkan*, referring to the completion of the *Mishkan* in the wilderness.

MONTH	ASTROLOGICAL NAME	SIGN	PLANET	TRIBE (ARIZAL)	TRIBE (ZOHAR)	SYMBOLS AND OCCURENCES
Nissan	Aries	Sheep	Mars	Yehudah, king, leader	Reuven	
Iyar	Taurus	Bull	Venus	Yissachar, knowledge	Shimon	"ox" referring to Yosef
Sivan	Gemini	twins	Mercury	Zevulun, commerce	Levi	Peretz and Zerach (Moshe and Aharon)
Tammuz	Cancer	Crab	Moon	Reuven	Yehudah	
Av	Leo	Lion	Sun	Shimon	Yissachar	The lion refers to the merit of Daniel, from Yehudah
Elul	Virgo	Virgin	Mercury	Gad, Goodness	Zevulun	Chananiah, Mishael and Azariah dedicated their lives to Hashem like a woman to her husband
Tishrei	Libra	Scales	Venus	Ephraim	Dan	Iyov's tribulations serve as a merit and atonement
Cheshvan	Scorpio	Scorpion	Mars	Menashe	Naftali	merit of Yechezkel who is referred to as Akrav
Kislev	Sagittarius	Archer (Bow)	Jupiter	Binyamin	Gad	Merit of Yosef who is referred to as a bow
Teves	Capricorn	Goat	Saturn	Dan	Asher	Yaakov wore the skins of a goat when he attained Yitzchak's blessings.
Shevat	Aquarius	Bucket	Saturn, Uranus	Asher	Yosef	Torah, water and Moshe. (The name Moshe means being drawn from water.)
Adar	Pisces	Fish	Jupiter	Naftali	Binyamin	Oral Torah, water, Menashe and Ephraim, two months of Adar

The Death Decree

13

Haman was so confident of his plan that he had not even bothered to clear it with Achashverosh before he cast the lots. He was not stupid, though, and he understood full well that he would have to tread carefully. Mordechai was still an important minister in the palace, a formidable foe who would maneuver to bring down his adversaries before he allowed himself to fall.[1] There was also a risk that Achashverosh might recall Mordechai's role in foiling the plot of Bigsan and Seresh, and he might resent Haman's ungrateful attack. Furthermore, Achashverosh might object to the eradication of an entire nation in his empire. No, it will not be easy, thought Haman, but it can be done. It has to be done![2]

There was only one prudent approach, Haman realized. He would not name the nation he intended to destroy. In fact, he would not even mention the death decree explicitly. He would attack every

---

1. *Yishai Elokim; Akeidah.*
2. *Lachmei Todah; Gra; Yosef Lekach; Alshich.*

aspect of this unnamed nation, and he wouldn't even talk about penalties until the Jews were painted with a black brush. This approach would penetrate the king's defenses and gain his approval. As a master at deceit, a cunning conniver, second to none in slander, Haman was confident he could pull it off. If everything worked according to plan, the Jews would fall into his hands like a ripe plum. And if Esther also turned out to be a Jew, she would go down with the rest of them.[3]

His new status as prime minister gave him virtually unlimited access to Achashverosh, and he took advantage of it.

"Good morning, my dear Haman," said Achashverosh. "I got your urgent message. Is there an emergency?"

Haman rocked back on his heels and squinted. "I would not quite call it an emergency, your majesty. But it is certainly a matter of some urgency." He chuckled at his own pun. "There is a very serious problem developing in the empire, and I have been giving it a lot of thought. I have done studies and analyses, and I feel that something must be done. There is no time to waste."

"All right. I'm listening. What's on your mind?"

"Your majesty, you chose me as prime minister for my political and strategic talents. I believe you have chosen well, and I intend to do everything in my power to justify your choice. In my opinion, the key to political success is foresight. If you deal with a crisis only after it explodes in your face, you will not be very successful."

"True, true. A wise observation, Haman."

"Exactly. The key is to anticipate a crisis well before it reaches the boiling point, and to clamp a lid on it. To nip it in the bud. To pull the rug out from under its feet."

"I get the point, Haman. Go on."

Haman squinted again. "Your majesty, there is a crisis brewing in the empire, and I believe the time to deal with it is right now. If we don't work hard well in advance it will grow and mushroom until it becomes unmanageable."

Achashverosh drummed his fingers on the arm of his chair. "You are making me nervous, Haman. Speak up. What is this all about?"[4]

"It is about a group of people in the empire who are not really part of the empire. I would like to spell out the problem only in

3. *Megillah* 13b *with Sifsei Chachamim; Gra; Malbim; Yosef Lekach; Lachmei Todah.*
4. *Yosef Lekach.*

broad strokes, since I do not want to belabor you with all the sordid details. Suffice it to say that I have the situation under control, your majesty, provided that you give me your stamp of approval. I think you will be pleased with the result."

"Well, I hope so. Fine, Haman, let's hear your broad strokes. I'll decide if I want to be belabored with the sordid details."

"Of course, your majesty, I would not have it any other way. You see, there is one nation in your realm that is completely intolerable. They are scattered all over the empire. They have strange and different laws, and they don't feel obligated to obey the king's laws. They are a blight to your empire, and there is no reason you should tolerate them."[5]

"And who are these people?" asked Achashverosh.

"I would rather not say at this point, your majesty. For your own protection, of course. You will not have to dirty your hands with what needs to be done. I will present you with a *fait accompli*. I, Haman, your loyal and devoted servant, will single-handedly remove this blight from the body politic of your empire, making it stronger and reinvigorated. With your permission, of course."

"It seems to me," said Achashverosh, "that what you propose is a little risky. Since this is an internal affair, I do see the wisdom in not involving me in the early stages. But based on the little you have told me, I have reservations. You say they have different laws. That must mean that they have a different god. If you will remove this blight, as you call them, it stands to reason we will antagonize this alien god of theirs. Now, why would we want to do something like that? That's one problem. Another problem is the risk of sparking a rebellion. The blight will fight, won't they? Then what happens? Civil war. Rebellion. Disruption of commerce, travel and tax collection. And even if you are successful, the empire will be depleted, with parts of it depopulated and ruined. Is it worth it?"[6]

"These are exactly the issues, your majesty. It would appear that the proposal is too difficult, beyond practicality." He lowered his voice. "But it is not. I have it all figured out. They will fall into my grasp like a ripe plum. The empire will not suffer. On the contrary, it will gain in happiness and prosperity once the blight is removed."

---

5. *Esther* 3:8 with commentaries.
6. See *Megillah* 13b with *Maharsha*.

"All right, Haman. Tell me about the blight. Why are the concerns I mentioned baseless?"

Haman rubbed his hands together with relish. Now he was in his element. "As you deduced, your majesty, these people do indeed have a different God. But this God is unlike any of our gods. He makes many demands of them. In fact, He has a whole set of laws for them to follow, and if they are lax in their observance, He does not protect them. And right now their level of observance is very low. Believe me, your majesty, they are not in their God's good graces these days."[7]

"Perhaps that holds true for the simple people," said Achashverosh. "But surely they must have sages, holy men who are on a higher level. Surely these select few will ensure the protection of their God."

"It would seem so, your majesty, but it is not. First of all, many of the sages have also become lax in their observance of their religious laws. And even if there are some who have not, it won't help them. Their God judges them as a group, and the innocent must suffer along with the guilty.[8] He also puts great stock in the internal unity of His people, and right now, they are a people in disarray. They do not respect their sages and elders, and there is incessant bickering and dissension on every subject, even on the essence of the religious laws. In this state, their God usually turns away from them."[9]

"I see you've done your research, Haman," said Achashverosh. "All right, let's assume for the moment that we don't have to worry about their God. What about my other concerns?"

Haman waved them aside with his hand. "They pose absolutely no threat to us. First of all, as I mentioned, their internal dissension has left them in complete disarray. How could they mount an effective rebellion or resistance if they are so disorganized? And even if they did, they are such a weak and debilitated people that any uprising would be totally ineffective.[10] And there's no need to be concerned about others coming to their assistance, not a chance. Everyone hates them, and I mean everyone. As for depopulating part

---

7. See *Megillah* 13b. Hashem never sleeps (*Tehillim* 121:4), and He vowed to arouse His wrath against Haman and the enemies of the Jews (*Midrash Panim Acheirim*).

8. See *Maharsha; Sefas Emes.* Haman was referring to the Sages' teaching, *Kol Yisrael areivim zeh lazeh,* all Jews are guarantors, and thus responsible, one for the other.

9. *Sifsei Chachamim; Ibn Ezra; D'na Pishra; Ma'amar Mordechai.*

10. *R' Elisha Galico; Chomas Anach;* see *Ben Yehoyada.*

of the empire, that would not happen, since these people are scattered all over the king's provinces.[11] They could disappear tomorrow, and they would not be missed. That's the beauty of it. They are troublesome, and getting rid of them would be no trouble."[12]

"All right, all right, Haman," said Achashverosh. "Let us say for argument's sake that you've convinced me that these people can be eliminated without serious consequences. But why should we? After all, the greatest asset of any kingdom is its people, and diversity of the people in my empire just adds to its strength. Why eliminate one of my assets?"

"Your majesty, did you ever hear the expression that with friends like these you don't need enemies? I'm sure you did. Well, with assets like these you don't need liabilities! These people scorn the laws and customs of your kingdom.[13] Their laws actually forbid them to follow the laws of Egypt and Canaan, and I'm sure this extends to Persian as well.[14] And if they scorn our laws, their law promises them a portion in a world of the spirit that will follow life in this world. What a ridiculous fantasy! Your majesty, it is downright insulting." He paused for effect.[15]

"I'm listening, Haman," said Achashverosh. "Go on."

"These people do everything they can to keep apart from us. They speak their own language. They dress in different garments. They do not eat our foods or marry our women or allow us to marry theirs.[16] If one of them marries one of our women, the children are rejected as outsiders by their people.[17] When you were searching for a queen, your majesty, they hid their daughters, because they did not consider you fit for them. They have meaningless laws like forbidding mixing wool and linen in one garment, or burning red calves, all to differentiate themselves from all the other peoples of your empire.[18] They even have a barbaric custom of mutilating

---

11. *Midrash Panim Acheirim; R' Avigdor Kohen Tzedek; D'na Pishra; R' Elisha Galico; R' Shmuel di Uzidah*. This was a blessing in disguise for the Jews; their dispersion makes it difficult to destroy them (see *Pesachim* 87b).

12. *Rashi* to *Megillah* 13b; *Yosef Lekach; R' Elisha Galico; R' Shmuel di Uzidah; Yad HaMelech*.

13. *Megillah* 13b; *Midrash Tehillim* 17:8; *Pirush Megillas Achashverosh; Targum Rishon; Yosef Lekach; Alshich*.

14. *D'na Pishra*; see *Vayikra* 18:3 and *Chiddushei HaRim*.

15. *Einei HaEidah; Megillas Sefer*.

16. *Megillah* 13b; *R' Yosef ibn Yachia*.

17. *Menos HaLevi*.

18. Ibid.

infant boys on the eighth day of life, leaving a mark on their bodies that will identify them as being different.[19] At the same time, they try to convince other people to abandon their gods and lifestyles and join them, to become one of them."[20]

"I'm listening."

"Your majesty, they are barbarians! They go down to the rivers in the late hours of the night to clean their grime by ritual washing, and they befoul our pristine waters.[21] They are uncivilized in their business dealings. Their law commands them to cheat other people and discriminate against them.[22] And try collecting taxes from them! Forget it! The expense of collecting taxes from them would be greater than the taxes themselves.[23] Tell me, is that civilized behavior? But wait, that is not the worst of it. When they go to war, they exterminate their enemies, men, women and children. They leave no survivors. What did the women and the infants do? Why do they deserve to be murdered? My ancestors hundreds of years were the victims of this policy. They attacked our cities and killed almost everyone. Thankfully, my grandfather got away and was able to revive our Amalekite people."[24]

"Aha, Haman!" Achashverosh exclaimed. "Now I hear the real story. You aren't so concerned with my empire but with exacting your own vengeance for the wrong committed against your ancestors."

Haman squinted at Achashverosh. "I beg your pardon, your majesty, but who would bear a grudge for centuries? No, I no longer seek vengeance. I just mentioned the incident with my ancestors as an illustration of their customs, no more. No, what gets me about them more than anything else is their hypocrisy. After putting out so many detailed laws that require them to separate from us, they ignore their own laws! Where are their ethics? Their morals? What kind of people are these? They preach to us about the inviolability of their laws, but when it suits them, they just trample their laws at will. It is a disgrace."[25]

19. *Targum Sheni; Pirush Megillas Achashverosh.*

20. *Einei HaEidah; Ma'amar Mordechai.*

21. *Targum Sheni; Sipur HaNeis (Yosef Shabchi).*

22. *R' Chaim Abulafia; Chida; R' Avigdor Kohen Tzedek.*

23. See *Megillah* 13b; *Midrash Lekach Tov; Yosef Lekach; R' Elisha Galico; R' Shmuel di Uzidah; Alshich.* As mentioned earlier, the Jews were the only ones who were not relieved of paying taxes in Esther's honor.

24. *R' Chaim Abulafia;* see *Yoma* 22b.

25. *R' Elisha Galico; Sifsei Chachamim; K'Sav Sofer; Chomas Anach; Me'am Loez.* Haman was concerned that the Jews would strengthen themselves and not sin any further. If this were to happen, the few good deeds they did would provide enough merit for them to be saved (*Ya'aros Devash*).

"I see they have offended your sense of morality, Haman."

"And my sense of decency, your majesty. Your empire is so powerful, your majesty, because your people work hard and conscientiously, but these people are a bunch of slackers. They always have an excuse for avoiding work or commerce.[26] Three times a day they run to their prayerhouses, and on Mondays and Thursdays they spend additional time there. Every time they eat something they pray beforehand and afterwards.[27] Every week, they have a day of rest, or this festival or that festival or the other.[28] Every year, they claim they have to supervise the wheat harvest in the spring, set aside special waters and scour out the last crumbs from their homes. What a waste of precious, productive time![29] And that's not all. In the autumn, they have a festival for the new year and a fast day for talking about their sins ands then — listen to this — a nine-day festival! Can you imagine how much time just goes to waste in this fashion? It is outrageous! Criminal! Why do these hypocrites need a day of rest every week? What do they rest from? They never work anyway. All they do is rest. Do they have to rest from resting so much?"

"It is strange, Haman," said Achashverosh.

"Wait a minute, your majesty. They're not finished resting yet. Because they're so exhausted from resting all the time, they also need a full year of rest every seventh year and, on top of that, another full year of rest every fiftieth year. I mean, is this ridiculous or what?"

"It is rather hard to believe."

"And on top of that, they are so careful with their holidays and events and things, but they have absolutely no commitment to our festivals and important days. They don't celebrate the birth of the Persian Empire, for instance. Nor do they celebrate the winter solstice, as we do."[30]

"Well, I wouldn't hold this against them, Haman. After all, they're so busy resting on their own holidays, if they would rest on ours as well, they would never have any time to work."

---

26. *Maharsha; Targum Sheni; Ramban.*

27. *Targum Sheni; Aggadas Esther; Midrash Abba Gorior; Rambam; Alshich.*

28. *Megillah* 13b; *Yalkut Shimoni; R' Chaim Abulafia.*

29. *Ben Yehoyada.* Because Haman mocked the holidays that the Jews honored and celebrated, Hashem gave them another holiday, the two-day celebration of Purim, celebrating Haman's destruction and the cancellation of his decrees (*Yalkut Shimoni; Midrash Lekach Tov*).

30. *Targum Rishon; Esther Rabbah; Aggadas Esther; Midrash Abba Gorion* 7:12; *Yefei Anaf.*

"Shall I go on?"

"You mean, there's more?"

"I'm afraid there is, your majesty. Very serious stuff. Now we come to their attitude toward you."

Achashverosh leaned forward, his interest piqued.

Haman rubbed his hands together. "Your majesty, their laws explicitly state that only one of their own can be a king over them. To me the implication is clear. They do not recognize you as their sovereign. They would gladly overthrow you and place one of their own on your throne. They mock you and your throne. Do you know what they pray for in their prayerhouses every day, your majesty?"[31]

"I don't, but I'm sure you will tell me."

"I certainly will. They pray that they regain their freedom and that their enemies go down to destruction. And who do you think these enemies are? You, your majesty, and the entire Persian Empire. They despise you, your majesty. If a fly would settle on their wine, they would scoop out the fly and drink the wine. But if you would touch their wine, they would spill it out. Can you imagine, your majesty? They consider you lower than a housefly." Haman shuddered. "Oh, I cannot take these affronts to your honor. They make my blood boil."[32]

"All right, Haman. You've brought my blood to a simmer as well. Do you do this much research on all your projects?"

Haman smiled. "Of course, your majesty. It is my duty to find out all the information available so that I can serve you well. I apologize for making your blood simmer. At least, a simmer is not as disturbing as a boil. But once again, I felt obligated to bring these things to your attention. Let me sum up. They do not work or pay taxes, yet they live off the fat of the land. They are parasites![33] Everyone in the empire despises them for their aloofness and their disgusting habits and customs. There can be no peace in the empire with these people scattered though every corner of it. Their own God has abandoned them. I tell you, your majesty, they are ours for the taking. As I said, they will fall into our hands like a ripe plum. If you rid the empire of this blight, your majesty, you will be a hero. They will write ballads and poems about you. Many years from now, grandfathers will still be telling their grandchil-

---

31. *Yad HaMelech.*

32. *Megillah* 13b; *Targum Sheni; R' Shmuel di Uzidah;* see *Tosafos, Avodah Zarah* 33b, s.v. *kassi.*

33. *Megillah* 13b; *Gra.*

dren how the great King Achashverosh saved the empire from the scourge of the arrogant parasites."[34]

Achashverosh drummed his fingers on the arm of his chair and scowled at Haman. "So what do you propose, Haman? I haven't said yes, and I haven't said no. But I'm listening. What's on your mind?"

Haman drew himself up to his full height and squinted at Achashverosh. "I have crafted a plan, your majesty. It is perfectly clear that we need to . . . ahem . . . eliminate these people from the empire, but I think we need to move slowly and carefully. I want to begin by outlawing their laws, thereby throttling the arrogant soul of these people. Then we can break their spirits by selling them into slavery.[35] Within a year or even less, they will be so dispirited and broken that we may even want to consider just putting an end to their misery and killing them swiftly and mercifully.[36] After all, we are not without compassion, even for arrogant parasites who are a blight on the empire. With their spirits and physical presence . . . um . . . eliminated, we will, of course, confiscate all their possessions. Nothing will remain of them, not their souls, not their spirits, not their bodies, not even their possessions as a remembrance that these people once existed."

Ultimately, when the miracle of Purim would deliver the Jewish people from Haman's hands, the observances of Purim would address these four areas of intended destruction. The Jewish people would read the *Megillah* to refresh the soul, sing and dance to refresh the spirit, eat and drink to delight the body and give charity to the poor to include their possessions in the festival.[37]

"It all sounds good and well, Haman," said Achashverosh, "but I am still concerned. Even people such as you describe pay taxes to the government. I know that you explained how the cost of collection would be greater than the taxes, but I think this was somewhat of an exaggeration. It seems to me that I would sustain a loss to the treasury if an entire people were . . . ahem . . . as you say, eliminated. Besides, the elimination itself could become quite an expensive process, and I am not sure it would be cost-effective."[38]

34. *Menos HaLevi; Megillas Sesarim; Kisei David; Maharal; Rishon LeTzion; Gra; Yosef Lekach; Targum Sheni; Maharsha; Malbim.*

35. *Akeidah; R' Shmuel di Uzidah.*

36. *Rokeach; Menos HaLevi; Alshich; Malbim.*

37. *Gra.*

38. *D'na Pishra.*

Haman looked Achashverosh directly in the eye. "Your majesty, I may have exaggerated a little before, but hardly. Nevertheless, I understand your concerns. And I have the answer." He paused for effect. "I am prepared to give you ten thousand talents of silver. I will pay this money into your treasury, and all you have to do is sign these people over to me. One stroke of your pen and it is all done.[39] The people are transferred into my power, and the ten thousand talents of silver are transferred into your treasury. This money will easily cover any lost taxes the treasury might incur. Furthermore, I will give the treasury a large share of the confiscated properties and possessions that these people leave behind when they . . . ahem . . . leave us. I will, of course, compensate the government for the time of the functionaries and laborers I will use to carry through my plans."[40]

"You're talking about quite a lot of money, Haman."

"Your majesty knows how wealthy I am. These sums are piddling for me. But to tell you the truth, I don't even think I will have to use so much of my own money.[41] When word of what I intend to do gets out in the empire, I will be able to raise untold sums for the project. People will be thrilled to participate through contributions, and plenty of them will volunteer for hands-on work, if you know what I mean. Can you imagine the popularity of a real religious crusade? The people will be glad to pay to participate."[42]

"I see you have this all figured out," said Achashverosh. "You have an answer for every question I ask you. Tell me then, how did you arrive at the figure of ten thousand talents of silver?"

"It's a complicated formula, your majesty."

"I can handle complicated formulas, Haman. We have time."

"Well, at one time in the history of these people, there were six hundred thousand men who donated a half-*shekel* to their God. That adds up to a total of ten thousand talents of silver. The number ten thousand is also significant, because Nevuchadnezzar drove ten thousand of them into exile. It is a number that works well in my

39. *Targum Sheni; Esther Rabbah* 7:19; *R' Zechariah HaRofei; Ma'amar Mordechai.*
40. *Megillas Sesarim; Sha'ar bas Rabbim; Gra.*
41. *Midrash Panim Acheirim; Ibn Ezra; Menos HaLevi.* Some suggest that the 10,000 talents of silver was half of the ready cash he owned. This did not include real estate and other assets (*Midrash Talpios*). Haman would give Achashverosh this money only after the letters were written (See *Pirkei d'Rav Eliezer; Yad HaMelech; Tzuf Devash*).
42. *Malbim; Menos HaLevi; Zera Baruch.*

occult calculations.[43] By the way, since you asked, your majesty, I would like to mention that if there are more than six hundred thousand of these people, I will gladly give you the additional silver. And if there should be fewer than six hundred thousand, you are welcome to the entire ten thousand talents."[44]

"How very generous of you," said Achashverosh. "Look, Haman, what's the point of beating around the bush? If I were a stable boy, I could not help figuring out the identity of these people you call a blight on my empire. We're talking about the Jews, of course, so why not be open and frank about it? You have made a powerful case, and I have to tell you that I am convinced. But I am still worried."

Haman arched his eyebrows. "Oh?"

"The prospect of uprisings and rebellion don't concern me. The empire is strong enough to deal with any disturbances. No, it is their God that worries me. Why, He absolutely loves them. Don't you know what He did to Pharaoh, to your Amalekite ancestors, to Og and Sichon, to Sisra, to Sancheriv? Well, I certainly don't want to end up like them."

"Your majesty, I assure you that it is safe," said Haman. "You will see. In fact, traditionally, all the kings who have taken on the Jews have risen in power and stature. If you accept my plan, you will become even greater than you are right now. It's all ups and no downs."

"You're so sure," said Achashverosh. "And what if you are wrong? What then? Will you give me back my kingdom? My life?"

"But you agreed that I am right!"

"Nevertheless, I want to consult my wise men. Summon my astrologers, wizards and magicians right now. Let us hear what they have to say."

An hour later, Achashverosh's leading practitioners of the occult stood before the king listening to Haman's presentation with exaggeratedly grave expressions on their faces.

---

43. *Megillah* 13b; *Targum Sheni; Rokeach; R' Saadiah Gaon.* See *Tosafos* to *Megillah* 16a and *Bach's* note there. See *Pnei Yehoshua; Chizkuni* to beginning of *Parashas Ki Sisa.* See *Melachim* II ch. 24. See *Selichos* for Ta'anis Esther, which mentions that the weight of the silver Haman gave Achashverosh equaled the amount of *adanim* (sockets) in the *Mishkan.* Haman was hoping that Achashverosh would disburse the extra money as charity. His distributing the money to the people would gladden them, especially as the funds came from the decree to destroy the Jews. Haman thought he would deserve to annihilate the Jews through Achashverosh's giving to charity a sum corresponding to the number of Jews.

44. *Menos HaLevi; D'na Pishra.*

An old magician with a stringy white goatee wearing long crimson robes spoke up. "How can we get rid of the Jews? If there will be no Jews, then there will be no Torah. And if there is no Torah, the world will cease to exist."

"Who says so?" asks Haman.

"The God of the Jews," said the magician.

"Bah! Don't believe it," said Haman. "It's just not true."

"Well, maybe, maybe not," said the magician. "But you cannot deny that their God loves them like an only child. How do you expect to destroy them? Do you want us to end up like the others who tried and failed?"

"Things have changed, my friend," said Haman. "Did you happen to notice that these Jews, so beloved of their God, are in exile, scattered among the nations? Did you happen to notice that Nevuchadnezzar destroyed their Temple? Where were the miracles? Where was the intervention of their God?"

The magician scratched his nose. "Hmm, good questions, Haman. So what do you say? How do you explain it?"

"In one word," said Haman. "Age! That's right, the God of the Jews has grown old. He just isn't what He used to be. He doesn't see well, and His powers are weakened. With no Temple in which to bring sacrifices or the yearly *shekel*, the Jews cannot even awaken the weak powers of their old God. I tell you, my friends, after so many years of pulling them out of the troubles they get into, their God is tired of them. We will be doing Him a favor by ridding Him of the Jews. He will thank us."[45]

"Interesting point, Haman," said Achashverosh. He turned to his advisors. "Do you agree with him, gentlemen?"

"We need to confer, your majesty," said the magician.

"Then go confer in that corner over there." Achashverosh pointed to the far end of the room. "You have fifteen minutes."

They were back in less than the time allotted. Once again the old magician with the goatee spoke for the group. "Your majesty, we endorse Haman's plan. He is well known to all for his wisdom, and for this project, we have to admit that his research and planning are nothing short of incredible. His arguments are airtight and utterly

---

45. See *Megillah* 13b; *Yad HaMelech*; *Esther Rabbah* 7:13; *Midrash Abba Gorion*; *Midrash Panim Acheirim*; *Aggadas Esther*; *Midrash Lekach Tov*; *R' Elisha Galico*; *Midrash HaGadol*. See *Gittin* 50a. Some suggest that the lotteries were first done now, with the approval of the royal cabinet.

persuasive. We all agree that his plan is safe and desirable. We do, however, have one reservation."[46]

Achashverosh leaned forward, and Haman tensed.

"Speak up," said Achashverosh.

"Your majesty," said the magician, "because of assorted auras and confluence of celestial influences, we believe that you yourself should have no direct involvement in this project. Even Pharaoh did not want blood on his hands, and therefore, he assigned the midwives to snuff out the infant Jewish boys. We feel it would be inauspicious for you to get blood on your hands in this manner, your majesty. After all, this is not the battlefield."[47]

Achashverosh nodded. "Haman, what do you have to say?"

Haman rubbed his hands together. "Your majesty, I fully agree with your advisors on this point. I would not want you to get blood on your hands. Of course not. You are the king! No, all you have to do is issue the decree turning them over to my power. Letters will go out to all the governors of the provinces, and we'll see how to take it from there. I'm sure we will have plenty of volunteers for the work. From that point on, you need have no involvement. On the contrary, I would also advise against your involvement. Most emphatically. Leave it to me, your majesty. I know exactly what to do."

Achashverosh leaned back and smiled. "Then it looks like we have a deal. Show me the money, and I'll sign on the dotted line. You will have my seal of approval, but I will know nothing about your activities. Done!"[48]

Haman threw back his head and laughed with delight.

"Not so fast, Haman," said Achashverosh. "I'm not totally sure yet. I want to put the question to another test."

Haman's face turned green. "Another test?"

"Yes, Haman, I want to be absolutely sure. Magicians! Devise another lottery for me. We will cast lots once again right here."

"I can suggest a simple lottery, your majesty," said the old magician in the red robe. "We will put two scraps of paper in a cup; on one will be written 'silver' and on the other 'people.' Haman will draw one of these slips of paper. If he draws 'people,' the Jews are his, and the silver is yours. If he draws 'silver,' he keeps his silver, and you keep the people."

---

46. *Gra.*

47. *Rashi; R' Elisha Galico; R' Shmuel di Uzidah; Maharal.*

48. *Menos HaLevi.*

The magician prepared the lots as Haman looked on nervously. Sweat poured from his brow, and he chewed his lip until it bled. When the lots were ready, he reached gingerly into the cup and withdrew one of the scraps. Slowly, breathlessly, he unfolded it.

"People!" he cried triumphantly, and he laughed again.[49]

But who would have the last laugh? Hashem had anticipated this event many years earlier. He had already taken possession of the Jews for Himself when He brought them forth from Egypt, and therefore, Haman was powerless to take control of them. Moreover, the annual collection of half-*shekels* from the Jews for the *Beis HaMikdash* had already given them the merit to be saved from Haman's collection. "Let us see whose silver talents will succeed," said Hashem, "Haman's or the Jewish people's?"[50]

In the meantime, Achashverosh had closed his eyes and was leaning back, his brow furrowed in thought. Haman and the king's advisors stood by respectfully, barely daring to breathe lest they disturb his concentration.

Achashverosh was doing some serious thinking. In truth, he hated the Jews as much as Haman did. Even more! Ironically, when Vashti was on trial he had called on many people to speak in her defense, but here he had condemned an entire nation without allowing them to speak a single word in their defense.[51]

His stargazers had once told Achashverosh that a Jew would ascend to his throne, and ever since then, he had hated the Jews with a passion. Little did he know that the Jew who would take his throne was his own son by Esther. Ironically, even if he killed all the Jews, this Jew would survive. Pharaoh also wanted to kill all the Jewish boys, because his stargazers had told him the Jewish savior was about to be born. Ironically, Pharaoh himself brought up Moshe in the palace.[52]

Despite all Haman's assurances and the concurrence of his advisors, Achashverosh was still not secure in his decision. He was still worried about dissension in the empire. But even more, he was wor-

---

49. *Midrash Abba Gorion; Midrash Panim Acheirim.*

50. See *Megillah* 13b; *Maharsha; Targum Sheni; Midrash Abba Gorion; R' Shmuel di Uzidah.* The Jews had continued to donate *shekalim* towards the *Beis HaMikdash* fund so that when it would be rebuilt the expenses of the public sacrifices would be covered. This show of faith served as a merit to thwart Haman's plan (*Ya'aros Devash*).

51. *Rashi* to *Esther; Menos HaLevi; R' Yosef ibn Yachia.*

52. *Ya'aros Devash.*

ried about the God of the Jews. How could he protect himself? Achashverosh had an idea.

He opened his eyes and leaned forward.

"Gentlemen, I have given this matter a lot of thought," he said, "and as you see, I still have my reservations. So this what I have decided to do. I cannot have even the slightest connection to this affair. Absolutely nothing, do you understand?"

They all nodded.

Achashverosh removed his signet ring from his finger and gave it to Haman. "Here you are, Haman. For the time being, you have my ring, and you can give the seal of approval to any decree you wish without consulting me. You are now effectively the independent ruler of the empire, co-equal with me for the time being. You have the power to make whatever decisions you wish about the Jews, just don't tell me anything about it. I have nothing to do with it."[53]

"Very good, your majesty," said Haman as he took the ring. It felt hot in his hands. He could not believe his good fortune. When he had risen from low in the ranks of the king's advisors to the office of prime minister, he though he had reached the pinnacle of power. And now he was virtually king! This was a far cry from being Mordechai's slave. He held all the power in his own hands now. Even Achashverosh was powerless to stop him now.[54]

"There is more," said Achashverosh. "I am returning your ten thousand talents of silver to you."

"But your majesty," Haman protested, "the money seals the deal."[55]

"Don't worry, Haman," said Achashverosh. "The deal is on. The money goes to my treasury to seal the deal, as you say.[56] But then it goes right back to you as a gift. I don't want any of that money sticking to me. All the booty you capture from the Jews is yours. I don't want even one plugged *dinar* of it. I will even allow you to use royal manpower and take all your expenses from the royal treasury. All

---

53. The word *hamelech*, "the king," has the same numerical value as *Haman*, 95. This suggests that Haman and the king were equals (*Sha'arei Binah*).

54. *Ya'aros Devash.*

55. *Targum Rishon.*

The word *hakesef*, the money, has the same numerical value as *ha'etz*, the tree, 165, which implies poetic justice. The money Haman used for persecuting the Jews would lead to his being hanged on the gallows (called *tree* in *Esther*). See *Esther Rabbah* 7:21; *Tosafos* to *Megillah* 13b; *Minchas Yehudah.*

56. *R' Elisha Galico; Ya'aros Devash.*

profits go to you, Haman. Nothing to me. No one will be able to say that I sold an entire people for money. No way."[57]

"Very prudent, your majesty," said Haman.

"You see, Haman, I know what's in your heart. Much as you care about the empire, you are doing it to avenge your Amalekite people. You have never forgotten the disaster with Agag. And now you want to settle your old scores with the Jews. I can see right through you, Haman."[58]

"But your majesty," Haman cried out, "you know how loyal I am. Why, every time —"

"Enough, Haman! Don't contradict me!"

Haman bowed his head. "Yes, your majesty."

Achashverosh smiled. "Yes, I have nothing to do with this. I gain nothing from it, and I will have no knowledge of anything that will go on. In fact, this whole affair has nothing to do with my empire. It is Haman's private vendetta against the Jews. I don't want to know anything about it. I absolutely don't want to know what's in store for these people, good or bad. It is beneath me to get involved in the petty squabbles of my subjects, don't you agree?"[59]

The old magician with the stringy goatee bowed from the waist. "You are very wise, your majesty. You have found the perfect path to enjoy the best of all worlds. I wish I had thought of this advice. It would have brought me honor."

A broad grin broke across Achashverosh's bearish features. He knew Haman had a difficult task ahead of him, that somehow he would run up against the God of the Jews, and he wanted no part of it. Unlike any other seller, Achashverosh had sold the Jews to

---

57. *Alshich;* see *R' Yosef ibn Yachia; Akeidah;* see *Targum Sheni; Maharsha; Pirkei d'Rav Eliezer* 50; *R' Shmuel di Uzidah; Menos HaLevi.* Others suggest that Haman never even gave the money to Achashverosh; rather, Achashverosh just told him to keep it (*D'na Pishra*). Achashverosh would later claim to Esther that he had never given Haman permission to kill the Jews. He had only agreed to exile them or sell them as slaves and confiscate their property, which would fall under the title of eradicating them and their memory. As incredible as this seems, Achashverosh convinced himself that he had never agreed to kill the Jews in a literal sense.

58. *Eshkol HaKofer; Yad HaMelech.*

59. *Midrash Panim Acheirim; Midrash Abba Gorion; Yedei Moshe; D'na Pishra; Yishai Elokim; Akeidah; Yosef Lekach; Melo HaOmer; R' Elisha Galico; R' Shmuel di Uzidah; Menos HaLevi; Eshkol HaKofer.* He also wanted to leave himself the option of reconsidering his policy. If he were to take the money, people would say, "You sold them; how can you take them back from Haman?" (*Aggadas Esther*). Some further suggest that Achashverosh did not want to be labeled as the king who killed an entire nation just for money. That is why he gave it back (*Chasam Sofer*).

Haman without getting anything in return but rather doing everything in his power to support the buyer's side.[60] He would get what he wanted without taking any of the risk or the blame, without getting involved. He was satisfied. He dismissed everyone and called for a glass of wine.

As Haman bowed and made his exit, he thrust his hand in his pocket and fingered the royal signet ring that nestled there. He was ecstatic.

The Talmud states that when Achashverosh "removed the ring" from his finger and gave it to Haman it was a far greater impetus to the Jewish people to repent than the rebuke of the forty-eight prophets and seven prophetesses who had lived up until that time. The people never asked for the prophecies nor did they pay particular heed to them. Perhaps they thought that the predictions would never materialize, that somehow or another disaster would be averted. But when Achashverosh removed his ring, they saw dire reality staring them in the face, and they were terrified. And there is nothing like terror to inspire repentance. The removal of the ring set in motion the apparatus of their destruction, but at the same time, it also triggered their ultimate repentance and redemption.[61]

---

60. *Esther Rabbah* 7:20; *Yalkut Shimoni.*
61. *Yishai Elokim;* see *Megillah* 14a; *Maharsha; Sifsei Chachamim; D'na Pishra;* see *Me'am Loez; Selichos* to Ta'anis Esther.

The Word Goes Out

14

Haman knew there was no time to waste if he wanted everything done on 13 Nissan, a date he considered auspicious for his designs. He had cast the lots on the morning of that day. He had immediately presented his project to the king. The king had called in his advisors, and he had given his approval. Now he would have to rush to get the letters sent out to the provinces before the sun set on that same day.

According to Haman's calculations, 13 Nissan presented a narrow window of opportunity against the Jewish people. During the first twelve days of Nissan, the twelve princes had brought offerings at the inauguration of the *Mishkan* in the Desert, which effectively eliminated those days. On 14 Nissan, the Jews brought the *korban Pesach*, which eliminated that day. But 13 Nissan seemed to be without Jewish merit and, therefore, an auspicious day for Haman.

But Haman had miscalculated. He did not realize that right before the Exodus from Egypt the Jewish people had been busy with the preparations for the *korban Pesach* from 10 Nissan through 14 Nissan, to their eternal merit. There actually was no window of opportunity on 13 Nissan.[1]

As the sun moved lower in the western sky, Haman gathered one hundred and twenty-seven scribes in the palace's vast scriptorium in order to write letters to each of the one hundred and twenty-seven provinces in its own language and in a style so clear that even children would understand them without any assistance.[2] Haman assumed that the poor response to his letters regarding domestic rules nine years earlier would be forgotten.[3]

With his customary cunning, Haman prepared two separate letters; one spoke in the name of the king to the common people and the other, in Haman's name, spoke to each individual government officials of any standing. Kings, princes, governors, legislators, satraps, aristocrats, ministers, mayors, aldermen – all would get a personalized, confidential letter. Haman wanted each official to receive his own letter, because it would give him a sense of importance and involvement.[4]

Furthermore, sending letters to each official guaranteed their widest distribution. A single letter going to a particular province might be waylaid or lost, but hundreds would get through.[5] Paradoxically, it would actually increase the confidentiality of the letters. A single letter passed around was more likely to be leaked to the people than individual closely held letters.[6] The increased secrecy would also foster the impression that the decree was for the local province only rather than for the entire empire.[7]

---

1. *R' Elisha Galico; Nachal Eshkol; Menos HaLevi; Pirkei d'Rav Eliezer; Aggadas Esther*. See *Radal's* detailed explanation of this matter. See also *Tehillim* 22:22. However, Haman thought it was an opportune time. His decree would last from 13 Nissan to 23 Sivan, 70 days, until Mordechai sent out his letters repealing the decree. The Persian nation benefitted from the Egyptian people's kindness many years earlier, when they had shown their respect for Yaakov by mourning his death for 70 days. Haman's decree thus endured for 70 days until it was anulled (*Yerushalmi Sotah* 1:10; *Bereishis Rabbah* 100:6; *Krovetz L'Purim*). The number 13 is significant as the numerical equivalent of the word *echad*, one, which refers to Hashem Who is One, as in *Kerias Shema*. Hashem would save the Jews in the merit of their saying *Shema* (*Rokeach*).

2. *Targum Sheni* 4:1; *Targum Rishon; Nachal Eshkol; R' Yosef ibn Yachia*. Others suggest that Achashverosh himself wrote these letters, while still others hold that it was Haman who wrote them.

3. *R' Shmuel di Uzidah.*

4. *Rambam; R' Yosef ibn Yachia; Yalkut Shimoni; R' Elisha Galico; Alshich; Malbim.*

5. *Menos HaLevi; Alshich.*

6. *Yosef Lekach.*

7. *Malbim.*

When all the scribes had settled in their seats, Haman rapped on the table for attention. "Gentlemen, I will dictate two letters to you. I will speak in Persian, but you will instantly translate and write in the language of your assigned province. Work quickly, because time is of the essence. The first letter will be in the name of the king. You will write only one copy. The second will be in my name. You will be given a list of addressees, and you will copy and personalize the letter as many times as need be. Leave a place on top for the addressees. Is that understood?"

There was a murmur of assent.

"Good!" said Haman. "We begin. First letter: My esteemed people! This is to inform you of a minor transaction that has taken place in the palace. The new prime minister, the illustrious Haman, has requested that he be given personal dominion over an alien people that dwells in our midst. These people have a long history of dissension and ingratitude, and in his devotion and loyalty to the empire, Haman has taken upon his own soldiers the responsibility of dealing with them effectively. We have granted Haman's request and have consigned these people to his power. We call on all loyal citizens of the empire to assist Haman in every way possible so that his campaign will be a success. The date on which the final solution is scheduled to take place is next 13 Adar. Please stand to arms on that day should your assistance be needed in any way. Keep in touch with your local officials for further instructions. We send you our personal greetings and the blessings of the gods. [signed] Achashverosh, King of the Medes and the Persians, and Emperor of the Persian Empire."[8]

Achashverosh's letter was deliberately vague to protect the king from involvement in Haman's actions. It was also important to contain the hot-blooded commoners who might attack the Jews prematurely before the designated, auspicious date of 13 Adar, to prevent the Jews from mounting a credible defense and to avoid a sympathetic reaction among the more liberal-minded people in the empire.[9]

"Very well, gentlemen," said Haman. "Now for the second letter: Esteemed citizens of the glorious Persian Empire! I humbly address

8. *Malbim; Megillas Sesarim; Esther Rabbah* 7:24; *Gra; Menos HaLevi; R' Shmuel di Uzidah; Alshich; R' Elisha Galico; Esther Rabbah* 7:13; *Targum Sheni; Tehillim* 10:16 with *Rashi; Midrash Abbah Gorion; Midrash Lekach Tov; Me'am Loez*. See *Yefei Anaf* for an explanation of the contents of this letter and its purpose. The authorship of this letter is a matter of debate among the commentators; were the words composed by Haman or Achashverosh? As mentioned earlier, many suggest that Achashverosh knew full well that Haman intended to destroy the Jews, and he granted his permission.

9. *Yedei Moshe; Gra; Yosef Lekach; R' Elisha Galico; Alshich; Malbim; R' Yosef ibn Yachia; Menos HaLevi; R' Shmuel di Uzidah.*

you as your prime minister, viceroy to his exalted majesty King Achashverosh, on an important matter of state. There was once a great eagle who spread his wings over the entire world so that no animal or bird could stand before it. One day, a lion came and struck down the eagle, breaking its wings and legs. Peace, calm and salvation returned to the world once again. But now the eagle stirs once again. It threatens to recover its old power and strangle us as it strangled our ancestors. His majesty King Achashverosh has granted me permission to deal with this crisis as I see fit, and I intend to destroy the eagle before it can rise again. We are, of course, talking about the Jews. They are poised to destroy the empire, but together, we will avert this disaster and guarantee the freedom and prosperity of the peoples of the empire. The day of reckoning for the Jews is next 13 Adar. Be prepared. [signed] Haman, prime minister and viceroy of the Persian Empire."[10]

Haman attached an addendum describing the exact process by which the Jews were to be exterminated with maximum cruelty. Everything had to begin and end on that auspicious date. The threat of killing the children should be used to force parents to reveal their hidden treasures, and then, children would be put to the sword in front of their fathers and infants in the laps of their mothers. No plunder was to be taken until after every last Jew had been slaughtered; no distractions could be allowed to interfere with the critical work.[11] The corpses were to be left unburied for the dogs to eat. In one day, the Jewish people would be obliterated.[12]

---

10. *Midrash Panim Acheirim;* see *Vayikra Rabbah* 27:11; *R' Elisha Galico.* According to some, Achashverosh's letter was sent to all the dignitaries and government officials, while Haman's letter was sent to the general population. Others suggest that both letters were sent out together to everyone. Yet others have an entirely different text of the letter sent by Haman. According to all commentators, Haman's letter was clear to some recipients and unclear to others. Many suggest that to some extent Haman acted without Achashverosh's knowledge, expressing his own wishes rather than the King's. Some are of the opinion that Achashverosh intended only to destroy the Jewish faith and its practices; only Haman wanted to physically annihilate them, and his attempt did not have the king's consent. See *Akeidah; Yishai Elokim; Megillas Sesarim; Malbim; Esther Rabbah* 7:13; *Midrash Lekach Tov; Midrash Abba Gorion; Midrash Panim Acheirim; Alshich; Yosef Lekach; Gra; Menos HaLevi.*

11. *D'na Pishra; Rokeach; Alshich; Targum Sheni; Gra; Yosef Lekach.*

12. *D'na Pishra; Alshich; R' Shmuel di Uzidah* to *Esther* 4:1; *R' Yosef ibn Yachia.* Some suggest that Haman permitted the people to take the booty rather than designate it for the king, as was customary in war, to refute skeptics from claiming that the Jews were killed specifically for their money. This would cause the king to appear greedy; moreover, the common people might fear that they would be the next targets should the royal treasury be in deficit. Such thoughts could lead to political disaster, and thus Haman allowed the people to keep all spoils of war (*D'na Pishra; Maharal*). Others suggest that the monies taken from the Jews would be earmarked for government officials. Since they would eventually be receiving their wealth in any case, they could not be bribed by the Jews.

All this information was carefully omitted from the letters sent out to the commonfolk in the name of the king. Those were left deliberately vague, not identifying the Jews, nor stating explicitly that the unnamed people had effectively been sentenced to a national death. In Shushan, however, the death decree was publicized to all the people, not only the government officials. The power of the king in Shushan was so pervasive that no one would dare stand against him or protest, not the Jews, nor any of the other citizens. Therefore, Haman preferred to publicize it so that it should become a *fait accompli* before the king would have a chance to reconsider at the last minute.[13]

Under Haman's personal supervision, all the letters were properly addressed, sealed and sent off before sundown to their proper destinations by special imperial couriers.[14] He wanted them to at least be on their way before the close of the auspicious date of 13 Nissan — and before the king had time for second thoughts.[15]

It did not take long for the news to spread throughout the empire. In Shushan especially, the news spread like wildfire and inflamed the population.[16] The residents of the capital city treated the Jews like condemned criminals. "Why are you spending your money?" they would say to Jews they met in the market. "Soon you'll be dead, and we will get all your money. Why waste it on yourself? You're dead men anyway! Save the money for us!"[17]

Other residents of Shushan weren't quite so impressed with the letters. They remembered the letters that went out after Vashti was executed. "Let every man be master in his own home." Hah! What a joke![18]

Tragically, there were also some people across the empire who embraced the letters but could not bring themselves to wait for the appointed date. They began killing Jews immediately, causing many casualties in the early days of the decree.[19]

---

13. *Menos HaLevi; Melo HaOmer; Alshich*. Others, however, suggest that Shushan was the last place where the letters were distributed. According to these opinions the king never knew Haman's true intentions; he would conceal his plans from the king as long as possible (see *Malbim*).

14. *Targum Rishon; R' Saadiah Gaon; Midrash Lekach Tov*.

15. *R' Yosef ibn Yachia; R' Elisha Galico; Menos HaLevi; Malbim; Chasam Sofer*.

16. *Ma'amar Mordechai*.

17. *Esther Rabbah* 7:25; *Radal; Yalkut Shimoni*.

18. *Megillah* 12b with *Rashi*.

19. *Yad HaMelech*.

During these dark days, Haman strolled the streets of Shushan, his face aglow with happiness. One day, he saw a somber Mordechai approaching from afar and decided to confront the Jewish minister. How sweet it would be to savor his moment of triumph at Mordechai's expense.[20]

As Haman watched, he saw Mordechai turn aside to a schoolyard where little Jewish children played. Mordechai bent down to speak to a few of the children, and Haman drew closer to watch.

"Tell me, my child," said Mordechai, "what verses did you study today in the Torah?" This was an age-old method of receiving divine messages.

"Do not fear the sudden terror when the wicked attack," the children replied in unison. "If they should plan a conspiracy or evil councils, they will not stand. Hashem is with us. I have made you. I will rescue you, carry you and bear you in your old age."

Mordechai knew, through divine inspiration, everything that had transpired — the lottery, the decree, the letters; he knew the Jews were in extreme danger. But the words of the children gave him encouragement. The three verses they had quoted all related to victory over Amalek. Just as the Jews had been victorious in the first two confrontations with their archenemy, they would be victorious once again. The frown left his face, and he smiled from ear to ear. Hashem had not forgotten His people. No matter how dark it seemed, they must not despair of redemption.[21]

Haman was perplexed. What could have made Mordechai smile?

"So, Mordechai," said Haman, "you are no longer riding so high, are you? Not you, not your accursed people. Your day of reckoning has come. At long last, the accounts will be balanced. By the way, what did those children tell you?"

"Why, these children brought me good tidings from Heaven," Mordechai replied. "Your sadistic decree will cause my people to repent and seek forgiveness from our God, and He will grant us atonement. Then the decree you have issued will no longer be effective against us, and it will turn on you, its evil author, and devour you. You will fall into the selfsame pit that you have dug for us. We have nothing to worry about, Haman. You are the one who needs to worry."

---

20. *Yosef Lekach.*

21. *Rambam, Gra* 4:1. These three verses represent the two wars the Jews had fought against Amalek as well as this third confrontation with them. They would eventually overcome their foe this time, just as they had been victorious in the past (*Gra*).

Haman turned beet-red. His eyes bulged and he sputtered but could not immediately speak. "W-w-why, you arrogant Jew!" he finally screamed. "Even when you swing from the gallows your ego will still reach to the sky. Don't fool yourself, Mordechai. This is the end. Just wait until 13 Adar. The empire will make you a farewell celebration. We will dance over your corpses! As for these children, I will remember them. They will be first to die by the sword."[22]

Haman spun on his heel and marched off in a huff. As he neared the palace, he saw demonstrators milling about outside the gates, shouting and shaking their fists. Haman approached quietly, hanging back in the shadows where he could not be seen. For several long minutes, he listened to the complaints and protests of the demonstrators, and his blood chilled. Things were not going as perfectly as planned. Many Persians objected to the decree authorizing wholesale slaughter of the Jews. They also objected strenuously to the sporadic killings that had already begun. They were demanding that the king rescind the decree immediately.[23]

Although the king had given Haman his signet ring, Haman knew that this was no guarantee. It only gave him moral authority, and any time the king asked for the return of his ring, Haman would be forced to give it back. He ruled only at the pleasure of the king. And if these demonstrators gained the ear of the king, the entire plan could collapse. More people were streaming to the palace, raising the noise level progressively.[24]

Haman quickly passed through the palace gates, with the shouts of the protesters still ringing in his ears. He gave a few sharp orders to the chef and the butler. Then he asked for an immediate audience with the king and found him in an expansive mood.

"Your majesty, would you do me a great honor?" Haman asked. "Would you let me join you in a special meal to celebrate our . . . er . . . my accomplishment? I have ordered up special delicacies from the kitchen."

"Of course, Haman. I hope you have also sent for some good wine."

"Certainly, your majesty."

---

22. See *Esther Rabbah* 7:13; *Yedei Moshe; R' Shmuel di Uzidah; Mishlei* 3:28; *Yeshayahu* 8:10 and 46:4.

23. *Yalkut Shimoni; Midrash Panim Acheirim; Aggadas Esther; R' Avigdor Kohen Tzedek.*

24. *Midrash Chaseros V'Yeseiros.*

The door opened, and the food and the wine were brought in. Right behind them came an orchestra which set up their instruments quickly and began to play. [25]

"Louder, louder!" shouted Haman to the musicians, and as the music reached din level, he relaxed. Achashverosh would never hear anything over this ruckus, not even the loudest demonstrators in front of the palace.[26]

And so, Haman and Achashverosh sat down to break bread, while an entire nation was condemned to death.[27]

In Heaven, this callous act recalled another similar act when Yosef's brothers sold him into slavery and then sat down to break bread. The recall of this terrible sin militated against the Jews even after all the centuries that had passed since that fateful day. But there was a ray of hope. Besides Reuven, the only one of the brothers who had not participated in the sale was Binyamin. Therefore, the Jews would be saved by the merit of Binyamin, through his descendant Mordechai.[28]

Word of Achashverosh and Haman feasting and drinking together reached the city and beyond and drove the final nail into the coffin of the decree. If they were drinking over the sale, surely it would not be rescinded.[29]

Shushan was plunged into chaos. The people remembered that Achashverosh had promised to stop drinking after he killed Vashti. If he had broken his promise and was now prone to drunkenness, there was no telling what he would do.[30] As for the decree, if he had at least transferred the signet ring while he was drunk, he could have been expected to take it back when he sobered up. But he had, in fact, given Haman the ring while he was still sober, and there was no hope that he would take it back.[31]

---

25. R' Elisha Galico; Menos HaLevi.

26. R' Elisha Galioc; D'na Pishra; R' Shmuel di Uzidah.

27. D'na Pishra. Many cite this as proof that Achashverosh was unaware of Haman's true intentions. It is incongruous, to say the least, for a king to celebrate the proposed annihilation of a major group of his subjects. Rejoicing would be warranted if a sector of the people who had not obeyed the king's laws were now compliant; this would enhance his power and demonstrate his authority. See Malbim and Megillas Sesarim.

28. Esther Rabbah; 7:25; Targum Sheni; Maharal.

29. D'na Pishra.

30. Ma'amar Mordechai.

31. Ya'aros Devash. Some, however, were unsure, which added to the confusion in Shushan.

The demonstrations in the streets swelled. Some of the demonstrators were Persians of good will who truly liked the Jews and respected them. But they were also joined by many enemies of the Jews who believed the decree would cause economic disaster in the empire.[32]

At the same time, many strange things were happening around Shushan. People drying foods and clothing on their roofs fell mysteriously to their deaths. Others drawing water from wells toppled in and drowned. There were too many incidents to ascribe to circumstance. Apparently, the God of the Jews was not so old after all. In a short time, the cries of numerous mourning Persians mixed with the anguished cried of the condemned Jews, stoking the fires of dissension against the decree.

More and more intelligent people stopped to think seriously about the decree and concluded that it was ridiculous. How could a king be so ruthless as to order the destruction of an entire people? How could he kill Mordechai, his trusted friend and advisor? Perhaps he hadn't. But then why was he celebrating with Haman? It was terribly confusing.[33]

Confusion also reigned outside Shushan in the provinces of the empire. The ambiguity of Achashverosh's letter left the people with many unanswered questions. True, the indications were that the Jews were the condemned people, but who could be sure? Each distinct people worried if perhaps they were the condemned, if they were slated to be killed, man, woman and child, on 13 Adar. The empire was in turmoil. Once again, Achashverosh's letters were greeted with mockery and disdain.[34]

But in Shushan, the pain and the agony were beyond measure. The people cried. The city wept; the very stones and trees shed tears over the coming destruction. The Torah itself wailed over the Jewish people. Such a decree could not have come from a mortal man like Haman. It was clearly a Heavenly decree, with Haman merely its herald.[35]

---

32. *Mechilta, Parashas Beshalach; Yalkut Shimoni Shemos* 230; *Targum Rishon*. Others were simply confused, not understanding the exact contents of the letter (*Yad HaMelech*).

33. See *Yalkut Shimoni; Midrash Panim Acherim; Aggadas Esther; Menos HaLevi; Maharal*.

34. *Pirush Megillas Achashverosh; Maharal*.

35. *Rokeach; Yosef Lekach; Me'am Loez*.

Sackcloth and Ashes

15

Up in Heaven, the Jewish people were also facing judgment. Satan stood before the Heavenly Throne and argued for a decree of annihilation. "How long will You tolerate this rebellious nation, Almighty?" he asked. "So much time has passed since they have eaten at Achashverosh's feast, not to mention that they bowed to Nevuchadnezzar's idols, and they still haven't repented. They deserve to be destroyed."

"Then what will be with the Torah?" asked the Almighty.

"The angels in Heaven will learn the Torah."

"Very well," said the Almighty. "Bring me a scroll, and I will issue a decree of death against the Jewish people."

Happily, Satan brought the scroll, and the deed was done.

The Torah saw that it might soon be separated from the Jewish people to whom it had been married since Mount Sinai. It donned mourning garments and sat in bereavement. The angels wept bitterly. The sun, the moon and the stars of the galaxies and constellations also felt there was no purpose in their continued existence if they could not serve the Jewish people. They, too, dressed in sackcloth and went into mourning.

Eliyahu *HaNavi* had also witnessed the terrible decree, and he hurried to get help. He approached the patriarchs and pleaded with them to come to the aid of their descendants.

"How can you sleep when your children are in distress?" he demanded.

"What can we do?" they said. "They are guilty."

Eliyahu ran to Moshe *Rabbeinu*. "How many times have you interceded with Hashem on behalf of the Jewish people? When they worshipped the Golden Calf, you came to their defense. When they listened to the Spies, you turned away the evil decree. They need your help again. Please pray for them. Please save them!"

"Are there any righteous people among them?" Moshe asked.

"Yes," said Eliyahu. "There is Mordechai."

"Very well then," said Moshe. "Go see how the decree was sealed. If it is sealed with clay, we have a chance. If it is sealed with blood, all is lost."

What was the significance of the clay and the blood? Clay is a physical sign, meaning that the Jewish people had been condemned for the physical contamination of participating in Achashverosh's feast. This could be overcome. Blood, however, is a spiritual sign, indicating that the contamination had penetrated to their souls, and that the only atonement was with their blood. Such a decree could not be overturned. Perhaps also, the clay recalled the food at the feast, while the blood recalled the *yayin nesech*, the gentile wine, that the Jews had drunk, which was far worse.

Eliyahu returned with good news. The decree was sealed with clay.

"Good," said Moshe. "Go tell Mordechai that he should pray from the earth while I will pray from the heavens. Together, we may reverse this decree."[1]

Down in the lower world, Mordechai was painfully aware of Achashverosh's decree against the Jewish people. Rumors and reports had swept through Shushan and the entire empire.

---

1. *Esther Rabbah* 7:4; *Targum Rishon*; *Midrash Abba Gorion*; *Aggadas Esther*; *D'na Pishra*; *Menos HaLevi*; *Yad HaMelech*. See *R' Elisha Galico*; *Alshich*; *Krovetz L'Purim*; *Selichos* for Ta'anis Esther. See *Midrash Talpios* who points out that *l'avdam,* to destroy them, contains the word *dam,* blood, although the decree was not sealed in blood. R' Chaim of Volozhin is said to have noted that *l'avdam* is actually a contraction of *lo badam* — *not with blood*.

Mordechai himself also heard the prophecies of Chaggai, Zechariah and Malachi. When Eliyahu delivered Moshe *Rabbeinu's* message, Mordechai recalled a dream he had had during the second year of Achashverosh's reign.[2]

He dreamed he was looking down at a desert. On one side was a huge crowd of angry people, on the other a small group huddled together in fear. A giant serpent arose from the midst of the huge crowd. It rose higher and higher, growing larger and larger as it rose, until it loomed large as a mountain. It arched out, as if to devour the huddled group, but suddenly, another serpent of equal size rose up to face the monster. The two serpents locked in battle right over the huddled group. Banks of heavy thunderclouds moved across the sky, obscuring the sun, adding the gloom of darkness to the battle raging below.

In the heat of the battle of the serpents, the huge crowd strapped on their weapons and prepared to attack the small group huddled helplessly beneath the warring serpents. The people in the small group cried out in terror and prayed for their lives. Miraculously, a small stream appeared in the path of the attackers, and within no time at all, it swelled into a roaring, turgid river that blocked their way. But the small group still trembled in fear, because the battle of the serpents continued to rage overhead. Then swirling tempests arose from the four corners of the earth and converged on the attacking serpent, tearing it into strawlike shreds. The thunderclouds also passed away, and the small group found itself standing safe in the bright sunshine. They grew in strength and numbers and brought peace and serenity to the world. Mordechai awoke.

The dream, Mordechai had understood, was a heavenly message. The huge crowd was the gentile nations, and the group was the Jewish people. There would be an evil decree against the Jews, but with the power of prayer, all would turn out well in the end. But what did the two serpents represent?[3] He told Esther about the dream, and they wrote it down for safekeeping. Now, Mordechai fathomed the symbol of the two serpents. They represented none other than himself and Haman, the two who were now locked in the

2. See *Yishai Elokim; Targum Sheni; Pirkei d'Rav Eliezer; R' Yosef ibn Nachmiash; Yedei Moshe; Yad HaMelech.* Some point out that Mordechai could not have received a prophecy at this time since he was in a state of sadness. See *Ir David; Yismach Lev; Chagigah* 5b.
3. *Yalkut Shimoni* 1056; see *Torah Sheleimah* 383; *Esther Rabbah* 8:5; *Rashi; Midrash Megillas Esther.*

struggle for the future of the Jewish people. Mordechai knew he had to tell Esther about the decree and the message of the dream.[4]

The Jewish people were in mortal danger, with the decree hanging over their heads. Having bowed down to Nevuchadnezzar's idols, eaten at Achashverosh's feast and become lax in Torah study, they were exposed and vulnerable. The situation was desperate.[5] Mordechai knew that if the Jewish people would come to their senses and repent, the decree would be rescinded before the day it was to go into effect, but in the meantime, the attacks were already beginning. Here and there, zealous gentiles were already killing Jews.[6]

It is comparable to a king who condemned an ailing man to death. He turned the condemned man over to his soldiers to bring him to the place of execution. The ailing man, too sick to walk properly, reeled and stumbled as the soldiers pushed him along. They struck at him viciously, prodding him without mercy every time he tripped, stumbled and fell.

The king was observing the scene from his window, and when he saw the cruelty and brutality of his soldiers, he became enraged. He ran after them, and pulled the soldiers off their hapless victim. He issued orders that the offending soldiers be executed and that the chains be removed from the prisoner. He then ordered that the prisoner be brought into the palace and nursed back to health. When he fully recovered his health, the king set him free and sent him home.

In later years, when the man would look back at those days, he would not recall what had ailed him when he first appeared before the king. He would only recall and remember his death sentence, the persecution of the soldiers and the royal reprieve. Similarly, when the decree against the Jews would be removed, they would recall the miracle of their deliverance with joy. They would not recall the eleven months of terror and sporadic murders that had preceded the abolishment of the decree.[7]

Mordechai confronted the task that faced him, fully aware that the survival of the Jewish people depended on him. The first step he took was to express his grief and sorrow at the terrible situ-

---

4. *Yedei Moshe; Krovetz L'Purim.*

5. See *Midrash Abba Gorion; Yalkut Shimoni; Midrash Panim Acheirim; Rashi* to *Megillah* 12a. See ch. 2, where mention is made of the *bitul Torah* which led to the Jews' attending the feast (*Pri Tzaddik*).

6. *R' Shmuel di Uzidah; D'na Pishra; Gra; Yad HaMelech.*

7. *Rambam; Yad HaMelech.*

ation of his people. He viewed the sporadic killings as an immediate death warrant against the Jewish people, and he went into mourning. He tore his garments to expose his heart, then he donned sackcloth and placed ashes on his head.[8]

Mordechai saw a parallel between this decree and the selling of Yosef by his brothers. Just as Achashverosh and Haman had sealed the decree by sitting down to eat and drink, the brothers had broken bread right after they had cast Yosef into the pit. Therefore, just as Yaakov had donned sackcloth to express his grief when he heard that Yosef had been killed, Mordechai also chose this way to express his own grief.[9] As for the ashes on his head, they were reminiscent of Avraham, who compared himself to "dust and ashes," and Yitzchak, who was placed on the *Akeidah* as a sacrifice.[10]

In a sense, Mordechai felt personally responsible to save the Jews from their predicament, since King Shaul, his ancestor, had spared Haman's ancestor Agag, the Amalekite king. He also felt that he should rend his garments, because his ancestor Binyamin had recognized the Egyptian viceroy as his long-lost brother Yosef and remained silent, thereby causing his brothers to rend their garments.[11]

Although it would be demeaning to do so, Mordechai resolved to sit in sackcloth and ashes and pray until the decree was abolished.[12] This was not a time to be concerned with decorum. He hoped his prayer would atone for the sin of the Jews bowing to Nevuchadnezzar's idols and the sackcloth for their participation in Achashverosh's feast.[13]

In the end, it was the merit of Mordechai's tearing his garments that resulted in Haman being hanged. In Heaven, Mordechai's ripping the cloth was considered symbolically as if he had torn up the decree.[14]

---

8. See *Targum Rishon; Pirkei d'Rav Eliezer; R' Shmuel di Uzidah.*

9. *Esther Rabbah* 8:1; *Bereishis Rabbah* 84:20 with *Yefei To'ar; D'na Pishra.* See *Yerushalmi Ta'anis* 3; *Taanis* 15a, 16a.

10. *Sha'arei Binah.*

11. *Esther Rabbah* 8:1; *Bereishis Rabbah* 84:20; *D'na Pishra; Bereishis* 44:13; see *Matnos Kehunah.*

12. *D'na Pishra.* The numerical value of the word *sak* (sack) is 400, the number of people who had come with Eisav to wage war against Yaakov (*Bereishis* 31:7). Mordechai's sackcloth would overpower the strength of Eisav with which his descendant Haman was now threatening the Jews (*Kav HaYashar*).

13. *R' Elisha Galico;* see his commentary for further allusions in the rending of garments, sackcloth-wearing and crying.

14. *Rokeach; Aggadas Esther; Midrash Panim Acheirim.*

Having prayed to the Almighty, and having donned sackcloth and ashes, which is another form of prayer, Mordechai went to enlist Esther's help in dealing with the crisis. He learned these priorities from Yaakov's actions when Eisav threatened him. First, Yaakov prayed, and only afterward did he seek ways to deal with Eisav.[15]

People gawked in amazement as Mordechai walked through the streets of Shushan in sackcloth and ashes. He approached the palace, but clad as he was, it would have been inappropriate to enter the gates, especially since the king had a superstitious fear of people in mourner's attire.[16] Mordechai urgently wanted to speak to Esther. First of all, he wanted to tell her about the decree. Secluded in her chambers and preoccupied with her preparations for Pesach, she had no inkling of what had happened. But he couldn't enter the palace in sackcloth, so he remained sitting outside the gates, hoping that word would reach her that he was there.[17]

It also crossed his mind that when the Jews of Shushan would see him sitting outside the palace gates, unable to enter, they would realize that their only hope was to pray to the Almighty. In other cities, where the Jews were not accustomed to relying on Mordechai, they had already come to the realization that they were in desperate need of prayer and repentance.[18]

---

15. *Aggadas Esther; Pirush Megillas Achashverosh; Yosef Lekach.*

16. *Esther* 4:2; *Akeidah; Rashi; Pirush Megillas Achashverosh; Menos HaLevi; Eshkol HaKofer.* Some suggest that the King's gates refer to the gates of Heaven. Mordechai would continue to mourn and cry until his prayers would break through the gates and be answered (*D'na Pishra; Megillas Sesarim*). When Yosef was mourning his father's death he also could not enter the palace; he could only communicate with Pharaoh indirectly (*Sechel Tov* to *Bereishis* 50:4; *Bereishis Rabbah* 100:4 with *Maharzu*).

17. *Koheles Rabbah* 8:5; *Yalkut Shimoni* 978; *Midrash Lekach Tov; Gra; Menos HaLevi; Malbim.* The commentaries disagree as to the date. Some say it was the night of 13 Nissan, while others hold that it was 14 Nissan; the difference of opinion centers on when the three-day fast began, 13 or 14 Nissan. See *Sh'eilos U'Teshuvos Radvaz* 1:284 and *Ya'aros Devash*, who maintains that 14 Nissan came out on Shabbos. See *Maharal* who explains the fasts according to both *Rashi* and the *Midrash*. Others suggest that since *chometz* represents the *yetzer hara* (evil inclination), Esther was symbolically demonstrating that she had repented of her sins and thus was worthy of being saved from the decree (*Chida*). Some hold that Mordechai was in the women's courtyard, actually inside the palace gates (*Melo HaOmer*).

18. *Melo HaOmer; Alshich.* Some suggest the opposite: The Jews blamed Mordechai for the decree since he had refused to bow to Haman. They also did not trust Esther, viewing her as having abandoned her brethren now that she was married to Achashverosh. Furthermore, since she was a relative of Mordechai's they partly blamed her as well (see *Me'am Loez*). Some suggest that in other locations, where the facts of the decree were unclear, they worried that they could be murdered at any time. In Shushan, where they knew the details, the Jews would have remained unconcerned until Adar, without Mordechai's guidance.

The bizarre spectacle of Mordechai sitting outside the palace gates in sackcloth and ashes had the intended effect. When Esther heard what was going on she trembled with fear and actually swooned; she may even have miscarried, according to some views.[19] She understood that something terrible must have happened and that Mordechai needed to reach her, but she had to be discreet. She couldn't quite go out in her royal attire to meet with him in the street. She could not even send him an explicit message to come to her in the palace. She had to be subtle.[20]

Esther decided to send Mordechai a change of clothes. The implied message, that she wanted him to come to her, was clear. Furthermore, he would not have to waste time going home to change in order to enter the palace. He would have a change of clothes in his hands right away. And no matter what else happened, at least he would not be arrested for behavior disrespectful to the king.[21]

The maid bearing the change of clothes found that a group of Jews had congregated around Mordechai, joining him in his lamentations. They also wore sackcloth in mourning.

She approached respectfully and cleared her throat. "Sir, her majesty sent these to you. She requests that you put them on immediately."

"Tell her majesty," Mordechai replied, "that I have taken it upon myself to wear sackcloth until the evil decree is rescinded."[22]

"Her majesty mentioned that you might be reluctant," said the maid. "If you insist on wearing the sackcloth, she said to ask if you would at least wear these elegant garments on top."[23]

Mordechai pointed to the men around him. "Do you see these men?" he said. "They are Jews. We are mourning and praying

---

19. *Megillah* 15a; *Targum Rishon*; *Pirkei d'Rav Eliezer*; *Esther Rabbah* 8:3; *Yalkut Shimoni* 1051; *R' Yosef ibn Nachmiash*; *Sechel Tov to Shemos* 15:14. There is much discussion regarding this *Midrash* and Esther's son Daryavesh. Some suggest that she could no longer bear children after this, but Daryavesh had already been born. Others suggest that she was still able to have children, and Daryavesh had not yet been born.

20. See *Pirush Megillas Achashverosh*; *Akeidah*; *Ohr Chadash*.

21. *Targum Sheni*; *Yedei Moshe*; *Menos HaLevi*; *Alshich*; *Maharal*; *Gra*. Others suggest that these were not royal garments but garments respectable enough for Mordechai to be permitted to enter the palace. Others suggest that they were intended for Mordechai to wear to see the king personally. (See *Menos HaLevi*; *Yishai Elokim*; *Akeidah*; *Megillas Sesarim*.) Some suggest that she sent Daniel (*Rokeach*). See *Sha'arei Binah*; *R' Shmuel di Uzidah*.

22. *Midrash Panim Acheirim*; *Aggadas Esther*; *D'na Pishra*; *Maharal*.

23. *Yosef Lekach*; *D'na Pishra*; *Melo HaOmer*; *Malbim*; *Ma'amar Mordechai*. Some suggest that she required he take off the sackcloth entirely, and come with his regular clothing torn in mourning (*Alshich*).

together. Should I accept your garments, I would be turning away from my brothers. Then an angel would place his hands on my head and declare, 'Just as this man did not share the sorrow of his community, so will he not share in its salvation.' So you see, I cannot accept the garments. Please take them back."[24]

When the maid reported back, Esther became frantic. What could have happened? She knew no one had died, because Mordechai would have accepted consolation. So what did happen?[25]

It must be a crisis facing the entire Jewish people, she thought. It must have something to do with that Amalekite prime minister, that evil Haman. But why would such a thing happen? Amalek only gains power over the Jewish people when they become lax in Torah. Had they transgressed all the *mitzvos* of the Torah? Was it because they had eaten at Achashverosh's feast? Or was it perhaps because they had bowed to Nevuchadnezzar's idols? Even though that had happened in the previous generation, perhaps the Almighty had waited for the Jewish people to repent, and when they didn't, He was punishing them for everything at once.[26]

How could she find out? How could she communicate with Mordechai? She would have to call on one of her staff, a courtier by the name of Hasach whom she used only for special missions.[27]

Hasach was none other than the prophet Daniel. In the account of the *Megillah*, he preferred Hasach to his own name, because Daniel and Haman have the same *gematria*, numerical value.[28] The name Hasach was particularly appropriate, because it means cut off.[29] Daniel consistently had his power shorn, or cut off. Under Nevuchadnezzar, he had been the chief royal advisor. Under Belshazzar, Darius and Cyrus, however, some of his powers had been removed and transferred to others.[30] Under Achashverosh, his

24. See *Aggadas Esther*; *Ta'anis* 11a; *R' Chaim Abulafia*.

25. *Ma'amar Mordechai*; *Melo HaOmer*; *Alshich*.

26. *Megillah* 15a; *Esther Rabbah* 8:4; *Rokeach*; *R' Elisha Galico*; *Alshich*; *Melo HaOmer*. See *Shemos* 17:1; *Sanhedrin* 106; *Megillah* 11a.

27. *Pirkei d'Rav Eliezer* 50.

28. *R' Yosef ibn Yachia*; *Menos HaLevi*. Others suggest that Esther had many officers from different nations serving her, and Daniel was the one representing the Jewish nation (*Melo HaOmer*). The name Hasach is discussed by the commentators; was it the name given after his demotion, or merely an alias?

29. *Megillah* 15a; *Esther Rabbah* 8:4; see *Bava Basra* 4a; *Maharsha*.

30. See *Daniel* 2:48, 5:29.

powers were even further reduced, and he had been attached primarily but not exclusively to the queen's staff; the king had anti-Jewish designs, and he sought to limit the powers of his Jewish advisors.[31] His name memorializes the injustice done to him. Others say that he still retained broad powers, as reflected by an alternate translation of Hasach as rendering a final decision.[32]

"Go to Mordechai," Esther told Hasach. "He is sitting near the palace gates in sackcloth and ashes. But be careful. No one must suspect that you are my messenger or that the meeting is planned. Since you are also an advisor to the king, people will not immediately think of me if you just happen to meet Mordechai by chance."[33]

As Hasach left the palace, he saw Mordechai sitting with his followers, but he gave them a wide berth. He went off on a long, circuitous tour of the city, stopping here and there, and glancing over his shoulder to see if he was under observation. Presently, he worked his way back to the palace, passing within earshot of Mordechai.[34]

"Perhaps you would like to take a walk to the market square," he said just loudly enough for Mordechai to hear. Then he continued walking through the city streets until he reached the market from a different direction.

The market was controlled chaos, the stench and the noise overwhelming. Farmers hawked their wares from overflowing stands. Old women waved squawking chickens over their heads, offering them for sale. Thieves bumped up against merchants and buyers and fled with their ill-gotten gains. Sad-eyed urchins begged for coins. Amidst this pandemonium, Mordechai in his sackcloth did not even draw a glance. Hasach sidled up to him. He picked up a melon, and as he was examining it, he spoke out of the side of his mouth.[35]

"Good morning, Mordechai," he said. "Esther sends her greetings. Do you have a message for her? I think we can speak safely

31. *Ma'amar Mordechai*; see *Ibn Ezra* who discusses whether this refers to Daniel.

32. *Midrash Megillah*; *Megillah* 15a; see *Ben Yehoyada*; *Me'am Loez*. Some say that, according to this view, it was not Daniel. See *D'na Pishra*; *Pirush Megillas Achashverosh*.

33. *Yosef Lekach*.

34. *Targum Rishon*; *Aggadas Esther*; *D'na Pishra*; *Yedei Moshe*; *Melo HaOmer*; *Maharal*; *Alshich*. Others suggest that they communicated through *ruach hakodesh* and did not actually speak (*Midrash Panim Acheirim*; see *Yalkut Shimon*). This was the place where they had gathered with the Jewish people to read from the Torah and spur them to repentance, and was thus safe due to its merit (*Menos HaLevi*).

35. *Alshich*; *Ma'amar Mordechai*; *R' Shmuel di Uzidah*; see *Yedei Moshe* for a different explanation of this.

here. The noisier the place, the less likely to be overheard. She fears that our people are in danger."

"Her fears are well founded. We are endangered by the descendant of *Karahu*." For security reasons, Mordechai did not want to say Haman's name. Instead, he alluded to him with a form of the word *karcha*, which appears in the Torah's account of Amalek. "Years ago, I had a dream about two serpents. I told Esther about it. Now I have discovered the identity of the serpents."[36]

"Karahu and you?"

"I'm afraid so. Eliyahu *HaNavi* told me."

"Why didn't you accept the garments Esther sent you?"

"Because the struggle will take place in the spiritual world," said Mordechai. "The sackcloth, which represents prayer, fortifies me there as armor fortifies a soldier on the battlefield."[37]

"Of course," said Hasach.

"Please tell Esther that she and I are responsible for Karahu, because our ancestor King Shaul spared King Agag. I also bear personal blame, because I refused to bow down to him. In any case, Esther is in a position to help her brethren. Her responsibility is very great."[38]

"I will tell her."

Mordechai handed Hasach a few scrolls. "Here, give these to Esther. They are copies of the decrees. Tell her to maintain top security, not to trust anyone. Anyone!"[39]

Hasach nodded. He glanced at the crowd around him and slipped the papers into his pocket.

"Tell Esther," Mordechai continued, "that the decree is not irreversible. It is based on lies and falsehood. She will be able to overturn it."[40] He went on to tell Hasach about the verses spoken by the schoolchildren and Haman's payment and Achashverosh's refund of the

---

36. *Esther Rabbah* 8:5; see *Midrash Rabbah* to *Devarim* 25:18; see *Torah Sheleimah*, pg. 383.

37. *Alshich*. Mordechai stressed that while the dream foretold destruction, it also held hope for redemption. He wanted to inform Esther that the punishment could be averted by prayer and repentance, as suggested in the dream.

38. *Targum Rishon; Megillas Sesarim; Midrash Lekach Tov; Eshkol HaKofer; R' Chaim Abulafia; Menos HaLevi.*

39. *Targum Sheni; Yosef Lekach; D'na Pishra; R' Shmuel di Uzidah; R' Yosef ibn Yachia;* see *Malbim; Megillas Sesarim.*

40. *R' Yosef ibn Yachia; R' Shmuel di Uzidah; Ma'amar Mordechai.* Some suggest that Mordechai based this on the fact that the king was ignorant of the decree's goal of wiping out the entire Jewish nation. Informing him that Haman had acted without his full knowledge would help convince him of Haman's personal interest in the decree (*R' Shmuel di Uzidah*).

money. "That is very good for us. Since there was no money given, the merit of the *shekalim* still stands. Prayer and repentance will help."[41]

"I will tell her all this. But how is she to overturn the decree? Do you have any instructions for her?"

"Yes, I do," said Mordechai. "Tell Esther that the time for dissembling is over. Her reign as queen now enters a new phase. No more of this secrecy about her national origin. Now it is time to tell the king she is Jewish and to use every weapon and subterfuge in her power to save her people. Until now, she has never gone to Achashverosh willingly but always in response to his summons. Now she must go to him of her own free will. She must plead for herself, because she too has been condemned to death. After she pleads for her own life in private, she can plead for her people even in public. No one would dare speak against the Jewish people once it is revealed that the queen herself is also Jewish. Will you remember to tell her all this?"[42]

"Rest assured, Mordechai," said Hasach. "I will tell her everything. But it will be a shock."

"It will and it won't," said Mordechai. "We knew something like this was coming. Despite all her efforts to avoid it, Esther was chosen queen. The Almighty was clearly placing her in the palace for a higher purpose. Now the time has come to use her position to save her people. I risked my life by wearing sackcloth. She must also be prepared to sacrifice her life, if that is what must happen."

"I will tell her. Do you have any words of encouragement for her to help through this terrible time?"

"Yes. Tell her to pray to the Almighty right before she goes to Achashverosh. If she pours out her heart, He will watch over her and guide her safely to success."[43]

---

41. See *Targum Rishon; Sha'arei Binah; Melo HaOmer; Yedei Moshe*. He pointed out the extent of Haman's wickedness: he wished to eliminate their merit by superceding the *shekalim* they had given so that he could succeed in destroying them.

42. *Midrash Lekach Tov; Gra; Yosef Lekach; Menos HaLevi; D'na Pishra; Yad HaMelech; Alshich.* Others suggest that Esther was not told to divulge her heritage to Achashverosh, but only to plead for the Jewish nation to be spared (*Midrash Panim Acheirim*).

43. *Menos HaLevi; R' Shmuel di Uzidah.*

Fasting and Prayer

16

When Esther finished reading the papers Hasach had given her, there were tears in her eyes. Hasach stood at a respectful distance, waiting for her reaction to his report.

"Oh, why did Mordechai have to antagonize Haman?" she said as she wrung her hands. "He didn't have to bow down, but he could have been nice to Haman. He could as a senior palace official have gotten a royal exemption from bowing."[1]

"I really couldn't say."

"Well, were you careful about security? Did anyone see you meeting with Mordechai?"

"I think I was successful. We met in the market, coming from different directions, and we didn't really talk face to face but rather out of the sides of our mouths. No one would have suspected we were conversing unless he was watching us intently." He paused. "Still, I get the uneasy feeling that we were observed. I've noticed a few furtive glances in my direction. Perhaps it means nothing. I certainly hope so."

"So do I," said Esther. "Be careful."

---

1. *Targum Rishon; Menos HaLevi; Kedushas Levi.*

"What shall I tell Mordechai? Are you prepared to reveal your identity to Achashverosh, as he wants you to do?"

"It is not as simple as Mordechai thinks," Esther replied. "True, he risked his life by appearing in mourners' garb in front of the palace, but that is not a security breach. He could have been arrested and put on trial. He would have had the opportunity to hire defense counsel. But to come to the king unbidden means instant death. When Belshazzar was assassinated, Darius decreed that no one might come unbidden to the king. Other countries have similar laws, instituted when Ehud assassinated King Eglon of Moav with a concealed weapon. You can't violate these laws. It would be a major breach of security.[2] Haman has really taken control of the king's schedule. He has added many provisions to the law, and he personally screens all the king's visitors. He wants to make sure no one reveals to the king that he had once sold himself to Mordechai, and he doesn't want anyone to advocate with the king for the Jews or the rebuilding of the *Beis HaMikdash*. Do you think he will let me set up an appointment? He hates me! Whenever he sees me, he remembers that if it hadn't been for me, he might have had his daughter sitting on the throne."[3]

"Is it certain death if you would come without a summons?"

"Not certain. If the king extends his golden rod, the visitor is spared. But who says he will extend it to me?[4] It's been thirty days since he's called for me. How do I know what his reaction would be if I suddenly appeared? Maybe he doesn't care for me anymore. Then I would really be in trouble if I came unbidden, and besides, if he doesn't care for me, it wouldn't do any good for me to argue for the people or even for myself."

"I hear the problem," said Hasach. "But Mordechai was quite firm."

'Look, the king has never let thirty days go by without calling me. He will probably call me any day, any minute. What's the point of going to him if he will call me anyway very soon? The decree is still eleven months away. Eleven months! Why is there such urgency? Why can't we wait a few days just to be on the safe side?[5] In any

---

2. *Aggadas Esther; Menos HaLevi; Akeidah.* Haman had reinstituted this law when he advocated punishing Vashti for rebelling against the King.

3. *Targum; Rokeach; Targum Rishon; Menos HaLevi.*

4. *Targum Rishon, Pirush Megillas Achashverosh.*

5. *R' Elisha Galico; Maharal; Sha'arei Binah; Targum Sheni; Megillas Sesarim; Gra; Yosef Lekach; D'na Pishra; Yishai Elokim.* Even after 7 days' separation a man usually venerates his wife, so Achashverosh was sure to call for her some time soon (see *Tzofnas Pane'ach* to *Niddah* 31b). According to *Rokeach*, this discussion refers not to Achashverosh but the King of Kings, Hashem, and Esther's place in the World to Come. The *Shechinah* (Divine Presence) had left Esther on the day of the decree and Esther was concerned that this signified Heaven's approval of the decree. See *Tzofnas Pane'ach; Chasam Sofer.*

case, he will be more favorably disposed if he calls for me than if I come unbidden. Don't forget, I have to ask for myself and for the people. We need the king to be in a perfect frame of mind. If I go now, he may just spare me but not the people."[6]

"Perhaps it would be an idea to send a message to the king," said Hasach, "asking for permission to see him."

"It's a big risk. If he sees me he may warm up to me, but if he gets a message, he may just say no. Then if I will have no options left. He won't call me. And I go without permission, I will surely be executed, just as Vashti was executed for breaking the law. Then what good would I be to the people?"[7]

"So what shall I tell Mordechai?"

"Tell him that the time is not yet ripe. We cannot rely on miracles. The opportunity will come soon, and in the meantime, the people should concentrate on prayer and repentance."[8]

"I don't think Mordechai will be happy with this reply," said Hasach.

"I know," said Esther. "I don't mean to disobey him. But I must speak my mind. Maybe he will come around to my way of thinking."

"Perhaps."

"Please give him my message. One more thing. Tell him to please, please stay out of Haman's way. The tensions are so high, we don't want them to get any worse."[9]

"If he is near the palace gates I will," said Hasach. "But if he has gone I will have to send it with someone else. I am on duty tonight, and I must stay near the palace."

"Thank you, Hasach."

Mordechai, assuming that Esther would follow his instructions without question, was nowhere to be seen when Hasach emerged from the palace. He returned to Esther to make arrangements for someone else to deliver the message. The most he could do was escort the messenger to Mordechai's house, but he would have to leave immediately to avoid being absent from the palace for too long. He would walk ahead with the messenger following a discreet distance behind.[10]

---

6. *Gra; R' Elisha Galico; Maharal.*

7. *Yedei Moshe; Malbim.*

8. *R' Elisha Galico.*

9. *Menos HaLevi; R' Elisha Galico; D'na Pishra.*

10. *Iyun Yaakov; Ben Yehoyada; Megillah* 15a with *Rashi.* Others suggest that Esther was concerned lest Hasach be caught, and sent another messenger instead (*Malbim*). See *Maharasha; Targum Rishon.*Others posit that Esther's maidens overheard her conversation with Hasach and related her thoughts on the matter to Mordechai (*Yad HaMelech*).

As Hasach strode through the palace gates, he heard the thunder of hooves, and he looked up. Haman was approaching on horseback, escorted by his retinue of retainers. Their eyes locked for an instant, and Haman pulled up sharply. Something had clicked in his cunning mind. Earlier, he had heard suspicious reports about Hasach wandering through the city and spending a lot of time in the farmer's market, and now he was off on some nocturnal adventure. It could only mean one thing. He was carrying messages between Mordechai and Esther. They were plotting against him. This was no time for niceties but for action.

Haman struck at his horse's flanks with his riding crop and charged straight at Hasach. At the last moment, the horse reared up and struck Hasach with its flying hoof and killed him. Haman sneered at the body sprawled on the ground and rode off.[11]

Despite Hasach's tragic death, Esther's message did get through to Mordechai. It may have come to him in the form of a letter from Esther. The angels Gavriel and Michael may have delivered it. Or perhaps it was communicated to him through divine inspiration.[12]

Mordechai responded to the message with sharp words of rebuke. "Do not be so concerned about your personal safety. There are no guarantees for you even if you do not go to the king. Are you so sure that you are secure in your position? Vashti thought she was secure, and look what happened to her. Do not think you are safe in the palace. Belshazzar thought so, too, and he was assassinated. Do not think you are safe because you did not sin at the feast of Achashverosh. It makes no difference. If the Jewish people perish, you will perish along with them.[13]

"Esther, providence brought you to this unlikely station for the sole purpose of rectifying the sin of our ancestor Shaul in sparing Agag's life. Now is the time for you to speak up on behalf of our people. There is no time to waste. The month of Nissan is a time of redemption. We must seize this opportunity.[14]

---

11. *Pirkei d'Rav Eliezer 50 with Radal; Midrash Abba Gorion; Targum Rishon; Yalkut Shimoni; Menos HaLevi; R' Avigdor Kohen Tzedek.* According to this view it is questionable whether Hasach was another name for Daniel. Some suggest that Daniel continued to prophesy after this period of time, and thus Hasach was a different person.

12. *Targum Rishon; Targum Sheni; R' Yosef ibn Yachia; Rokeach; Yalkut Shimoni; Midrash Panim Acheirim; Minchas Yehudah. Pirkei d'Rav Eliezer* writes that Esther herself went to speak to Mordechai. *Radal* has difficulty with this view; how could she leave the concealment of the palace to speak with Mordechai in public?

13. See *Rashi; R' Yosef ibn Nachmiash; Midrash Lekach Tov; R' Shmuel di Uzidah; D'na Pishra.* Some suggest that Mordechai wanted Esther to go to Achashverosh now, when she was still ill from the shock of the edict, so Achashverosh would not make any advances (*Ya'aros Devash*).

14. *Targum Sheni; R' Chaim Abulafia; Megillas Sesarim; Menos HaLevi; Maharal;* see *Malbim.*

"Esther, if you remain silent now out of fear for your life, you will lose your share in the world to come. Your silence will be counted as an endorsement of the evil decree, and the sin of our ancestor will be forever unforgiven.

"Don't think you have time to tarry. You must speak to the king while the decree is still fresh in his mind, before it settles in as an accepted fact. You have to nip this decree in the bud. Besides, every day the decree remains in force there is the danger of some Jews abandoning the Torah and trying to pass as gentiles. Do you want the responsibility for this?[15]

"If you have other concerns, let me address those as well. If you are afraid the Jews will pin their hopes on you and pray less, all you have to do is be discreet and private. No one has to know about your mission. You might wonder how you may put yourself in danger when you are not assured that your mission will be successful. You might also wonder how it is permitted for you willingly submit yourself to the king. None of these issues come into consideration when the safety of the whole people is at stake. If there is any chance of success, you must make the attempt. Besides, if you should be killed, that itself may save the Jewish people. There is a royal custom in Persia as well as many other countries that the death of a member of the royal family is taken as an ill omen and then evil decrees are rescinded.[16]

"No, Esther, there is no way out for you. You are there for a purpose and you must fulfill it. Believe me, if you don't, the Almighty will find another way to send His salvation to the Jewish people, but you and your family will perish."[17]

---

15. See *Targum Sheni; R' Yosef ibn Nachmiash; Rokeach; R' Chaim Abulafia; Gra; Menos HaLevi; Esther Rabbah* 8:6; *D'na Pishra; Maharal; Yosef Lekach; R' Elisha Galico; Yishai Elokim; Me'am Loez.*

16. *R' Chaim Abulafia, Nachal Eshkol; Gra; Yosef Lekach; Yedei Moshe;* see *Rambam* (*Hilchos Yesodei HaTorah* 5:5); *Shabbos* 4a. The halachic ramifications are discussed at length by the Gemara and commentaries. They have been overly simplified in the narrative, and no halachic conclusions may be reached from our discussion.

17. *Targum Rishon; Rokeach.* It is noteworthy that Mordechai did not say that Hashem would save them some other way, but *revach v'hatzalah ya'amod laYehudim mimakom acher,* relief and deliverance will come to the Jews from some other place. The word *mimakom* is generally explained as an allusion to Hashem, Who is called *HaMakom,* a reference to His Omnipresence. Thus Mordechai was telling Esther that Hashem had many messengers at His disposal, and if she refused to fulfill the mission, someone else would be sent instead. Mordechai was careful not to use Hashem's Name openly in the *Megillah,* since he knew that it would be recorded in the Persian-Medean chronicles (*Esther* 10:2) and he feared that they would replace His Name with those of their idols. Therefore he referred to Him in a way that would not lend itself to such revision. See *Taz, Orach Chaim* 364, *S'if Katan* 11; *Midrash Lekach Tov; Pirush Megillas Achashverosh; Midrash HaGadol; Minchas Yehudah; R' Yosef ibn Nachmiash.*

When Esther received Mordechai's message, she was taken aback. Mordechai had misunderstood her. She had never been overly concerned with her own safety to the detriment of her mission. Rather, she had wondered if there might be a better way and time to approach the king.[18] Nevertheless, she did not respond to Mordechai with excuses, recriminations or a defense of her motives. In her response, which she sent with the angels Gavriel and Michael, she accepted Mordechai's rebuke with grace and reassured him that she was ready to do exactly as he instructed. And she asked that he assemble the Jews of Shushan to hear the message she would soon send to them.

Her purpose in calling for this assembly was threefold. First, she hoped the assembly would disprove Haman's accusation that the Jews were scattered and dispersed. Second, she hoped Achashverosh would suspect a revolt was brewing and rescind the decree. But most important, she knew that to gain divine favor the people needed to unite in peace, harmony and friendship. She hoped the assembly would set them on that road.[19]

As for herself, she realized with a sad heart that she would be taking a step from which there was no return. By submitting to the king of her own free will, even though he had not called for her, she could never return to Mordechai as his wife. She shuddered at the thought. But she consoled herself that she was doing this for the people and that her own reward in the world to come would compensate for her suffering in this world.[20]

The message Esther wanted Mordechai to deliver to the people of Shushan was a call to three days and three nights of fasting. Everyone, men, women, children, were to fast, even pregnant and nursing mothers. The fast was to be known in her name — the Fast of Esther — to ensure that no one would interfere.

---

18. See *Alshich; Menos HaLevi; R' Elisha Galico; Midrash Panim Acheirim.*

19. *Tana d'vei Eliyahu* 1; *Yedei Moshe; Nachal Eidah; Chomas Anach; Menos HaLevi.* Unity promotes peace, the symbol of Yaakov. Only through this can the divisiveness, *pirud,* of Eisav be overcome. The numerical equivalent of the work *k'nos,* gather, is 136, the same as *kol,* voice. Esther wanted the voice of Yaakov to overpower the *pirud* of Eisav (*Nachal Eshkol; Kisei David*).

20. See *Megillah* 15a with *Rashi; Targum Sheni; Midrash Panim Acheirim; Pirush Megillas Achashverosh; Rabbeinu Bachyei; Yedei Moshe; R' Elisha Galico.* Some suggest that Esther was also concerned about losing her share in the World to Come (*Pirush Megillos Achashverosh*). There is some discussion about whether Mordechai's divorcing Esther would have made her staying with Achashverosh less sinful (see *Tosafos, Megillah* 15a, *Menos HaLevi, Ya'aros Devash*). See also *Ben Yehoyada* and *Nachal Eshkol* who treat this issue in other ways.

A three-day and night fast is quite long, and only those who were physically capable did so. The others broke their fast shortly before sundown, ate a light meal and continued the fast after nightfall.[21] Others suggest that they only fasted during the days and spent the nights in prayer and weeping, giving them the status of fast periods as well.[22]

The burden of the fast fell particularly on the people of Shushan. They had sinned at Achashverosh's feast, and they now had to fast to atone for it. The fast, therefore, did not include other customary fast day restrictions, such as washing or wearing leather shoes. Only eating and drinking were forbidden to highlight the connection of the fast day to their eating and drinking at Achashverosh's feast.[23]

Esther limited the fast to three days, in emulation of the ways of Hashem, who does not allow suffering and distress to continue for more than three days.[24] The three days and nights were also significant. They were to counteract Haman's decree, which had mentioned three devastations — to destroy, to kill and to eradicate.[25] Esther personally felt she had to atone for the three cardinal sins: the collective sin of the Jewish people for bowing to Nevuchadnezzar's idols; her guilt, albeit under duress, of being with the king; and what she perceived as her inadvertent cause of Hasach's death. The three days and the three nights were also meant to atone for the six days the Jews had spent at the feast.[26]

---

21. *Midrash Tehillim* 22; *Yevamos* 121b; see *Ran (Rosh Hashanah,* end of ch. 1*); Tosefta Ta'anis* 1:5; *Sha'arei Binah; Pirush Megillas Achashverosh; R' Elisha Galico; Tosafos.* The three-day fast is widely discussed by the commentators. *Maharal* explains that it was not for three full days, but only for part of each day.

22. *Menos HaLevi; Akeidah; Eshkol HaKofer.* Others suggest that the three days of fasting were not consecutive, but on Monday, Thursday and the following Monday, like *Bahab* (see *Teshuvas Rivash* 416), which was instituted in the time of Iyov. This raises other questions: according to this view the Jews did not fast on *yom tom;* furthermore, Haman's demise would have occurred before the series of fasts was completed.

23. *Midrash Panim Acheirim; Midrash Lekach Tov; Yalkut Shimoni; Midrash Tehillim* 22:5; *Rokeach; Sha'arei Binah; Yosef Lekach.*

This seems to exclude communities outside Shushan from fasting. Others are of the opinion that the people in other places fasted as soon as they received Mordechai's letter. Others suggest that any outsiders then living in Shushan fasted together with the locals. See *Yosef Lekach; Gra. Sefas Yam* points out that the first letters of *lech k'nos es kol haYehudim* (go gather all the Jews) can be rearranged to spell *k'achlah* (like eating); the fast was in atonement for their having eaten at Achashverosh's feast and thus was "like eating." Other suggest that the fast, like Yom Kippur, restricted all five areas of pleasure; see *R' Shmuel di Uzidah.*

24. *Midrash Tehillim; Esther Rabbah* 9:2; *Yosef Lekach.*

25. *Rokeach.*

26. *Ya'aros Devash; Kisei David; Shabbos* 149b; *Menos HaLevi; Rokeach.*

The number three also had significance in that it encompassed the three types of Jews — the righteous, of whom Mordechai was the greatest, the eighteen thousand wicked people who participated in the revelries at the feast to the fullest extent, and those in between who came to the king's feast but left early.[27]

The total number of hours of the three-day fast was 72, the numerical value of *chessed*, kindness, adding yet another dimension to this desperate call for Hashem's mercy and kindness.[28] If we also count the first hour before sundown, the number of hours is 73, the numerical value of *yayin*, wine, when the three letters of the word are also included. This was an allusion to the gentile wine the Jews drank at Achashverosh's feast.[29]

All these events took place on 13 Nissan, the day on which the death decree was published. Late on that very same day, Mordechai had already contacted Esther and she had already instituted the fast day. There is question, therefore, as to whether 13 Nissan was the first day of the three-day fast (in which case it did not last a full seventy-two hours), followed by 14 and 15 Nissan, or if the fast began on 14 Nissan and stretched through 15 and 16 Nissan.[30]

At first, Mordechai objected to Esther's plan for the three-day fast, since it would prevent the people from the *mitzvos* of Pesach, *matzah*, *maror* and the four cups of wine. Esther, however, insisted that it was better to forfeit one Pesach in order to ensure that the Jewish people would survive to celebrate Pesach many times in the future. The very existence of the Jewish people was at stake. In fact, the necessity of foregoing not only physical pleasures but also the *mitzvos* of Pesach would

---

27. See *Menos HaLevi*.

28. *Keren Yehoshua* in sefer *Sefas Yam*. 72 also represents the 72-letter name of Hashem. This was a signal of prayer and hope that Hashem would redeem them from their plight (*R' Elisha Galico*).

29. *D'na Pishra;* see *Maharal* 10:11 who says the fast of Esther lasted 70 hours; she ended it two hours early.

30. *Esther Rabbah* 8:7; *Rashi; Midrash Panim Acheirim; Yalkut Shimoni.* See *Rashash; Anaf Yosef; Pirkei d'Rav Eliezer* 50; see *Radal.* Some suggest that Mordechai did not fast because it was *erev* Pesach, while others who received the letters after Pesach fasted even after Haman had been hanged (*Melo HaOmer*). According to the opinion that they fasted from 14 Nissan, when Esther went to Achashverosh on the third day (*Esther* 5:1), it was three days from when the letters had been written, not from the beginning of the fast. It is a matter of debate whether Esther ate at the parties with the King and Haman. Many suggest that at the first party she did not, but at the second one which was at the end of the day, she did. Haman was killed on 16 Nissan at night after the party. See *Eitz Yosef; Sifsei Chachamim; Radal* to *Pirkei d'Rav Eliezer; Rambam.* See *Menos HaLevi,* who explains the various possibilities. *Alshich* comments that it is difficult to suggest that the decree became known on 12 Nissan when it had only just been declared. He therefore suggests that the fast began the next day, on 13 Nissan. See *Shelah* on his view when the fast began and when Haman was killed.

make the Jews painfully aware of the devastation of sin. Esther was confident and took the responsibility for the decision upon herself.[31]

According to some views, the Jewish people did not fulfill the *mitzvos* of Pesach that year, which was a violation of the Torah to some degree. Only for Mordechai himself was there no violation at all, because he was fasting a *taanis chalom*, a fast in response to an ominous dream, which is permitted even on Shabbos.[32] According to other views, the Jewish people were still able to fulfill the *mitzvos* of Pesach on the most basic level by eating small portions of *matzah* and *maror*. An olive-sized portion is sufficient for fulfillment of the *mitzvah*, while only a date-sized portion, which is larger, is considered a violation of the fast.[33]

After writing to Mordechai to institute the three-day fast, Esther remarked that she and her maidens would also be fasting in the palace. She would take off her royal garments and crown and don sackcloth and ashes in their place.[34] These were the Jewish maidens who had attended Vashti and suffered persecution at her hands. Now they were attending the Jewish queen. According to other views, these were gentile maidens who fasted along with their mistress out of sympathy. In fact, they may not even have known that Esther was Jewish, only that she was fasting because she intended to go the king unbidden.[35]

Esther asked Mordechai that the Jewish people should "fast for me." She was going to the king of her own free will, which was a violation of the Torah. She was going before the king without being summoned, which was a violation of Persian law. And by joining in the fast, she would be coming to the king looking drawn and haggard, a further violation of Persian law. She knew she was in mortal danger.[36]

Having received Esther's final instructions, Mordechai immediately set out to implement them. He crossed the stream that separated the government center from the residential areas in which the Jews lived.[37]

---

31. See *Pirkei d'Rav Eliezer; Megillah* 15a; *Targum Rishon; Midrash Panim Acheirim; Gra; R' Elisha Galico; R' Shmuel di Uzidah; Meilitz Yosher.*

32. See *Megillah* 15a; *Sifsei Chachamim; Gra; R' Yosef ibn Nachmiash.*

33. See *Aruch L'Ner.*

34. *Targum Sheni; Esther Rabbah* 8:7.

35. See *R' Yosef ibn Nachmiash; Rambam; R' Shmuel di Uzidah; Maharal.* Others suggest that these maidens had been converted by Esther (*R' Yosef ibn Yachia*).

36. *R' Yosef ibn Yachia; Yishai Elokim; Megillas Sesarim; Yosef Lekach.*

37. *Megillah* 15a with *Rashi; Menachem Meishiv Nefesh; Yishai Elokim.* See *Maharsha.* Some suggest that this stream, which separated Shushan *HaBirah* from Shushan, was called Ulay. This was the stream in Mordechai's dream which separated the two battling serpents (see *Ya'aros Devash; Daniel* 8:2; *R' Saadiah Gaon*).

Dressed in sackcloth and ashes, he walked up and down the streets and alleyways, knocking on the doors of all the synagogues, calling together Jews wherever he could find them.[38]

Many of the people were shocked to see Mordechai in sackcloth and ashes. "Why are you dressed this way?" they wanted to know.

"Haven't you heard?" he replied. "Haman has engineered a terrible decree against the Jews. The letters have already gone out to every corner of the empire. We are all to be killed!"

His words were greeted with stunned disbelief and abject wailing. There had been sporadic attacks on the Jews for a good part of the day. Now everyone understood what had triggered them.

"What will we do, Mordechai?" they pleaded.

"We can only turn to the Almighty," he replied. "Esther has established a three-day fast. We will fast, we will pray, and we will weep, and Hashem will hear us and take pity on us. That is what we will do."

Tens of thousands of people gathered in the square, even the children. Twelve thousand young *Kohanim* lined up behind Mordechai, each holding a *shofar* in his right and a Torah in his left. Mordechai brought out a Torah, which was also covered in sackcloth and ashes, and read to the people from the *Tochachah* (*Devarim* 30:2) which says that when the Jewish people encounter suffering and distress, "you will return to Hashem your Lord and obey Him."

After the reading, Mordechai stood up to address the people. "Hashem, it was in Your honor that I did not bow down to Haman," he said. "Please accept my deed as a *kiddush Hashem*, a sanctification of Your Name."

Then he turned to the people and began, "You, who are Hashem's beloved and precious nation, are in danger. What must you do? Let us take a look at Nineveh, the capital of the Assyrian Empire, which had incurred the wrath of Hashem by its corrupt practices. Hashem sent the prophet Yonah to warn the city that He planned to destroy it. How did they react? The king of Nineveh stepped off his throne, removed his crown and donned sackcloth and ashes. He went through the city urging the people to fast and repent. They heeded his call, and Hashem forgave them and spared the city. We must do the same, my dear brothers and sisters. Each of us feels the pain, because we have all been condemned to die. With every passing day, with every passing hour, the pain intensifies, because the day of execution draws near. We must marshal our strength together as one. We must repent and pray, and even though we do not have a

---

38. *R' Yosef ibn Yachia; Rokeach; Maharal; Alshich; Selichos* for Ta'anis Esther; *Krovetz L'Purim; Malbim.*

Beis HaMikdash in which to bring sacrifices, Hashem will accept our prayers and forgive us."[39]

Word of the decree and Mordechai's exhortation spread beyond Shushan to wherever there were Jews. Everywhere, Jews went into mourning and wept. Many donned sackcloth and ashes, and all fasted and said lamentations.[40] According to some views, only the elders and community leaders wore sackcloth and ashes, while according to others everyone but the youth did. The young men were more inclined to respond by fighting against Haman.[41] These six acts — mourning, weeping, sackcloth, ashes, fasting and lamentations — were meant to atone for the six days the Jewish people sinned at Achashverosh's feast.[42]

In the meantime, the Jews of Shushan were already coming under attack by overeager gentiles. Even those who did not participate shut their doors to the persecuted Jews, refusing to harbor a Jewish fugitive from street violence. If they were caught harboring a Jew in their home they too would be killed together with the Jews. Worst among the gentiles were Haman's children who rode through the streets of the Jewish neighborhoods, laughing and taunting, "Soon all of you will executed and hanged."[43]

The Jews prayed to Hashem to take pity on them for the sake of the Torah. Who would study it if the Jews were destroyed? Hashem had saved the Jews of Egypt, when only the males were condemned to death and even those were accorded the dignity of burial. Surely, He should save the Jewish people now from the decree that they all should die and that their bodies should be thrown to the dogs. The gentiles were not interested in the money of the Jews. They just wanted their lives. There was no way out, other than miraculous divine intervention. They pleaded with Hashem to save them, just as He had saved Chananiah, Mishael and Azariah from the fiery furnace. Hearing the heartrending prayers of the Jews, the angels in Heaven joined in their supplication, begging Hashem to save the Jews from extinction.[44]

39. *Targum Sheni; Esther Rabbah* 8:7; *Yad HaMelech; Yishai Elokim; Midrash Abba Gorion; Menos HaLevi; Malbim.*

40. *Ibn Ezra; Midrash Panim Acheirim; Aggadas Esther; Targum Sheni; Rokeach; Yosef Lekach; Rashi; R' Elisha Galico; Malbim.*

41. See *Targum Rishon; R' Saadiah Gaon; Gra; Yosef Lekach; Menos HaLevi; Rokeach.*

42. *Ya'aros Devash; Sha'arei Binah.* According to this opinion the Jews did not attend the feast on the seventh day, which was either Shabbos or Yom Kippur, as mentioned earlier.

43. *Targum Sheni; Yad HaMelech;* see *Rashi* to *Megillah* 10b; *Midrash Tehillim* 22:21; *Yalkut Shimoni* 686.

44. *Midrash Tehillim* 22:6, 17; *Targum Sheni.* See *D'na Pishra; Rokeach* ch. 3; *Midrash Lekach Tov.*

The situation was desperate. Mordechai got up to pray in front of the assembled Jews. He could have prayed silently, as Chanah had done in the times of Eli, the *Kohein Gadol,* but he was going up against the ancestral power of loud weeping. When Yaakov had taken his father's blessings, Eisav had reacted with loud, pitiful cries. Now, his descendant Haman was drawing on the merit of those tears to attack the descendants of Yaakov. Therefore, Mordechai cried out to Hashem with loud weeping and prayers in front of all the people. He would be the messenger of the people to remove the evil decree. He also wanted to make a public display to show other nationalities residing in Shushan that everyone was endangered by such policies. Today, it was the Jews, tomorrow it would be someone else.[45]

"Hashem, how bitter it is for us that Haman has secured the king's ring," he cried out. "Achashverosh may have hated us even more than Haman does, but he would never have condemned a people to death. But he gave his ring to Haman and gave him permission to do as he pleases. Hashem, although I know it is not so, it appears to the world that the earthly king has won out against the Heavenly King. Please show them this is not so. Hashem, You promised our forefather that we would be as numerous as the stars in the sky, and now we are being led like sheep to the slaughter. Not a few of us, not many of us, but all of us! We have never faced such an evil decree.[46]

"Master of the Universe, I know that my refusal to bow down to Haman was the straw that broke the camel's back, but I did it to honor You. As You commanded, I will bow down to no other god. Hashem, do not abandon us. Do not let the nations of the world say that the God of the Jews has no power. Rescue us from Haman's decree, and let him fall into the web he himself has spun. Sanctify Your Name before all the nations of the world. Show them You have

---

45. *Bereishis Rabbah* 67:4; *Menos HaLevi; Yalkut Shimoni; Midrash Panim Acheirim; R' Shmuel di Uzidah;* see *Esther Rabbah* 8:1; *Malbim. Alshich* writes that Mordechai did not make a public display so that Haman would not find out that the Jews knew of the decree. Haman had striven to conceal the extent of the decree from the Jews.

46. *Megillah* 15a with *Rashi, Maharsha, Rif, Iyun Yaakov, Ben Yehoyada; Midrash Lekach Tov; Menos HaLevi; Aggadas Esther; Targum Sheni.* Some suggest that Haman had designs on the throne. He still bore great animosity towards Achashverosh for not choosing his daughter to be queen. Haman concluded that Achashverosh would be punished by Hashem for the destruction of the Jews; as King, he should bear the ultimate responsibility for the deed. As highest-ranking minister and possessor of the King's ring, Haman assumed that he would succeed Achashverosh to the throne.

The holiday of Purim will never be abolished. Unlike Pesach, which commemorates the redemption from Egypt where a decree had been only against the Jewish males, Purim celebrates the rescue of the entire nation. See *Megillas Ta'anis; Tikunei Zohar* 21; *Yerushalmi Ta'anis* 2:12; *Sefer Chassidim* 369; *Likutei Gra; Purim.*

not forgotten the oath You made to our forefathers that You would only be sent into exile to awaken us to repentance. Show the nations of the world that we are Your beloved nation, the one that stands apart from all the others to love You and sanctify Your Name."[47]

The people listened to Mordechai's prayers and were inspired to continue praying on their own.

In the palace, Esther offered her own special prayers to Hashem. "Take pity on Your maiden who was left orphaned without a father or a mother, who wanders from window to window like a beggar girl going from door to door. Hashem, please rescue Your flock from their enemies. Rescue us from that menacing dog. Haven't I fulfilled the three *mitzvos* of a Jewish woman, *nidah*, *challah* and candle lighting? Then why have You forsaken me? Please rescue me. I am desperate. You heeded the prayers of the Jews in Egypt when only the males were condemned to death. Surely, You must heed our prayers now when we are all to die. Do not forsake us. Even if we do not have the merit, rescue us out of Your boundless kindness alone."[48]

The pleading of the Torah, the angels, the stars in the heavens all could not break Haman's evil decree. Only the prayers of the Jewish people were able to accomplish this. They had bowed down to Nevuchadnezzar's idols, but in their hearts they had not accepted them as gods. They had done it out of fear, although this too was a sin. Measure for measure, Hashem made it appear externally that He had abandoned them to Haman's evil decree, but in His heart, so to speak, He still loved them. When they repented, He forgave them.[49]

---

47. *Otzar Midrashim,* p. 64, cited in *Torah Sheleimah,* pg. 384; *Gra; Yosef Lekach.* Mordechai felt a degree of personal responsibility for the decree. He felt perhaps he was partially to blame for acting beyond the letter of the law in not bowing to Haman even when he wore no idol. He had even gone further and shown disrespect when Haman had come to talk to him. Although in principle he was correct, Mordechai reflected that, considering the danger pending over the Jews, perhaps he should have acted differently.

48. *Esther Rabbah* 8:7; *Yalkut Tehillim* 685; see *Megillah* 15b; *Aggadas Esther.* See *Kli Chemdah.*

49. *Megillah* 12a; *Ohr Yechezkel* 3:195; see *Toldos Am Olam* for a further description.

The Golden Rod

17

On 15 Nissan, three days after Haman's decree was issued, Mordechai sent word to Esther that it was time to approach Achashverosh. It was the first day of Pesach, a time of salvation for the Jewish people. It was a day of miracles, and right now, the Jewish people needed miracles.[1]

Esther had been fasting for two days, and it showed on her. She was weak and drawn. Her complexion had lost its luster, and her greenish tinge was unusually strong.[2] But Hashem clothed her in a divine radiance that made her glow with beauty. She assumed an ethereal grace, like an angel, a pure spirit unencumbered by a body similar to what her grandfather King Shaul experienced.[3] It was a heav-

---

1. *Ya'aros Devash.* See *R' Yosef ibn Nachmiash; Midrash Lekach Tov; Menos HaLevi* for an explanation of two opinions regarding this point. See *Rashi* to *Megillah* 16a. Others suggest that it was the third day of fasting, which had begun on 13 Nissan. See *Esther Rabbah* 9:2; *Pirkei d'Rav Eliezer;* see *Pirush Megillas Achashverosh; Targum Rishon;* who say it was Chol HaMoed, the third day of Pesach.
2. *Eshkol HaKofer.*
3. *Bereishis Rabbah* 56:1; *Matnos Kehunah; Yefei To'ar; Zohar* 169; *Gra.*

enly reward for maintaining her silence through all the years she had lived in the palace, and it was also a testimony to the virtue and chastity of her conduct.[4]

Although she had been wearing sackcloth and ashes along with the rest of the Jewish people, out of respect to the king, she now donned majestic royal garb. However, because she was still observing the fast day, she used just the barest touch of makeup.[5] Her gown was of the finest woven silk, with gold sequins, adorned with jewels and pearls, and a long diamond-studded train. She wore gold sandals and a golden crown on her head in the place from which she had just removed the ashes.[6]

The walk from her chambers to the king's throne room was in a straight line that passed through seven chambers, each ten cubits long. The chambers, each of which had its own contingent of guards, were separated from each other by courtyards.[7]

Esther set out with a firm stride, accompanied by three maidens, one on either side to support her and one behind to carry the train. Bolstered by the divine spirit, she passed through the first three chambers with such poise and confidence that it never occurred to the guards to ask if she had been summoned or not. But just as she was about to enter the fourth chamber, she suddenly felt disoriented. The divine spirit had departed from her![8]

What could the reason be? She looked around and saw to her dismay that she was in a shrine full of idols. The divine spirit had not entered this corrupted place, leaving her alone and unprotected.[9] Esther also understood it as a message that the Jewish people were being judged for bowing to Nevuchadnezzar's idols.[10]

Swooning with weakness, she cried out, "Hashem, Hashem, why have You forsaken me? I have not come here of my own volition. Am I to be punished for this? Are You judging me for going to Achashverosh of my own free will? You know I have no choice in

4. *Megillah* 14b, 15a; *Zohar* 3:183b, ibid. 275b.

5. *Yosef Lekach; Targum Sheni* with *Rashi; R' Saadiah Gaon.* It is suggested that Esther changed only after she had neared the king, in the inner chambers. She had waited to remove her sackcloth and ashes until the last possible moment..

6. *Esther Rabbah* 9:1. *Targum Sheni; Rokeach; Menos HaLevi.*

7. *R' Yosef ibn Yachia; Aggadas Esther.*

8. *Megillah* 15b; *Esther Rabbah* 9:1; *Midrash Lekach Tov;* see *Ibn Ezra; R' Elisha Galico; Maharsha; R' Shmuel di Uzidah.*

9. *Megillah* 15b.

10. *Sifsei Chachamim* to *Megillah* 15b.

the matter. And if I am guilty, then why did the divine spirit accompany me until here? Am I guilty for speaking disrespectfully of my husband, calling him a dog? Is it demeaning to You that You should be victorious over a mere dog? Very well, I accept the blame. From now on, I will call him a powerful lion. Am I guilty for praying to be saved from Haman but not to be saved from Achashverosh? I accept blame for that as well, and I will pray to be saved from him, too."[11]

Standing motionless in the courtyard on the threshold of the fourth chamber, weak and haggard, her lips moving in prayer, Esther no longer presented the façade of the confident queen. It dawned on the guards that she was approaching the king without having been summoned, that she was liable to be executed on the spot for her breach of security.[12]

"Corporal, should we cut her down?" a guard asked his squad leader.

"That's right," said a second guard. "Let's do it! I get her rings."

"Not so fast, laddies," said the corporal. "I will decide who gets what. The gown, of course, is mine."

"But that has most of the jewels," protested a guard.

"Indeed it does," he replied.

The stamp of boots heralded the arrival of Haman's hand-picked palace guard. "Wait a minute," the leader declared. "You men shouldn't be in such a rush to divide up the booty. We have just as much right to it as you do."

"So what do you suggest we do?" asked the corporal.

"We will cast lots right here and now."[13]

Esther heard all this, and she blanched. "Hashem, don't abandon Your orphaned daughter," she cried out. "This is the third day of the decree, and I have with me a number of auspicious threes. I call out to You in the merit of the three forefathers, the three parts of *Tanach*; *Torah*, *Neviim* and *Kesuvim*, Avraham's three-day journey to the *Akeidah*.[14] Hashem, Sarah was detained in Pharaoh's palace for one night, and You worked miracles for her.

---

11. *Maharsha to Megillah* 15b; with *Rashi; Maharik Shoresh* 165; *Midrash Talpios; R' Shmuel di Uzidah;* see *Kli Chemdah; Ya'aros Devash.* Others suggest that when Esther prayed to be saved from the dog, she seemed to be minimizing Hashem's power. It would be more miraculous to save the Jewish nation from a powerful lion rather than a simple dog.

12. See *Midrash Tehillim* 22; *Yalkut Shimoni* 687.

13. *Midrash Tehillim* 22:7; *Esther Rabbah* 8:7 *Aggadas Esther.*

14. *Tosafos* to *Megillah* 15a; *Targum Sheni; Rambam; Bereishis Rabbah* 56:1.

But for all these years I have been detained in Achashverosh's palace, You have worked no wonders for me. Please save me now. Deliver me as You delivered Chananiah, Mishael and Azariah from the fiery furnace. Deliver me as You delivered Daniel from the lion's den. Please save me from the wicked Haman. He brought down Vashti, and he hates me for taking the place he thought would go to his daughter. Don't let him bring me down as well. Please let me complete the mission for which I was placed here."[15]

Esther looked up and, because of the straight sight lines, saw Achashverosh sitting in his throne room far away, listening to people presenting cases and petitions for his review. The king turned his head and saw her where she stood, and they made eye contact. The guards immediately backed off. They would leave it to Achashverosh to deal with this matter as he saw fit.[16]

Achashverosh's eyes widened with shock when he saw Esther. Although he couldn't see clearly at that distance because of a cyst in his eye, he recognized her as his queen. He flew into a rage. The blood rushed to his face, and he turned beet-red. How dare she come without a summons? "Look what is happening!" he shouted. "Vashti didn't come when I summoned her, and this one comes when I don't summon her."[17]

Esther saw Achashverosh's anger, and she fainted dead away. But just before she fell, three angels — Chasiel, Chaniel and Rachmiel — caught her and held her up. They had come to accompany her in the merit of the three-day fast she had instituted.[18]

Achashverosh took one last look at Esther and turned his head away. The guards took this as a signal of royal disfavor, and they sprang forward to carry out their perceived duty. It looked to be the end.[19]

At the very last moment, however, one of the angels grabbed Achashverosh and slapped him sharply across the face.

---

15. *Yalkut Tehillim* 685; *Targum Rishon*; *Targum Sheni*; *Aggadas Esther*.

16. *Yosef Lekach*; *Yad HaMelech*; *R' Elisha Galico*; see *Gra*; *Alshich*; *Malbim*. Some suggest that the king was not in the innermost chamber, but was far enough outside to see Esther. Thus she was not legally violating Haman's edict; see *Ma'amer Mordechai* and *Yad Hamelech*.

17. *Esther Rabbah* 9:1; *Midrash Tehillim* 22; *Yalkut Shimoni* 687; *Minchas Yehudah*.

18. *Midrash HaGadol*; *Yad HaMelech*; *Midrash Eliyahu*; *Esther Rabbah* 9:1; *Midrash Lekach Tov*; *Yosifun*.

19. *Midrash Panim Acheirim*; *Targum Sheni*; *Aggadas Esther*.

"You evil man!" the angel whispered in his ear. "Your wife stands before you, faint and trembling, and you sit nonchalantly on your throne and turn your head away? What kind of a heartless beast are you?"[20]

The angel turned Achashverosh's head until he was looking directly at Esther. Suddenly, the cyst in his eye began to shrink, and he could see clearly even from a distance. Achashverosh was overjoyed at his newfound sharp vision, and he leaned forward to get an even better look. As soon as the guards saw this, they fell back. Obviously, the king had taken matters back into his own hands. Their moment had passed.[21]

This was the first of many miracles. The chain of events that would lead to the deliverance of the Jewish people had begun.[22]

The three angels now set to work. One of them raised Esther's neck so that she would appear tall and erect. The second bathed her in a special divine radiance that instantly touched Achashverosh's heart. The third pulled at the end of Achashverosh's golden rod, which miraculously appeared in his hand without his lifting it from the table, stretching it out like a piece of elastic until it almost reached Esther. All the courtiers and the guards gaped at the marvelous drama unfolding before their eyes.[23]

Esther was suffused with an extraordinary, otherworldly charm. It was no longer recognizable that she had been weakened by fasting or that she had just had the fright of her life. Achashverosh's mood also underwent an instant change. His wrath vanished, and he sought to defend her. She had not, he decided, violated any laws, for she had never entered the throne room without permission. In fact, she had exhibited a commendable modesty by remaining standing several chambers away and awaiting the pleasure of the king.[24]

Achashverosh was once again filled with concern for Esther. Esther's life would be spared, and she would be allowed to plead for her people. At the same time, she would be spared having to sin with him. She would have the best of both worlds, a true blessing from Hashem.[25]

20. *Midrash Panim Acheirim; Midrash Tehillim* 22; *Aggadas Esther.*
21. *Midrash Panim Acheirim; Midrash Talpios; Chomas Anach; D'na Pishra.*
22. *Maharal.*
23. *Megillah* 15b; *Midrash Lekach Tov; Alshich.*
24. *Esther Rabbah* 9:1; *Maharal; Alshich; R' Elisha Galico; Gra.*
25. *Yosef Lekach; Alshich.*

The golden rod stretched toward where Esther stood, and it expanded gradually. The rod itself was two cubits long, representing Mordechai and Esther. It extended to twelve cubits, representing the twelve tribes of Israel. Then it extended to sixteen cubits, representing the thirteen tribes with Yosef subdivided into Ephraim and Menashe and the three patriarchs. Then it extended to twenty-four cubits, representing the number of books in the *Tanach*. Then it extended to sixty cubits, representing the number of tractates in the Talmud and the number of ten thousands of Jews in the desert.[26]

As Esther reached out to touch the tip of the golden rod, it receded. She stepped forward to touch it, and it receded even further. Each time she stepped forward, it receded further, until she approached the king. With the help of the angel's assistance, she reached out and touched the golden rod. She was now safe. Moreover, she also had the right to have a request granted.[27]

Achashverosh looked at his queen, frail, weak, sad-eyed, and his heart filled with compassion. "Esther, don't be afraid. The law of not coming unbidden does not apply to you. Why, you are my queen, my companion, my mate, my very own wife. You can come see me any time you wish. There is no reason to be afraid."[28]

---

26. *Megillah* 15b; *Zohar Chadash*; *Yalkut Shimoni*; *Midrash Tehillim* 22; *Ben Yehoyada*; *Midrash Talpios*; *R' Elisha Galico*; *Alshich. Midrash Talpios* explains the different views of the commentators regarding the length of the scepter. See *Maharsha* and *Maharal* for explanations of the different views. Some suggest that Hashem Himself extended the scepter (*Rokeach*). The scepter reached a length of sixty cubits which represented the sixty *masechtos* of the Mishnah, which alluded to the *kiy'mu ve'kiblu*, the Jews' reacceptance of the Torah in the wake of the Purim miracle, when they would willingly accept the Oral Torah in addition to the Written Law. See *Rokeach* and *Maharal* for further explanation of the various measurements. Others suggest that the first 10 cubits the scepter extended represented the merit of the Ten Commandments. The next 14 cubits, until it reached 16 cubits long, alluded to the merit of David, whose name's numerical value equals 14. The following 22 cubits it lengthened represented the *aleph-beis*, and the 26 cubits from the original 2-cubit length to 28 hinted at the numerical value of Y-K-V-H, one of Hashem's Names (*Ben Yehoyada*). Some say that it first lengthened 15 cubits, which hinted at the *Yud-Kay* of one of Hashem's Names. Then it extended 8 more cubits, representing the eight *kerashim* (boards) of the western portion of the Mishkan (Tabernacle) and then 16 cubits, alluding to the *adanim* (sockets); see *Eshkol HaKofer*. Others say that the scepter elongated as much as two hundred cubits.

27. *Targum Rishon*; *Aggadas Esther*; *Maharal*; *Einei HaEidah*; *Akeidah*; *Eshkol HaKofer*; *Midrash Panim Acheirim*. Others suggest that the mere motion to hold out the scepter was sufficient to demonstrate that the king had granted permission to the person to enter (*R' Yosef ibn Yachia*; *Menos HaLevi*).

28. *Esther Rabbah* 9:1; *Menos HaLevi*; *Ma'amar Mordechai*; *Yosifun*; *R' Shmuel di Uzidah*; *Malbim*. This is the first time Achashverosh referred to Esther as queen. In the past she was called "Esther the Queen" as opposed to "Queen Esther"; now that she approached him of her own volition, he graced her with the title of queen.

"Thank you, my lord," said Esther.

"Why didn't you speak up when I caught sight of you? Why did you just stand there as if dumbstruck?"

"I was silent out of respect for you," said Esther. "It was for you to speak first."

"How thoughtful, my dear Esther. But why are you so pale? You look as if you haven't eaten in days."

"I haven't, my lord."

"But why not?" asked Achashverosh. "Aren't you feeling well? Do you want me to call for the royal physician? And look at your eyes and your tear-stained face. You look so sad, yet so strangely beautiful, more beautiful than ever. What can I do for you, Esther?"

"I am fine already, my lord. Don't worry."

"But I cannot accept that," said Achashverosh. "Something is clearly bothering you. Something is troubling your mind, and I want to relieve your anxiety. You can have anything you desire. Just ask for it. I would even give you half my kingdom if that would bring a smile to your face."[29]

"Really?" asked Esther. "Half of your kingdom? And no more?"

"No more. If you ask me to allow the Jews to rebuild their temple, I would not agree to it. I took an oath not to allow it to be rebuilt. It would only lead them to rebel. It already caused a rebellion once before when I still ruled over the entire world, and as a result, I lost half my kingdom. I would not take such a risk again. But in any case, why should you want to ask for the Jews, or anyone else for that matter. I want to do something for you and you alone. Ask and it is yours!"[30]

---

29. *Yalkut Shimoni; Megillah* 15b; *Rashi; Rambam; Gra; Yishai Elokim; Nachal Eshkol; Menos HaLevi; Yad HaMelech;* see *Maharsha* for a different interpretation. Many suggest that Achashverosh was offering Esther half the world as the *Beis HaMikdash* was at the midway point. Others argue that, since he had lost half his kingdom years earlier, this would not be likely. We have followed the opinion that Achashverosh was offering half the kingdom, and the divisioin was at the site of the *Beis HaMikdash* (see *D'na Pishra*). Achashverosh would never offer more than half his kingdom, as that would give Esther majority control (*Maharal*).

30. See *Targum Rishon; Ya'aros Devash; Maharal; Megillas Sesarim; Malbim.* See *Gra* for a different explanation. Achashverosh knew that the Jews would be redeemed from exile by first destroying Amalek and then building the *Beis HaMikdash*. By declaring his unwillingness to allow the rebuilding of the *Beis HaMikdash*, Achashverosh meant that Haman, whom he liked, would remain alive and well. Others suggest that Achashverosh, who thought Esther lacked for nothing, assumed that she came on behalf of someone else, either an individual or a nation in his kingdom. He was willing to give Esther half his kingdom on behalf of the one for whom she was making her request. See *R' Shmuel di Uzidah; Pirush Megillas Achashverosh; Yedei Moshe.*

"You are so kind, my lord," said Esther, thinking furiously. She felt it was not yet time to ask for the Jewish people, since the three-day fast was not yet complete. Also, it did not seem appropriate to ask just when her life had been miraculously spared. Better to give Achashverosh some time to get into an expansive mood, when he would be more serene and open-minded. She would bide her time.[31]

"Well, Esther? What is your request?" Achashverosh prompted her.

"I accept your kind offer, my lord. But I must think for a while about what I will request. It must be something very special, and I don't want to squander it with an impulsive request. In the meantime, I do have a rather small request."[32]

"Granted!" cried Achashverosh. "Even before I hear it, I grant it!"

"How wonderful. Actually, I want to invite you and Haman to a banquet in your honor in my chambers. In fact, I have already prepared it."

"I accept. Why Haman?"

"Oh, the banquet is in your honor, my lord. I just want Haman to be in attendance."[33]

Achashverosh shrugged. "As you wish, Esther. As you wish."

Why did Esther choose to make this seemingly outlandish request? How did she expect this to help her overturn the decree and save the Jewish people? She actually had very good reasons.

Esther wanted to lull Haman into a false sense of security, as it is written, "Pride goes before the fall." The special honor afforded Haman would go to his head and cause him to let down his guard. In addition, taking her cue from Mordechai, she had asked school-children for a verse and they had quoted, "If your enemy is hungry, give him bread." She also applied the verse (*Tehillim* 69:23), "Let their table become a trap before them."[34]

Esther knew that Haman had designs on the throne, and she wanted to keep a close eye on him to make sure he did not attempt to assassinate or overthrow Achashverosh. She was also afraid that Haman might try to convince Achashverosh that she had indeed violated the law and should be put to death. In case Haman was har-

31. *Yosef Lekach; Menos HaLevi; Yad HaMelech.*

32. *Megillas Sesarim; Gra; Yosef Lekach.*

33. *D'na Pishra.*

34. *Megillah* 15b; *Menos HaLevi* and *Mishlei* 16:18. See *Mishlei* 25:22; *Ben Yehoyada*. It was common practice for the children to regularly recite verses from *Mishlei* at this time, just as we learn *Pirkei Avos* between Pesach and Shavuos. See *Midrash Shmuel* on *Avos*.

boring any such thoughts, she knew that plying him with good food and fine wines would make him more mellow and less likely to act precipitously. Also, by flattering Haman she hoped to make him better disposed toward her, considering her a possible friend rather than an obstacle to power. She wanted him to become complacent and vulnerable. Besides, if she expected Achashverosh to rescind the decree, he would need to retrieve his ring from Haman. Having Haman close by when she made her plea would ensure the recovery of the ring.[35]

Furthermore, Esther was concerned that Haman had guessed she was Jewish, if only because of her association with Mordechai. If he told his suspicions to Achashverosh, he could prevent Esther from arguing against the decree, since she herself would be subject to it. He might also change the Adar deadline. Better to invite him to the banquet, thereby dispelling any suspicions he might be harboring.[36]

Having Haman at the banquet, Esther felt, would also give her many opportunities to maneuver him into a mistake, especially with his tongue loosened by wine. If he did or said something that enraged the king, he would not be able to defend himself fully in front of the queen, since this would be disrespectful. Long investigations and inquiries would also be avoided, since the king himself would be witness to the infraction. Haman would have to beg the queen for mercy, and this would lead to his downfall, as indeed it did.[37]

It was very important to Esther that Haman be exposed as a villain and that Achashverosh should not think she had some grievances against him and was conducting a personal vendetta. Achashverosh would not have changed public policy to satisfy Esther's personal grudges. Therefore, by inviting Haman to the banquet, she would show Achashverosh that she bore Haman no personal ill will.[38]

Furthermore, Esther was counting on the impulsiveness Achashverosh had displayed when he had ordered Vashti executed. If Haman incurred his wrath, it would be best if he were right there

---

35. *Megillah* 15b with *Rashi* and *Sifsei Chachamim; Menos HaLevi; R' Shmuel di Uzidah; Maharal.*

36. *Megillah* 15b; see *Chidushei Geonim; Sifsei Chachamim; Menos HaLevi.*

37. *Megillah* 15b with *Rashi; Zeis Ra'anan; Ben Yehoyada; Yedei Moshe; Yosef Lekach; Maharal.* See *Malbim* and *Maharal.* Some express surprise that Esther never told Achashverosh of Haman's secret pact with Mordechai wherein he had sold himself as a slave to Mordechai. This would surely have aroused Achashverosh's suspicion about the decree.

38. *Malbim.*

to bear the brunt of his instant vengeance. Later, Achashverosh might cool off and change his mind. He had changed his mind over Vashti, too, but it had been too late.[39]

The invitation was also designed to isolate Haman politically. Although he had been elevated to viceroy, the highest post in the empire, an invitation to a private banquet with the king and queen would surely arouse the jealousy of the other courtiers and turn them against Haman. Achashverosh would also resent Haman's further elevation to practically equal status with the king, further undermining Haman's position.[40]

Having Haman at the feast would also help her steer the conversation in the right direction. She would express her gratitude to Haman for toppling Vashti so that she could become queen. Once the topic of gratitude was on the table, she could bring up what Mordechai had done to save the king's life and how he was owed a debt of gratitude. From there, it would be just a short step to pleading for herself and her people. If it turned out that, in spite of everything, Achashverosh maintained his high regard for Haman, Esther considered begging Haman for mercy at the banquet. To keep her options open, she clearly needed both of them to come.[41]

From a different perspective, Esther knew that feasts had historically resulted in royal deaths. Belshazzar and Vashti had both died during feasts. For the Jewish people, too, eating had been a harbinger of tragedy and sin. Yosef had been sold into slavery, while the brothers broke bread. In Shitim, the Jews had turned to sin while eating. Perhaps this feast would also cause the death of Achashverosh.[42] According to royal custom, the violent death of a high personage associated with a decree would cause it to become invalidated. Achashverosh or Haman's death would thereby accomplish a dual purpose. It would cancel the decree and also set Esther free.

As a fallback position, Esther wanted to raise suspicions in Achashverosh's mind that there might be an illicit liaison between her and Haman. If his wrath could be aroused he would have them both killed; she was ready to sacrifice her life for her people should the need arise. After all, he had killed Vashti for far less than that.

---

39. *Megillah* 15b with *Rif.*

40. *Megillah* 15b with *Maharsha* and *Ben Yehoyada.*

41. *R' Elisha Galico.*

42. *Megillah* 15b with *Rashi; Maharsha; Zeis Ra'anan; Maharal* to *Yirmiyahu* 51:39; *Bamidbar* 25:1-9.

Once Haman was killed, the decree would automatically be abolished. As a last resort, Esther also felt it might be better that Haman be executed on these charges than to die for some other pretext without being fully disgraced, making him a martyr.[43]

Esther wanted to show Hashem that, for the benefit of the Jewish people, she was enduring the humiliation of sharing a table with Haman. Perhaps then Hashem would put an end to this *chilul Hashem* and take pity on her people.[44]

She also felt that since the decree had been sealed by Achashverosh and Haman at a private feast, it was only fitting, measure for measure, that a similar feast should bring about its reversal.[45]

Inviting Haman was also a psychological ploy to inspire the Jewish people to new heights of prayer and repentance. Despite all their protestations, they might still feel a certain reliance on having a friend in the palace, a Jewish queen who could plead for them. But if they saw her consorting with Haman, inviting him not only to one feast but to two while the people were fasting, they would suspect that she had abandoned them. Then they would finally be convinced that they could rely on no one but the Almighty, and they would pray as they had never prayed before.[46]

Esther did not want to be alone with Achashverosh when she won his favor, because she did not want him to make advances. Having Haman there with them at the banquet would prevent that from happening.[47]

Even as she awaited Achashverosh and Haman at the first banquet, Esther was already planning to use this night only as a prelude to a second banquet the following night. By then, the Jews would have completed their three-day fast. By then, Haman would also have been lulled into a false sense of security so that he would be caught unawares and brought down.[48]

---

43. *Megillah* 15b with *Rashi* and *Sifsei Chachamim.*

44. *Megillah* 15b with *Rashi*; see *Pirush Megillas Achashverosh; D'na Pishra; Menos HaLevi.* The initial letters of the words *yavo hamelech veHaman hayom"* spell the Y-H-V-H name of Hashem. Esther was going into this feast with the security of Hashem's spirit with her (*Kad HaKemach*)

45. *R' Shmuel di Uzidah.*

46. *Megillah* 15b with commentaries; *Alshich; R' Shmuel di Uzidah.*

47. *Yosef Lekach.*

48. See *Alshich; Megillas Sesarim; Yishai Elokim.*

Esther's Banquet

18

Achashverosh was very eager to get to the banquet as quickly as possible. He was beside himself with curiosity about Esther's mysterious request,
which would supposedly be presented at the banquet.[1] Moreover, his interests in her were stronger
than ever, and he wanted to grant her wish, to make
her genuinely happy.[2] And of course, since the food
was already prepared, Achashverosh, enthusiastic
trencherman that he was, did not want it to lose its
flavor and freshness.[3]

Achashverosh was quite pleased that Esther had
invited Haman to the banquet. Technically, she had
violated Haman's law by coming to the throne room
without being summoned, but the invitation would
surely mollify him; undisturbed peace would reign
in the palace.[4] Besides, it would be useful to have

1. See *Gra; Yosef Lekach; Melo HaOmer.*
2. *Maharal.*
3. *Sha'arei Binah; Menos HaLevi.*
4. *Menos HaLevi; Midrash Mishlei 9:2.*

Haman, the king's closest advisor, on hand when Esther made her request. Should any question arise, Haman would be right there to resolve it.[5]

Pleased with the way things were turning out, Achashverosh sent one of his courtiers with a message to Haman. "Tell him he is invited to a private banquet with the king and queen in the queen's quarters. And tell him specifically that the invitation did not come from me but from the queen herself. He is to come immediately. Everything is ready and waiting. We will not begin without him, so he must hurry."[6]

Haman received the message with mixed feelings. On the one hand, he was honored and excited that the queen had chosen to invite him to such an intimate dinner. At the same time, he was uneasy about the queen's sudden solicitude, since relations between the two of them had been strained, to say the least. Why the sudden change of heart?[7]

Wasting no time, Haman hurried off to the banquet chamber. He arrived there just as Achashverosh was walking through the door, and the two of them entered together.[8]

Esther greeted the two men with charm and grace and ushered them to their places. The chamber was exquisitely appointed and bathed in soft candlelight. The table was set for three. Servants stood against the wall at the other end of the chamber, close enough to be summoned with a snap of the fingers yet far enough to allow the celebrants privacy.

To give even greater honor to her guests, Esther herself poured wine for them. They insisted that she pour wine for herself as well, which she did, but she did not drink it; she was still fasting. The men drained their cups, and she refilled them.[9]

Then, as Achashverosh watched with mild irritation, Esther turned towards Haman. She took her untouched cup of wine and offered it to Haman, who accepted it with a diabolical gleam in his eye and instantly drained it to the last drop.

---

5. *Melo HaOmer.*

6. See *Ibn Ezra; R' Elisha Galico.*

7. *Alshich.*

8. *R' Shmuel di Uzidah.*

9. *Menos HaLevi.* Some suggest that she was concerned that Haman might poison her food, and therefore did not eat at the feast.

Achashverosh's eyes immediately narrowed. What was this? Why was Esther paying special attention to Haman? Was something unsavory going on? But then he shook his head, as if to clear it of these disturbing thoughts. No, it couldn't be. He dismissed the thoughts as merely the product of wine and an overactive imagination, and he plunged again into the pleasures of the banquet. But his sense of unease refused to be completely dispelled.[10]

He stood up on shaky legs, lifted his cup high in the air and declared, "I propose a toast to the most gracious queen in all the world. Long life, happiness and glory!"

"A toast!" shouted Haman and drained his cup again.

Esther just smiled. She did not lift her cup.

"Esther!" cried the king, taken aback. "Why don't you join in the toast? In fact, it would do me great honor if you would offer one of your own."

"Do not be offended, my lord, if I do not drink any wine," she replied. "I am still feeling a bit faint. But I welcome your toast, and I thank you and Haman for your good wishes. And I toast you in return, but not with wine."[11]

"Esther," said Achashverosh, "it pains me to see you in such a subdued mood. Surely, your spirits will rise when I grant you your request. Then let us do it now! What do you need? Money? Up to half my kingdom, and it is yours. In fact, we have Haman, who is also the royal treasurer, right here with us. Your wish can be fulfilled as soon as you express it. What's more, I grant you both a request for yourself and a plea for someone else. Don't hold back, Esther. What is on your mind? What is making you sad? Do you want someone killed? No problem. Just tell me who it is, and he is as good as dead already!"

Esther lowered her eyes. "You are most kind, my lord."

"And one more thing. If you need help with some law or regulation, Haman is right here. Just state your need and it is done. The two highest personages in the empire are right here with you. You can have anything you wish. Just ask for it. I can't bear to see you so miserable."[12]

"Thank you so much, my lord," said Esther. "Your concern for my welfare touches my heart. As you know, first and foremost, I wish to find favor in your eyes. As for my request, at the moment I

---

10. *Midrash Panim Acheirim; Aggadas Esther.*
11. *Midrash Lekach Tov; Menos HaLevi; Yosef Lekach.*
12. *R' Yosef ibn Yachia; R' Elisha Galico; Yad HaMelech.*

do indeed have another request. It would give me great honor if you and Haman would join me tomorrow night once again for another private banquet I will give in honor of both of you.[13] Hopefully, I shall be feeling better then, and I will be able to join more actively in the festivities. I will also tell you my request at that time. You were right to an extent, my lord. It does involve issues of life and death and money. I will explain tomorrow."[14]

Her request for life was, of course, for the survival of the Jewish people. Her request for death was to have Haman executed. Her mention of money was a reference to the ten thousand talents of silver Haman had offered to pay for the right to do with the Jews as he pleased.[15]

But why did Esther ask for another banquet? Achashverosh was so eager to grant her request. Why then didn't she make the request right away? Why wait until tomorrow?

Primarily, Esther was taking her cues from Jewish history. Yaakov had prepared to defend himself against Eisav in three stages — prayer, appeasement and battle. Esther had begun with prayer and fasting. The first feast had been like a gift to Haman. At the second, she would engage him in battle. Moreover, Yehoshua had prepared to battle Amalek at Refidim "tomorrow." Apparently, the battle with Amalek could only be joined successfully after a day's delay. She also knew that Hashem does not let anyone suffer more than three days. By the next night, she would have been fasting for three days, and she was sure Hashem would guide her to success.[16]

Esther's instincts also told her than the time was not yet ripe. The first banquet had been an ice-breaker, but it hadn't accomplished everything she wanted. Haman had warmed to her a little, but he was still a dangerous enemy, who could turn on her in a moment and convince the king to kill her. He had not yet let his guard down fully so that he would be vulnerable to her attack. She needed to shock him to his very core.[17]

---

13. See *Targum Rishon; Malbim; D'na Pishra.*

14. *Rashi; R' Yosef ibn Nachmiash; R' Yosef ibn Yachia; Yosef Lekach; Menos HaLevi; Yad HaMelech.* Since Haman had bought the rights to the Jews, it was also a financial issue.

15. See *Targum Rishon; Menos HaLevi; Gra; Yosef Lekach; Akeidas Yitzchak.*

16. *R' Meir Armah.* See *Yalkut Shimoni; Menos HaLevi; R' Shmuel di Uzidah.*

17. *Targum Sheni* provides this as a basic reason for inviting Haman to the first party. Others suggest that Esther was concerned lest Achashverosh himself prosecute her for breaking the law. She wanted to allow more time to elapse and distance herself from the incident (*Akeidah*).

Furthermore, Haman did not yet feel fully equal to Achashverosh at the banquet, and therefore, Achashverosh's jealousy was not sufficiently aroused. The first banquet had been in honor of Achashverosh, with Haman attending in a subordinate role. The second would be given in honor of both Achashverosh and Haman equally, swelling Haman's head and discomfiting Achashverosh.

Another important aspect was Esther's participation. Because she was fasting, she had not been able to join in the spirit of revelry, but at the second she could eat and drink with them. She would thus lull Haman into thinking her feeling towards him were warm, thereby inviting Achashverosh's jealous rage.[18]

Finally, Esther was waiting for some sign from Heaven that she should make her request. She had hoped that Mordechai's name would come up during the conversation, perhaps providing a signal for her. But it did not. Therefore, she decided to wait until the next night. As it turned out, the very next day provided an ample sign. Afterward, there was no question in her mind that the time to act had come.[19]

Achashverosh and Haman bid Esther good night and departed, each to his own destination, each accompanied by his own thoughts. Achashverosh was uneasy. What was really the point of the second banquet? Was Esther's request so complex and involved that she needed days to articulate it and present it? In fact, was there really a request at all? Or was everything just a ruse between Esther and Haman to collude against him? Was there anything inappropriate going on between those two? Were they making a fool of him? Were they plotting to do him harm? What was going on? The questions plagued Achashverosh until he seethed with frustration and rage. The more he thought about it, the further Haman fell in his esteem and affections. There was something going on. He could feel it. And Haman was behind it. He was sure of it.[20]

Haman, for his part, felt nothing of the sort. On the contrary, he was gay and carefree, his heart enormously expanded by wine and good fortune. He had considered himself fortunate earlier, but it was nothing compared to the new heights he had reached. He was no longer a mere official, but practically a member of the royal fam-

---

18. See *R' Yosef ibn Yachia; Midrash Lekach Tov; Yosef Lekach; Yedei Moshe; Menos HaLevi.*
19. *Ibn Ezra; Yedei Moshe; R' Shmuel di Uzidah; Maharal; Chiddushei HaRim.*
20. *Midrash Lekach Tov; Yad HaMelech.*

ily. As for the queen, he had obviously judged her unfairly, and he was ashamed of any suspicions he had harbored about her when he heard she had come to the king unbidden. But then she had been so warm to him that she couldn't possibly have been plotting to save the Jews.[21]

What an incredible person she was, thought Haman. So clever, so refined, so gracious. And her most endearing virtue was the high regard in which she held the prime minister of the empire. She could not be a Jewish woman, and I no longer hear of any contact between her and Mordechai. There must have been an innocent explanation for all those reports, and now, they are a thing of the past. I would have liked to see my own daughter on the throne, and maybe I will someday. But if it had to be someone else, Achashverosh couldn't have chosen a better woman for his queen than Esther.[22]

Haman finally felt fully secure in his decree. Esther, who had grown up in Mordechai's home, had now come completely over to his side. The Jews could no longer pin their hopes on any help in the palace. Mordechai would have to come on his knees and beg for mercy. But he would get none, just the blade of the sword.[23]

Haman felt as if he were walking on air. He was on top of the world, at the pinnacle of power and prestige. He had the king in his hands, and now he was on the verge of having the queen as well. The queen had specifically stated that the next day's banquet would be in his honor, raising him up to a level equal with the king.[24] As if it were not enough to invite only him to the exclusion of all others, she had also singled him out to give the banquet in his honor. The queen apparently likes me a lot, thought Haman. Wouldn't it be wonderful if I could count the queen among my conquests? Wouldn't that be the crowning touch to a brilliant career?[25]

---

21. *Yefei Anaf; Menos HaLevi; Alshich.* It never occurred to Haman that his suspicions were in fact true, and that it was no coincidence that Esther had invited him at this time in an unusual manner. Hashem allowed him to be lulled into complacency, and this would lead to his downfall. See *Midrash Mishlei.*

22. *Menos HaLevi; Yosef Lekach; Gra; Melo HaOmer; Yefei Anaf.*

23. *Midrash Panim Acheirim; R' Avigdor Kohen Tzedek; Menos HaLevi; Gra; D'na Pishra; Alshich.*

24. *Esther Rabbah 9:2; Alshich; Malbim.*

25. *R' Yosef ibn Yachiah;* see *Pirkei d'Rav Eliezer* with *Radal; R' Elisha Galico; Menos HaLevi; Megillas Sesarim; Malbim.*

Haman Seeks Revenge

19

Haman was in an ebullient mood when he left Esther's banquet, but as soon as he rode out of the palace on his horse, it was immediately dispelled. Directly ahead of him, Mordechai was sitting with his colleagues on the Sanhedrin, surrounded by schoolchildren, learning Torah. He did not bow down to Haman. Nor did he retreat before him. He simply did not give him a second glance.[1]

What an outrage! This time there was no excuse for it. Haman was dressed for a visit with the royal family. He was not wearing any idols or images that might prevent a Jew from bowing down. What reason could Mordechai offer now for not bowing down to show respect to the highest official in the empire?[2]

---

1. *Targum Rishon; Gra; R' Yosef ibn Yachia.* Some suggest that this was the first time Haman had seen Mordechai since the letters had been sent about the decree. Moredechai could not appear at the palace gates in his sackcloth (*Yosef Lekach*).

2. See *Alshich; Gra; R' Shmuel di Uzidah.* Mordechai wanted to avoid giving the impression that he was bowing to an idol or acknowledging it in any way. Even if Haman was not wearing any idol, people might think he was. Therefore, Mordechai refused to bow to Haman under any circumstances.

As Haman drew closer, Mordechai finally stirred. He extended his boot upon which Haman had acknowledged in his own hand that he had sold himself to Mordechai as a slave.[3]

Haman exploded with rage, but he did not allow the people around him or Mordechai to see his inner feeling. What prodigious effrontery![4] Mordechai should be crawling on his hands and knees to beg for mercy. Instead, he was learning Torah right in front of the palace gates. He should at least show some respect to the prime minister by rising when he passed by, as he did when other princes passed by. At the very least, he should have made the pretense by rising for some other purpose at that very moment. But instead, he extended his boot in a show of arrogant contempt.[5] Clearly, the issue was not idolatry, or some other supposed violation of Jewish law. It was just a personal vendetta, but one that Mordechai would surely lose. Perhaps he thought he had the support of the queen, but he was mistaken. The queen had shown very clearly where her sympathies lay. Mordechai and his people were doomed.[6]

A flicker of doubt crossed Haman's mind. Could Mordechai's fearlessness be a sign of some private knowledge, some information the government informants had not yet discovered? Could there be a secret conspiracy between Mordechai and Esther after all? Could it be that Esther would ask the king to spare Mordechai's life at the second banquet?[7]

Haman felt a strong urge to spur his horse straight at Mordechai and trample him, as he had trampled Hasach.[8] It was simply too risky to allow Mordechai to live. He was simply too clever, too bold, too dangerous. But it would be beneath his dignity to trample Mordechai himself right in front of the palace

---

3. *Pirush Megillas Achashverosh; Targum Rishon*. Mordechai trusted the message of the children's *pesukim* that Hashem would save the Jewish people, and this faith made him fearless of Haman (*Alshich*).

4. *R' Shmuel di Uzidah; Me'am Loez*. Some suggest that although he was filled with anger, this did not detract from the joy and happiness he had experienced earlier (*Maharal*).

5. *D'na Pishra; Menos HaLevi; R' Shmuel di Uzidah; Sifsei Tzaddik; R' Elisha Galico; Ta'ama D'kra*.

6. *Targum Rishon; R' Yosef ibn Yachia; R' Meir Armah; D'na Pishra; R' Elisha Galico*. We see Haman's utter foolishness. He had everything he could possibly want, including the respect and adulation of the entire world, yet he allowed one person's defiance to ruin his mood and cause him to act recklessly. Privately, Haman realized how crucial Mordechai's subservience was; as long as he didn't bow, he was still Haman's master (*Me'am Loez*).

7. *Ma'amar Mordechai*.

8. *R' Yosef ibn Yachia; R' Avigdor Kohen Tzedek*.

gates. He would have to bring his complaint to the king and ask that Mordechai be executed.[9]

But then he laughed nervously. Mordechai was probably sitting near the palace gates because he wanted the queen to plead his case and get the decree abolished. But he was laboring under a fatal illusion. The queen was not on his side. True, she had not eaten at the first banquet, but she was not feeling well. She would certainly not refrain from eating at the second banquet. Yes, there could be no doubt about it. Esther favored him over Mordechai. And if there was any wavering, he would take care of it. He knew how to handle women. After all, hadn't he handled Vashti perfectly? No one would foil his plans, not Mordechai, not anyone else.[10]

Having come to the decision to get rid of Mordechai once and for all, Haman made a conscious effort to bring his temper under control. He was clever enough to understand that an impulsive act could backfire on him.[11] Should he rush to Achashverosh with complaints about Mordechai, he might come across as a bit of a fool. First of all, Achashverosh might recall that Mordechai had saved his life and refuse to act against him. That would undermine Haman's power and might start his downfall. But even if he didn't, how could he justify a campaign against one insignificant Jew to the king and to all of Shushan? He would become a laughingstock.[12] There were also other factors to consider. Killing Mordechai might also trigger a riot among the Jews. And in the final analysis, could he be absolutely sure about where Esther stood in the scheme of things? There were too many unknowns for comfort.[13]

---

9. See *R' Shmuel di Uzidah; Malbim; Keren Yehoshua.*

10. *Yedei Moshe;* see *Alshich; R' Elisha Galico.*

11. See *Midrash Lekach Tov; Rashi; Sha'arei Binah; Ibn Ezra; Pirush Megillas Achashverosh; D'na Pishra; R' Shmuel di Uzidah.* We have given various explanations of the word *vayisapak.* See *Shem Efraim* to *Bereishis* 45:1.

12. *Akeidah; Yosef Lekach; R' Yosef ibn Yachia;* see *Yedei Moshe; Malbim.* Haman's thoughts, enabling him to control himself, came from Hashem, part of the Master Plan leading to his downfall. In fact, this point figured in Achashverosh's concerns which contributed to his dream that night. He could not fathom why Haman had not come to him immediately to report Mordechai's failure to obey the law (*D'na Pishra*). Haman feared that any mention of Mordechai as an individual would be a clue that his motivation in wanting to kill the Jews was only to eliminate Mordechai out of personal hatred. Achashverosh would not approve of this, and thus Haman had to restrain himself.

13. *Megillas Sesarim; Me'am Loez.*

All these thoughts did not deter Haman from his decision to destroy Mordechai. They just gave him pause regarding the method. It clearly needed much careful thought. It would also be prudent to seek the counsel of his family and advisors. The deed had to be done right. He had always kept his feelings about Mordechai bottled up inside. It was time to speak about them with those he loved and trusted. It was time to seek some help.[14]

Being a man of action, Haman wasted no time putting his plan into action. Coming home from the banquet, he did not take any time off for a short rest. As soon as he walked through the door, he called for Zeresh, his wife, but she was not home.[15]

Zeresh was the daughter of Tatnai, governor of a province beyond the Euphrates River. She had a history of being unfaithful to her husband, and had taken advantage of his attending the party. Nonetheless, she was Haman's most important and trusted advisor. Haman would not make a move under these circumstances without consulting her.[16]

Haman also wanted to hear the advice of everyone who knew him, who could contribute any small insight to the discussion, from the leading government ministers to the maidservants in his house. Therefore, he drew up a list and sent off messengers to assemble everyone immediately in his house. The meeting would wait until all were present. In the end, three hundred and sixty-five people gathered in Haman's salon, eager to hear the serious crisis for which he sought their help. The buzz was deafening.[17]

Haman stood up and raised his hands for silence. The buzz came to a grudging end. Haman glanced around the room with satisfaction.

"I'm sure you are all curious to hear why I called you here," he began. "Rest assured, you will find out before you leave."

There was a titter of laughter, then silence again.

Haman continued. "Now it's time to get serious. Believe me, there is no mirth in my heart right now.[18]

---

14. *Rashi; Sha'arei Binah; R' Shmuel di Uzidah; Yad HaMelech.*

15. *R' Shmuel di Uzidah.*

16. See *Esther Rabbah* 9:2; *Targum Rishon; Aggadas Esther; R' Shmuel di Uzidah; R' Yosef ibn Yachia; Yismach Lev; Menos HaLevi; Maharal.* See *Ezra* ch. 5 and 6.

17. *Rokeach; Rambam; Midrash Panim Acheirim; Pirush Megillas Achashverosh; R' Shmuel di Uzidah.*

18. *Yedei Moshe; D'na Pishra; R' Elisha Galico.*

"My dear friends and family, you see here standing before you one of the most fortunate men who ever lived. Who in this world is more fortunate than I? Let us take money. Who doesn't want money? Why, everyone in the world wants money, the more of it the better. Well, I have about as much money as one can possibly have. I have looted and plundered and pillaged and amassed an incredible fortune. I have rooms filled with money, rooms filled with treasure, gold, silver, precious stones. And I know every cent I possess. I carry an account with me in a special belt, and whenever I am depressed, I look at the belt, and my heart is refreshed."[19]

"We get the message, my dear husband," said Zeresh. "You have money."

"You figured it out? Good. I was afraid I was not making myself clear. So much for money. I also have many fine children. Two hundred and nineteen to be exact. My sons are up-and-coming officials, scribes in the palace and future leaders of our government. I am very proud of them."[20]

Haman rubbed his hands together and squinted.

"So! I have money and children. These are wonderful things. But I also have honor and power. Oh-so-much honor and power, more than most people can even imagine in their dreams. I am second only to the king in all the Persian Empire. I have more honor than Avraham, an ancestor I share with the Jews, more money than Yitzchak, another common ancestor, and more children than Yaakov, the third of the Jewish patriarchs. I am the most powerful person in the empire, other than the king. When I walk through the streets or the corridors of the palace, everyone bows down to me. Everyone! My power is uncontested and absolute." He did not add that he was secretly contemplating exploiting the tensions between the Greeks and the Persians, toppling Achashverosh and ascending the throne himself.

---

19. See *Megillah* 15b; *Midrash Lekach Tov; Menos HaLevi; R' Shmuel di Uzidah; Yismach Lev; Ben Yehoyada* to *Megillah* 15b; see *Maharal*.

20. See *Megillah* 15b; *Ben Yehoyada; Targum Rishon; Yalkut Shimoni; Yeshayahu; Pirkei d'Rav Eliezer; Rokeach; Midrash Tehillim; Yotzer* to *Parashas Zachor; Pirush Megillas Achashverosh*. There are many opinions regarding how many children Haman had. Some suggest that he had 210. Seventy were scribes in Shushan, seventy lived in other places, and seventy were government officials on the islands of Achashverosh's empire. Others suggest that only his son Shamshai was a scribe. The *Gemara* (*Megillah* 15b) states that Haman had thirty children; ten died, ten were hanged, and ten had to beg from door to door for food. This last group, which was composed of Haman's illegitimate offspring, numbered, according to some opinions, 70 or 80 children.

"Not quite absolute, sir," one of his younger advisors spoke up. "Don't forget that Esther opposes you."

"You are a clever young fellow," Haman retorted. "One of the new breed of government officials that know everything. Well, you may know everything, but you don't know anything else."

"But isn't it true?" asked the young advisor. "It is a well-known fact that Esther disapproves of you. And it is also a well-known fact that she is the queen. So your money, children and honor are not as secure as you might think. Forgive me for speaking this way, sir, but you want honesty, don't you?"[21]

"Of course I want honesty, young fellow," said Haman. "You're a smart one, aren't you? Listen, you are right in saying that with the queen against me I would not be entirely secure. But she is not against me! In fact, just this night she invited the king and me to a private banquet. Why, barely two hours ago, we were sitting around a table, just the three of us, talking and drinking wine. And Esther was so kind and gracious to me. I tell you, she has come around to accepting my power and position. She now sees me as an ally rather than a rival."

"My dear Haman," said an older man, "I don't think it is wise to jump to conclusions. How can you be so sure about the queen's sympathies after just one night? So what's one banquet? Maybe she had some kind of angle she was playing, something that required your presence. And of course, if she invites you, she has to be hospitable. Don't forget she's a queen. She can't exactly behave like a barmaid, you know."

"I fully agree, uncle," said Haman. "One banquet does not a friendship make. But it is not just one banquet. At the end of the banquet, the queen invited us again to a banquet tomorrow night. And not only that, she said specifically that the banquet was in my honor."[22]

"Two banquets?" said the old advisor. "Hmm. That seems to bear out your theory, Haman. I would tend to agree with you. If she couldn't stand the sight of you, why should she subject herself to your company twice? Once would be more than enough for whatever purpose she might have."

"Exactly my reasoning," said Haman.

"I accept it as well," said the young advisor.

---

21. *Yedei Moshe; D'na Pishra; Maharal; Ya'aros Devash.*
22. *Targum Rishon; Menos HaLevi.*

"Yes, I believe we all agree that Esther is finally on my side. My power is complete and secure."[23]

Haman paused to take a sip of water.

"But there is a dark cloud behind this silver lining," he continued in an ominous tone. "There is one thorn in my side that turns all this sweetness to ashes in my mouth. There is one man who defies me, who positively taunts me every chance he gets. He makes me feel like a bath attendant, a beggar, a slave. You all know how far I have come. I started poor and penniless and worked my way to the top. This person reminds me of those dreadful days and makes me forget how much I've accomplished. He makes me feel poor and destitute. He robs me of my pleasures, of the joy of living. Even the thought of him makes me depressed. And that is why I have called you together here tonight. I need advice on how to deal with him."[24]

"What's the problem, sir?" said the young advisor. "Just chop off his head and be done with him. Now how's that for some sharp advice?"

"Sharp indeed," said Haman, "but not so simple."

"I think it would help," said Zeresh, "if you told us who this fellow is. Do we know him? And why isn't it so simple? Why can't you take our young friend's sharp advice? If you want blunt advice, then I suggest you hit him over the head with a hammer."

"Very funny, Zeresh," said Haman, "but this is no laughing matter. The man is Mordechai the Jew. He has planted himself outside the palace gates, and every time I pass I see him studying the Torah of the Jews, teaching the Jewish schoolchildren or consulting with the judges of the Jewish Sanhedrin. It is insulting, an affront to the laws of the king, and I know why he is doing this. He thinks the gates of the palace symbolize the gates of Heaven. He is trying to overturn the decree through study and prayer. Hah! A lot of good it will do him. He behaves as if he will pull something off within the next eleven months that will save the Jews from the royal decree, which is, of course, ridiculous."[25]

---

23. A heavenly voice declared, "Today you are full of greatness and superiority; tomorrow you will be hanged and impaled!" (*Midrash Panim Acheirim; Rokeach*). Esther's prediction was correct; the haughty Haman's ego would trip him. He was proud and conceited, as Esther intended, and he would soon meet his downfall (*Mishnas R' Eliezer*).

24. See *Megillah* 15b; *Ben Yehoyada; Rashi; R' Yosef ibn Yachia; D'na Pishra; Yosef Lekach; Maharal*.

25. *Targum Rishon; Menos HaLevi*.

"Is that what is driving you crazy, sir?" asked the maidservant.

"No, if that was all, I could bear it. In eleven months, the whole business will be history anyway. The only records of the Jews will be in the imperial museums. Perhaps. But this Mordechai deliberately insults me. Of all the people in the empire, he is the only one who won't bow to me when I pass by. He bows to other princes, but not to me. He just ignores me. But not always. Sometimes, he extends his foot to show me his boot."[26]

"His boot?" squealed the maidservant. "Why would you be interested in seeing his boot, sir?"

"Of course I have no interest in a Jew's boot. But this Mordechai has written things on his boot, insinuations that I am his slave. Can you imagine such an outrage?"

"An absolute outrage!" offered the old advisor.[27]

"Exactly. Why can't the fellow just stay out of my sight? Why must he deliberately provoke me? People cannot help but see what he is doing. My prestige and reputation are suffering. Because of him, I have lost confidence in our gods. And I have grown to hate the Jewish God with such a burning passion that I sometimes find it hard to breathe. I must put an end to this torture. I cannot wait eleven months for Mordechai to die. I also want to kill him to avenge the deaths of my cousins Bigsan and Seresh, and the death of my ancestor King Agag of Amalek. I will feel much better once he is dead."[28]

The young advisor cleared his throat. "We still haven't heard why you can't just cut off his head or hit him over the head with a hammer. What exactly is the problem?"

"How can I just kill him without losing face?" asked Haman. "People will laugh at me for allowing this piddling Jew to get under my skin. How will the king look at it? It is beneath me to get down to Mordechai's level, but on the other hand, I cannot bear to ignore

---

26. *Rokeach, Yedei Moshe; Yosef Lekach.* Haman was beginning to worry that Mordechai's *mazal* might be greater than his. If so, his concerns were justified, and Mordechai would ultimately prevail. Therefore Haman sought a foolproof method of eliminating Mordechai (*Melo HaOmer*).

27. *Megillah* 15b; *R' Chaim Abulafia.* Haman was most disturbed by the knowledge that all his wealth actually belonged to Mordechai, since a slave's possessions belong to his master. If Mordechai had bowed before Haman, he would have implicitly emancipated him, thereby relinquishing all rights over his property. Since he refused to do so, Haman decided he would have to die so that the secret would be protected (*Iyun Yaakov; Ben Yehoyada; R' Shmuel di Uzidah*).

28. See *Maharsha* to *Megillah* 15b; *Rambam; Ma'amar Mordechai; Yosef Lekach; R' Elisha Galico; R' Shmuel di Uzidah; Menos HaLevi; Alshich; Hillel ben Shachar* as cited in *Torah Sheleimah.*

his provocations.[29] I understand that my response is emotional rather than rational, but what can I do? The emotions are a powerful force. And then there's the question of the queen. It seems she has completely turned away from Mordechai and is exploring an alliance with me. A very wise move, if I say so myself. So does this make it easier for me to get rid of that horrid Jew? Should I just have him bodily removed from the palace gates? I really don't know what to do. And I'm afraid that if I rely on myself for the answer, I will decide with my gut rather than my brain. I need some cool-headed advice. My friends, I invite your comments and suggestions."[30]

There was a moment or two of pregnant silence, followed by a low murmur as the advisors put their heads together and conferred in hushed tones. There were many erudite and wise people in attendance, but none was quick to offer an opinion. None except for Zeresh, who was the lowest among them and also the brightest.[31]

"My dear husband," she began, "I agree that you must without question get rid of Mordechai. I also don't think you need to worry about the political repercussions — unless you fail, that is. Failure would certainly be a disaster. So, in my opinion, the issue is not if but how. We have to find a way to commit the perfect murder, so to speak."[32]

Haman snickered. "As usual, Zeresh, you speak with exceptional insight and wisdom. Very well, let us consider the question as you put it. How? Do you have suggestions?"

"Of course I do, Haman. I always have suggestions. You know that. This Mordechai, he's not just your regular Jew. He's one of the big fish. Of course, when we turn the pail over, all the fish will perish, big and little alike. But until then, we have to be especially careful with the big fish. So let's take a look at the history of these Jews for some clues on how to land their big fish."

"Sounds like a good idea," said Haman.

"Should we throw him into a fiery furnace?"

"Great idea!" shouted Haman.

---

29. *Sefer HaChaim.*

30. *Gra; Yosef Lekach; Midrash Eliyahu; Malbim.* Little did Haman know that his life would end less than 24 hours later.

31. *Yalkut Shimoni; Esther Rabbah* 9:2; *Eshkol HaKofer; Midrash Lekach Tov; Menos HaLevi.* Some suggest that Haman had divorced Zeresh and now wished to reestablish himself in his father-in-law Tatnai's good graces. One way was to allow Zeresh to speak first before the large audience (*R' Yosef ibn Yachia*).

32. *Yalkut Shimoni; Esther Rabbah* 9:2.

"Not such a great idea," said Zeresh. "Nimrod threw Avraham into a fiery furnace, and he didn't even get a tan. Same with Nevuchadnezzar and Chananiah, Mishael and Azariah. So should we stab him to death?"

"Marvelous idea!"

"Not such a marvelous idea. Yitzchak survived the knife at the *Akeidah,* and Moshe survived the sword of Pharaoh. So should we lock him up in a dungeon and throw away the key?"

"A pretty good idea," Haman said carefully.

"Not such a good idea. Yosef was thrown into the dungeon, but then he was released and even became viceroy — just like you! So should we chain him up, put him into a copper caldron and roast him over the coals?"

"Now you're talking sensibly, Zeresh!"

"But not so sensible. The Babylonians did this to Menashe, and he survived. So should we throw him into the lions' den?"

"Finally, Zeresh! You've hit on the perfect idea!"

"Not quite perfect, Haman. Daniel was thrown into the lions' den, and he survived. So should we hang him from the gallows?"[33]

"Bad idea?" said Haman tentatively.

"No, good idea this time, Haman. There is no case history of an unsuccessful gallows death. And there is a special beauty to a gallows death."[34]

"You mean because the faces turn purple, mistress?" asked the talkative maidservant.

"Maybe that's it for you, silly goose," said Zeresh. "Stick to the kitchen from now on. Haman, there is a great political and psychological advantage in hanging Mordechai from the gallows. First of all, we will hang him high, fifty cubits high. We will set up the gallows right here on our estate and string up this Jewish big fish, so that all the world can see him as he twists in the wind. All the Jews will see what you have done, and they will tremble before you. In addition, the ministers will certainly not think you were involving yourself with trivial matters by killing Mordechai when they see him hanging high from the tree; it will clearly be an important political statement. It will also be a good omen. If you ever dreamed

33. See *Yalkut Shimoni; Esther Rabbah* 9:2; *Aggadas Esther;* see *Divrei HaYamim* II 33:11; *Pesikta d'Rav Kahana* 162; *Yerushalmi Sanhedrin* 10:2, 11:17; *Midrash Abba Gorion; Midrash Panim Acheirim; Targum Rishon.* See *Yalkut Beshalach* 256.

34. *D'na Pishra.*

about Mordechai being over you in any way, this will be the interpretation. His body will swing from a noose high over your head. Think of it, Haman, you will experience such joy and relief every time you look up and see the corpse dangling high overhead. When you go to the queen's banquet tomorrow night, Mordechai will be in a, ahem, high place and you will be in high spirits. The thought will add special flavor to the foods and wines you will enjoy there.[35] What's more, any magical abilities Mordechai may practice to prevent his demise will be fruitless. It is a known fact that one whose feet are off the ground can't perform any magic. Mordechai will be helpless once the gallows hang him, similar to the Egyptians in the plague of lice who could do nothing to stop it when their feet were off the ground."[36]

"Brilliant, Zeresh, absolutely brilliant," said Haman. "We will do exactly as you say. I feel better already. And I like the number fifty. As a demigod, I have mastered the fifty gates of defilement and the fifty gates of wisdom, while Moshe could only master forty-nine gates of wisdom.[37] I also have sons who command battalions of fifty. The fifty-cubit-high gallows will be a sign of my superiority over Mordechai in the astrological arena."[38]

"Just one moment," said the young advisor. "I hate to put a damper on things, but there is one factor that still disturbs me. Should I just keep it to myself, or should I speak up?"

"Speak up, young fellow," said Haman.

"I can accept that a successful execution of Mordechai will not have adverse political ramifications," he said. "No one will care. No one will even give it a second thought. Except maybe for one person. One very significant person. The queen of the land, Esther. How can you be so sure that she and Mordechai are not still close?"

"Good question," said Haman. "Zeresh? What do you say?"

<hr/>

35. *Midrash Lekach Tov; Yalkut Shimoni; Yedei Moshe; Gra; Targum Rishon; Akeidah; R' Shmuel di Uzidah.*

36. *Einei HaEidah;* see *Let My Nation Go,* ch. 13 footnote 195. Some suggest that Haman wanted the gallows to use as a last resort in case his plans backfired. If he were found guilty of treason he would hang himself there and avoid the humiliation of a public execution (*Midrash Eliyahu*).

37. See *Menos HaLevi; Maharal; Midrash Talpios.* The numerical value of *adam,* man, is 45. The numerical value of *Haman* is 45 plus the *nun* which is 50. Haman believed that he was a god, supreme above man. Furthermore, Haman believed that just as Noach's Ark had the ability to save a person, so this beam from the ark would save him. He did not realize that the ark had only saved those who were righteous; in this case Mordechai.

38. *Rokeach; D'na Pishra; Maharal; Melo HaOmer.*

"I think it is absolutely clear that they have parted ways, Haman, just as you suspect. I detect a note of desperation in the fasting and the prayers of the Jews, don't you?"

"Oh, absolutely."

"Well, then, it is simple psychology. If Mordechai and Esther were still friends, why would they feel so desperate? A high friend in the palace, especially the queen herself, is like money in the bank!"[39]

Haman slapped his forehead. "Zeresh! Now that you put it that way, it is as clear as daylight. In fact, I'm surprised I didn't think of it myself. Fine! All is settled then. We will string up Mordechai. Now we just have to find good lumber and skilled carpenters and build this beautiful gallows."

Much discussion followed about the type of wood to use for the gallows. The vine, apple, nut, citron, pomegranate, myrtle and willow were all ruled out, because the Jewish people are compared to them in one place or another. The final decision fell on the cedar. The Jewish people are never compared to the cedar, because it shatters in a strong wind instead of bending.[40] (Some suggest that Hashem asked all the trees during Creation for a volunteer to have Haman hanged from it. All the trees demurred, but the thorn said, "I am useless. I only cause damage. Let the evil Haman who is a thorn in the side of the world be hung from me." Others say that all the trees volunteered, but Hashem chose the thorn as the most appropriate.)

The discussion now turned to very practical matters. "We now know that we should use a cedar tree," said Haman. "Where do we get a cedar beam fifty cubits long?"

Once again, Zeresh provided the answer. "May I remind you, my dear husband, about the gift our son Parshandasa, the governor of Kardunia, sent us when we built this house? He took a day trip to Mount Ararrat, which is in his district, removed a cedar beam from Noach's ark and sent it to us. It is fifty cubits long and twelve wide. We built it into the width of the vestibule of our house. You can easily take it out and stand it up erect."

"Excellent, Zeresh!" Haman exclaimed. "I don't mind if I have to rebuild half my house. I will rip out that beam and use it. Imagine!

---

39. *Midrash Eliyahu.*
40. See *Esther Rabbah* 9:2; *Aggadas Esther; Midrash Panim Acheirim; Targum Sheni; Esther* 7:9.

I will hang Mordechai from a beam of Noach's Ark. What a touch of poetic flair!"[41]

Another man of extreme wealth, Korach, had also followed his wife's advice, and she had led him to his downfall. Now, Haman would meet the same fate. He followed his wife's advice, and in the end, it was he who was hanging from the tree. All his fabulous wealth could not help him. He had risen to greater heights than any other man had, and now he would plunge to the bottom. He would hang from a tree.[42]

Although darkness had already fallen, Haman insisted that the work on the gallows begin immediately. There were already hundreds of people in the house who could help with the work. Craftsmen were summoned, even if they had to be roused from their beds, and ordered to come immediately. They would be paid whatever they asked, but they had to complete the work that very night.

All through the night, Haman and his sons drove the construction forward. Nor did they hesitate, despite their high station, to roll up their sleeves and pitch in with the work. The men pried the huge cedar beam loose from the house and raised it up erect. Then they set about building the gallows structure around it. Haman walked about, exhorting the workers, "Hurry, men! The sooner we finish, the sooner we can celebrate when Mordechai is swinging in the wind." In the meantime, Zeresh and her friends were playing music and singing songs, entertaining the workers as the work progressed.[43]

Finally, the work on the gallows was complete. It was a magnificent structure, towering over the house and the whole neighborhood. Haman stared at it in awe. "I wonder how well it will fit Mordechai," he said. "He and I are about the same size. I will step onto it and see how it fits."

Haman climbed up onto the gallows and stood against the beam. It was a perfect match. "Hey, it's perfect," he shouted down to the

---

41. See *Megillah* 10b; *Maharsha. Yalkut Shimoni* 1059; *Yotzer* to *Parashas Zachor; Krovetz L'Purim; Midrash Panim Acheirim; Midrash Abba Gorion; Esther Rabbah* 9:2; see *Eruvin* 2b. See *Rokeach* for a different opinion.

42. *Midrash Mishlei* 11:27, 28.

43. *Targum Rishon; Gra; Yosef Lekach; R' Shmuel di Uzidah; Alshich; Midrash Abba Gorion; Midrash Panim Acheirim; Yalkut Shimoni.* See *Bereishis* 22:3 and *Shemos* 14:6 on the concept of *sinah* and *ahavah mekalkeles es hashurah* – the tendency of emotions of love and hate to distort clear judgment. Some suggest that these men were making arrows and spears with which to shoot Mordechai (*Rambam*).

others. "It will fit Mordechai like a glove. Gentlemen, I want to congratulate you on a job well done. And in record time to boot!"

In Heaven, the angel Gavriel called out, "Haman! You were right the first time. It fits perfectly. Yes, it does. It fits you perfectly, you and your ten leading sons. Cyrus issued a curse that anyone who prevents the construction of the *Beis HaMikdash* should die by hanging. You will have that honor."[44]

Meanwhile, back on Earth, Haman was beside himself with glee. His heart was pounding so loudly that he could actually hear it from inside. There stood the tree, and in just a few hours it would be crowned with Mordechai's corpse. The deaths of Bigsan and Seresh and the slaughter of his ancestors would finally be avenged. All he had to do was get Achashverosh's permission to proceed with the execution, which should not be too difficult. He would go to the palace in the predawn hours and tell the king that he wanted to execute a rebellious citizen who would go unnamed; there was no point in burdening the king unnecessarily with unpleasant details.[45] There would be no other advisors with the king at that time, since they would all still be asleep. Consequently, the king would accept his

---

44. See *Aggadas Esther; Midrash Panim Acheirim; Yalkut Shimoni; Midrash Abba Gorion; Targum Rishon* 9:14; *Tosafos* to *Yoma* 31a; *Shabbos* 92b; *Midrash Talpios*. One opinion makes the following calculation for the 50-cubit gallows: each hanged man occupied 3 *amos* plus a *zeres*, which multiplied by ten equals 35 *amos*. Haman himself took up three and one-half *amos* bringing the total to 38.5. Between each body there was a space of a *zeres* and an *etzba*, for a total of 43 *amos*. Add to this sum the 3 *amos* that the gallows was buried underground, 2 *amos* plus 1 *zeres* above ground to prevent dogs from reaching the corpse, plus 1 *amah* above Haman's head to keep away birds, and the total is 50 *amos*. Others suggest that each person occupied 4 *amos*, which accounted for 44 *amos*; each one was separated by a half-cubit, adding 5 cubits for the sum of 49; and there was half an *amah* each at the top and the bottom, bringing the total to 50 *amos*.

The word *kesef* (money) has the same numerical value as *Yosef* if one adds the four letters of the name, a common practice in *gematria*. This suggests that Haman felt that he had the right to own the Jews, and thus kill Mordechai, in punishment for the tribes having sold Yosef. He was unaware that Mordechai was a descendant of Binyamin, who did not participate in the sale, and thus was innocent of the act and did not deserve to die for it (*Nachal Eshkol*).

See *Chida* in *Devarim Achadim*, where he discusses the concept of *ein shaliach l'dvar aveirah* and its relevance to non-Jews, including Haman. Some suggest that the merit of Avraham having served the angels under a tree protected Mordechai from this "tree" and instead led to Haman being hung (*Midrash Talpios*; see *Bereishis* 18:4).

This was all predestined from the beginning of Creation, and it is alluded to in the words *hamin ha'etz*, from the tree (*Bereishis* 3:11); the word *hamin* can also be read as *Haman*. It is thus not surprising that Hashem had asked the trees during the first six days of Creation which species would be willing to have Haman hanged on it (see *Chullin* 139b; *Ya'aros Devash*).

45. *D'na Pishra; Yosef Lekach;* see *Gra; R' Elisha Galico; R' Shmuel di Uzidah; Yedei Moshe; Ma'amar Mordechai; Menos HaLevi; Malbim; Yismach Lev.*

request as a matter of course without giving it too much thought. And if he refused for some reason, there would no one in attendance to see his embarrassment.[46]

Yes, a predawn visit would be perfect. By morning, Mordechai would be charged, arrested and hanged. Even if Esther had some residual sympathy, it would be too late to do anything by the time she awoke. Haman also considered it important to arrest Mordechai before his morning prayers, since the *Shema* was reputed to have strong protective powers.[47]

Haman set out for the palace, but he could not resist peeking in on Mordechai on the way. He rode to the *beis midrash* and found Mordechai dressed in sackcloth and ashes, learning Torah with the children, who were also wearing sackcloth and ashes and fasting into their third day.

He stormed in with his guards and arrested the children. A sweep through the Jewish district brought in thousands more fasting children.

"So we meet again, Mordechai," said Haman, "but for just about the last time. My patience has run out. These children who foretold my demise shall die first, but you will not be far behind. Look out the window, and you will see the high gallows I have erected on my estate in your honor."

The children were led off to the dungeons with their scrolls clutched tightly in their little hands. Word of the catastrophe spread quickly. Soon the parents came running to the dungeons to bring their children food and water to sustain them in their hardship.

"Here, take my scroll," said one boy to his father. "We did not earn long life through our Torah study, and we will not be needing these any longer."

---

46. See *Midrash Lekach Tov; R' Elisha Galico; Gra; R' Shmuel di Uzidah.* Haman perceived that nighttime was auspicious for him. The angel of Eisav was more powerful at night, as illustrated by his begging Yaakov to release him before the sun came up (*Bereishis* 32:27). Haman also sensed that his power was strongest at night (*Alshich*). Divine Providence had led Haman to think this way to lead to his own downfall. When Achashverosh awoke after his disturbing dream, Haman himself was conveniently available to honor Mordechai. The Divine Hand was later evident as well, when the king became angry with Haman. Charbonah pointed out the large gallows visible from the palace windows, and the king declared that Haman be hanged from it, which was easily arranged (*Yosef Lekach*).

47. See *Midrash Talpios* under letter *aleph*, Achashverosh; *R' Yosef ibn Yachia; D'na Pishra; Midrash Lekach Tov; R' Elisha Galico; Malbim; Ya'aros Devash.* See *Sotah* 42a-b with *Maharsha; Ein Yaakov; Vayikra Rabbah* 28:6; *Tanchuma Kedoshim* 6. Yaakov said *Shema* before meeting Eisav, Haman's grandfather, who was marching toward him with 400 armed soldiers, and Yaakov prevailed in the merit of this prayer.

"Take some food and water, my son," the father pleaded.

"We have made an oath not to break our fast," the son replied. "We will die hungry and tired."

The moaning of the children grew louder as the minutes passed.

Up in Heaven, the angels remarked that they could hear "the crying of lambs and young goats."

"Those are not lambs and young goats you are hearing," Moshe told them. "Those are the cries of young Jewish children who are giving their lives for the Torah and the honor of the Almighty. They are suffering and dying, while Haman and his henchmen are laughing."

The pure voices of innocent young Jewish children forced open the heavenly gates, and the sweet sounds and breath of their learning and praying came before the heavenly throne.

"I am breaking the seal of the evil decree," the Almighty declared. "Haman will not carry out his plan. His fortunes will fall, and the fortunes of the Jewish people will rise. Haman will hang from the very tree he prepared for Mordechai. It has been destined to be so since Creation. On this day, Haman will die, and joy will replace the weeping."[48]

---

48. See *Midrash Abba Gorion; Aggadas Esther; Midrash Panim Acheirim; Yalkut Shimoni; Esther Rabbah* 9:2; *Targum Rishon; Midrash Tehillim* 30. See *Shabbos* 119b.

A Sleepless Night

20

It was nearing the end of the second night of Pesach, the third night of the Fast of Esther. In Heaven, the cries of the Jewish children had awakened Hashem to the plight of the Jewish people, so to speak. The forefathers, Avraham, Yitzchak and Yaakov, together with Moshe, Aharon and the heavenly angels, spent the night in prayer and supplication, also foregoing sleep, so to speak.[1]

In Shushan below, it was also a night of widespread sleeplessness. Haman, his family and associates had spent the whole night building the giant

1. See *Esther Rabbah* 10:11; *Tehillim* 78:65; *Megillah* 15b; *Targum Rishon; Midrash Panim Acheirim; Yalkut Shimoni*. For the first time, Hashem demonstrated to Achashverosh that, although he perceived himself as a *"melech bekipah"* (King over the entire world), he was mortal after all (*Sifsei Chachamim*). It was in the merit of Pesach that the redemption of the Jews would begin (*Tzuf Devash*). See *Pesikta d'Rav Kahana* ch. 17, pg. 129; *Midrash HaGadol Shemos* 157; *Krovetz L'Purim; piyut* to *Haggadah "Az rov nissim"*; see *Let My Nation Go*, ch. 17, pg. 290, 291, footnote 7. See *Targum Rishon; Rokeach; Sha'arei Binah*. On this night Avimelech had taken Sarah; the firstborn of Egypt were killed; and the army of Sancheriv miraculously perished. For a detailed explanation of the different opinions, see *R' Elisha Galico*.

gallows. Mordechai was learning and praying in the *beis midrash* with his colleagues and students, all fasting and dressed in sackcloth and ashes. Esther was up early to make sure her maidservants did not inadvertently allow any *chametz* into her apartments when they were preparing the food.[2]

In the palace, Achashverosh was also having a sleepless night. He had returned bone tired to his quarters after Esther's banquet and more than a little intoxicated from all the wine he had poured into his belly. It had been a long and stressful day, and he was ready to slide between the satin sheets and sink into a few hours of blissful sleep. But it wasn't happening.[3]

In Heaven, Hashem had summoned the angel in charge of sleep and befuddlement and commanded, "Wake this ingrate up! My children are suffering, and he dares to sleep!" The angel descended and began to torment Achashverosh. Just as the king's eyes were drooping shut, the angel struck him a mighty blow that sent him tumbling to the ground and drove any thoughts of sleep from his mind.

The dazed king picked himself up and climbed back into bed, wondering what could possibly have disturbed his rest to such a degree. Perhaps it had been the beginning of a bad dream; he simply didn't know. He tried to return to sleep, but the same thing happened again. No warning, just a violent thrust tossing him out of his bed. What could be causing this? Could it be that he was in the midst of a most bizarre, incredibly realistic dream? Achashverosh berated himself for drinking so much. The strong wine had no doubt addled his brain to the point that he did not know what was happening, even though it seemed to him that he was awake.[4]

Suddenly, he began hallucinating. Through his alcoholic haze, he thought he heard the rumbling of a voice, but he couldn't be sure. He looked around the bedchamber but saw no one. He looked in the closets and under the bed, but all he found was dust. He rubbed his ears and shook his head. That wine! Gingerly, he got back into his

---

2. See *Esther Rabbah* 10:11; *Megillah* 15b; *Targum Rishon*; *Chiddushei Harim* on *Pesach*; see *Tehillim* 44:24, 121:4.

3. *Rashi; Yedei Moshe; Alshich.*

4. See *Yalkut Shimoni; Targum Sheni.* It is possible that there were actually two angels, one appointed over sleep and one for *behalah*, confusion. Others suggest the king was struck 365 times, because of the 365 advisors Haman had consulted about how to kill Mordechai (*Midrash Talpios*). Others suggest that he was hit 366 times. Some say that the angel appointed over Achashverosh was Michael, not Gavriel (*Targum Rishon*).

bed and grabbed onto the bedclothes, braced for the next convulsion that would cast him out.

An eerie mist rose up in the room. It was invisible to the eye, but he could feel it in his bones. The air trembled and vibrated, and a rumbling voice reverberated through the chamber. The voice was saying something, and Achashverosh strained to make out the words. "Ingrate . . ." he heard. Then something unintelligible, then again, "Ingrate . . . repay . . . old debts . . ." He did not get the whole message, but he got the gist of it. It had something to do with old debts he had not yet repaid. What old debts? He could think of no old debts. Was his imagination playing tricks on him again? Was the wine causing him to hallucinate as he never had before?

Achashverosh gave up trying to fall asleep. He stumbled to an overstuffed chair and sat down. His head was throbbing from sleep deprivation and disorientation. What was happening to him?

A disturbing thought occurred to him. Someone must have slipped him a potion that robbed him of his sleep and caused him to hallucinate, and it could only have happened at Esther's banquet. He would get to the bottom of this, and right away. He immediately summoned every member of the palace kitchen staff that had enjoyed access to the food and drink served at the banquet. Within minutes, they were all assembled in front of the king, bakers, butchers, stewards, most of them groggy, bleary-eyed and rumpled.

"Listen here, you scoundrels," Achashverosh shouted. "One of you did something to my food or wine last night, and now I am having hallucinations. If the guilty one comes forward, admits his crime and gives me full details, I will execute him and let the others go. Otherwise, you will all die. You have one minute to decide. Who is the culprit? Answer me!"

The kitchen workers shrank back in fear, but none of them stepped forward. Achashverosh snapped his fingers, and his guards sprang forward.

"Wait a minute, your majesty," a young butcher burst out. "None of us has come forward, because we are all innocent. I know these, your majesty. None of them would dream of harming you."

"Pah! The character reference of a butcher mean nothing to me," said Achashverosh as he waved a haughty arm. "Guards, take them away."

"Wait! Your majesty!" the butcher screamed in desperation. "I can prove we are innocent."

Achashverosh held up his hand, and the guards stood back. "Prove it."

"Your majesty, if any of us poisoned your food or drink at the banquet, Esther and Haman would also have been affected. Why don't we just check if they are also having hallucinations."

"Esther did not eat or drink at the banquet."

"Then Haman, your majesty."

"Very well, we will check." He pointed to one of the guards. "Go right now and check on Haman."

The guard returned in less than fifteen minutes. "Haman seems perfectly fine, your majesty," he reported.

"Did you wake him? Was he sound asleep?"

"Actually, he was wide awake and busily engaged in building some kind of structure near his house."

"Is that the cause of all the infernal banging and hammering I've been hearing for the last few hours?"

"I'm afraid so, your majesty."

"But otherwise he seemed well? Did he appear to be hallucinating?"

"He seemed perfectly fine. No different from always."

Achashverosh grumbled. He turned to the cowering kitchen staff. "All right. You men can go back to your jobs. But don't let this happen ever again."[5]

Achashverosh sank deep into thought after everyone left. What could be the explanation of his insomnia and hallucinations? He began to have the glimmer of a suspicion that Haman might be at fault. Esther had invited Haman to a private banquet not once but twice. Was something going on between them? And if so, was Haman plotting to kill Achashverosh, take the crown and marry the queen?

But if this were true, someone would have caught an inkling of it, some word would have reached Achashverosh. Why, the king wondered, was no one telling him anything? Could it be that the information was being withheld from him because he had failed to repay an old debt? Was that what the disembodied voice was trying to tell him? But who had done this favor for him without being repaid? This called for some research.

He pulled his bell rope, and an attendant appeared.

5. *Midrash Abba Gorion; Targum Rishon; Yalkut Shimoni;* see *Rashi; R' Yosef ibn Yachia; R' Elisha Galico; Menos HaLevi; Koheles Rabbah,* ch. 5; *Pirkei d'Rav Eliezer* 50 with *Radal;* see *Sha'arei Binah;* see *Rokeach; Pirush Megillas Achashverosh; R' Chaim Abulafia; Ya'aros Devash;* see *Yeshayahu* 21:15.

"Go bring my book of records," said Achashverosh. "I need to look up something.[6] Besides, I can't fall asleep. I might as well read. Perhaps the reading will help me fall asleep. Also, bring a good scribe to read for me."[7]

The attendant went off to fetch the book and the scribe, and Achashverosh's thoughts turned to Esther once again. She had risked her life to approach him, but then she had refused to divulge her request. Logic said she wanted to plead for someone else. It couldn't be for her own needs, because she had everything she could possibly want. Who could this someone else be but Mordechai, who had taken her in as a child? Kind woman that she is, she has not forgotten her debt of gratitude to Mordechai even though she has progressed far beyond her erstwhile Jewish benefactor. But how could the king grant leniency or pardon to Mordechai when all the Jews were under an irrevocable decree of death? There was only one way. He would have to look for a mention of Mordechai in the book of records. If Mordechai had ever done something advantageous for the throne, he could be exempted from the general decree. The book of records would tell the story.[8]

The Persian royal archives had a voluminous book of chronicles, which recorded, to the best of the Persian historians' knowledge, every significant event that had happened in the world since creation and every even insignificant event that had happened in the Persian-Medean Empire since its inception. There was also a second archive, called the book of records, which was essentially an index to the book of chronicles. Favors done to the king were recorded in the book of records and remained there until the provider of the favor was rewarded, at which time it was erased.

Presently, the guard returned with the book of records and several royal scribes, sons of Haman, who would read from it to the king. Shimshai stepped forward and bowed.[9] Achashverosh settled

---

6. See *Megillah* 15b; *Yalkut Shimoni*; *Malbim*.

7. *R' Yosef ibn Yachia; R' Yosef ibn Nachmiash.* When he could not sleep, it was the king's custom to play, relax or read, especially the book of chronicles. Others suggest that it would have been more likely for him to request music to ease him to sleep, but since he wished to investigate the unpaid debt, he asked for this book (*Maharal*).

8. *Gra; Yosef Lekach;* see *R' Shmuel di Uzidah,* in the name of *Yedei Moshe; Yishai Elokim; Malbim.*

9. See *Ben Yehoyada* to *Megillah* 15b; *Gra; Yosef Lekach; R' Elisha Galico; Menos HaLevi; Yad HaMelech; Alshich.* This book of records is referred to in Esther as the *sefer hazichronos.* This was also a symbolic reference to Hashem recalling the merit of the *Avos* (forefathers); in the *Mussaf* prayer of Rosh Hashanah this is included in *Zichronos* (*R' Shmuel di Uzidah*). Others suggest that while Haman had altered the public record, he could not tamper with Achashverosh's private diary or his own book of records, and this is the book which was now being read to him (*Malbim*).

back to listen. At the least, he would be entertained by stories of the glorious past, and his own memories of thrilling adventures and sweet victories would be reawakened. Perhaps he would also discover the unpaid debt of gratitude that might be responsible for his bizarre discomfiture on this awful night.[10]

"Read, Shimshai!" Achashverosh commanded. He leaned back and closed his eyes.

Shimshai droned on for a while without incident, but then he reached the part where Mordechai had saved Achashverosh from the assassination plot of Bigsan and Seresh. Shimshai despised Mordechai as much as his father did, and he did not want to read such a favorable report to the king. Quickly, he rolled the scroll forward and began reading the next entry. Miraculously, however, the scroll returned to the account of Mordechai's service to the king. Shimshai tried to roll the scroll forward again, but it flipped right back again.[11]

After five attempts, he gave up in frustration. Instead, he erased Mordechai's name and replaced it with Haman's, but the angel Gavriel undid everything Shimshai did, restoring Mordechai's name as it was before. In desperation, Shimshai tried at least to minimize the favor, replacing the conjunction "and" with "or" between the names Bigsan and Seresh. At least, the king would think there had been only one assassin rather than two. But the angel Gavriel corrected this corruption as well.[12]

"What is going on, Shimshai?" Achashverosh asked. "Why aren't you reading? What are you fussing about over there?"

"There is some problem with the text, your majesty. I was just trying to correct it." He laughed nervously. "It was really nothing."

"Good! Then go on reading. I am becoming impatient."

"Ahem, your majesty, I'm afraid I cannot read any more of this."

Achashverosh leaned forward. "Why not?"

---

10. *Yad HaMelech.*

11. *D'na Pishra.* This was the same Shimshai who was involved in convincing Koresh not to allow the rebuilding of the *Beis HaMikdash* (*Rashi* in *Megillah;* see *Ezra* 4:6,8).

12. See *Sifsei Chachamim; R' Chaim Abulafia; Midrash Talpios; D'na Pishra; Menos HaLevi; Malbim; Melo HaOmer.* Some suggest that it was only Gavriel who understoood all 70 languages, and would be able to make the necessary changes in the book (*Ya'aros Devash*). Shimshai wanted to make it seem like two people were exceuted when only one was guilty of attempted assassination. This would greatly minimize Mordechai's deed, since while he saved the king he had also caused the death of an innocent man, so he entered *Bigsan oh Seresh* — Bigsan or Seresh — into the record. The angel Gavriel, however, would not permit the lie to remain, and made it clear that both were guilty and deserving of death, changing the spacing of the letters so it read *Bigsana v'Seresh,* Bigsana and Seresh.

"Because there seems to be some problem with this scroll. The writing is not at all clear. Perhaps I can read something else to you, your majesty."

Achashverosh frowned.

"It is written here," said a voice.

Shimshai jumped from his chair. "What is that voice?" he screamed.

"It seems to be the scroll speaking," said Achashverosh. "How interesting. Be quite and sit down, Shimshai. I want to hear this."

"It is written here," the scroll repeated, "that Bigsan and Seresh, two of the king's servants assigned to guard his chambers, plotted to assassinate the king. Mordechai the Jew discovered the plot and reported it, thereby saving the king's life."[13]

This was absolute news to Achashverosh. All along, he had thought Esther had discovered the plot, perhaps on her own, perhaps with the help of Haman. All the pieces began to fall into place. If Esther was not fully loyal to her husband, then Mordechai would never have saved his life. So Esther was really loyal, and Mordechai was owed a debt of gratitude. Haman had deceitfully taken the credit for Mordechai's deed and achieved his high status under false pretenses. What a devious schemer that man was! What a snake in the grass![14]

---

13. See *Targum Rishon; Targum Sheni; Megillah 15b; Aggadas Esther; Midrash Abba Gorion; Midrash Panim Acheirim.* Some suggest that it did not actually read itself, but it became so easily read that it was as if the words "leaped off the page" (see *Maharal*). Others suggest that the King took it from Shimshai and read it himself, while still others say it was Eliyahu *HaNavi* who kept rewriting the correction. Some further suggest that what Mordechai did was not written in the book at all, but only spoken, which was symbolic of the Jews' acceptance at this time of Torah *sheb'al peh* (Oral Law); *Ya'aros Devash.* It seems unlikely that Shimshai would attempt to erase a complete story or alter the details in an official book which was well known to many people. It is more probable that the book from which he was reading and which he attempted to falsify had been used for casual note-taking (*R' Shmuel di Uzidah; Menos HaLevi; Alshich*).

14. *R' Shmuel di Uzidah; Ya'aros Devash; Malbim; Melo HaOmer; R' Chaim Abulafia; Malbim.* It is actually not unprecedented that an inanimate object called out words. When the Jews had cast lots to determine which portion of *Eretz Yisrael* would go to each tribe, the papers called out the name of each tribe (*Yalkut* to *Esther;* see *Bamidbar* 26:56 with *Rashi* and *Sifsei Chachamim*). Some say that Achashverosh had known that Mordechai had been the one to save him, but it had slipped his mind. Now he regretted his forgetfullness and his failure to reward Mordechai. As mentioned earlier, some suggest that in order to keep Mordechai's involvement secret, the incident was written giving credit to Esther. Now it miraculously appeared with Mordechai's name instead (*R' Chaim Abulafia*). Some suggest that it was necessary for Mordechai to be saved first; once his life was spared he would be able to pray more freely and act as an advocate for the Jewish people. In keeping with the principle of *ein chavush matir atzmo mibeis ha'assurim* (a prisoner cannot free himself from prison), Mordechai's prayers would not be effective while he was in Haman's power, under the enforcement of the decree (*Ya'aros Devash*).

"All you scribes are dismissed," shouted the king. "Not just for now but permanently. You are a bunch of bumbling fools. How could you make such an omission, not telling me that I had an unpaid debt to Mordechai. I don't care that you're sons of the prime minister. You're all fired."[15]

The scribes shrank back in fear, and Achashverosh roared with laughter. He was feeling much better. He was no longer drunk or disoriented or hallucinatory. He was gaining control of his life again.

A pleasant drowsiness came over him. He left the servants and scribes in the outer chamber and he went back to his bed. There was still time to snatch some sleep before dawn. Somehow, he knew he would now be able to sleep. And he did.[16]

In his dream, Achashverosh saw Haman standing over him. In one hand, the wily prime minister held a drawn sword while with the other hand he was removing the king's crown and purple cloak. Achashverosh awoke in a cold sweat and jumped out of his bed. What message had he seen in this frightening dream? Clearly, Haman wanted to kill him. Haman was emerging as a major problem.[17] It did not occur to him that all dreams have inaccuracies and that Haman was really trying to kill Mordechai, Esther's legitimate husband.[18]

Although he had barely slept at all, Achashverosh decided not to go back to bed. The first rays of the sun were already touching the horizon, and there was much to be done. The first order of business was to reward Mordechai immediately.[19] It was important that people know that the king gives reward as soon as he hears someone deserves it; it would encourage them to come forward when they had important information.[20] There was also a second advantage in rewarding Mordechai immediately. If, as he suspected, Esther was going to plead at the banquet that evening that Mordechai deserved to be rewarded, which could become problematic, he could reply that he had already given him his reward.[21]

15. *Tosafos Berachah, Shoftim.*
16. *Aggadas Esther; Rokeach; Menos HaLevi.*
17. *Midrash Abba Gorion; Esther Rabbah* 10:1; *Rokeach.*
18. As seen in *Talelei Oros.*
19. *Rambam; R' Elisha Galico.*
20. *R' Yosef ibn Yachia.*
21. See *Gra; Yosef Lekach.*

As Achashverosh mulled over these matters, there was a loud knock on the gates of the inner courtyard, within easy earshot of the king's chambers. Achashverosh was perplexed. Who dared to disturb the king's sleep by knocking at such an early hour? He sent a servant to investigate.

Moments later, the servant returned. "It is Haman, your majesty. He says he has urgent business that cannot wait."

"Hmmph," said Achashverosh. It was most unusual for Haman to come to the palace so early. Usually, he took advantage of his high station to come last, and now, he was coming at the crack of dawn while everyone else is still asleep. The dream was right, thought Achashverosh. He's come to kill me.[22]

"Leave him waiting in the courtyard," Achashverosh said aloud. He would see how long Haman's patience lasted before he took the liberty of entering the king's chamber unbidden. He would see if Haman's intentions were really murderous, as the dream had suggested.[23] At the same time, it occurred to Achashverosh that Haman's present might just be useful, since he would need some advice as to the proper reward for Mordechai.[24]

Achashverosh stepped into the outer chamber where the dismissed scribes were cowering. "You scribes, sons of Haman," he declared, "I want to know if Mordechai ever received a reward for the great service he did for me. His loyal deed is recorded but there is no mention of a reward was there one? Did he receive any special honors or riches?"

Some of the scribes pretended they hadn't heard the king. Others simply shrugged their shoulders. None wanted to admit that Mordechai was still owed a reward.[25]

Achashverosh turned to his servants. "Does any one of you know the answer to my question? Did Mordechai ever receive a reward?"

"No, your majesty," his valet replied. "Nothing was ever done for the man for the last five years."[26]

---

22. *Aggadas Esther; Esther Rabbah* 10:1; *Midrash Panim Acheirim; Pirkei d'Rav Eliezer* 50 with *Radal;* see *Yosef Lekach; Yad HaMelech; Kli Chemdah* to *Parashas Tetzaveh; Gra.* Secretly, Haman did indeed want to kill the King. He thought that if he could kill Achashverosh and Mordechai, he could gain the support of the rebellious Greeks and gain the throne for himself (*Ya'aros Devash; Yosifun*).

23. *R' Chaim Abulafia; Menos HaLevi; Yad HaMelech.*

24. *Yishai Elokim; Menos HaLevi.*

25. *R' Shmuel di Uzidah.*

26. See *Rambam; R' Yosef ibn Yachia; Yedei Moshe.* They spoke more out of hatred for Haman than love for Mordechai. If it were the latter, they would have mentioned him at the outset (*Megillah* 15a).

"The man meaning . . . ?"

"Mordechai, your majesty," said the valet. "No riches, no honor, not even simple words of praise."[27]

"But wait," said a butler. "Perhaps the king did not want to reward Mordechai. Perhaps he felt that he was duty-bound to tell in any case and, therefore, did not deserve a reward."

"Nonsense," said the valet. "The king would be in great danger if people thought the way you did. People would perceive him as ungrateful, and they would not be forthcoming with important information. Anyway, I can prove it to you. Someone was rewarded for uncovering the assassination plot, only it wasn't Mordechai. It was Haman! He was honored by a law that required all people to bow to him. And he was elevated to a position of power second only to the king. I would call that serious reward, wouldn't you?"[28]

"One minute, my good fellows," said Achashverosh. "Wasn't Mordechai given the privilege of sitting in the palace gate? Doesn't that constitute a reward?"

"It would certainly be considered a reward," said the valet, "but he received that privilege as soon as Esther became queen, well before the assassination plot. In fact, looking back, that appointment actually led to the discovery of the plot, since Mordechai overheard Bigsan and Seresh while sitting in the palace gate. But even had he received that privilege it would not be considered sufficient reward according to royal custom."[29]

"Protocol, your majesty," said the butler, "would call for special dress or a title at the very least. The key to the city for a day would also be an option. Or a promotion to a higher office. Or the grant of a fiefdom."[30]

"These are good suggestions," said Achashverosh, "but you are not objective. You know all the circumstances of the case. I will ask Haman for his opinion without telling him what is involved. He will give me an objective opinion." Achashverosh frowned. "Enough. I must think."[31]

---

27. R' Yosef ibn Yachia. R' Avigdor Kohen Tzedek; Gra; Yosef Lekach; R' Shmuel di Uzidah; Chomas Anach; R' Elisha Galico; Menos HaLevi; Malbim.

28. See R' Chaim Abulafia; Maharal; Alshich.

29. Menos HaLevi; Malbim. Some suggest that Achashverosh felt that Mordechai deserved an additional level of honor. He had already bestowed greatness on Mordechai by allowing him to sit at the palace gates; he now wished to confer honor upon him as well (Yosef Lekach).

30. R' Shmuel di Uzidah; Sha'arei Binah.

31. Ibid.

Things are becoming clearer and clearer, thought Achashverosh. Esther had reported the plot, but she had not mentioned Mordechai's role in it. Mordechai probably didn't let her tell me, because he is a pious man uninterested in reward. He saved my life out of the goodness of his heart. Esther, however, is upset that he was never rewarded. But how could I reward him if I didn't know about him? I wanted to reward Esther, but there was no point. She has everything. Instead, I rewarded Haman, because I thought that would please Esther.[32] After all, Haman was instrumental in removing Vashti and opening the way for Esther. Meanwhile, Haman wants to kill me in revenge for killing his cousins Bigsan and Seresh. He also wants to kill Mordechai for thwarting the assassination plot, which would have killed me. Perhaps Haman put them up to it in the first place. I can see that all my earlier assumptions are open to question. Anything is possible. Well, let us see what Haman is up to. I will keep my guard up.[33]

"Why was I never told that Mordechai had never been rewarded?" Achashverosh asked his servants. "After all, it is written in the book of records. Why was it never brought to my attention?"

The servants shrugged.

"Did anyone tell you not to tell me?" Achashverosh persisted.

They both nodded and inclined their head toward the courtyard.

"Say no more," said Achashverosh. "I know exactly whom you mean."[34]

Outside in the courtyard, Haman was growing increasingly impatient. He had heard the king ask who was there. He had heard people stirring, and the palace awakening. And still he was cooling his heels in the courtyard. It was unseemly![35] He thought about Esther entering unbidden the previous day. The king had not punished her for it. On the contrary, he had granted her any request she asked for, until half the kingdom. Surely, the king would also receive him favorably and be happy to grant his request.

Having thus reassured himself, Haman squared his shoulders, took a deep breath and entered the king's chambers.

---

32. *Alshich.*

33. See *Alshich; Megillas Sesarim; Me'am Loez;* see *Kli Chemdah* to *Parashas Tetzaveh.*

34. *Alshich; Tehillah L'David;* see *Yosef Lekach.*

35. See *Me'am Loez; Sipur HaTa'anis;* see *D'na Pishra.* See *Rokeach,* who discusses what time it was when this occurred. Some further suggest that two angels escorted Haman to the palace, towards his eventual downfall (*Menos HaLevi*).

"A good early morning to you, your majesty," he said with a hearty cheer he did not feel.

"Oh, Haman," said Achashverosh. "Good to see you."[36]

Then the king fell into a brooding silence, absorbed by suspicions of Haman's murderous intent and his desire to usurp the throne. He knew he would have to be clever to deal with Haman and trap him into exposing his true intentions. He would ask him about the reward in such a way that Haman would think he was the intended receiver and perhaps make a serious blunder. Furthermore, since Haman already had as much power as possible, he would ask only for additional honors. Based on this advice, Achashverosh would feel comfortable repaying his debt to Mordechai, for whom he had no great love, with honors but no grants of power.[37]

"You're just the person I want to see, Haman," Achashverosh said at last. "I need sage advice, and no one surpasses you in wise counsel. Tell me, Haman, what should be done for someone the king wants to honor?"[38]

"Hmm," said Haman. "Can I have a moment or two to think about it?"

"Of course. Take your time. I need a good answer, not a quick one."

Haman held the question up in his mind's eye and examined it from all sides. What is the meaning of this strange question? Why didn't the king mention the person who was to be honored? Also, why did the king ask only about honor and not about reward? It would appear that the person he wants to honor is already beyond reward; he already has all the wealth and power to which a person can aspire. Who is this person?

It can only be me, thought Haman. I have already achieved everything. All that is left is honor. Therefore, I must give an answer that is suited to me. What would I enjoy? Ah, the pleasures that are coming.[39] But wait! I must not let myself be carried away by my emo-

---

36. See *Midrash Lekach Tov; D'na Pishra.*

37. See *Yedei Moshe; Gra; Yosef Lekach; Malbim.*

38. *Midrash Abba Gorion; Pirkei d'Rav Eliezer.*

39. See *Megillah* 7a; *R' Shmuel di Uzidah; Targum Sheni; Yedei Moshe; Yad HaMelech; Gra; Yosef Lekach; Malbim.* It is suggested that from here one can infer that the *megillah* was written with *ruach hakodesh*; there is no other way we would know what Haman was thinking. Others suggest that it does not require great wisdom to discern what the conceited Haman thought. Others posit that Haman later told people what he had thought (*Ibn Ezra*). Haman resembled Yeravam and Eisav; their thoughts of evil also did not materialize. In fact, their thoughts were the very vehicle leading to their downfall (*Bereishis Rabbah* 72:9).

tions. What if the king has someone else in mind? Would I want to be responsible for raising someone else up above me? Impossible! I must think of something that would be very valuable and memorable for me but which would pass quickly and be forgotten for someone else, should the king not be thinking of me.[40]

"Your majesty, I have an idea," said Haman.

"Don't you always, Haman?" said Achashverosh. "Out with it. What is your idea?"

"I think we should begin by announcing that the king wishes to honor this person.[41] Once this has been publicized, an officer of the king should dress him in the king's royal garments — purple robes, hat, belt, shoes."

"But I have innumerable garments," said Achashverosh. "Which ones would we choose?"

"The ones you wore on the day of your coronation might be one possibility," said Haman. "Cyrus' green robes or the robes of Adam, the first man, might be another. Or the garments you wear when you sit on your throne and receive people. All these are possibilities. Whichever you choose would be fine."[42]

"Go on. What else?"

"He should ride the king's horse," Haman continued, "the one upon which the king rode on his coronation day. And yes, the king's coronation crown would also be a very lovely touch."[43]

The king's face, pale and drawn from lack of sleep, turned as purple as his royal robe. "My crown?" he spluttered. Now he was convinced he had been right about Haman. The man was after his crown. He was not satisfied with all his vast powers and riches. He wanted the crown and the throne.[44]

Haman, cunning as always, instantly realized his blunder and sought to cover it. "Of course, the crown would not be worn by the man you seek to honor," he said smoothly. "That would be too much, I think. It would not be respectful to the king and would send the wrong message. No, what I meant was to place the crown on the

---

40. See *R' Elisha Galico; Yad HaMelech; R' Shmuel di Uzidah; Menos HaLevi; Sefas Emes.*

41. *Malbim.*

42. *Koheles Rabbah* 5:2; *Targum Rishon; Yosef Lekach; Alshich; Ibn Ezra; Ma'amar Mordechai;* see *Aggadas Esther; Midrash Abba Gorion; Midrash Lekach Tov; R' Saadiah Gaon; Yedei Moshe.*

43. *R' Yosef ibn Nachmiash; Rambam.*

44. See *Koheles Rabbah* 5:2; *Pirkei d'Rav Eliezer; R' Avigdor Kohen Tzedek.* This is what is meant by *foolish talk [comes] from many words (Koheles 5:2).*

pommel of the horse's saddle as a reminder of the king, to show the favor of the king for this fortunate beneficiary of the king's honors. The whole point of the crown on the saddle would be to remind people that the man on the horse was not the king, even though he was being honored by being allowed to wear the royal garments."[45]

Achashverosh grudgingly accepted Haman's explanation, but his trust had been further undermined. He looked at Haman with ever-growing suspicion.[46]

"Go on," he said.

"The officer," said Haman, "would lead the man on the king's horse through the streets of Shushan, shouting, 'This is what is done for a man the king wishes to honor!' The people will be required to bow down, and anyone who doesn't will be instantly executed. The man would also be deemed worthy of marrying the king's daughter."[47]

Haman had chosen honors he would enjoy immensely. He also hoped to have Mordechai assigned as the officer to lead him through the streets. What a delicious touch of irony that would be! The icing on the cake![48]

It never dawned on Haman that the person Achashverosh was speaking about was Mordechai; he thought all his enemies were also the enemies of Achashverosh. Had he suspected it for a moment, he never would have mentioned those things.[49]

Haman was very careful with his suggestions, because he could not be absolutely sure the king was thinking of him. He therefore suggested honors he had not yet received that, if given to others, would not elevate them over him. He did not suggest that this mystery person receive the king's ring, because he already had it. In the end, however, Mordechai would get more honors and power than Haman ever had.[50]

---

45. See *Menos HaLevi; R' Shmuel di Uzidah; Alshich; Yishai Elokim;* see *Ibn Ezra, R' Yosef ibn Nachmiash; R' Elisha Galico.*

46. See *Menos HaLevi; R' Shmuel di Uzidah; Alshich; Yishai Elokim.*

47. See *Esther* 6:9; *Midrash Abba Gorion; Aggadas Esther; R' Yosef ibn Nachmiash;* see *Menos HaLevi; R' Elisha Galico;* see *Alshich; Me'am Loez.* Assuming that he himself was the person to be honored, Haman saw in this an excellent opportunity to kill Mordechai the next time he refused to bow to him.

48. *Rokeach; Yedei Moshe; Yishai Elokim.*

49. *Ma'amar Mordechai.*

50. *R' Shmuel di Uzidah.*

The Tables Are Turned

21

Haman's suggestion pleased Achashverosh. Whether or not his motives were pure, the proposal itself enhanced the honor of the king even as it honored the beneficiary. If wearing the king's garments was such a great honor, then surely the king himself is regarded with the highest esteem and respect. "Yes," he decided. "I will accept this suggestion, and I will have it carried out immediately before anyone can argue against it and introduce doubt into my mind."[1]

While the king was thinking, Haman indulged himself in pleasant daydream. He could already imagine himself sitting astride the horse in the public square of Shushan, resplendent in the royal garments, gazing down disdainfully at the mere mortals who looked up to him in awe.

"I have made up my mind," said Achashverosh, interrupting Haman's pleasant reverie. "Take the garments and the horse and go immediately to

1. *Ma'amar Mordechai.*

Mordechai. I want you to do for him exactly as you said. Do not omit a single detail. And hurry! I fear Esther may make a request on behalf of Mordechai at the banquet tonight. I want him to have been paid off by then."[2]

Haman was thunderstruck. Could the king have possibly chosen to honor his archenemy and to have him provide the honors? It couldn't be!

"Mordechai? Mordechai?" said Haman in desperation. "Who is Mordechai? There are many men named Mordechai in Shushan."

"Don't waste time, Haman. It is Mordechai the Jew."[3]

"Oh, that one. But legally he cannot be honored, since all the Jews are under a sentence of death. And anyway, may I respectfully remind your majesty that I have acquired the right to the Jews of the empire, and I am not inclined to shower them with honors."

"Don't trifle with me, Haman," said Achashverosh. "Mordechai is a high palace official, a distinguished general and diplomat. I have never sold you the rights to any of my officials, regardless of their religion. I only gave you the rights to the Jewish commonfolk. Now, stop wasting time, and go do as I say. Right now!"[4]

The awful reality that there was no way out of this predicament finally sank into Haman's consciousness, and he fainted dead away. He lay on the ground for a minute or two before he regained consciousness. He opened his eyes and saw Achashverosh staring at him balefully.

"Well, how long do you intend to lie there, Haman?" Achashverosh snapped. "Get going already! Get out of my sight!"

Haman's head swam as he scrambled to his feet. "Please, your majesty. I understand that you want to honor Mordechai, but why through me? Why humiliate me by making me do this?"

"Look around you, Haman. Do you see any other officials here? If you choose to come to the palace at the crack of dawn when no one else is here, you must be prepared to undertake all sorts of tasks."

Haman opened his mouth to reply, but Achashverosh stopped him with a raised hand.

2. *Iyun Yaakov; Gra; Yosef Lekach; Melo HaOmer; Yad HaMelech.* See *Bereishis Rabbasi,* which points out that in the merit of Sarah hurrying to provide food for the visiting angels (*Bereishis* 18:6), her descendant Mordechai would have Haman to hurry to honor him.
3. See *Megillah* 15a; *Pirkei d'Rav Eliezer.*
4. See *Megillah* 15a; *Pirkei d'Rav Eliezer; Targum Sheni; R' Avigdor Kohen Tzedek; Yad HaMelech; Alshich.*

"I don't want to hear your arguments, Haman," he said. "The truth is that even if you hadn't been here I would have called on you to do this task. You are not half the man Mordechai is. He may be exiled from his native country, but he saved my life. You threatened it. Mordechai sits on the Sanhedrin. He speaks seventy languages. He understood what Bigsan and Seresh were saying when they plotted to assassinate me. But instead of honoring him, I mistakenly honored you, because you fooled me. When you walk in front of Mordechai's horse, think of this humiliation as your atonement for taking an honor that belonged to another man, a better man than you."[5]

Haman had pulled himself together somewhat while the king was talking. He had gathered his wits about him, and now he made another attempt to extricate himself from this awful situation.

"Your majesty, I have a confession to make." he said, pausing for effect.

"Go ahead," said Achashverosh. "Confess."

"When you asked me how to honor a man you favor, I thought you meant me. I realize now that it was presumptuous of me to jump to that conclusion, but I have served you so faithfully and so well that I cannot be faulted for thinking you wanted to show me some gratitude. The answer I gave you was with myself in mind. I spoke of things that would mean a lot to me. But if it is Mordechai you wish to honor, your majesty, and by all means far be it from me to object to such a plan, the advice I gave was inappropriate. What does wearing the king's clothes mean to Mordechai? Nothing. What does riding on the king's horse mean to Mordechai? Again nothing. He is a Jew. Give him some money, a lot of money, and he will be a thousand times happier. Give him orchards. Give him a village from which to collect taxes. Give him a river from which to collect bridge tolls. He wants riches. He will laugh at the honors."[6]

"Excellent idea," said Achashverosh.

Haman breathed a sigh of relief. At last!

"I will do all these things as well," Achashverosh continued. "I will make him a governor and have him rule over land and sea. You are

---

5. *Aggadas Esther; Lekach Tov; Targum Rishon; Melo HaOmer; Malbim; Iggeres Purim; Yosef Lekach; Maharal*. This is a further example of how Haman himself contributed to his debasement. Had he not come to the palace at such an early hour, someone else would have been selected for the task.

6. *Sifsei Chachamim* and *Ben Yehoyada* to *Megillah* 15a; *Pirkei d'Rav Eliezer* 50 with *Radal; Targum Sheni; Aggadas Esther; Rambam*.

right. It is not fitting for me to honor a poor man. I must make him rich first, and then we will bestow upon him the honors you described."[7]

Reinvigorated, Haman tenaciously persisted in his attempt to avoid humiliation. "Mordechai is a commoner, a Jew. He does not need aristocratic honors. I will give him the ten thousand talents of silver I offered you originally. Mordechai will be the happiest man in the world with so much money. He never imagined there was so much money in the world. That will be ample repayment of your debt to him many times over. He doesn't need anything else, your majesty."

"We will give him that, too," said Achashverosh, "and the honors as well."

Haman was aghast. "I am pleading with you, your majesty, not to subject me to such humiliation. Let my sons run in front of Mordechai's horse, but not me."

"Then that, too, shall be included in my repayment of my debt to Mordechai. I will make him master of you, your sons and all your household. It would not be the first time you were Mordechai's slave, Haman. Do you think I don't know what transpired in India during the famous three-year siege?"[8]

"Let someone else honor him, your majesty," Haman pleaded. "Why does it have to be me?"

"It is just," said Achashverosh. "You deceitfully took the honor that Mordechai deserved. Now the tables are turned.[9] Now listen very carefully, Haman. Go to the royal storehouse and choose my finest purple robe and a long silk chemise embroidered with precious stones and fringed with bells and pomegranates. Get the armor and sword I got from the Ethiopians and the pearl-studded veil I got from the Africans. And the crown I wore at my coronation, a gift from the Macedonian district of Carrane. Then go to the royal stables and get my trusty steed Shifregaz, the one I rode to my coronation. Make sure you do exactly as I say."[10]

---

7. *Megillah 15a* with *Sifsei Chachamim; Targum Sheni;* see *Epilogue.*

8. *Targum Sheni; Aggadas Esther; Alshich.* Some suggest that Achashverosh told Haman that his words had unwittingly predicted that it was Mordechai who deserved to be honored; he had said, "*ish asher hamelech chafetz bikaro,*" and Mordechai is referred to as *ish Yehudi (D'na Pishra).* In the end, Mordechai indeed owned all Haman's property, when he was appointed to oversee Haman's house and all his possessions.

9. *Yad HaMelech.*

10. Targum Sheni; Alshich; Aggadas Esther; Menos HaLevi; Mishtei Yayin; see Me'am Loez. It is interesting to note that when the Torah describes the me'il, the robe the Kohen Gadol wore, it uses the word sachra, which Targum Onkelos translates as siryan, the same word used here for armor. See Shemos 28:32 with Targum Onkelos

"Your majesty, Mordechai is my greatest enemy. Our enmity stretches back deep into the mists of the past. Our ancestors were also mortal enemies. In truth, I came here this morning to ask you for permission to hang him from the gallows I constructed on my estate, and now this! It is breaking my heart. If you wish to honor him, your majesty, by all means do so. But please do not humiliate me by ordering me to run before him. I would rather die. Substitute his name for mine in all my honors and associations with you, kill me if you must, but don't force me to do this."[11]

Achashverosh shook his head. "I will indeed give Mordechai all the honors you mention, and this one as well. I have decided. If you want to die, go ahead and kill yourself. I will not stop you. But I will not execute you. I understand what you want. If you kill yourself, the decree will be rescinded according to royal custom because of the untimely death of an important personage associated with it. But if I execute you, the decree will remain in force. No, I will not execute you. Now go do as I have commanded."

Haman made one more last-ditch attempt. "But your majesty, the decree against the Jews has already been sealed and delivered throughout the empire, and Mordechai is included in the decree. So how can we honor him so? Your majesty, let us talk facts for a moment. Both of us know that I have risen as high as I have only because you and I see eye to eye on most issues, including the Jewish problem. Especially the Jewish problem. You will be just as happy as I will be when the empire is rid of the Jews. So now you have an issue with an unpaid reward. So pay it. But don't forget the big picture. Don't tear down everything that we've built up so carefully together. Think it over carefully, your majesty. An impulsive mistake would have very damaging consequences."

and Rashi. Earlier Achashve rosh was enraged at Haman's mention of the crown, yet now he willingly offered it for Mordechai. Some suggest that Achashverosh was suspicious of Haman's taking it for himself, especially after the dream he had had. However, the king did not feel threatened by honoring Mordechai with it. Others offer a more direct approach. Achashverosh had long been concerned with his astrologers' prediction that a Jew would ultimately reign on his throne, not realizing that his successor would be his son born to a Jewish mother — Esther. Achashverosh viewed their words as a warning that the Jews would one day revolt. Thus he now attempted to satisfy the vision of the astrologers by honoring Mordechai as king for a day (*Ya'aros Devash*).

11. *Midrash Panim Acheirim, Targum Rishon; Yalkut Shimoni.* Some suggest that Haman responded differently: "You know that I would not commit suicide, no matter how pained I am, since I want to see the day when the Jews are destroyed. Furthermore, if I were to kill myself, the decree would automatically be revoked according to Persian law because of my death." See *Sefas Emes; Sifsei Tzaddik.*

Achashverosh glared at Haman. "You forget yourself. I am still the king, and you are still my subject. Speak with respect!"

"I apologize, your majesty. I meant no offense."[12]

"For the last time, listen to what I am saying and do not respond. Do you understand? Do not respond. I don't want to hear any more of your endless arguments and mental maneuvers. Enough! If you want to kill yourself, go right ahead. I will even give you a dagger. Otherwise, you are to obey my command. I want you to do the honors for Mordechai. He is a distinguished man who deserves the attentions of a high officer, which you are. You also know your way around the royal storehouse and can be trusted with my things.[13] But most important, I want to cut you down to size. I may not be a great friend of the Jews, but to eradicate an entire nation? To build gallows in the middle of the night to string up high palace officials? That is the work of a power-hungry, bloated egomaniac. It was your idea, and you talked me into it. Well, it's time to bring back a little sanity. Do you understand? Don't answer! Just shake your head."[14]

With great effort, Haman kept his lips sealed and nodded.

"Good," said Achashverosh. "Now, I understand your heart may not be completely in this mission, but I don't want you to be lax in anything I have commanded you to do. Do not cut corners! And take off that idol you're wearing. It's disrespectful to Mordechai."[15]

Achashverosh summoned several of his trusted officers and addressed himself to one of them. "Charvonah, my good man," he said, "I am assigning you men to escort Haman and make sure he does not neglect to do a single thing he suggested. Now, go and keep and eye on him."[16]

Escorted by the officers, Haman walked away slowly, still hoping against hope that Achashverosh would have a last-minute change of heart and call him back. But as he passed through the door with no summons, he realized that he was doomed to fulfill the king's command. "Foolish king," he muttered under his breath. "He doesn't know what he is doing."[17]

---

12. *Targum Sheni; Midrash Abba Gorion; Aggadas Esther; Rambam; see Gra.*

13. *Pirkei d'Rav Eliezer* with *Radal; Melo HaOmer; R' Elisha Galico; Me'am Loez.*

14. *R' Meir Armah; see Me'am Loez.*

15. *R' Yosef ibn Yachia; Rambam; Pirush Megillas Achashverosh; R' Shmuel di Uzidah; Alshich; D'na Pishra; Ya'aros Devash.*

16. *Pirkei d'Rav Eliezer* with *Radal; Midrash Abba Gorion.*

17. *Midrash in Otzar HaMidrashim, pg. 58.*

Word of the king's command spread through the palace quickly. By the time Haman was entering the royal storehouses, Esther was already fully apprised of all the details. She immediately proclaimed that day a national holiday with all schools and businesses closed. There would be a major parade, and all citizens were required to attend, on pain of death.[18] She also dispatched numerous young men to march in the parade behind Mordechai, carrying golden goblets to commemorate Achashverosh's escape from the poisons of Bigsan and Seresh.[19]

Meanwhile, Haman was staggering through the royal storehouse, crushed and depressed. Charvonah and his officers dogged his every step, as the king had ordered. Esther's proclamation had also piqued a lot of interest, and many curious courtiers and officials were congregating around Haman, just adding to Haman's discomfiture.[20]

After Haman assembled all the royal accoutrements, he placed them in a cart. Then he mounted his horse and set off to meet with Mordechai.[21]

Sitting in his usual place in the palace gate, Mordechai saw Haman, followed by a large retinue, riding towards him from afar and immediately sensed something was different.

"Quick, it is time to run!" he told the students gathered around him. "Haman is coming, and I fear he has finally run out of patience. I fear he intends to kill me with his horse's hooves, just as he killed Hasach. Run for your lives! Scatter in every direction."[22]

But the students refused to flee. "Life or death, we will share your fate. We will stay with you until the end."

Mordechai wrapped himself in his *tallis*, closed his eyes tightly and began to say *Shema*. Moments later, Haman rode up and dismounted, but he did not interrupt Mordechai's prayers.[23] He was actually in no hurry to commence with his own humiliation. Watching the prayer, however, made him restive. He moved closer to Mordechai and shuffled his feet in order to disturb his concentra-

---

18. *Esther Rabbah* 10:4; *Yalkut Shimoni*; see *Vayikra Rabbah* 28:4 with *Radal*; *Pirkei d'Rav Eliezer* with *Radal*; *Menos HaLevi*.

19. *Targum Sheni*; *Menos HaLevi*. According to one opinion there were 27,000 young men.

20. See *Midrash Abba Gorion*.

21. *Targum Sheni*; *Rambam*; *Yalkut Shimoni*.

22. *Midrash Abba Gorion*.

23. *Megillah* 16a; *Yalkut Shimoni*; *Esther Rabbah* 10:4; *Radal*; *Midrash Abba Gorion*; *Midrash Panim Acheirim*.

tion and interfere with the effectiveness of his prayer. Presently, Mordechai finished and opened his eyes. He saw Haman.[24]

"Peace to you, Mordechai," said Haman. He turned to his retinue. "Rise for the righteous son of great ancestors, Avraham, Yitzchak and Yaakov."[25]

Mordechai looked at him strangely, but he remained silent.

"What were you studying here?" asked Haman.

"The laws of the *Omer* offering."

"What is that?"

"Today is 16 Nissan, the second day of Pesach. When the *Beis HaMikdash* was still standing, we used to bring a special offering for the new harvest. Now that it is destroyed, we study its laws instead."[26]

"How charming," said Haman. "And how large is this *Omer*?"

"Three fingers."

"Three fingers of what? Gold? Silver?"

"No," said Mordechai. "Three fingers of barley."

"Barley! Why, that's not worth more than a few pennies!"

"That is correct," said Mordechai.

"How ironic," lamented Haman, "that your few grains of barley and your cheap sackcloth should push aside and overpower the ten thousand talents of silver I offered the king."

Mordechai glowered at him. "You fool! Have you forgotten about India? Have you forgotten that you are my slave? Well, according to the law, whatever the slave acquires goes to the master. If you acquired the Jewish people, they are mine. If you have ten thousand talents of silver, they are also mine. What do you want? Why have you come here? Just to annoy me? If you've come to take me to your gallows, then do it."[27]

---

24. *Sifsei Chachamim* to *Megillah*.

25. *Targum Sheni; Pirkei d'Rav Eliezer* with *Radal*.

26. See *Maharsha* to *Megillah* 16a; *Yefei To'ar* to *Esther Rabbah* 10:4. See *Menachos* 110a with *Rashi*; see *Vayikra* 23:9.

27. See *Megillah* 16a; and *Sifsei Chachamim; Yalkut Shimoni; Targum Sheni; Rambam; Esther Rabbah* 10:4. Some suggest that when Achashverosh had reimbursed Haman, he gave all the money to charity. He knew that Daniel had advised Nevuchadnezzar that the way to regain power was to give charity, and Haman therefore thought that by giving charity his power would be assured and he would be successful in his plot to annihilate the Jews. Mordechai was now telling him that, as master of his slave, Mordechai truly owned all Haman's wealth. Thus Haman's money — and the merit of having donated it to charity – belonged to Mordechai. Since *charity saves from death* (*Mishlei* 10:2), Haman had actually helped ensure that Mordechai's life would be spared (*Ya'aros Devash; Anaf Yosef*).

Much as he would have enjoyed to hear those words under other circumstances, Haman could take no pleasure in them now. "No, righteous Mordechai," he said. "I had prepared a gallows for you, but your Father in Heaven has prepared a crown for you instead. I have come here on orders from the king to dress you in royal garments and give you honor." He turned to one of his attendants. "Bring the robes."[28]

"Wait a minute," said Mordechai. "You don't think I would put on the king's precious robes in my present state, do you? I have fasted for three days, worn ashes on my head and refrained from washing. Before anything, I must have a bath. It would be disrespectful to the king to do otherwise."[29]

"Fine," said Haman. "Let's go to a bathhouse. There's one in the next street and three more in the one after."

There were indeed many bathhouses in Shushan, but because of Esther's proclamation, they were all closed. The only open bathhouse was in the palace itself, but because of the parade, all the attendants had left. There would be no one to prepare the bath and attend to Mordechai while he was taking it.

"I guess that leaves you, Haman," said Mordechai. "You will have to be my bath attendant."[30]

"But why does it have to be me?" Haman whined. "I'll give you one of my attendants here. Any of them will do just fine."

"I'm afraid not, Haman," said Mordechai. "I insist that you do it yourself." Mordechai suspected that an attendant might attempt to kill him in the bathhouse, and Haman would protest his innocence to the king. But Haman himself would not dare lift a finger against him and arouse the wrath of the king. Mordechai also did not mind bringing Haman down another notch or two.[31]

Haman seethed and fumed. The ordeal had not yet begun, and already he was being humiliated. But in the end, he had no choice. He lit the fires in the bathhouse, heated up the water, washed Mordechai and dried him.[32]

---

28. *Targum Sheni; Rambam.*

29. *Megillah* 16a; *Yalkut Shimoni; Targum Sheni; Rambam; Esther Rabbah* 10:5; *Pirkei d'Rav Eliezer* with *Radal.*

30. *Megillah* 16a; *Yalkut Shimoni; Esther Rabbah* 10:4.

31. *Pirkei d'Rav Eliezer* 50; *Rambam;* see *Anaf Yosef;* see *Ben Yehoyada.* Some say that Mordechai would not permit a defiled person like Haman to touch him, and he found someone else (see *D'na Pishra*).

32. *Vayikra Rabbah* 28:4; *Matnos Kehunah; Pirkei d'Rav Eliezer; R' Avigdor Kohen Tzedek.* Others say that Haman also performed bloodletting, since it is beneficial to one's health and appearance (*Rambam*).

"All right," said Haman. "Let us get the garments."

"Not so fast, my dear Haman," said Mordechai. "Do you think I would put on the king's garment without having my hair barbered? It would be disrespectful."[33]

Haman threw up his hands in frustration. "Fine!" he said. "Let's go to a barber shop. There's a fellow around the corner who's nimble with the scissors. He does a good job, and he's quick."

But Esther's proclamation had closed all the barbershops as well. There were none to be found in Shushan.

"Haman," Mordechai drawled.

He didn't have to say anything else. Haman knew what he had to do. He found a pair of rusty old scissors belonging to his father, sharpened the blades on a stone and set to work.[34]

"Look what's happened to me," he groaned as he trimmed Mordechai's hair. "Here I am, the most powerful man in the empire, and I've been reduced to a bath attendant and a barber. Oh, how could such a thing be?"

"Perhaps I should refresh your memory, Haman," said Mordechai. "Have you forgotten that you were a barber and a bath attendant in the province of Kartzoum for twenty-two years? You should feel perfectly comfortable in this profession. It's not something one forgets so easily.[35] Actually, I have to compliment you on your work so far. It's quite good. You must have been popular back in Kartzoum."

"You don't have to remind me," said Haman. "Look, this was not part of the king's orders. It's unfair that I should have to lower myself so much."

"Is it now? And was it fair to issue a death decree against the Jews? You brought all this on yourself, you know. You got us to

---

33. *Yalkut Shimoni;* see *Megillah* 16a.

34. *Yalkut Shimoni; Targum Sheni; Rambam;* see *Megillah* 16a; *Esther Rabbah* 10:4; *Vayikra Rabbah* 28; *R' Avigdor Kohen Tzedek.* Some question the permissibility of Mordechai having a haircut on the *yom tov* of Pesach. Some offer that since Mordechai had been in danger and was thus fasting and in mourning, it was as if he were imprisoned in jail until now. Under such circumstances *halachah* would permit one to take a haircut. See *Maharitz Chiyus; Orach Chaim* 531:4; *Ya'aros Devash; Anaf Yosef; Sifsei Chachamim* for detailed explanations and differences of opinion on the issue. Some question how Esther could have closed all the barbers, bathhouses and the like – and other shops – in Shushan. Her plan included feigning friendship to Haman. It is thus suggested that Esther had cast a spell on them, preventing them from being able to work (*Gra;* see *Shabbos* 81b).

35. *Megillah* 16a; *Yalkut Shimoni; Pirush Megillas Achashverosh.* Some suggest that the place was called *Kreinus,* others say it was the ancient village of *Circesium.* Some hold that he was there 21, not 22, years.

fast and wear sackcloth and thereby reverse the Heavenly decree onto you."[36]

Haman clamped his jaws shut and spoke no more. He finished barbering Mordechai, dressed him in the royal garments until every part of his body was covered, and he placed the crown upon his head.[37] Then he adorned him with the royal scents of perfumes, spices and other fragrances. Mordechai was ready to be displayed to the public.[38]

The starting point of the parade was in the main square of Shushan. Mordechai and Haman made their way there through side streets so as not to arouse too much attention.[39]

Huge crowds were already gathered in the square when they arrived. The king's great steed, adorned in royal fashion, with jewel-studded saddle and bridle, snorted and pawed at the ground, reacting to the excitement in the air.

Mordechai looked up at the giant horse. "Haman, I'm afraid I need your help again."

"What is it this time, Mordechai?"

"I can't climb up onto this horse without a boost. Could you bend down? Then I can step on you like a stool and reach the horse."

"You must be joking. I'm too old for that sort of thing."

"Well, I'm too old to climb up onto horses."

Haman sighed. He knew there was no way out, no point in arguing further. He got down on his hands and knees and offered his back to Mordechai. Holding up the royal garments in his hands, Mordechai stepped onto Haman and catapulted himself into the saddle. At the last second, he stepped hard on Haman's neck, driving him face down into the mud.

"Why did you do that?" squealed Haman. "Doesn't your own Torah say that 'you must not rejoice when your enemy falls'?"

---

36. *Esther Rabbah* 10:4; see *Pirkei d'Rav Kahana,* pg. 71, where it is discussed at length; see *Maharzu; Matnos Kehunah* to *Vayikra Rabbah* 28:4.

37. There was no concern regarding the prohibition of wearing *shatnez;* Mordechai was permitted to do so since he would be endangering himself by not obeying the King's request (*Sifsei Chachamim* to *Megillah* 16a).

38. *Targum Sheni; Rokeach.* Yosef had enjoyed the same treatment when he was taken out of jail and introduced to Pharoah. While Mordechai surely did not object to Haman's discomfiture, this was not the only motivation behind his request. It was fitting that a descendant of Rachel's son Binyamin be treated in the same manner as Rachel's son Yosef (*Sifsei Chachamim* to *Megillah* 16a).

39. *Alshich.*

"That refers to a Jewish enemy," said Mordechai. "But with an implacable enemy such as you, the Torah tells us to 'tread on their high places.' Would you consider your neck a high place?"[40]

"Can we go now?" asked Haman, drained and exhausted. "Are you ready?"

"I am ready."

The procession began. Haman walked ahead with lit candles in his hand, shouting at the top of his lungs, "This is what is done for a man the king wishes to honor!"[41] Every time he sang out those words, the thousands of young men Esther had dispatched repeated the shout to ensure that the assembled crowd heard every word. Mordechai, however, accepted everything with humility and diffidence. He was uncomfortable with the honors, but he could not refuse the king.[42]

As he rode through the thoroughfares of Shushan, Mordechai recited the verse, "I will exalt You, O God, for You lifted me up, You did not allow my foes to gloat over me" (Tehillim 30:2).

His students responded with the succeeding verses, "Sing melodies to God, O His pious ones, give thanks at the mention of His holy Name. For His anger lasts a moment, His favor a lifetime, retire weeping at night, greet the dawn with hymns" (ibid. vs. 5-6).

The Jews in the crowd that lined the streets, overawed by the miraculous reversal of their fortunes, also joined the sequence, "Hear, O God, grant me favor, O God, be a helper for me. You transformed my laments into dancing for me, You undid my sackcloth and fortified me with joy" (ibid. vs. 11-12). Esther, watching from a vantage point high in the palace, joined in as well, "I call out to You, O God, I plead with my Master" (ibid vs. 9). Even Haman found a reference to himself, "In my tranquil times, I said, 'I shall never falter' "(ibid. v. 7).[43]

The procession neared its end in the posh district near the palace where Haman's lavish home overlooked the parade route. Both men were looking down to conceal their faces, Haman out of humiliation, Mordechai out of humility. Haman's daughter

---

40. *Megillah* 16a; see *Mishlei* 24:17 and *Devarim* 33:29; *Esther Rabbah* 10:4 with *Yefei To'ar; Midrash Panim Acheirim.*

41. *Midrash Abba Gorion; Maharal.*

42. *Targum Sheni;* see *R' Saadiah Gaon; Menos HaLevi.*

43. See *Yalkut Shimoni; Tehillim* 30; see *Targum Sheni* for an alternate interpretation of the praises Mordechai and Esther sang.

Shaknehaz, the one he had hoped would become queen, watched from a window on the highest story as the parade approached. She did not know exactly what was happening, only that Mordechai and her father were coming. She saw below her a man dressed in royal robes being led by another man dressed in simple clothing, but she couldn't see their faces. The man leading the horse was shouting, "This is what is done for a man the king wishes to honor!" His voice, however, was hoarse and unrecognizable from hours of shouting during the parade.[44]

Naturally, Shaknehaz assumed that her father, the glorious Haman, all-powerful prime minister, was riding on the horse and that Mordechai, the despised Jew, was leading him. With a shout of glee, she ran to get the chamber pot, which was filled to the brim with a mixture of hot excrement and other wastes, and she tossed its contents out the window onto the man she thought was Mordechai. Her aim was perfect, and it splashed onto his head and scalded him.[45]

The man bent over, and his shoulders trembled and shook. Then he looked up to see who had thrown the excrement. Father and daughter looked at each other in absolute shock. Shaknehaz screamed and leaped from the window, plunging to her death right in front of her father.[46]

The death of Shaknehaz completed the stunning turnaround of the parade with an exclamation point. Haman was devastated, because Shaknehaz had symbolized his ambitions. Through her, he had hoped to lay claim to the throne itself. Now her death dashed his hopes, just as they were being dashed on all sides. But there was no time to deal with his grief and frustration. He had to finish his mission.[47]

He brought Mordechai to the palace and retrieved the royal garments. Mordechai dressed in ordinary garb and went back toward the palace gate. He avoided entering the palace, because he was afraid the king would invite him to return to his ministerial duties. He was reluctant to do this, because he did not want any more confrontations with Haman. Instead, he returned to his place

---

44. *Sifsei Chachamim* to *Megillah* 16a; *Ben Yehoyada, D'na Pishra.*
45. *D'na Pishra; Sipur HaNeis; Sifsei Chachamim.*
46. *Megillah* 16a; *Esther Rabbah* 10:5; *Midrash Lekach Tov; Sipur HaNeis.*
47. *Maharal.*

in front of the palace, donned his sackcloth and ashes and resumed his praying and fasting. The great honors the king had bestowed on him worried him. The debt had now been repaid, and he could no longer ask the king for the safety of the Jewish people as his reward. He assembled the Sanhedrin and told them to spread the word among the people that the crisis was far from over, to tell everyone to continue to fast and pray until the final deliverance would materialize.[48]

For his part, Haman went off to return the horse, garments, armor and crown. The stable hands pushed him away as soon as he brought them the horse, because they couldn't bear the stench. At the royal storehouse, they didn't even let him come close.[49] His humiliation was total. In a few hours, he had fallen from prime minister of Persia, the most powerful minister in the world, to bath attendant, barber, groom, crier, and now he was not even accorded the welcome due the lowest peasant.[50] Furthermore, he had been stricken with *tzaraas* because he had spoken against Mordechai. He was at rock bottom. Stumbling and staggering like a vagrant drunk, he found his way home. He was a shattered hulk, an ephemeral shadow of his former self. He did not believe he could fall any further.

"My dear husband," Zeresh greeted him, "we must have a conference immediately. We face a terrible crisis. What happened to you in the palace? Why did you deserve this kind of treatment?"

"I will explain it to you soon. I just need to wash up and change."[52]

"You can do that soon," said Zeresh. "We have our advisors here, and we have to talk. I feel a little responsible myself for advising you to go to the palace this morning, so I will just listen for the most part. But others have a lot to say. By the way, this time the maidservants have not been invited." She smiled ruefully. "We

---

48. *Esther Rabbah* 10:6; *Maharsha; Sifsei Chachamim; Yefei Anaf; Shemos Rabbah* 38:4 with *Maharzu; Targum Rishon; Midrash Panim Acheirim; Pirush Megillas Achashverosh; R' Elisha Galico; Maharal; Ma'amar Mordechai.* Some suggest that he returned to the palace to thank Achashverosh for having bestowed this honor upon him (*Iggeres Purim*).

49. *Talelei Oros,* citing *Ta'ama D'kra.*

50. *Esther Rabbah* 10:7 with *Matnos Kehunah; Targum Sheni; Midrash Abba Gorion; Midrash lekach Tov; Midrash Panim Acheirim; Gra.*

51. *Midrash Lekach Tov; Iggeres Purim; Menos HaLevi; Nachal Eshkol; D'na Pishra; Yad HaMelech; Sha'arei Binah; Rokeach; R' Avigdor Kohen Tzedek; R' Yosef ibn Yachia; Pirush Megillas Achashverosh; Gra.*

52. *Eshkol HaKofer; Yedei Moshe.*

need a plan. Come inside, Haman. Everyone awaits you. At last, you are among friends."[53]

Haman thought for a moment and nodded. He needed the warm embrace of his friends more than anything right now. Figuratively, of course. No one in his right mind would embrace Haman literally in his present condition. He took a deep breath, squared his shoulders and strode into the room.

"My friends," he began, "I appreciate that you have all come here to help me. And yourselves, too, of course. Before we discuss plans for the future, I have to fill you in about this morning."

He then related the entire episode in great detail, greeted by gasps and groans at every turn.

"Pretty awful, isn't it?" he continued. "But I am not one to wallow in self-pity. This was the worst day of my life, but it is over. I am a resilient person, and I will make a comeback. True, I have suffered incredible humiliation, worse than anyone in my position has ever suffered, but I will recover. The king gave me the opportunity to kill myself, and I have to admit that the prospect seemed rather attractive. But it is not like Haman to give up and commit suicide. I bounce back from adversity."

"Hear! Hear!" the crowd cheered.

Haman swelled with renewed confidence. "I look at it this way. There is a bright side to what happened today. The king owed Mordechai a debt of gratitude, and who knows what Mordechai might have collected for it? Perhaps even the reversal of the decree. But now there is nothing to worry about. The king has repaid his debt, and Mordechai no longer has any claim on him. I stuck my foot in my mouth, because I thought the honors were for me. I should have kept my mouth shut. So everything that happened was a coincidence, but it works out for the best. We now have Mordechai where we want him, stripped of his last defense."[54]

An old respected minister was the first to speak after Haman. "It seems to me," he said, "that we must determine what the king had in mind when he issued these orders. Did he want to raise Mordechai up? Did he want to put you down, Haman? Or perhaps it was both. If it was the second or both, I'd say your goose is cooked,

---

53. *R' Yosef ibn Yachia; R' Shmuel di Uzidah; Menos HaLevi; Ma'amar Mordechai.*
54. *Gra; D'na Pishra; Yosef Lekach; Midrash Eliyahu; R' Shmuel di Uzidah; Eshkol HaKofer; Malbim.*

Haman. My advice for the immediate future is to stay away from Mordechai like the plague."[55]

Another old advisor also spoke. "I disagree with you, Haman, when you say that what happened today was a coincidence. It is well known that the God of the Jews protects the tribes of Yehudah, Binyamin, Ephraim and Menashe. Mordechai is descended from the tribe of Binyamin, who never bowed to your grandfather Eisav. This is a bad omen for you. Throughout history, these last three tribes, the descendants of Rachel, have prevailed over Amalek, starting with Yehoshua. King Shaul of Binyamin almost wiped out Amalek."[56]

Yet another advisor picked up on the theme of Jewish history. "There is too much supernatural protection there for my tastes. Avraham was saved from the fiery furnace. Yitzchak prevailed over Avimelech. Yaakov prevailed over Eisav's angel. Moshe and the Jews prevailed over Pharaoh. Daniel was saved from the lions' den. I can go on and on. The Jews are beyond the rule of the zodiac. I am afraid you will fall, Haman, like Nevuchadnezzar."[57]

The young advisor who had spoken up the previous time offered his opinion once again. "With all due respect to my elders, I think we are missing a crucial point. Where does Esther fit into things? Is she a Jew herself? Is she related to Mordechai? If the answer is yes, do you think for a moment the queen would allow a decree of death against her own people? It is preposterous. Look, she is already making moves. Who closed the bathhouses and barber shops today? It was Esther! I'm afraid the adversary is not Mordechai but the queen herself. I say we are in deep trouble."[58]

"You are a clever young fellow," said the first speaker. "There is definitely something to worry about in that quarter. I want to return to my first point, however. What was the king's intention? I've been thinking while this discussion has been going on, and I think it is clear that the king wanted to do both, elevate Mordechai and demote you, Haman. The way it works with the Jews is that when they fall, they fall all the way to the dust, and their enemies rise. But when they rise, they rise to

---

55. *Menos HaLevi; Iggeres Purim.*

56. See *Megillah* 16a with *Maharsha; Aggadas Esther; Midrash Pirush Achashverosh; Akeidah.* The last letters of the names *Menashe, Ephraim* and *Binyamin* spell *Haman,* indicating that they and their descendants will prevail over him (*Ben Yehoyada*).

57. *Midrash Panim Acheirim; Targum Rishon; Targum Sheni; Pirkei d'Rav Eliezer; Menos HaLevi.*

58. *Rokeach; Yedei Moshe; R' Elisha Galico; Ma'amar Mordechai.*

the stars, and their enemies fall. Mordechai is clearly on the rise, which means that you, Haman, are in free fall. I would advise you to flee."

"Well, I don't think we should be so extreme, Haman," said another advisor. "You do not yet have to abandon everything you've built up over the years. And what about the rest of us? If you flee, where does that leave us? No, I say you should swallow your pride. Humble yourself before the king and beg forgiveness from the queen."

Haman laughed harshly. "Swallow my pride? As if I have any left!"

"Well, phrase it as you wish. Just get it done. Bow down to Mordechai as well. Make him think he has won. Maybe his ego will swell, and then his prayers will be ineffective. I understand that the God of the Jews despises arrogant people."[59]

"I agree with much of what has been said here, Haman," said Zeresh. "I think our position for the moment is weak. How do you hang a man who's just been paraded through the capital in the king's crown and garments? The king has switched sides. He is with Mordechai now and against you. The struggle with Mordechai has to come to an end. Think of your children, Haman. They are the future. Much as I loathe saying this, I think you should flee for your life, Haman. Some of your sons are imperial governors in outlying provinces. Surely one of them would offer you a place to hide. In time, you can muster an army and overthrow Achashverosh."[60]

Haman looked around the room and sighed. "How things have changed in one day," he remarked. "But what can you do? Life goes on. I have to thank all of you for your kindness and concern. I've heard a number of views tonight. Some want me to apologize to Achashverosh and Esther. Some want me to befriend Mordechai. Some want me to make a run for it. Everyone apparently wants me to give up the fight and tear down the gallows. Myself, I am inclined to flee. But before I make a decision, I have to take care of important business, critical business. I have to wash myself and change my clothes. I must go upstairs and — what was that?"

A loud pounding on the door had interrupted him. The door burst open, and Charvonah and a contingent of the palace guard rushed in. Esther had sent them to bring Haman before he had a chance to flee. She also had Haman's ten leading sons detained to

---

59. See *Megillah* 16a; *Maharsha; Shabbos* 75a; *Midrash Panim Acheirim; Midrash Lekach Tov; Pirush Megillas Achashverosh; Akeidah; Gra; R' Elisha Galico; R' Chaim Abulafia; R' Shmuel di Uzidah; Maharal; Chasam Sofer; Yosef Lekach; Me'am Loez; Malbim. D'na Pishra.*
60. *D'na Pishra; Yosef Lekach* with *commentaries; Eshkol HaKofer; Ein Yaakov.*

prevent a conspiracy. Through an open window, Charvonah and the guards had heard Haman's last comments about the gallows.

"Haman, you must come with us immediately," said Charvonah. "The king summons you to Esther's banquet. You are late already, and the king is annoyed. He thinks you may have decided not to come."[61]

"Not to worry, officer," said Haman. "Not going never crossed my mind. Have a seat, and I'll be with you before you know it."

"There is no time to sit," said Charvonah. "You must come right away."

"Very well, suit yourself," said Haman. "Stand if you wish. I just need to wash up a little and change my shirt. I can not present myself before the king and queen smelling and looking like this."

"Absolutely not. You had time to clean up, but you chose to have a meeting instead. My orders were very specific: 'Bring him the moment you walk through the door. Do not waste a second and keep the king waiting.'"[62]

"What's the matter with you?" said Haman. "I cannot come to the king like this. It would be a slap in his face. I'd rather not go at all."

"You don't have a choice in the matter, Haman," said Charvonah. "The queen told us specifically that even if you are still wearing today's clothing you are to come as you are. It is outrageously late. The king and queen are waiting. Our orders are to carry you if we must."[63]

And carry him they did. They planted him in the street and shoved him ahead like a common peasant until he was running. Shocked to his very core at the incredible turn of events, he felt that he was running to his doom.[64]

---

61. *Pirush HaMeyusad LeRambam; Gra; Yosef Lekach; R' Elisha Galico; Yad HaMelech; Chida; Malbim; Akeidah; Chasam Sofer; Iggeres Purim.* See *Yalkut Shimoni; Sha'arei Binah; Menos HaLevi; R' Avigdor Kohen Tzedek; Yedei Moshe; Ma'amar Mordechai.* At the moment that Haman was concerned with falling further, the guards entered to take him to the palace. It was fitting that the last words of his friends and family to him were "*nafol tipol,*" you shall surely fall. Some suggest that the guards believed they were summoning Haman to his execution and therefore rushed him, to ensure that the condemned man not remain alive longer than his time.

62. *R' Yosef Ibn Yachia; Maharasha* to *Megillah* 16a; *R' Yosef ibn Yachia.* Others suggest that Haman did want to go. He thought that his only remaining ally in the palace was his recently acquired friend, Queen Esther. He hoped that at the feast all misunderstandings would be resolved (*Me'am Loez*).

63. See *Rashi* to *Megillah* 16a; see *Rif* to *Ein Yaakov; Targum.* Esther wanted to ensure that Haman would not be wearing anything related to idol worship. Knowing that Achashverosh had demanded that Haman remove such items before escorting Mordechai, she wished to ensure that he remain this way (*Ya'aros Devash*).

64. *Maharsha* to *Megillah* 16a; *Otzar Midrashim,* pg. 57; see *Sechel Tov* to *Parashas Beshalach* 15:15; *D'na Pishra; Melo HaOmer; R' Elisha Galico; Menos HaLevi.*

Haman Is Defeated

22

Somehow, Haman's remarkable resilience sur-faced again. The king had insisted that he come to the banquet. Why? The queen may have had some private agenda in inviting him, but why did the king want him to come? Obviously, to a certain extent, he was still in the king's good graces; something of the relationship still survived.[1]

Haman entered the banquet hall happy and at peace. There was still hope. All was not lost. And what he encountered did not cause him to lose heart. On the contrary, it confirmed his speculation. The king and queen both greeted him cordially, not making any remarks about his tardiness or the state of his hygiene. Achashverosh seemed in a relaxed and expansive mood. He was happy to know that his debt of gratitude had been repaid. The suspi-cions of a liaison between Esther and Haman were long forgotten. He smiled at both Esther and

---

1. See *Rambam; Yotzer* to *Parashas Zachor.*

Haman, apparently with genuine affection for both. Haman breathed a sigh of relief.[2]

Esther was participating in the festivities, eating a little but still not drinking, but Achashverosh and Haman let the wine flow freely into their cups. Soon, they were both quite intoxicated and in high spirits, although still a little tense from the events of the day.[3]

"Come, my queen," said Achashverosh. "Tell me your request. As I already told you once before, I will give you up to half my kingdom. My curiosity grows by the minute. What is your desire? Do you want money? As much as you want, it is yours."

But Esther still demurred. The feast progressed, and the king did not give up. He kept pressing Esther again and again to tell him her request, but she still said nothing. She was waiting until Achashverosh was drunk enough to lose his temper when she finally broke her silence.[4]

As the feast neared its end, Achashverosh finally lost his temper. "Once and for all, Esther, I demand to know the nature of your request. You've pushed me off again and again, from last night till tonight, and many times tonight that I've asked you to tell me. I told you I would grant you up until half my kingdom for your request, and I told you I would grant a petition on behalf of others as well. And still, you refuse to tell me. It cannot have anything to do with Mordechai, because I have already rewarded him. You have no family of your own, so what can you possibly want that you are willing to risk your life for it? I've had enough of this mysterious nonsense. Tell me right now, or I will uproot you from the face of the earth!"[5]

At last, Esther felt sure the time had come to break her silence. Haman, although still a formidable foe, had fallen from his impregnable position of power, and Achashverosh was simply bursting with eagerness to grant her secret wish.[6]

"My lord, your wish is my command," said Esther. "I will be silent no longer. All I ask is to be allowed to live in peace and favor before you, to have you look kindly upon my request. My lord, I request that my life be spared, and I petition for the survival of my people. Please, please, let my nation live. I ask for nothing else, no

2. *R' Elisha Galico; Menos HaLevi; Maharal; Malbim.*

3. *Gra;* others say Esther did not eat at this feast, either (*Midrash Lekach Tov*).

4. *Targum Rishon; Rokeach; Yad HaMelech; Menos HaLevi; D'na Pishra.*

5. *Midrash* in *Torah Sheleimah,* pg. 194, *Yosef Lekach; Midrash Panim Acheirim; Midrash Lekach Tov; Yishai Elokim.*

6. *R' Shmuel di Uzidah; Yad HaMelech.*

riches, no rewards, no power, no domains, just my life, for if one is not allowed to live everything else is meaningless."[7]

Achashverosh stared at her in astonishment.

"My lord, I have always concealed my background from you," she continued. "But now the time has come to speak up. I am a Jewish woman, descended from Jewish royalty, the granddaughter of King Shaul, the first king of Israel. My enemy has engineered a death decree against my people and me. Eleven months from now, we are all to be killed. In fact, my people are already under attack. Sporadic killings have already begun. If you will not grant me both my request and my petition, then grant just the petition alone. At least, my people will survive. As for me, if my people are destroyed I would have no desire to remain alive."

Esther began to sob, but she quickly regained control.

"Had we been sold into slavery," she continued, "I would have remained quiet. Perhaps there would have been a temporary benefit to the empire in such a thing, just as the Egyptians prospered during the early years of Jewish bondage. I don't know if I would have had a right to disturb the king with my own personal pain and sorrow. Also, there would have been no urgency if we had been sold into slavery. If it were unjust, the passage of time could have led to ultimate justice. But what is the good of ultimate justice when the people are threatened by a death decree? What does it help to reverse a decree after the condemned have been executed?[8]

"Perhaps if we had been sold into slavery, you would have realized eventually that the loss to the empire is too great to bear and you would have rescinded the decree. But if we had all been killed, would it have helped to rescind the decree? Death is final.[9]

"But even slavery would have had its drawbacks for you, my lord. If the Jews had been sold into slavery, then I would also have become a slave woman. How would it look to the world if they found out that the king is married to a slave woman?"

"In any case, the sale is not valid. In my humble opinion, although I am not a trained attorney, I would say that a sale made under false pretenses is worthless. You might have agreed to have the Jewish

7. *Esther Rabbah* 10:8; *Targum Rishon; see Pirkei d'Rav Eliezer; R' Yosef ibn Yachia; Ibn Ezra; Yishai Elokim; R' Shmuel di Uzidah.*

8. See *Megillah* 16a; *Rashi* to *Esther* 7:5. See *Aggadas Esther; Yad HaMelech. Pirush Megillas Achashverosh; R' Yosef ibn Yachia; Yosef Lekach; D' na Pishra; Menos HaLevi; Ya'aros Devash; Akeidah; Chomas Anach; Melo HaOmer; Alshich.*

9. *R' Elisha Galico; Akeidah.*

people eradicated, but that could have meant slavery or exile, not outright murder. And anyway, had you known your own queen was Jewish, surely you would not have sold her people into slavery."[10]

Esther dabbed at her eyes and continued.

"My lord, my enemy is intent on destroying me, because I stand in his way to grabbing the throne for himself. Do you remember how I thwarted the assassination attempt by Bigsan and Seresh? With Mordechai's help, of course. I am loyal to the king, and my enemy cannot contend with an alert and loyal queen. Therefore, he feels he must destroy me, as he has already destroyed one queen before me. How do you destroy the queen? By condemning her entire nation to death! When my people die, I will die, too. That is his intention.[11]

"But what kind of madness is this, my lord? Who would destroy an entire nation in order to murder his enemy? Look at this! Think of the tremendous loss the king would suffer by the destruction of the Jewish people. The Jews are the only people still paying taxes, and the loss of the Jews would be a huge loss of revenue for the treasury. Even more, the loss of the talents and industry of the Jews would cripple the imperial economy. The damage would be immeasurable, far more than the ten thousand talents he offered, and never even paid![12]

"And think of the embarrassment to the throne. What would the rest of the world say to an empire that would slaughter an entire innocent, law-abiding people? What would they say about a king that slaughters the family of his own queen? You would be a laughingstock. And think about the risk of divine retribution. Do you think the Jewish God would let you get away with murdering His chosen people? Surely such a dastardly deed could not be done with impunity.[13]

"My enemy fooled you into thinking the Jews were bad for the empire. He passed a law that anyone who saves or protects a Jew must die. Well, wouldn't you protect your Jewish queen? Don't you see? It was just another way to engineer your death. He wants to kill you and sit on your throne. He toyed with you and used you for his own ambitious purposes. I think he actually enjoys manipulating

---

10. *R' Chaim Abulafia*; see *R' Elisha Galico; Yosef Lekach; Alshich; Malbim.* It would be considered a *mekach ta'us*, an erroneous transaction.

11. *Megillah* 16a; *Maharsha; Rambam; Melo HaOmer; Menos HaLevi; Alshich; Malbim;* see *Ya'aros Devash.*

12. *Midrash Lekach Tov; Targum Rishon; D'na Pishra; Rashi; Gra; Pirush Megillas Achashverosh.*

13. *Rambam, D'na Pishra.*

you and maneuvering you toward a downfall. My enemy is the peril to you, my lord, not the Jews!"[14]

"I appeal to you, my lord. Break free from my enemy's diabolical influence. Shake off this parasite that sucks your blood and awaits the day he can sit on your throne. Take pity on your poor queen whom he is trying to murder because she is so loyal to you. Take pity on her innocent people who have always brought you blessing and benefit and never one bit of rebellion or harm. My lord, I beg of you, please tear up the death decree!"[15]

With those words, Esther burst into tears, sobbing so uncontrollably that her shoulders shook.

Achashverosh was deeply moved. He had always despised the Jews because he saw them as a threat to his throne. But now he realized that the queen and her people were steadfast in their loyalty to him, and that the threat to his throne came from other directions.[16]

Who was this enemy of whom Esther spoke? It could only be Haman. Could it be that Haman would issue a death decree in his name when the most he had authorized was slavery? Could it be that he would construe the king's words as permission to slaughter an entire people, men, women and children? Could it be that he had incurred the wrath of the awesome God of the Jews? Could it be that he authorized the slaughter of the queen's people? Could it be that he had given permission for the killing to begin already? Now word would get out, and the Persian emperor would become the laughingstock of the world.[17]

---

14. *R' Saadiah Gaon; Ibn Ezra; R' Chaim Abulafia; D'na Pishra; Mishtei Yayin; R' Shmuel di Uzidah; Malbim.*

15. *Rambam; Menos HaLevi; Malbim.*

16. *Ya'aros Devash.* Now that he knew Esther was descended from royal lineage, Achashverosh would no longer use a translator to speak to her. She was worthy of respect and entitled to have the king speak directly to her (*Megillah* 16a; *Rashi* to *Esther* 7:5; *Yalkut Shimoni*).

17. See *Akeidah; Yad HaMelech; Menos HaLevi; Pirush Megillas Achashverosh; Tzofnas Pane'ach; Nachal Eshkol; R' Shimon Ashterak* in *Torah Sheleimah*, pg. 196; *Sefer Oheiv Yisrael; Chasam Sofer.* Some suggest that Achashverosh truly did not remember the letters that had been sent four days earlier, and wished to know what it was all about (*D'na Pishra*). Others say that Achashverosh had known that Haman's decree to kill the Jews had been enacted but he had not realized that this would include Esther. Therefore he wondered who else could have been responsible for such an edict (*Ma'amar Mordechai*). Some posit that Achashverosh surely knew what Esther was telling him; he himself had implemented the decree together with Haman. Embarrassed that his own designs were now threatening his queen, he feigned astonishment and ignorance (*Iggeres Purim*). Others say that Achashverosh had only granted permission for the Jews to be sold. Esther told him that, were this the extent of the decree, she would have remained silent; such was an expected experience in exile and not unfamiliar in our nation's history. However, Haman altered the decree, changing the word לְעַבֵּד, *le'abeid*, written with the letter *ayin*, meaning to enslave them, to לְאַבֵּד written with an *aleph,* which means to destroy them.

Achashverosh looked at Haman with revulsion. This rascal must have changed the letters, he thought, and then forged my signature to it.[18]

He turned back to the queen and declared, "Who is this man, Esther? Who has filled his heart with hatred for you and the Jewish people? Who is this man who has become my enemy by attempting to harm my queen? Who is this mutinous man who rebels against my authority?[19] Is he an officer? A guard? A nobleman? Where does he live? We must find him! We must kill him and cut his body into tiny pieces. We must wipe out his entire family for what he has done. We must take a terrible revenge for the crimes he has committed. Who is this man? I must know!"[20]

Esther lifted a trembling finger and pointed it straight ahead to where Achashverosh and Haman were sitting together.[21] Overcome by a spirit of absolute honesty, she actually pointed her finger at Achashverosh and spoke with conviction. "This is the man who has done this," she said. "This enemy of the Jews is despised by the Almighty above and by people below. He is the enemy of the empire, not the Jews. He is evil through and through, full of hate and ambition, grasping jealously for what anyone else may possess."[22]

Achashverosh shuddered at these accusations, which Esther seemed to be directed against him for authorizing and signing the decree, but at the last moment, an angel pushed Esther's hand so that her finger now pointed at Haman instead. Achashverosh breathed a sigh of relief.[23]

---

18. See *Yedei Moshe; Yishai Elokim; Yosef Lekach.*

19. *Melo HaOmer.*

20. *Targum Rishon; Targum Sheni; Menos HaLevi; Midrash Lekach Tov; R' Saadiah Gaon; Rambam; Yedei Moshe; Sipur HaNeis.*

21. *Megillah* 16a, see *Ein Yaakov.*

22. See *Shemos Rabbah* 38:4; *Midrash Panim Acheirim; Alshich; Akeidah; R' Elisha Galico; Nachal Eshkol; Midrash Lekach Tov; Malbim.*

23. *Megillah* 16a, see *Rashi, Bach, Rif* and *Maharal.* When Esther referred to the King, she meant Hashem, King of the Universe. Achashverosh, too, was an enemy of Hashem. Many question how Esther could risk not only her life, but the lives of the Jews for whom she was pleading, had the angel not moved her pointing finger. Many say that Esther held Achashverosh as equally guilty. Her desire for truth was so deeply ingrained in her heart that even if it meant her death, she could not hold back from the truth. Others suggest that Esther wanted to point out her grievances to Achashverosh but attributed them mainly to Haman. The angel moved her hand to eliminate any misunderstanding about the subject of her words (*Anaf Yosef; Ben Yehoyada;* see *Lev Eliyahu* and *Talelei Oros* in the name of *Chazon Ish*). Others posit that Esther's intention was in fact for the King to become angry at her and have her killed. The decree would then automatically be revoked, as is royal custom when a distinguished person is killed because of a decree. Esther did not want to rely on Achashverosh rescinding it on her request, but Hashem wished her to do so, and thus sent the angel to prevent her inciting the king's ire (*Menos HaLevi*). See *Abarbanel, Mishpatim;* see *Gra* for further explanation.

"My lord, you do not have to search far for this villain," Esther cried. "He is right here in front of you. Yes, the enemy is this evil Haman![24] He schemed to have Vashti executed so that his daughter could become queen. He worked against your interests to further his own. He has hated me and my people from the day you chose me over his daughter to be your queen. There is no end to the man's ambition. He has always had a burning desire to kill you and take your throne. There is no doubt in my mind that he would have turned the slaughter of the Jews to his advantage and your disadvantage. He plans to pretend to the world that he is not responsible and that it is all your work. He plans to ridicule you to the rulers of the world as a foolish king who kills his own people. He plans to gain their support in leading a palace coup against you, overthrowing you and mounting your throne. He is also conspiring with those impossibly wily Greeks who want to swallow your whole empire. No doubt, he has promised to deliver your head to them on a platter. He was behind Bigsan and Seresh, his cousins, in their plot to assassinate you. He and his family are the source of all evil and dissension. Haman is the enemy!"[25]

Haman recoiled in shock at the accusation. For a moment, he actually thought he would pass out. He buried his face in his hands as he tried to compose himself.[26] He knew he was in deep trouble. He was all alone with no support, and no means of escape.[27] He would have to strain his wits to their utmost in order to escape from his present predicament. How could he defend himself against the charges of trying to undermine the king? How could he defend himself against the charges of endangering the queen? Miraculously, it did not occur to him to argue that he had never known Esther was Jewish since she had concealed her nationality, that he would never have persecuted the Jews had he known Esther was one of them.[28]

---

24. *Rambam.*

25. See *Rambam; Targum Rishon; Yosifun; R' Shmuel di Uzidah; Anaf Yosef;* see *Abarbanel, Mishpatim (divrei hamaschil "hinei"), Menos HaLevi; Melo HaOmer; Me'am Loez.*

26. See *Pirkei d'Rav Eliezer* with *Radal; Midrash Lekach Tov; Yedei Moshe; D'na Pishra; R' Yosef ibn Yachia; R' Yosef ibn Nachmiash.* The angel Gavriel threatened Haman's *mazal* with a sword, thus frightening Haman. Although a person does not see this happening, it nevertheless affects his emotions (see *Rokeach; Megillah* 3a).

27. *Rokeach; Yedei Moshe; Menos HaLevi; Maharal.*

28. *Yosef Lekach; Gra; R' Elisha Galico; Menos HaLevi; Yishai Elokim; Melo HaOmer.*

Haman realized he was fighting a battle on two fronts. On the one hand, he had to regain the confidence of the king who was judging him. On the other, he had to mollify the queen who was prosecuting his case. He could not do both at the same time. If he argued in his defense before the king, the queen would refute his arguments, and use the prestige of her position and her place in the king's affections to overwhelming effect. In the end, the king would hate him even more. If he were to ask Esther's forgiveness and plead for mercy in the king's earshot, he would be admitting his guilt and forfeiting all his defenses. Fortunately, an opportunity soon presented itself.[29]

Achashverosh was so furious that he stepped out onto the veranda for a breath of fresh air. His head swam from the wine, and his heart pounded with anger and frustration. He needed time to clear his head and think, to calm his nerves and slow the feverish beating of his heart. Experience had taught him that acting impulsively under the influence of wine would bring disastrous results. He had lost his first queen in this manner. He was now at risk of losing his prime minister or his new queen or both if he did not handle the situation in a calm and reasoned manner. This called for a long walk in the royal orchards, so that the soothing effects of nature would help him focus more clearly.[30]

As Achashverosh stepped out into the cool night air, Haman had to make a quick decision. Should he follow the king outside and mount a defense? Or should he stay inside and throw himself on the queen's mercy? He decided it would be too risky to engage the king in conversation in his present state of mind. His chances would probably be better with the queen. He would appeal to her soft heart.[31]

He knelt before the couch upon which Esther sat. "Please forgive me, most gracious queen. Believe me, I never meant to harm a sin-

---

29. Gra; Yosef Lekach; Malbim.

30. *Rambam; R' Yosef ibn Yachia; Ma'amar Mordechai; Alshich; Midrash* in *Torah Sheleimah* 197; *Alshich; Eshkol HaKofer.* Some suggest that Achashverosh went searching for an official to arrest Haman (*Tzuf Devash*). Others say that the king first met with Mordechai to verify Esther's claim. Mordechai confirmed Esther's words; furthermore, he told the king that Haman was an evil man who was acting solely for his own gain and not in the interest of the empire. Everything Haman had told him was false, especially his slander of the Jews, who were truly a good people. This infuriated Achashverosh and he stomped out to the royal gardens in a rage (*Yosifun*).

31. See *Ya'aros Devash; Yosef Lekach; R' Elisha Galico; Alshich; R' Shmuel di Uzidah.*

gle hair on your head. I did not know you were Jewish. How could I? You kept it such a secret. You can wipe out the decree.[32] You can have all my money, all my estates, all my treasures. You can demote me from my station and do anything you please with me. But please let me live. My life is in your hands; please do not snuff it out. Can't I find any favor in your eyes?[33] Didn't I indirectly lead you to the throne by having Vashti executed? And even if you feel you owe me no debt of gratitude, can't you find it in your heart to forgive me out of pure mercy and compassion? You are Jewish and a woman; both are known for compassion.[34] Can you find any compassion for me in your heart? Think of how you felt when the death decree was in force. That is how I feel now. You can feel my pain, can't you? Can you also forgive me?[35] Can you also intercede for me with your God, the King of the Universe, and with Achashverosh, the King of Persia, who once looked upon me as a friend but is now my enemy?"[36]

Haman's face contorted with pain as he realized that his life hung by the thinnest of threads. He began to tremble violently.

"Your most gracious highness," he screamed in anguish, "please let me live!" Then he pitched forward and grabbed Esther as if by shaking her he could cause his supplications to penetrate to her heart.[37]

Meanwhile, a bizarre drama was unfolding in the royal orchard. As Achashverosh was taking his stroll, trying to bring his emotions under control, he heard the sound of wood chopping and went to investigate.[38] To his amazement, he saw Haman's ten sons uprooting some of his finest and rarest trees. In reality, they were angels who had taken on the appearance of Haman's sons, but Achashverosh did not know this.[39]

"What is going on here?" he said to the figure he identified as Haman's son Vayzasa, who was actually the angel Michael.

---

32. *Rambam, Yosef Lekach; R' Yosef ibn Yachia.*

33. See *Midrash Panim Acheirim; Yishai Elokim; R' Shmuel di Uzidah; Yad HaMelech.*

34. *R' Yosef ibn Yachia; Ma'amar Mordechai; Alshich.*

35. *D'na Pishra.*

36. See *Rokeach; D'na Pishra; Ma'amar Mordechai.*

37. *Ibn Ezra; Midrash Lekach Tov; Rabbeinu Bachyei; Gra; Me'am Loez.*

38. See *Targum Rishon; Midrash* in *Torah Sheleimah* 197; *D'na Pishra.*

39. See *Megillah* 16a; *Targum Rishon; Sipur HaNeis.*

"We're uprooting some trees!"

"But why?" asked Achashverosh.

"Our father sent us to do it."

"Haman said so?"

"Yes."

"But why?"

"He said they are so beautiful he wants them in his own garden."[40]

"Arghh," shouted Achashverosh, spluttering with drunken rage but unable to get a coherent word out of his mouth. He spun on his heel and hurried off to confront Haman with this latest outrage. He also needed a drink to calm his nerves.[41]

As Achashverosh tottered back to Esther's banquet hall, his head foggy with wine even as his blood percolated with anger, a very disturbing thought occurred to him. He remembered how Haman had sat near Esther the night before drinking her wine and how the scene had discomfited him. After everything Esther had just said, it was clear that she despised Haman and that she would not dream of any impropriety with him. The guilty party, therefore, must be Haman. And now he was alone with Esther![42] Achashverosh bid his wine-soaked muscles to go faster.

Huffing and puffing, he burst into the banquet hall he had left scant minutes earlier. His eyes couldn't believe the scene that confronted him. Esther was reclining on her couch, and Haman was apparently leaning towards her.

"Haman!" shouted Achashverosh.

Haman was gripped by a fright such as he had never felt before. He tried to stand up and jump from his compromising position, but

---

40. See *Megillah 16*; *Esther Rabbah 10:9* with *Yefei Anaf*; *Pirkei d'Rav Eliezer* with *Radal*; *Midrash Panim Acheirim*. Some say that these were *malachei chabalah* (angels of destruction; *Rambam*). Hashem's intervention was necessary at this point to ensure that Achashverosh remained angry, as the salvation of the Jews depended on it. Once he calmed down, his natural hatred of the Jews would reassert itself. While he was angry and drunk, however, Achashverosh would not control himself or consider the ramifications of his actions (*Etz Yosef*). Some point out that the angel's lie was a payment, measure for measure, for Haman's lying about the Jews. He was innocent of this crime, just as the Jews were innocent of the charges against them, but he would pay for the king's anger regardless (*Gra*; *Menos HaLevi*).

41. See *Megillah 16a*; *D'na Pishra*; *Menos HaLevi*; *Midrash* in *Torah Sheleimah*, pg. 198; *Midrash Panim Acheirim*. Some suggest that although the king's ire was aroused by the incident in the royal orchards, he had calmed down after his walk outside. The scene that greeted him upon his return to the palace reignited the flame of his fury (*R' Shmuel di Uzidah*).

42. *Ma'amar Mordechai*; *Yad HaMelech*.

he felt a force of supernatural strength driving him down onto Esther; the angel Gavriel was pushing him down.[43]

Esther screamed, "Save me from Haman!"

Haman struggled hard to break free, making it seem even more as if he were attacking Esther.[44]

"Haman!" shouted Achashverosh. "Stop immediately!"

The force suddenly released Haman, and he fell to the ground.

"I've had enough of you, Haman," hissed Achashverosh. "Would you force yourself upon the queen right here in front of me in my own palace? Are there no limits to your effrontery? Isn't the queen safe in her own house? First you buy my queen and her nation and now you attack her. When you came early this morning, you showed me that you coveted my royal garb and crown. And now you covet my queen![45] You really came because of the queen this morning, didn't you? But you had no opportunity to carry out your evil designs. So now, as soon as I step out the door and leave you alone with her, you attack her. And because she resisted you, you were ready to kill her.[46] First, you send your sons to ravage my garden, and then you come to ravage my queen! Look at you! So filthy, so stinking, so despised by the queen, and still you try to force yourself on her? What kind of a maniac are you?"[47]

Haman shrank back from the king's fury. His face was bright red with shame and guilt. He wished that the earth would open under his feet and swallow him up.[48]

"Oh yes, I see it all now," Achashverosh continued. "You are as evil as Esther claims, even worse. Just like you killed Vashti, who was actually innocent, you are now trying to kill Esther. Oh, you're the clever one, Haman. Always knowing how to twist things to your advantage, always using your wily wits to slither out of tight spots.

---

43. See *Megillah* 16a with *Rashi; Targum Rishon; Ibn Ezra; R' Yosef ibn Nachmiash; Pirush Megillas Achashverosh.* Some suggest that it was the angel Michael who pushed him (*Esther Rabbah* 10:9).

44. *Esther Rabbah* 10:9; *Pirush Megillas Achashverosh.*

45. *Esther Rabbah* 10:9; *Aggadas Esther; Yalkut Shimoni; Targum Rishon; Rambam; Midrash Lekach Tov; Rabbeinu Bachyei; Yedei Moshe; Yosef Lekach; Malbim; R' Shmuel di Uzidah; Menos HaLevi.* Some suggest that this was an illogical assumption. It did not make sense for Haman to risk himself in such a way, at such a time, in such a place. Achashverosh's anger did not allow him to think rationally (*Menos HaLevi*).

46. *R' Chaim Abulafia; Menos HaLevi.*

47. See *Megillah* 16a with *Maharsha; Esther Rabbah* 10:9; *Yefei Anaf; R' Yosef ibn Yachia.*

48. *Targum Rishon; Maharal; Eshkol HaKofer; Midrash Lekach Tov; Einei HaEidah.*

Well, this time you are cooked. What can you possibly say for your-self? I suppose you'll tell me you were on your knees in front of the queen begging for mercy." He laughed a harsh and bitter laugh. "Well, I've had my fill of you, Haman. The time has come for you to face the consequences of your duplicity and heinous crimes."[49]

Haman felt the air go out of him. All his feelings of shame and guilt were dwarfed by an immense, incredibly chilling fear. The *tzaraas* that had afflicted him earlier that day now spread over his face and body, and he covered his face with his hands. There was nothing left to do, nothing to say, no tricks and clever stratagems to employ. This was the end of the road.[50]

The king looked at his guards and then abruptly turned away. The message was unspoken but clear.[51] The guards sprang forward and grabbed Haman. One of them snatched Haman's cloak and wrapped it around his head so that the king would not have to see the condemned man's face. Another placed a hood over his head, a sign of impending execution. Then the guards stood at attention on either side of the prisoner to await the king's command.[52]

Just then one of the king's senior advisors stepped forward. His name was Charvonah. Some suggest that the speaker was actually Eliyahu *HaNavi* in the guise of Charvonah.[53] For years, Charvonah had served the king faithfully, mostly as a reliable bearer of royal messages. He had been one of the seven officers sent to summon Vashti on

---

49. See *R' Yosef ibn Yachia; D'na Pishra; Pirush Megillas Achashverosh*.

50. *Yedei Moshe; Gra; R' Shmuel di Uzidah; Menos HaLevi; Rokeach; Sha'arei Binah.*

51. *Rambam; R' Elisha Galico.*

52. See *Ibn Ezra; Akeidah; R' Yosef ibn Nachmiash; Rambam; Sefas Yam; Yad HaMelech.* Achashverosh and Haman had finalized the decree while drunk, and Haman's down-fall now came when they were in a similar state (*Menos HaLevi*).

53. See *Megillah* 16a; *Esther Rabbah* 10:9; *R' Zechariah HaRofei.* Many question the *Megillah's* change in the spelling of Charvonah's name. Earlier it is written with an *aleph* at the end, while here it ends with a *hei.* Some say that this shows that here it was not the real Charvonah who spoke, but Eliyahu *HaNavi.* Others hold that it was Charvonah himself; since he now switched his allegiance from supporting Haman to denouncing him, he also changed the spelling of his name (see *Pirush Megillas Achashverosh; Yosef Lekach; Menos HaLevi*). Furthermore, in the *piyut* of *Shoshanas Yaakov* we say that Charvonah is *zachur latov*, remembered for good. This would prove that it was not Eliyahu *HaNavi* who spoke here, since, as our Sages state, Eliyahu is already remem-bered for good (as in *Berachos* 3a and *Birkas HaMazon*). See *Esther Rabbah* 10:9 with *Yefei Anaf; Pirkei d' Rav Eliezer* with *Radal; Rokeach; Maharal.* The name Charvonah also alludes to sword, *cherev*, since Charvonah caused Haman's destruction (*Rokeach*). The name can also suggest that first he was Haman's sword threatening Mordechai, and now he was Eliyahu to Mordechai and the means of death to Haman (*Kad HaKemach*).

the last day of the Shushan feast.[54] Charvonah was an old ally of Haman and an enemy of Mordechai. He had pressed Mordechai to bow down to his friend Haman, but to no avail.[55] He had also been among the advisors assembled in Haman's house the night before, and he had heartily endorsed Haman's plan to have Mordechai hanged. But now that Haman was doomed, he was afraid that he might go down with the sinking ship. He saw clearly that it was time to switch allegiances and change the tune he had been singing.[56]

"Your majesty," said Charvonah, "if I may say a few words before you pass judgment. This is a vile creature that we see before us. It is not just that he attacked the queen. Perhaps he would be able to offer some explanation. Perhaps the queen would even show mercy and forgive him. Perhaps even Mordechai would forgive him. But none of this should make a difference, because his sins run far deeper."[57]

"Go ahead," said Achashverosh. "I'm listening."

"I believe that evidence had come to light implicating Haman in the assassination plot of Bigsan and Seresh, his cousins. Mordechai and Esther foiled the plot, and Haman has never forgiven them. Ever since, he has conducted a personal vendetta against them. And I'll prove it. He built a gallows fifty cubits tall on his own estate and was preparing to hang Mordechai from it. Now, here is my proof. What did Haman have against Mordechai? That he was violating the law by refusing to bow down to him? Then he should have had him arrested and put on trial in a Persian court. Why didn't he just wait and let Mordechai perish along with all the Jews in eleven months when the decree takes effect? If Mordechai deserved to die, why did Haman build a gallows on his own estate instead of using government facilities?" He paused.[58]

"Good questions," said Achashverosh. "So what are the answers?"

"Because his campaign against Mordechai is all personal," said Charvonah. "He is furious that Mordechai thwarted his plans to assassinate the king. Would he be able to put Mordechai on trial in a Persian court for this terrible crime? Would he be able to hang

54. *Yosef Lekach.*

55. See *Yalkut Shimoni;* see *Midrash* in *Torah Sheleimah,* pg. 200; *Rambam; R' Yosef ibn Yachia.*

56. *Megillah* 16a; *Targum Sheni; R' Shmuel di Uzidah; Yad HaMelech.*

57. See *R' Yosef ibn Yachia; D'na Pishra; Menos HaLevi; Alshich.*

58. See *Yosifun; Menos HaLevi; Yedei Moshe; R' Chaim Abulafia;* see *Rokeach; Alshich; Ma'amar Mordechai; Midrash Panim Acheirim; Yalkut Shimoni;* see *Targum Sheni; Yosef Lekach; Maharal.*

Mordechai from government gallows? This is all a show of defiance of the legitimate power of the king. He builds a gallows on his own estate and executes a high official of the king while he and the king are feasting at the queen's banquet."[59]

"Go on."

"I was among the men sent to summon Haman to the queen's banquet earlier tonight, and I saw the gallows. I pleaded with him to take it down, but he laughed at me. He wanted to hang Mordechai high enough for all of Shushan to see what he had done in defiance of the king's authority. He even sent his sons into the king's orchard to get more wood to make the gallows more elaborate. Why such an elaborate gallows? I was told it is to accommodate the king and his loyal advisors as well." He paused. "May I offer one more comment, your majesty?"[60]

"Speak, Charvonah."

"If I may take the liberty, your majesty, I suggest that Haman should get exactly what he intended for Mordechai. He committed high treason against the king. Therefore, he should be hanged from his own gallows for all of Shushan to see."[61]

Achashverosh nodded. Deep down, he had always harbored a resentment against Haman for his role in the execution of Vashti, but at the same time, he had suppressed these feelings in order to avail himself of Haman's counsel and political skills. Now the truth was finally apparent, and he saw the monster for what he was.[62]

"Take him away!" he commanded. "Turn him over to Mordechai and tell him to hang him on his gallows. Tell Mordechai to hang him high. He is in your hands. Do with him as you please."[63]

---

59. See *Maharal; Alshich; Ma'amar Mordechai; Yad HaMelech.*
60. *Pirkei d'Rav Eliezer* with *Radal; Targum Sheni; Rokeach; D'na Pishra; Menos HaLevi; Iyun Yaakov.* Charvonah wanted to convince the king that he himself was not involved in the plot to hang Mordechai, and thus used the excuse that he had been sent to Haman's house. In fact, he had already known about the gallows because he was one of the conspirators. See *Maharsha; Ben Yehoyada.*
61. *Ya'aros Devash; R' Elisha Galico.*
62. *Sha'arei Binah* to *Esther* 1:16.
63. *Targum Sheni; Rambam;* see *Targum Rishon. Sefer Biurim V'Likutim* to *Megillas Esther* notes: There are 70 verses between 2:23, where Bigsan and Seresh are hanged, and 7:10, where Haman is hanged. This refers to the fact that it all occurred due to wine; the numerical equivalent of *yayin*, wine, is 70. Also, Haman's promotion to greatness lasted for 70 days. It is noteworthy that Haman is mentioned in the *Megillah* 54 times, while the names of his ten sons are comprised of 54 letters. The numerical value of *emcheh*, I will obliterate – the word Hashem uses to describe His ultimate eradication of Amalek – is also 54 (*Matei Moshe; Rokeach*).

The guards hustled Haman away and brought him to Mordechai with the king's instructions. Mordechai ordered the guards to clamp Haman in chains, and they set off for the gallows immediately.[64]

"Mordechai, listen to me," said Haman, his voice muffled by the hood over his head. "My life is in your hands. Take pity on me. Vengeance is not a Jewish trait, is it? Don't treat me like a common criminal. Remember who I am. Prime minister. Viceroy. One of the most powerful people in the world.[65] Now look how I have fallen. I am walking to my own execution. Who would have believed such a thing this morning? Well, isn't this bad enough for me? Don't treat me as Shmuel treated my grandfather Agag." He began to sob. "How much can one human being suffer? My head and heart are bursting with pain and sorrow. Can't you at least give me a little honor in my death? Please be merciful, Mordechai. Kill me by the sword. Chop off my head if you must. But don't string me up high on the gallows. The shame and humiliation are just too much."[66]

Mordechai thought for a moment and replied, "Haman, you are a wily snake until the very end. I know that the manner of your death doesn't really matter that much to you. So why are you crying crocodile tears over it? I see right through you. You think that if you die an honorable death, you may be remembered as a hero, and once all the ruckus dies down, the decree you engineered may be allowed to remain in force. But if you swing from the gallows, all your prestige and power will crumble like dust, and the decree along with it. Even in death, you want to make sure your evil designs are furthered. Not a chance, Haman. Not a chance."[67]

Haman gnashed his teeth in frustration. All the arguments were finally over. He had only one last hope. When he had built the gallows, he had cast a magic spell on it making it receptive only to Mordechai and no one else. Perhaps his enchanted gallows would save him by refusing to accept him.

As the small procession neared their destination, they were joined by *Kohanim* blowing trumpets to herald the arrival of the condemned Haman. The Jewish population of Shushan came out in force and lined the streets. The procession stopped at the foot of the

---

64. *D'na Pishra; Yosef Lekach; Ma'amar Mordechai.*
65. *Targum Sheni.*
66. *Targum Sheni; Kedushas Levi.*
67. *Kedushas Levi.*

gallows. The royal executioners removed Haman's hood and ring. They cut his beard and dressed him in his finest ministerial robes so that all should recognize the corpse dangling from the gallows. A netting was placed over him to prevent the birds from pecking at him and hastening his death.

The noose was placed around his neck.

Haman held his breath, hoping that the gallows would refuse to accept him, but the exact opposite happened. The fifty-cubit-high structure miraculously bent down and offered its highest tip to receive Haman. The rope was attached to the tip of the gallows, and the gallows slowly straightened itself, lifting Haman high into the air.

Haman kicked and flailed for a few minutes, but then his convulsions abated and he just dangled in the wind, a pathetic figure buffeted by the breeze. At long last Haman was dead. He was ninety-five years old.[68]

The Jewish people had sinned, and Hashem had threatened them with annihilation in order to cause them to repent. In that sense, Haman had been the agent of Hashem. But just like Pharaoh before him, Haman had taken pleasure in his divine mission, and for that he deserved to be punished and humiliated, as he was.[69]

There was much poetic justice in his demise. He had dressed as an idol and wanted to be worshipped, and now he was hung in shame in his best finery.[70] Haman had tried to prevent the rebuilding of the *Beis HaMikdash*, and now he was hanged from the kind of beam of which the Holy of Holies was built, at the hands of a descendant of the tribe of Binyamin in whose portion the *Beis HaMikdash* was located.[71] Haman had caused the death of Achashverosh's wife, and now Achashverosh's second wife had caused the death of Haman. Vashti had died when she deserved to live, while Esther lived when she had been condemned to die.[72] Most ironic, Haman was his own worst enemy. His daughter had died

---

68. *D'na Pishra; Yosef Lekach; Ma'amar Mordechai; Me'am Loez; Einei HaEidah;* see *Rambam* and commentary there; *Rokeach; Einei HaEidah.* See *Ta'ama D'kra* who says that Mordechai, too, was at least 95 years old. This assertion is based on his years in the *Sanhedrin.* Also, the *Midrash* says that Mordechai had told Haman that he was too old and weak to mount the horse. Haman replied that he, too, was old, and could not help him, implying that they were of similar age.

69. *Chasam Sofer.*

70. *Tzofnas Pane'ach.*

71. See *Aggadas Esther; Maharal.*

72. *Yalkut Shimoni; Me'am Loez, ch. 3.*

because of his own machinations, and he was hanged from his own gallows. The law he had formulated during Vashti's trial now allowed the king to act by edict and have Haman executed without benefit of a trial.[73] Memuchan, Haman's original name, meant destined, and he was indeed a man of destiny, destined to suffer retribution through his own actions.[74]

For Achashverosh, Haman's death was like the end of a nightmare. Ever since Vashti's death, Achashverosh had not enjoyed a moment of pure serenity. He had been torn apart by all sorts of conflicting needs and desires, ambitions and loyalties, fears and suspicions, and Haman had been at or near the center of all of them. He had befriended and relied on the man, but he had also feared and distrusted him. Now that Haman was dead, he felt incredibly relieved. At last, his inner anger and rage gave way to a feeling of pure serenity. At last, he was at peace.[75]

Haman's death also signaled the subsidence of the anger of the King of the Universe, aroused when the Jews had bowed to Nevuchadnezzar's idols. Prayer and repentance had earned them divine forgiveness. They did not have to work hard to bring about Haman's downfall once they had gained divine favor.[76] Esther did not have to move a finger to bring down Haman. All it took was prayer to Hashem and a plea to Achashverosh.[77] This is the great miracle the *Megillah* commemorates, and that is why we read portions of it aloud before the reader. That is why Charvonah is remembered in such a positive light. He was part of the miracle that happened on its own.[78]

The death of Haman brought a great sense of relief all around, and the Jewish people rejoiced. But there was still unfinished business. The decree still had to be abolished.[79]

---

73. See *Yosef Lekach; Yalkut Esther* 1:13.

74. *Megillah* 12. Ultimately, Haman had worked tirelessly to construct his own gallows, as the *Gemara* says on the words *asher heichin lo,* [the gallows] that he had prepared for him [Mordechai]: *lo heichen,* he [Haman] had prepared it for himself!

75. See *Megillah* 16a; *Esther Rabbah* 3:15; *D'na Pishra; R' Shmuel di Uzidah; R' Elisha Galico.*

76. See *Megillah* 16a; *Maharsha; Midrash Lekach Tov; Midrash Panim Acheirim; Maharal.*

77. *Aggadas Esther.*

78. See *Pirush Megillas Achashverosh; Midrash Tehillim* 9:14; see *Yerushalmi* 3:7.

79. *R' Shmuel di Uzidah.*

Out of Death's Shadow

23

A chashverosh and Esther were sitting together on the veranda when they heard a great cry in the distance. They looked up at the towering silhouetted against the moon and saw the figure of Haman dangling from a noose at the very top.

"What a relief!" said Esther. She laughed nervously. "It seems that Haman is finally finished, but with that snake, you can never be sure. I'll be glad to see him buried deep underground. Let him try his arguments and his conniving stories on the keepers of the netherworld, but I don't think it will do him any good."

Achashverosh nodded. "It is over, Esther. It is finally over. You know, I've been thinking, and I decided to give you a gift."

"There is no need, my lord. You have already given me the greatest gift of all, my life and the survival of my people. I don't need anything else."

"Oh, I know you don't need it. I just want to give it. I am giving you all of Haman's wealth. After me, he was the wealthiest in the empire, and everything he owned is now yours; his estate, his slaves, his treasures, his money, they are all yours.[1] I told you I would give you up to half the kingdom if you asked for it. You didn't take me up on my offer, but I want to do something along those lines anyway."

"But how can you give me Haman's wealth?" asked Esther. "Isn't there a law that the estates of people executed for political crimes go to the government?"

"Yes, there is. But my main purpose in executing him was his attack on you, my dear queen, and by giving you his wealth I am telling it to the world and showing them my esteem for you. I also want to show you that I harbor no ill will or suspicions against you.[2] I know that you never encouraged Haman's advances or led him on in any way. And besides, isn't it just that you should get his wealth? Haman tried to kill the Jews and plunder their wealth. Now, he is killed and his wealth goes to a Jewish woman. You are in full control, and not only of his wealth but also his family. Watch them; they are a dangerous bunch."[3]

"I accept your gift with gratitude, my lord."

"So tell me, Esther, what is Mordechai to you? I know that he raised you, but is he related to you?"

"Oh, yes. Mordechai is my uncle."

"Then he is my uncle-in-law," said Achashverosh with a laugh. "Tell him that he may come see me in the palace whenever he wishes. I have gotten back the signet ring I gave Haman; the executioners removed it. I have returned it to my own hand. I will give this ring to Mordechai now. He will replace Haman as prime minister and viceroy. First of all, I owe him a debt of gratitude for raising his niece so well."[4]

Esther lowered her eyes. "You are too kind, my lord."

"No, I am not. You are the most extraordinary person I have ever met. But I wouldn't give him the signet ring for that reason alone. The position of viceroy is important, but it can also be abused. Look

1. *Esther Rabbah* 10:9; *Pirkei d'Rav Eliezer* 50 with *Radal*; see *Midrash Shochar Tov* 47:22; *Pirush Megillas Achashverosh*; *Ibn Ezra*. Haman's amassed fortune, which had taken him five years to acquire, was now lost in an instant (*Midrash Lekach Tov; Seder Olam* 29).

2. *D'na Pishra*; see *Sanhedrin* 48b; *Chasam Sofer* to *Megillas Esther*; *R' Elisha Galico*; *R' Shmuel di Uzidah*; *Menos HaLevi*; *Malbim*.

3. *Yad HaMelech; D'na Pishra*.

4. *Rashi; D'na Pishra; Menos HaLevi; Ma'amar Mordechai.* Esther was loath to request special treatment for Mordechai from the King lest he suspect that it was all a scheme to elevate Mordechai's status. Instead she waited for Achashverosh to realize himself what Mordechai deserved (*R' Elisha Galico*).

at Haman! I am confident, however, that Mordechai can be entrusted with so much power. He is a humble and righteous man."[5]

"That he is, my lord. That he is."

Achashverosh stood up and began to pace back and forth. "Sometimes I wish I could relive certain times in my life. No one can do that, not even a powerful king such as I. But sometimes you can make partial restitution. Sometimes you can correct a wrong. Haman took the credit for foiling the assassination plot of Bigsan and Seresh, and that led to his rise in power and the office of viceroy. Now, years later, I discover that the credit really should have gone to Mordechai. The least I can do is give him what Haman got by stealing his credit. How ironic that Haman wanted to kill all the Jews in one day, and now everything he owned and achieved has been transferred to Mordechai in one day! How ironic that the signet ring that, on Haman's finger, signified the destruction of the Jews will now, on Mordechai's finger, signify their salvation!"[6]

In the days that followed, Esther appointed Mordechai to oversee Haman's estates that the king had given her. Mordechai also made a point of frequenting the palace as much as possible in order to solidify his new political power for the benefit of the Jewish people.[7]

Once again, Mordechai was the master of Haman's family. Haman's dream of Mordechai's ascendance had come true, not by Mordechai swinging from a high gallows, but by his trusteeship over all Haman had ever possessed. By controlling Haman's wealth, Mordechai in effect became the second richest person in the empire, barring only the king.[8]

The comparison between Mordechai and Yosef was now complete. Both were among the children of Rachel. Both had resisted corruption — Yosef by spurning the advances of Potiphar's wife and Mordechai by refusing to bow to Haman. Both were paraded through the streets in royal garb. Both rose to the office of viceroy, and both were entrusted with the king's signet ring.[9]

---

5. *R' Elisha Galico; Yad HaMelech.*

6. *Maharal; Yosef Lekach; R' Shmuel di Uzidah; R' Elisha Galico; Ma'amar Mordechai; Alshich; Einei HaEidah; Malbim.* Others suggest that Achashverosh gave Mordechai the ring at a later time (*Yad HaMelech*).

7. *Yedei Moshe; Melo HaOmer; D'na Pishra.*

8. *Targum Rishon; R' Saadiah Gaon; Yedei Moshe; Yad HaMelech; Melo HaOmer; Sefer HaChaim.*

9. See *Esther Rabbah* 7:7 with *Yefei Anaf; Bereishis Rabbah* 87:6; *Bamidbar Rabbah* 10:2; *Aggadas Esther.*

Mordechai put his enormous wealth and political power to good use. They gave him protection against his numerous enemies, now including all the friends of the fallen Haman. They also enabled him to provide some restitution to the families of the Jews who were killed during the sporadic pogroms the death decree had triggered. The fortunes of the Jews had turned around. But not completely.[10]

Although Achashverosh had ordered Haman executed and his estates turned over to Esther and Mordechai, the death decree had still not been officially abolished.[11]

"I appreciate everything you've done for me, my lord," Esther said to Achashverosh one day. "But the sword of death still hangs over my people. The decree is still officially in force."

"Don't you know that Haman's death cancels his decree?" Achashverosh replied.

"It is not so clear," said Esther. "Some may argue that only the ordinary natural death of a high official cancels the decree, not a political execution."[12]

"So what do you want me to do, Esther?"

"I want you to abolish the decree. Just wipe it out as if it had never been issued in the first place."[13]

"But you know I can't do that. It is against Persian and Medean law. A decree signed and sealed with the king's signet ring cannot be rescinded."

"I am sure there is some way to do it, my lord."

"Well, I am not sure of it at all. We will talk about it some more at a later time."[14]

Terrified that Achashverosh would content himself with all he had already done for her without actually rescinding the decree, Esther returned to her regimen of fasting and prayer.[15] For seventy days, she pleaded with Hashem for a reprieve of Haman's evil decree. She wept for the people that would die and for the Torah that would be lost if this tragedy were allowed to take place. During all this time, she also persisted in her campaign to persuade the king to rescind the decree, but she consistently ran up against the same

---

10. *Yosef Lekach; Alshich; Yad HaMelech;.* See *Midrash Tehillim* for a different view.
11. *Yedei Moshe; Yosef Lekach; Akeidah; Malbim.*
12. *R' Shmuel di Uzidah; Alshich.*
13. *R' Shmuel di Uzidah; Maharal.*
14. *Menos HaLevi; R' Elisha Galico.*
15. *Rokeach; D'na Pishra; Gra.*

stone wall. In Persian law, a decree sealed with the king's signet ring could not be recalled.[16]

Finally, she threw herself completely on Achashverosh's mercy. Weeping hysterically, she pleaded with him desperately to spare the Jewish people. Achashverosh's heart went out to her, and he extended the golden rod to her as a show of favor.[17]

"My lord, the golden rod is extended to me," she said, "but what about my people? Are they reprieved as well? In the past, you have received my requests with favor. You know they have always been in the best interests of the kingdom. Grant me this request as well. Rescind the decree."[18]

"I will write a letter to the provinces stating that no one is to harm the Jews. Will that satisfy you, Esther?"

"It is not enough, my lord. People will wonder why they should listen to the second letter over the first."

"But the people know that Haman has been executed and that I have given you and Mordechai control of Haman's estates. Is that enough proof for them about where my sympathies lie?"

"It is not a solution. First of all, this would help mostly right here in Shushan, but what about the rest of the empire? They are not so familiar with the latest political news in the capital. And even here in Shushan, they will conveniently forget everything and satisfy their bloodlust when Adar comes around. The decree has to be ripped out by its roots."[19]

"Esther, you know I want to please you, but what am I supposed to do? The law is very clear. The decree cannot be rescinded."[20]

"This case is an exception, my lord."

---

16. *Menos HaLevi; R' Elisha Galico; Nachal Eshkol.* Some suggest that Esther waited two months before making her request. She did not feel it was proper to ask immediately after all that Achashverosh had already granted her (*Ralbag*). Some say that Esther waited until the month of Sivan so that the merit of the Torah, given on 6 Sivan, would protect the Jews from the decree (*Nachal Eshkol*).

17. *R' Saadiah Gaon; R' Yosef ibn Yachia; Menos HaLevi; Aggadas Esther; Yosef Lekach; R' Shmuel di Uzidah.* Others suggest that, although Esther approached the King humbly, she spoke harshly because she felt justified in her request (*Menos HaLevi*). Esther beseeched, cried, fell and begged, performing four actions to remove the four aspects of the decree: *lehashmid, leharog, le'abeid,* to destroy, to slay and to exterminate, and *machshavto,* Haman's plans (*Alshich*).

18. *Targum Rishon; Menos HaLevi; Dana Pishra; Yosef Lekach; R' Elisha Galico.*

19. *Menos HaLevi; Nachal Eshkol; R' Shmuel di Uzidah; Malbim; Ma'amar Mordechai; Targum Rishon; R' Yosef ibn Yachia.*

20. *R' Yosef ibn Yachia.*

"And why is that?"

"First of all, it was engineered through false pretenses. Haman did not tell you the truth. You did not know the extent of the destruction directed at the Jews. Had you known you would not have signed. And there were two letters, one telling the people to be ready for action on 13 Adar, the other to remain sealed until that day. Since the first does not give a clear command it should be open to reversal. As for the second, since it was never opened, it does not yet have the force of a letter bearing the royal seal, and could be retracted unopened."[21]

Achashverosh scratched his jaw. "I don't know. I need to think about it. We still have plenty of time. It is still a long way to 13 Adar."

"There really is no time to waste," Esther replied heatedly. "The decree has leaked to the public. There are sporadic pogroms against my people. It has to be stopped right away, and the best way to do that is by wiping out the decree, by rendering it invalid, as if it had never been signed. There is no risk to you, my lord. There will be no damage to your prestige or to the legal system if you abolish the decree. At the very least, you can send out imperial letters stating that anyone who harms one hair on a Jewish head will swing from the gallows like Haman did."[22]

"Let me think about it."

"My lord, Haman issued the decree against my people because he hated me. If anything should happen to my people because of me, I could not bear it. If you won't save my people, then kill me now. I don't want to witness the destruction of my people."[23]

Achashverosh paled at Esther's words. "My dear queen, believe me – I would do anything for you. I thought I had done more than enough to protect you and your people from the decree. I had Haman executed. I gave you his estates. I made it known that persecuting Jews would not be tolerated. But your mind is not set at ease. So let us explore this further."[24]

"When?" asked Esther.

"Right now. Call in Mordechai. Let's get some good advice."[25]

---

21. *R' Yosef ibn Yachia; R' Elisha Galico; Menos HaLevi; Alshich; Melo HaOmer; D'na Pishra.*
22. *R' Yosef ibn Yachia; Maharal; D'na Pishra; R' Shmuel di Uzidah; Menos HaLevi; Alshich; Malbim.*
23. *Aggadas Esther; Targum Rishon; Menos HaLevi.*
24. *Rashi to Esther; Rabbeinu Bachyei; R' Yosef ibn Yachia; Pirush Megillas Achashverosh; Akeidah; Yosef Lekach.*
25. *Gra; Yosef Lekach.*

Presently, they came up with a plan. They would send out two letters. The first, signed by the king himself, would inform the people about Haman's disgrace and fall from power and the concomitant rise of Mordechai to take his place. The second would inform the people that the original letters had been sent out in error, that they were invalid and that the Jews were ordered to defend themselves vigorously should anyone dare to attack them. Achashverosh insisted on the extermination of all the attackers, because survivors might form the nucleus of a rebellion.[26]

The conflicting letters would undoubtedly cause confusion in some minds. Varying reactions could be expected. Some people would place both letters in doubt and cancel them out. Others would give credence to the second letter, because the king would sign it, while Haman had signed the first. In addition, the second letter would gain credence by its companion letter, which described the reversal of the Jews' fortune. Furthermore, since the first letter only allowed people to attack the Jews while the second made it mandatory for the Jews to defend themselves, it would appear that the second carried more weight. Finally, the decisive argument against the first letter would be the change in the situation. Haman had originally bought the Jews, but now that Esther had taken over all of Haman's property, the Jews belonged to her. The decree, therefore, could not affect Jews in the possession of the queen.[27]

"Very well," said Achashverosh. "We have a plan. Now go ahead and write these new letters in my name, and I will sign them and seal them with my ring. Remember, these letters are also irrevocable."[28]

There were seventy days from the time Haman sent his letters until the letters to rescind the decree went out. It was now late in the month of Sivan, the month during which the Torah was given, a month of merit for the Jewish people.[29] The number 70 is significant for many reasons. The Jewish people had been forgiven for bowing to Nevuchadnezzar's idols, but they were still not fully forgiven for drinking at Achashverosh's feast. The numerical value of *yayin*,

26. *Gra; Yad HaMelech; Yosef Lekach; R' Shmuel di Uzidah; Menos HaLevi; R' Yosef ibn Yachia; Pirush Megillas Achashverosh.*

27. *Rabbeinu Bachyei; R' Shmuel di Uzidah; Ibn Ezra; Yedei Moshe; Menos HaLevi; Malbim; R' Elisha Galico;* see *Alshich* to *Esther* 3:14. See *Yosef Lekach; R' Yosef ibn Yachia; Rambam; Akeidah; Melo HaOmer.*

28. *Aggadas Esther; Targum Sheni.*

29. *Yerushalmi Sotah* 1:10, *Midrash Lekach Tov; Rokeach.* The first letter was sent on the 13th of Nissan. The recision letters went out on the 23rd day of Sivan, a span of 70 days.

wine, is 70.[30] They also had to wait the 70-day period that the Egyptians had mourned Yaakov when he passed away.[31]

Most important, there was a Persian law that a prime minister's position was fully validated and confirmed only after 70 days in office. Haman had not waited the full 70 days after his accession to office to issue the decree, while Mordechai had waited 70 days to issue the reversal. This in itself gave Mordechai's letter more credibility than Haman's.[32]

By the time the 70 days were up, the original couriers had returned from the far reaches of the empire, and now, the new letters were sent out with these selfsame couriers, adding even more credibility to them.[33]

Achashverosh added further credibility to the new letters by composing the text himself rather than just placing his seal on someone else's text, as he had done with Haman's letter.[34] Furthermore, instead of turning the letter over to the copyists in the royal scriptorium, Mordechai took it upon himself to write all the copies with his own hand.[35] The new letters received the widest distribution possible, going to every government official, from the highest to the lowest, in every district, every city, every village throughout the one hundred and twenty-seven provinces of the empire.[36] The letters were sent out already translated into the language of their points of destination to ensure accuracy and immediate comprehension. These letters were also sent to Jews, unlike the first which had not been.[37] Instructions were also sent to the police throughout the empire to protect the Jews and offer them assistance should they come under attack.[38]

Time was getting short. Mordechai worked day and night to get the word out to every corner of the empire. Preparations had to be

---

30. *D'na Pishra.*

31. *Bereishis Rabbasi* 268; *Ya'aros Devash.* Yaakov *Avinu* died on Pesach.

32. *Ya'aros Devash.*

33. *Yosef Lekach; Gra; D'na Pishra; Maharal; Malbim.*

34. *Menos HaLevi; D'na Pishra; Maharal; Yad HaMelech.*

35. *Menos HaLevi; Yad HaMelech.* These scribes were not Haman's children; those had already been fired. They were newly hired scribes, but Mordechai still did not trust them (*Tosafos Berachah, Parashas Shoftim*).

36. *Targum Rishon; Yosef Lekach; Malbim; R' Elisha Galico.*

37. *Targum Rishon; R' Yosef ibn Yachia; Gra; Yedei Moshe.*

38. *R' Shmuel di Uzidah; Menos HaLevi; D'na Pishra; Maharal; Ma'amar Mordechai.* In addition, Hashem helps the Jewish people the most when they live together in harmony. The *Shechinah* dwells among them when they are united as one (*D'na Pishra*). See *Targum Sheni; R' Yosef ibn Yachia; Pirush Megillas Achashverosh; Maharal* for various versions of the letters' contents.

made for defense against any attacks that might materialize; they would need time to stockpile weapons and devise strategies.

In his instructions to the Jews, Mordechai differentiated between the potential attackers. Any Amalekite was to be considered a mortal enemy and put to death on the spot.[39] Others were only to be killed if they actually attacked. The Jews were permitted to fight with every means at their disposal, including the taking of hostages. The king forfeited his right to the booty, but the Jews were also not allowed to take any. Only others who fought alongside them were welcome to the spoils of war. The battles would take place on 13 Adar; on the very day Haman had considered auspicious for a victory over the Jews, they would enjoy their greatest victory. As an added bonus, the assurance and specificity of Mordechai's letter overshadowed the vague letter Haman had sent out, lending further credibility to the second letter.[40]

At last, the letters were completed and ready to be sent out. Swift steeds from the royal stables were prepared, and as soon as the couriers returned from delivering the original letters, they were turned around and sent back with the new ones. Time was of the essence; great haste and speed were needed to deliver these letters to their proper destinations.[41] Bone tired, most of the couriers were not eager to make the journeys again, especially when they discovered that they were for the benefit of the Jews.[42] But they were given no choice. They were ordered, on pain of death, to mount the fresh animals and be off immediately. There was no time to waste. The fateful day was drawing near.[43]

---

39. *R' Elisha Galico; Menos HaLevi; Yad HaMelech;* see *D'na Pishra* for different view.

40. *Esther* 8:10-13, *Yosef Lekach; Ma'amar Mordechai; R' Shmuel di Uzidah; Malbim.* See *Pirkei d'Rav Eliezer* 50; *Esther Rabbah* 10:10-11 with *Yefei Anaf* which explains why it was specifically the 13th of Adar.

41. Special animals were selected for the runs. Many suggest that they were swift horses, dromedaries or stallions. Mules of a special Greek breed known for their strength and endurance were also used; their speed was such that they could cover ten days' distance in only one day. See *R' Saadiah Gaon; Ibn Ezra* to *Esther; Yosef Lekach; Midrash Lekach Tov; Kela'im* 8:5. See *R' Yosef ibn Yachia; Metzudas Tzion* to *Michah* 1:13; *Chasam Sofer.* See *Sha'arei Binah; Menos HaLevi; Rashi* to *Kesubos* 55b, *divrei hamaschil "matnos."* Some suggest that they were mules or camels, a unique species found in the Persian-Medean empire of that time. They had two humps and eight legs. See *Sifsei Chachamim* quoting *Haga'os Ya'avetz* to *Megillah* 18a; *Rokeach; Sha'arei Binah* and *Rashi.* Some go so far as to suggest that the animals' spleens were removed to lighten their weight, and the soles of their feet carved out to give them greater speed. Couriers' feet were also carved to eliminate pain from stepping on thorns and thistles (*Targum Rishon; Rashi* to *Avodah Zarah* 44a).

42. *D'na Pishra; Alshich; Gra; Malbim.*

43. *Ma'amar Mordechai; Yosef Lekach.*

From Darkness to Light

24

Mordechai was a humble man who shunned honors. Even when the king had honored him with a parade for saving his life, Mordechai had immediately afterwards changed back into sackcloth and ashes and returned to his lamentations. After being appointed prime minister and viceroy in Haman's place, Mordechai had stayed inside the palace for months, concerned about retaliation by Haman's friends and uninterested in glory and honor for their own sake.[1]

But now things were changing. With the letters sent out to the entire empire, the danger to the Jewish people had abated to a great degree. Now the message had to be reinforced, and Mordechai knew that nothing would be as effective as showing himself to the public in his full regalia. When the gentiles would see the heights of power and prestige to which Mordechai had risen, they would abandon

1. *R' Yosef ibn Yachia.*

any thought of doing harm to the Jewish people. The danger of retribution would be too great.[2]

For his own people, too, Mordechai felt it was important to present himself in a royal manner. He knew that in order to rebuild the
Beis HaMikdash he would have to defeat Amalek, and that to be successful he would have to have the status of a Jewish king.[3]

Mordechai suppressed his personal aversion to pomp and
appeared in public for the first time resplendent in full regalia. He
wore a garment of purple embroidered with the likenesses of
beautiful birds under a cloak of precious silks from Tarshish; this
garment alone was worth four hundred and twenty talents of
gold.[4] His belt was studded with precious red stones. Over these
he wore a suit of gleaming armor wrapped in fine blue cloth and a
white linen robe lined with gold and jewels. His woven sandals
were trimmed with gold and emeralds. A large golden necklace
dangled over the front of his robes. On his head he wore a huge
golden crown atop a hat of many bright colors. A Medean sword
rode on his thigh in an intricately worked scabbard secured with
golden thongs and adorned with an engraving of Yerushalayim.
Tefillin sat proudly on his head directly in front of his crown, and
he wore a *techeiles*-fringed *tallis* over his shoulders. All in all, with
his flowing white beard and his penetrating eyes, he was a most
impressive sight.[5]

The streets were covered with sheets of purple fabric and myrtle
branches wherever he was to walk. Palace pages with trumpets
escorted him through the streets of Shushan and cried out, "Anyone
who does not give honor to Mordechai will be killed along with his
family!" Haman's children led the parade, shouting Mordechai's
praises to Hashem, and lauding Him for saving the Jewish people
and bringing down the wicked. They mocked their foolish father
who had trusted in his wealth and power but was defeated by
Mordechai's sackcloth and ashes.[6]

---

2. *R' Elisha Galico; Alshich;* see *Yosef Lekach* for a different approach.

3. *Ya'aros Devash.*

4. See *Menos HaLevi; Ralbag.* See *Ramban* to *Shemos* 28:2.

5. *Targum Rishon; Targum Sheni.* See *Toras Chaim* to *Parashas Tetzaveh* 28:19-20; *Rokeach;*
Midrash to *Shmuel* 27:4; *Yad HaMelech; Gra; Tikunei Zohar.* Some suggest that Mordechai
dressed in the same clothing he had worn earlier when he was honored by the King
on the streets of Shushan (*Menos HaLevi*).

6. *Targum Rishon; Rokeach.*

Esther observed the parade from a window in the palace; it would not have been dignified for the queen to join the parade. Mordechai looked up and saw her. He mouthed the words, "Blessed is God for not letting us fall prey to their teeth" (*Tehillim* 124:6). She read his lips and nodded, responding, "My help is from God, the Maker of heaven and earth" (ibid. 121:2). The Jews in the crowd added, "Salvation is for God, upon Your people is Your blessing for eternity" (ibid. 3:9).[7]

It was a moment of incredible triumph for the Jews. Mordechai had now achieved a status far higher than Haman had ever had. Haman had been the most powerful official in the empire, but Mordechai was that and much more. To his own people he was a true king, dressed in purple, with a golden crown on his head, feared and honored by all. In true royal manner, Mordechai even had a coin minted in his honor and put into circulation; sackcloth and ashes and Mordechai's name were represented on one side, and a golden crown and Esther's name were represented on the other. Mordechai had shied away from honors, but they pursued him in abundant measure.[8]

During those heady days, Mordechai and the Jewish people emerged from darkness to light. Where there had been agonized groans under Haman's rule, there were now relief and happiness. Where there had been anguished mourning — fasting, weeping, bitterness, rent clothing, sackcloth, ashes and lamentations — there was now honor fit for kings. Mordechai and the Jews had shared in the common suffering, and now they were worthy of sharing in the salvation as well.

There were joy and celebration throughout Shushan; even the trees and the stones rejoiced.[9] Haman had thought that 13 Adar, the day on which Egypt was plagued with darkness, was an auspicious time for his decree, but he forgot that the Jews enjoyed light even while the Egyptians were immobilized by the darkness.[10] The light of spiritual and physical happiness now suffused Jewish life in

7. *Targum Rishon*; see *Tehillim* 124.
8. *Esther Rabbah* 10:12; *Menos HaLevi; Yad HaMelech; R' Shmuel di Uzidah; Yosef Lekach.* Hashem, too, as it were, was rejoicing in the salvation of the Jews. It was as though He, too, was enwrapped in royalty to honor and rejoice with them (*Rokeach*). Mordechai wore five sets of clothing, which were alluded to in the five sets of clothing Yosef had given to Binyamin, since his descendant Mordechai would one day wear five sets of royal garments. See *Megillah* 16a; *Yalkut Bereishis* 152; *R' Shmuel di Uzidah.*
9. *Rokeach; D'na Pishra.* Some of the people who rejoiced did not even know why they were happy. It was a joyous time for everyone in the city of Shushan (*Kedushas Levi*).
10. *Nachal Eshkol.*

Shushan.[11] Many Jews who had gone into hiding could now literally emerge into the light.[12]

The spiritual light, happiness, joy and honor reflected three targets of Haman's evil decree — the Torah, the people and their money. Above all, the Jewish people were overjoyed that they were no longer restricted in their Torah observance. Haman had understood that the Jewish nation could only be destroyed by undermining its Torah foundation, and he had outlawed Torah study, the festivals, circumcision and *tefillin*. But now the Jews were free once again to study and keep the Torah in perfect safety, and they rejoiced. The Torah brought back light, the festivals brought back happiness, circumcision brought back joy and *tefillin* brought back honor. Moreover, they would now have an additional festival to celebrate every year — the supremely joyous festival of Purim.[13]

There were still some slight reservations which mitigated the happiness of the Jews. Mordechai was concerned about the few outlying districts where the letters had not yet reached. He knew they would soon be coming there as well. But in the meantime, the Jews in those districts were still sad, and this disturbed him.[14] Also, some of the Jewish women in Shushan were concerned that Achashverosh, having found such a wonderful wife in Esther, would counsel all his officers to take Jewish wives.[15] And of course, the most righteous could not experience complete happiness as long as there was no *Beis HaMikdash* and the Jewish people were in exile.[16]

At the opposite end of the spectrum, the turnaround had an electrifying effect on those Jews who had become weak in their faith and observance in their desire for acceptance by their gentile neighbors

---

11. *Gra; Megillas Sesarim.* Some suggest that the Jews erred in their celebration. They did not sing praises of Hashem for their salvation, but rather dined and feasted lavishly, and because of this their exile would last longer (*Menos HaLevi*).

12. *Yad HaMelech.*

13. See *Megillah* 16b with *Rashi; Targum Rishon; R' Chaim Abulafia; R' Elisha Galico; R' Shmuel di Uzidah; Kisei David; Menos HaLevi*. Because of this, we perform three *mitzvos* on Purim: Reading the *Megillah* represents the Torah, feasting represents the physical people, and giving *mishloach manos* and charity represent their money (*Menos HaLevi*). Years later, the Greeks issued decrees against Shabbos, Rosh Chodesh and *bris milah*. This was similar to Haman's intentions to destroy the foundation of the Jewish religion. Shabbos and *bris milah* are symbolic of the unique bond and covenant between Hashem and the Jewish nation. Not being allowed to keep Rosh Chodesh would cause the collapse of the Jewish calendar and the end of the festivals (*Menos HaLevi*).

14. *Sha'arei Binah; Megillas Sesarim;* see *Malbim.*

15. *Sha'arei Binah; Rokeach.*

16. *Rokeach.*

and associates. These former sinners now embraced the Torah with great joy and enthusiasm.[17]

Even the gentiles themselves were affected by the miraculous turn of events. These miracles were far greater than the survival of Chananiah, Mishael and Azariah in the fiery furnace or the Jewish children from drowning in Egypt; fire and water were mindless elements but a vicious human like Haman was a far more dangerous adversary.[18]

Many of the people of Shushan were genuinely happy for the Jews. Even during Haman's reign of terror, many gentiles had felt that an injustice was being done, but they were afraid to speak their minds. But under Mordechai they felt comfortable; they knew he was just and fair, and they admired his humility. And now that they had witnessed how the God of the Jews performs miracles for them when they are sincere and righteous, these gentiles were so amazed that many wanted to convert to Judaism.[19]

Other Persians, however, reacted to the new state of affairs with fear and apprehension. These were the ones who had mocked and taunted the Jews and threatened their lives, and now they feared retribution. If the powerful Haman could fall so precipitously before the Jews, they reasoned, what chance did they have to survive under Mordechai's rule?[20]

Some of these people asked their Jewish neighbors to take them as slaves. Others pleaded to be accepted as converts.[21] For the most part, they were accepted, even though their motivation was suspect. Mordechai wanted to show the gentiles that the Jews were not as insular and exclusive as Haman had claimed. Prospective converts from Amalek, among them some of Haman's descendants, were deemed Jewish but were not accepted into the community. Nonetheless, some of Haman's descendants would someday learn Torah in Bnei Brak.[22]

---

17. *D'na Pishra; Megillas Sesarim.*
18. *Alshich.*
19. *Ma'amar Mordechai; R' Shmuel di Uzidah; Yishai Elokim; Alshich; R' Elisha Galico.* Some people hated both the Jews and Haman's Amalekites, and would have been quite content to watch the two groups destroy each other (*Chasam Sofer*).
20. *Yishai Elokim; R' Shmuel di Uzidah; R' Elisha Galico; Alshich.*
21. *R' Elisha Galico; Melo HaOmer; Yishai Elokim; Yedei Moshe; Einei HaEidah.*
22. *Yevamos* 24b; *Maseches Geirim* 1:7; *Rashi; Targum Rishon; Menos HaLevi; Rokeach; R' Elisha Galico; Alshich; R' Yosef ibn Yachia; Gra; Bereishis Rabbah* 149; see *Sanhedrin* 96b; *Menoras HaMaor, ner* 5, *klal* 3, *ch.* 3. See *Rambam, Isurei Bi'ah* 13:15. This would be the greatest number of conversions performed at one time. The reason for this was that the defeat of Amalek, the embodiment of evil, tore down a spiritual barrier separationg the Jews from Hashem. Once Amalek was blotted out of existence, Hashem's sovereignty could be clearly recognized, and He could be acknowledged as the One and only (*Maharal*).

Yet others did not actually convert but only disguised themselves as Jews to avoid danger in the coming battle. They wore Jewish clothing and rejoiced along with the Jews, but they did not convert.[23]

There was also fear of a different kind among the gentiles who were devout adherents to their pagan religions. They knew they would one day have to answer for the corruption of their various cults, that they would be judged in comparison to the Jewish people, but they had the arguments ready. True, the Jews had accepted the Torah voluntarily at Mount Sinai, but that was only the Written Law. They had accepted the Oral Law, however, only when God had held the mountain over their heads and threatened them with annihilation. Now these gentiles would argue that they too would have accepted the Torah if they had been forced to do so. But now they would no longer be able to make this argument. In the aftermath of the miraculous events, the Jewish people embraced the Torah anew, of their own free will, with joy and fervor. What would these gentiles be able to say now in their own defense? They would shrink in shame before the shining example of the Jewish people.[24]

---

23. *Rokeach; Melo HaOmer; R' Shmuel di Uzidah; Menos HaLevi.* Some suggest that this is why we masquerade in costume on Purim (*Sefas Emes*). Perhaps that is also the reason many dress up as Haman, Achashverosh or Vashti, the opposite of who they are.
24. *D'na Pishra;* see *Sha'arei Binah; Chomas Anach; Nachal Eshkol; Alshich.*

War Breaks Out

25

Nine months had passed from the time Mordechai had sent out the second letters. Word had penetrated to the farthest corners of the Persian Empire. The momentous day of 13 Adar drew near, and everyone, Jew and gentile, waited with bated breath. Amazingly, during all this time Achashverosh, notorious for his fickle nature, had not wavered or reneged on his promises. His trust and confidence in Mordechai were complete.[1]

Haman and his wizards had chosen this day as the most auspicious for the destruction of the Jewish people; it fell during the mourning period for Moshe *Rabbeinu*, and it was also the date of the plague of darkness in Egypt, during which numerous Jews perished. But Hashem would show His complete mastery by making this very day one of unqualified Jewish victory and triumph.[2] It would be a total turn-

1. *Yosef Lekach; D'na Pishra; R' Shmuel di Uzidah.* Achashverosh was a *"melech hafuch,"* a king who always changed his mind.
2. *Aggadas Esther; Targum Rishon; R' Elisha Galico; Ma'amar Mordechai.*

about. Haman the Amalekite had reigned supreme; now Mordechai the Jew had replaced him and risen even higher. Haman's decree had sent many Jews running for cover; now their enemies were going into hiding. The Jews had trembled in fear; now the satraps, nobles, warriors and officials all feared the Jews. The enemies of the Jews had tried to buy them for money; now they minted and circulated coins in honor of Mordechai. The Jews who had once been like helpless sheep were transformed into roaring lions.[3] As the fateful day approached, the Jews came out of hiding and prepared to do battle.[4] Following Mordechai's instructions, the Jews from all the small towns and villages massed for battle in the cities.[5] In Shushan, the Jews left their own quarter and massed in the government center, where they felt more secure against ambush and treachery.[6] Jews even came from outside the empire to fight alongside their brothers. The royal armed forces also showed their solidarity with the Jewish defenders by offering military support, even though the Jews did not need it. The terror-stricken enemies of the Jews were nowhere to be seen. Many of them knew that gentiles are responsible just for their evil intentions, even if unfulfilled, and therefore, they stayed completely out of sight.[7]

Mordechai, however, instructed the Jews to fight only those who opposed them and also the Amalekites wherever they could be found, but the opposition never materialized. The streets were empty. No one came out to fight against them, except for Amalek who knew they were going to be killed and were determined to go down fighting.[8] The rest of the populace did not mourn the impending demise of the Amalekites. Many held all the Amalekites in disdain, having been antagonized by Haman's high-handed wielding of power. Nor did the Amalekites have any allies who were ready to come to their defense, since this would have been considered an act of rebellion against Achashverosh.[9]

---

3. *Esther Rabbah* 10:11 with *Yefei Anaf; Melo HaOmer; Zera Baruch; Dana Pishra; Yad HaMelech.* The word [ve]*nahapoch* can be read as *nun hapuch*, the 50 [– foot tree (gallows)] *turned* against Haman (*Rokeach*). As noted earlier, the word *hakesef*, the money, has the same numerical value as *ha'etz*, the tree, another example of the complete turn-around (*Chomas Anach*).

4. *Midrash Lekach Tov.*

5. *D'na Pishra; R' Shmuel di Uzidah; Megillas Sesarim.*

6. *Menos HaLevi; Ibn Ezra.*

7. *Rambam; Rokeach; Gra; Pirush Megillas Achashverosh; D'na Pishra; Menos HaLevi; R' Shmuel di Uzidah; Alshich; Ma'amar Mordechai; Kol Rinah;* see *Maharal* for a different assessment.

8. See *D'na Pishra; Rokeach; Yad HaMelech; R' Elisha Galico;* see *Ralbag* cited by *Menos HaLevi; R' Shmuel di Uzidah.*

9. *R' Shmuel di Uzidah; Megillas Sesarim; Yad HaMelech;* see *Menos HaLevi.*

As the Jews prepared for battle on 13 Adar, they emulated Moshe's preparations for war against Amalek and instituted a day of fast and prayer. This fast day would be commemorated for all future generations on 13 Adar as the Fast of Esther.[10]

The battle did not begin with a lightning strike or a surprise attack in any of the war zones. Rather, it began and progressed in a controlled and deliberate manner of people doing a job that had to be done.[11] There was no glee, no bloodlust, just the methodical elimination of the enemies of the Jews, regardless of age, gender or social status, each according to what he deserved, measure for measure.[12] Those who had attacked the Jews prematurely and killed them in pogroms were killed in the most horrible way, and their bodies were dismembered, as Shmuel had dismembered Agag; entire families were erased from the face of the earth.[13] Those implacable enemies who had not participated in the pogroms were killed more mercifully, by a single stroke of the sword.[14] Those who bore even less guilt were sold into slavery, deposed from their positions or simply humiliated in public.[15]

The battled against Amalek raged most fiercely of all, but the result was a foregone conclusion. Thousands of Amalekites perished throughout the empire. In Shushan alone, the Jews killed five hundred Amalekite dignitaries, including government ministers and generals.[16] The ten most prominent and prosperous of Haman's sons were also among the casualties.[17]

By midday, Mordechai called a halt to the killing in Shushan, leaving some of the work to be completed the next day. He did not want to give the impression that the Jews were bloodthirsty killers but rather that they were sober-minded, responsible people doing their duty, unpleasant as it might be. He also wanted to prove that

---

10. See *Rosh* to beginning of *Megillah; Korban Nesanel;* see *Mishnah Berurah* 686:2; *Rambam, Hilchos Ta'anis* 5:5, *Seder HaYom.*

11. *Menos HaLevi.*

12. *Targum Rishon; R' Shmuel di Uzidah; Maharal; Alshich; Menos HaLevi; Malbim.*

13. *Targum Rishon; Targum Sheni; R' Yosef ibn Yachia; Gra; Yosef Lekach; R' Shmuel di Uzidah; Maharal; D'na Pishra; Yad HaMelech; Megillas Sesarim; Alshich.*

14. *Gra; R' Shmuel di Uzidah; Maharal; Yad HaMelech.*

15. *R' Yosef ibn Yachia; Menos HaLevi; Megillas Sesarim; Maharal; Malbim.*

16. *Targum Rishon; R' Yosef ibn Yachia; R' Shmuel di Uzidah; Yad HaMelech; Menos HaLevi; Eshkol HaKofer.* Some suggest that 500 were killed in Shushan *HaBirah* besides the many others taken as prisoners (*Yad HaMelech*).

17. *R' Yosef ibn Yachia; Yosef Lekach; Tzuf Devash; see R' Shmuel di Uzidah.*

the success of the Jews was not due to the auspiciousness or inaus-
piciousness of any particular day.[18]

He also forbade anyone to take booty to avoid the impression that
they were intent on personal monetary gain, patterning Avraham,
who had defeated the Amorite kings but refused to take "as much
as a shoelace" for his efforts. Instead, they left the booty to those of
the gentiles who fought alongside them, and they themselves concentrated on the work of eliminating their enemies.[19] They ravaged
the homes of their enemies, destroying all the idols and objects of
worship, but not taking anything of value.[20] In any case, there was
really scant justification for taking booty since this was not a war in
the classic sense but a nationwide act of self-defense.[21] Still, by foregoing the booty they atoned for King Shaul's sin of taking the livestock when he destroyed Amalek.[22]

With the lull in fighting, Mordechai made an assessment of what
the day had wrought and presented it to Achashverosh. The casualty figures were calculated against the booty collected, and the numbers matched exactly; nothing had been taken.[23]

The other side also sent a body count to the king, hoping to
arouse him to anger and pleading with him to put an end to the
damage the Jews were doing to his kingdom.[24] Achashverosh read
the reports with increasing agitation. Many people had not shown
up for work in the palace that day. He had already noticed that
many seats formerly occupied by high-ranking Amalekite officials
were now empty, and now the hard figures told him that fully five
hundred had been killed.[25]

What did this mean for the rest of the empire? Was it possible to
extrapolate an estimate of casualty figures elsewhere? At first, the

18. *Rashi; Midrash Lekach Tov; Gra; Rokeach; Menos HaLevi; R' Yosef ibn Yachia; R' Shmuel di Uzidah; see Megillah 7a; Menos HaLevi; Megillas Sesarim.*

19. *Einei HaEidah.*

20. *Ibn Ezra; Menos HaLevi; Alshich.*

21. See *Mechilta Beshalach* 17; *Rabbeinu Bachyei; Binyan Ariel; Menos HaLevi.*

22. *Menos HaLevi; Yad HaMelech.*
Others suggest that in the large cities the people did not take the spoils, while in the smaller ones they did (see *Me'am Loez*).

23. *Me'am Loez.*

24. *Yad HaMelech.*

25. See *Megillah* 16b with *Rashi* and *Maharsha; Midrash Lekach Tov; Yosef Lekach; R' Shmuel di Uzidah; Alshich; Malbim; Menos HaLevi; D'na Pishra; Yosef Lekach; Eshkol HaKofer; R' Shmuel di Uzidah.*

king considered the mentality of the enemies of the Jews in Shushan. Knowing the king was on the side of the Jews, they most probably hadn't had the confidence and morale to mount a spirited resistance, and still, only five hundred perished. In other parts of the empire, where they had surely defended themselves more tenaciously, the casualty figures were probably proportionately lower.

On the other hand, there were probably fewer fighters against the Jews in Shushan, where the power of the king was strongest, and still five hundred people died. In other places, where the king's power was not so strongly felt, there must have been proportionately more fighters and, therefore, proportionately more casualties. What a disaster!

Just as these thoughts were crossing Achashverosh's mind, an angel struck him across the cheek. These unworthy thoughts instantly disappeared, and Achashverosh saw things in a more favorable light. He decided that five hundred Amalekite officials were not such a loss in the grand scheme of things. He also marveled at the miraculous manifestations of Hashem's power and congratulated himself on siding with the Jews. Moreover, he was pleased that the Jews had broken off the fighting early rather than pursue the battle tenaciously; it showed them to be calm, orderly and responsible, a stabilizing factor in the empire.[26]

As for tomorrow, the king decided to consult with Esther.

"So, my dear queen," he said after filling her in on everything that had happened that day, "where do we go from here? I promised you up to half my kingdom, and I want to know if I have fulfilled my obligation to you. Are you satisfied with today's results? Do you want anything else?" [27]

Esther furrowed her brows in thought. She wanted to give the Jews of Shushan a second day, because they had fasted and repented. They had sinned at Achashverosh's feast, they had been the focus of the death decree and they had suffered the most.

"Killing is distasteful, my lord," she said, "but sometimes it is necessary."

"My sentiments exactly."

"The Jewish fighters in Shushan stopped early today to demonstrate that they have no taste for killing, to inspire your confidence in them."

---

26. See *R' Yosef ibn Yachia; Yosef Lekach; Alshich.*

27. *R' Yosef ibn Yachia; Rokeach; R' Shmuel di Uzidah; Ya'aros Devash; Ma'amar Mordechai; Gra; Menos HaLevi; D'na Pishara; Megillas Sesarim.*

"I took note of it, and I am pleased."

"But I fear they may not have completed the job. There are left pockets of opposition that will fester and come back to haunt the Jewish people and the empire as well. If it pleases you, my lord, I would like to give them another day here in Shushan. In other places, where they fought all day, they probably finished the work, but not here in Shushan. I also think that the authorization of a continuation on 14 Adar, something not mentioned in any of the letters, would send a clear signal to the entire empire that you are fully behind the Jewish people in this and in everything."

"I grant your request, Esther."[28]

To strike fear into the hearts of the populace and to deter them from any hostile thoughts against the Jewish people, Esther immediately ordered that the ten sons of Haman be hanged alongside their father from the gallows he had built. According to some, Haman's sons had been brought down the day before by archers but not killed.[29] They were hanged from the gallows in one single string of Amalekites. The archers then simultaneously shot arrows into their hearts so that they should all die together.[30] Others believe that they fell on the battlefield, and their corpses were hanged from the gallows along with their father's.[31]

Starting from the bottom, the order of their position on the gallows was: Parshandasa, Dalfon, Aspasa, Porasa, Adalia, Aridasa, Parmashta, Arisai, Aridai, Vayzasa, with the line crowned by

28. See *Megillah* 16b; *Midrash Talpios*; *Yosef Lekach*; *Yad HaMelech*; *D'na Pishra*; *Einei HaEidah*. Many suggest that Haman's children were the first ones to be killed. See *Maharsha*, who holds that Haman and his children were killed at the same time. *Rambam* to *Esther* clearly states that Haman and his sons were all hanged together, although this contradicts the opinion of *Seder Olam*. Others say that Haman's children were decapitated; to ensure that everyone would know whose corpses they were, they were hanged next to Haman (*Chasam Sofer*).

29. *Rambam; Yad Hamelech*. This is why the names of Haman's ten sons are read from the *Megillah* in one breath – to signify that they had all breathed their last simultaneously. In addition the ten names are written in the *Megillah* in a column, one atop the other, to signify that they were all hanged from the gallows in the same way (*Orach Chaim* 690:15, 690:3).

30. See *Rambam; Menos HaLevi*. Some suggest that Haman's children committed suicide when they saw that escape was impossible. They hoped that avoiding execution would ensure that their wealth would descend to their heirs. However, the public display of the corpses was akin to a government execution, and their wealth was confiscated (*Einei HaEidah*).

31. See *Targum Rishon*; see *Aggadas Esther*; *Midrash Panim Acheirim*; *Yalkut Shimoni*; *Midrash Abba Gorion*; *Tosafos* to *Yoma* 31a; *Shabbos* 92b; *Midrash Talpios*; *Selichos* for Ta'anis Esther.

Haman himself in the topmost position.[32] Ten lesser sons, including Shimshai, were executed by the sword and hanged from another gallows, ten were fed to the dogs, and Zeresh and seventy other sons escaped. They survived for ten months, begging for food, then they too were captured and executed.[33]

The fighting in Shushan resumed toward evening on 13 Adar and continued into the next day, and the rest of the enemies of the Jews were destroyed.[34] When the dust had settled, three hundred more Amalekite dignitaries were killed, including more sons of Haman.[35] The total casualties for the Amalekites, their allies and other enemies of the Jews were seventy-five thousand, and as Mordechai had instructed, no Jew took any of the booty.[36] Although there were still some fugitives who had escaped death, the memory of Amalek was virtually obliterated.[37]

Haman had indeed made a decree, a decree of death that killed out his family, relatives and friends. If Haman could only have known the ramifications of his actions![38]

On the afternoon of 14 Adar, Mordechai stopped in front of the gallows Haman had built and looked up at the bodies twisting in the wind.

"Foolish Haman," he declared. "Look where your efforts have led. You tried to destroy the Jewish people, but Hashem caused you to being down disaster on your own head. And now, you hang here, with your ten sons under your wing."

Mordechai shook his head and walked away.

---

32. *Midrash Tehillim* 22; *Targum Rishon; Rokeach; Menos HaLevi; R' Shmuel di Uzidah; Eshkol HaKofer; Yotzer* to *Parashas Zachor* with *Iyun Tefillah; Krovetz L'Purim.* Some say that this is contrary to the opinion of the majority of commentators who hold that all of Haman's children were killed; indeed they had to be killed to fulfill the commandment of wiping out Amalek. Others offer the possibility that these 70 sons were the ones who converted to Judasim. See *Targum Sheni* regarding the prohibition of *lo solun nivlaso al ha'etz,* leaving a corpse hanged on the gallows overnight.

33. *Rokeach; Alshich; D'na Pishra; Melo HaOmer.*

34. *Targum Rishon; Rambam.* Some suggest that they were part of the group of 208 children of Haman. Others suggest that exactly 180 of them were killed. (See *Targum Rishon; Rokeach*). Others suggest that the low death toll in Shushan was only because they had minimized the number so as not to incur the king's wrath (*D'na Pishra*).

35. See *Targum Rishon; Rokeach; Melo HaOmer.* The number 75 is significant; it is the age at which Esther became queen. It is also the numerical value of *Hadassah* plus 1 (*Rokeach; Nachal Eshkol*).

36. *Yad HaMelech; Menos HaLevi.*

37. *Alshich.*

38. *Targum Sheni;* see *Al HaNissim.*

The Days of Purim

26

Jewish festivals celebrate the victory of the Jews rather than the downfall of their enemies.[1] Mordechai and Esther instituted the festival of Purim to celebrate the return of peace and serenity to Jewish life, and this did not take place until the day after the fighting.[2] There had been many miracles from the very beginning but they had not reached their final culmination until the middle of Adar. Therefore, they decided that the Jews in outlying areas, who had fought on 13 Adar, should celebrate Purim on 14 Adar, while the Jews of Shushan, who fought on 14 Adar as well, should celebrate Purim on 15 Adar.[3]

In future years, not only Shushan but also all cities walled since ancient times would celebrate

---

1. Some suggest that we do not celebrate on the 13th of Adar because this day marks the beginning of the thirty-day period during which the *Shechinah* left Esther, from the issuance of the decree until Pesach (*Chasam Sofer*).

2. *Rokeach; Alshich; R' Elisha Galico; Menos HaLevi; Ma'amar Mordechai; Megillas Sesarim.*

3. *R' Elisha Galico; R' Shmuel di Uzidah; Menos HaLevi.*

Purim on 15 Adar, while all unwalled cities would celebrate on 14 Adar. Therefore, even if someday Jews no longer lived in Shushan, Jews living in other walled cities would still commemorate the miracle of Shushan.[4]

In this aspect, Purim is unique among Jewish festivals, for all others are celebrated on the same day by all Jews regardless of where they live. Why is this so? At first glance, it would appear that the two days were to commemorate the different miracles that took place in Shushan and without. Still, one might have expected that the festival would be instituted for all Jews on 15 Adar, the day of the culmination of all the miracles when an enlightened peace descended on the Jewish people. Furthermore, two of the three Pilgrimage festivals take place on the 15th of the month, and it would be fitting that Purim should do so as well.

Nonetheless, Mordechai and Esther felt that to institute the celebration on 15 Adar would disregard the particular situation of the Jews outside Shushan. In Shushan itself, the Jews enjoyed the protection of the king. But the Jews elsewhere were in far greater peril, and their ultimate salvation was therefore far more miraculous. In order to preserve the memory of these additional miracles, they also instituted a celebration on 14 Adar in unwalled, unprotected cities. Furthermore, since the celebration of Purim involves excessive eating and drinking, there is a risk that Torah study will suffer. By dividing the festival into two days, however, they ensured that Torah would always be studied diligently somewhere. On 14 Adar, while the unwalled cities celebrated, the Jews of Yerushalayim would learn Torah, and on 15 Adar, when the Jews of Yerushalayim celebrated the others would learn Torah.[5]

Not every walled city celebrates on 15 Adar. Sanhedrin ruled that only cities that were walled in the times of Yehoshua are included.

---

4. *Menos HaLevi; Ya'aros Devash; Ran* to beginning of *Megillah*. See *Ramban*. A reference to this can be seen in Hashem's oath to annihilate Amalek, *ki yad al keis Kah*. The numerical value of *yad* (יד) is 14, and *Kah* (י-ה) is 15, an allusion to the 14th and 15th of Adar when the Jews would celebrate the destruction of Haman the Amalekite (*Yishai Elokim; Nachal Eshkol; Alshich*). Some point out that the miracle of Purim should actually have been celebrated on 16 Nissan, after Haman was hanged. That day was not designated, however, since it is the second day of Pesach, and the Purim miracle would not receive adequate recognition (*Einei HaEidah; Kedushas Levi*).

5. *Ramban; Menos HaLevi; Chasam Sofer, Malbim*. See *Akeidah; Gra; Yosef Lekach* for further distinctions between Shushan and other cities. Some suggest that the Jews in the walled cities were in greater danger, and consequently experienced the greater miracle, because they had no avenue of escape. The Jews in the open cities were not restricted in this way (*D'na Pishra*).

This might seem somewhat strange. Why should the criteria be the conditions that existed in the times of Yehoshua? Wouldn't it be more logical to establish the standard based on Ahashverosh's times? For example, if one city had walls in the time of Yehoshua and not in the time of Achashverosh while a second city had walls in the time of Achashverosh but not of Yehoshua, wouldn't the second city be more comparable to Shushan?

The answer is that the Sages of the Sanhedrin were concerned for the honor of Yerushalayim. During the time of Achashverosh, Yerushalayim lay in ruins, its wall demolished. Had the Sages set the standard according to Achashverosh's time, Yerushalayim would be grouped with the unwalled cities, a humiliating reminder of its shame and destruction. Therefore, the Sages chose to set the standards by the times of Yehoshua, the first Jewish general to fight Amalek. Since Yerushalayim was a walled city at that time, it would always celebrate Purim on 15 Adar along with all other walled cities.[6]

The original celebration of Purim was the result of the natural impulse of the people after having been pardoned and redeemed. No official laws were as yet formulated. The Jews outside Shushan made 14 Adar a holiday, a day of joy and feasting, a day to wear the finest festival clothes, a day on which there would be no fasting, eulogies or work.[7] The Jews of Shushan, who had experienced a somewhat lesser miracle, feasted joyously on 15 Adar but did not make it as much of a holiday.[8]

The original celebrants also sent gifts, delicacies and foods to each other, as was the custom among victorious Persian soldiers at the time.[9] The custom took on a deeper significance for the Jews who had risen to the crisis with unity and friendship.[10] Haman had maligned them as a scattered people, but they showed exceptional solidarity despite their geographic dispersal. The gifts were also a

---

6. *Menos HaLevi; Malbim; Ran* to beginning of *Megillah;* see *Ramban.*

7. See *Megillah* 4b with *Tosafos, divrei hamaschil "psak"; Megillah* 5a-b; see *Alshich; Yedei Moshe; R' Yosef ibn Yachia; Gra.* These three practices corresponded to the three-fold decree of *lehashmid, leharog, le'abeid.* This book intentionally does not deal with the halachic aspects of Purim. Nothing written here should be used to decide practical *halachah* or custom. Mention has been made only of those aspects of the Purim observance that pertain to the historical account. A minimum of halachically related points are cited to assist the reader in understanding the foundations of the Purim holiday.

8. *Ramban; Menos HaLevi; D'na Pishra; Malbim.*

9. *Targum Rishon; Rokeach; D'na Pishra.*

10. *R' Yosef ibn Yachia; Rokeach; Alshich.*

symbolic replacement of the spoils of the war they had declined to take. Haman had attempted to take the wealth of the Jews, but Hashem had not let him do it. By distributing some of the wealth of their own volition, the Jewish people wanted to demonstrate that ultimately all wealth belongs to Hashem.[11] Mordechai would later institute the practice of giving charity on this day, since it can be concealed with the food and given with utmost discretion.[12]

After the Purim celebrations were over, Mordechai recorded all the events in the Book of Esther, which would come to be known as the *Megillah*. Mordechai and Esther wrote letters to the Jews throughout the empire and beyond establishing the festival of Purim for all time on 14 Adar for unwalled cities and 15 Adar for walled ones.[13] If any Jew anywhere might have entertained the notion that Haman's decree affected only his mortal enemy Mordechai but not other Jews, the full disclosure of the events taught him otherwise.[14]

The Jewish people accepted this new festival upon themselves and took an oath to uphold it always regardless of location or political situation.[15] They could have continued celebrating Purim in commemoration of their deliverance without attaching to it the obligatory status of a *mitzvah*, but they agreed nonetheless out of their high regard for Mordechai. Moreover, since they would be celebrating anyway, they liked the idea of earning the merit of *mitzvah* performance.[16]

Mordechai did not have the authority to establish a full-fledged festival on the level of Pesach or Succos, on which weekday labors are forbidden and sacrifices are brought in the *Beis HaMikdash*; only Hashem can do that.[17] Rather, he instituted Purim as a minor festival, as Chanukah would be two centuries later, a day of joy and celebra-

---

11. *D'na Pishra; R' Shmuel di Uzidah*. Some suggest that the *manos*, portions (of food) were reminiscent of the *manos*, portions (of clothing) which Yosef had given Binyamin as a foreshadowing of the miracle which would occur through his descendant Mordechai (see ch. 24, ftnt 8).

12. *D'na Pishra.*

13. See *Targum Rishon; R' Yosef ibn Yachia; Yedei Moshe; R' Elisha Galico; R' Shmuel di Uzidah; Menos HaLevi; D'na Pishra.*

14. *Rashi; Gra; R' Elisha Galico; Alshich.*

15. See *Ibn Ezra; R' Yosef ibn Nachmiash; Maharal.*

16. See *Yedei Moshe; R' Shmuel di Uzidah; Menos HaLevi; R' Elisha Galico.* This included walled cities sharing the celebration on the 15th of Adar with Shushan, and the added *mitzvah* of giving charity.

17. See *Akeidah.*

tion with only a customary restraint from work.[18] In order to make the celebration uniform, they also ruled that during leap years, Purim should be celebrated in the second Adar rather than the first; since Haman was killed in the month of Nissan, it would be better to celebrate Purim during the month immediately preceding it.[19]

The central observance of Purim is *krias Megillah*, the reading of the *Megillah*, which publicizes the miracles that took place, as an expression of our gratitude to Hashem for His kindness and mercy.[20] It is also a source of solace and encouragement for Jewish people in all times and places who might find themselves beleaguered and endangered. Furthermore, publicizing these miracles to the world would discourage gentiles from persecuting the Jews.[21]

In addition, Mordechai instituted several other *mitzvos*:

- The *mitzvah* of *mishlo'ach manos ish lerei'eihu*, exchanging gifts with each other to generate and reinforce friendship among Jews. The minimum is two kinds of food to one person.[22]

- The *mitzvah* of *matanos l'evyonim*, gifts to at least two poor people, was a symbolic substitute for festival sacrifices.[23] These gifts would help the poor to participate in the celebration just as they had been included in the miracles.[24] On this day of celebration, there could be no greater experience of joy than through bringing happiness into another person's life.[25]

- The *mitzvah* of *seudah*, lavish feasting, drinking wine and merry-making, was to commemorate the miracles, especially since feasting had played such a critical role in the story.[26] The troubles

---

18. See *Orach Chaim* 69b.

19. *Megillah* 6b; *Rokeach; Ibn Ezra; Menos HaLevi; R' Shmuel di Uzidah; Midrash Eliyahu.*

20. *Rashi* to *Esther; Targum Rishon.*

21. *Aggadas Esther; Megillas Sesarim; Mechilta Beshalach;* see *Eichah Rabbah* with *Yefei Anaf; Maharzu* 3:400; *R' Yosef ibn Yachia.* Some suggest that Mordechai wrote the *Megillah,* while others say that it was authored by others. See *Rashi* to *Esther* 9:20 and *Rashi* to *Megillah* 7a. One of the reasons it is called *Megillas Esther* is that Esther risked her life for the Jewish people just as the Torah is called *Toras Moshe* because Moshe risked his life for them. This demonstrated her great righteousness, having survived spiritually after living with Achashverosh for so many years (*Ya'aros Devash; Einei Ha'Eidah*).

22. See *Megillah* 7a-b; *Menos HaLevi; R' Elisha Galico;* see *Me'am Loez* 248 for further reasons; *Manah* is the same letters as *Haman.* See *Chasam Sofer* for further symbolisms of *mishloach manos.*

23. *Menos HaLevi; Malbim.*

24. *Menos HaLevi.*

25. *Rambam, Hilchos Megillah* 2:17.

26. *Rashi* to *Esther; R' Shmuel di Uzidah; Menos HaLevi.*

began when the Jews had participated in Achashverosh's feast, which had also led to Vashti's demise and Esther's selection. Haman also made a feast after the death decree was finalized, and his downfall was at Esther's banquet. Afterward, the Jews celebrated with joyous feasts. Mordechai realized there was a risk of sin and debauchery in such excessive feasting and drinking, but he hoped the *mitzvos* of the day would be a counteracting influence.[27] Some suggest that the reason for the fast on 13 Adar is to mitigate beforehand the potential effects of the food and wine.[28]

Although Adar, the month in which Moshe died, was originally a sad one for the Jewish people, the joy of Purim suffused the entire month with boundless joy.[29] There were also positive aspects from earlier times. The day of Purim, 14 Adar, was also the day of Moshe's *bris milah*.[30]

The festival was called Purim in commemoration of the *pur*, the lot that Haman cast to determine the most auspicious time, from an astrological aspect, to destroy the Jewish people. This was the starting point of the events that culminated with the miraculous redemption.[31] Furthermore, by choosing a time that was still eleven months away, Haman inadvertently gave the Jews ample time to pray and repent and gird themselves spiritually for a great victory.[32] Some suggest that this was the central theme of the miracle. Haman found the least fortunate month for the Jews, and Hashem transformed it into a fortunate month.

The use of the plural Purim instead of the singular Pur recalls the many lots Haman cast until he found his supposed answer.[33] It also acknowledges the two different days of celebration, depending on

---

27. See *Malbim; Megillas Sesarim; Me'am Loez; Orach Chaim* 695; *Avudraham* on Purim.

28. *Kav HaYashar*, Purim; see *Maggid Meisharim* to *Parashas Vayakhel*. Another reason for fasting on 13 Adar, and for its name, Ta'anis Esther, is as a reminder of Esther's call to the Jews to fast after the decree was issued. Some have the custom to fast for three days following Purim to recall Esther's three-day fast from 13-16 Nissan. The fast is observed on the Monday, Thursday and following Monday (known as *Behab*) after Purim. See *Orach Chaim* 686:3; *Beis Yosef Orach Chaim* 429; *Matei Moshe; Maseches Sofrim* 21; *Machzor Vitri* on Purim.

29. *Gra; Ta'ama D'Kra; Melo HaOmer; D'na Pishra*.

30. *Ibn Ezra; Menos HaLevi; R' Shmuel di Uzidah; Midrash Eliyahu*.

31. *Menos HaLevi; R' Shmuel di Uzidah; Gra; Melo HaOmer; Me'am Loez; Ta'ama D'Kra*. See *Sha'arei Binah*, who points out that the numerical value of *Purim* is 336. The Jews' anguish lasted 336 days, from 13 Nissan until 14 Adar nearly a year later.

32. *Me'am Loez*.

33. *D'na Pishra; R' Shmuel di Uzidah*; see *Einei HaEidah*. Some say that the word may be read as *Pur-yam; yam* (ים), with a numerical equivalent of 50, hints to the fact that Haman's *pur* led to his eventual hanging on the 50-cubit gallows.

the locale. Some suggest that it commemorates the destruction of Haman as an individual and the general destruction of Amalek.[34] Others suggest that it indicates that the crisis began in Shushan and then spread to other places.[35]

The word *pur* is Persian. Wouldn't it have been more appropriate to name the festival *goralos*, using the Hebrew word for lots? Some suggest that it acknowledges the critical role the Persian language played in the events. Because Achashverosh had sent out letters ordering all women to speak the language of their husbands, Esther spoke Persian when she was taken to the palace. Had she spoken Hebrew he would immediately have know her nationality.[36] Others suggest that just as we use the Babylonian names for the months in commemoration of our redemption from Babylonian exile, so do we use a Persian name to honor the miracle that took place in Persia.[37]

Purim also commemorates the Jewish people's voluntary acceptance of the Oral Law; for this reason, the Sages ruled that one must interrupt Torah study in order to listen to the *Megillah* on Purim.[38] They had accepted the Written Law when they had said, "*Na'aseh venishma*. We will do and we will hear." But then Hashem had uprooted Mount Sinai and held it over them, threatening to bury them then and there if they did not accept the Oral Law. Thus, sinners would always be able to claim that they had never accepted the Oral Law willingly. But after the miracle of Purim, the Jewish people voluntarily embraced the Oral Law by accepting upon themselves the *mitzvos* of Purim. Just as they had accepted the Written Law after the first attack of Amalek, they accepted the Oral Law after the most recent one.[39]

True, the Jews did assemble on Mount Gerizim and Mount Eival to swear an oath to fulfill the Torah, but that too, according to some opinions, may have been under compulsion.[40] Others suggest that the oaths on the mountains were made conditional on the Jewish

---

34. *Nachal Eshkol.*

35. *Menos HaLevi.*

36. *Chasam Sofer.*

37. *Chasam Sofer;* see *Ramban* to *Shemos* 12:2.

38. See *Megillah* 3a; *Rambam, Hilchos Megillah* 1:1; *D'na Pishra.*

39. *Shabbos* 88a with *Rashi; Rokeach; Menos HaLevi; Chiddushei HaRim; Midrash Eliyahu; Sefas Emes.*

40. *Shavuos* 39a; *Tosafos* to *Shabbos* 88a.

possession of *Eretz Yisrael*. Once they were exiled, the oaths were no longer in effect.[41]

The introduction of Purim and the *Megillah* by Mordechai and Esther as obligatory *mitzvos* did encounter some opposition in the beginning. Eighty-five elders of the *Anshei Knesses HaGedolah*, the Men of the Great Assembly, among them thirty prophets, raised objections.

First, they argued that instituting a new festival might be considered adding to the Torah. Esther also wanted the *Megillah* to be included in the canon of the Written Torah, to have the sanctity of Scripture, like the other Books of the Torah. The elders, however, felt that the era of prophecy had come to an end and that no books could henceforth be added to the Written Torah. Furthermore, King Shlomo had instructed that the story of Amalek appear only three times in the Torah, and it already did. The *Megillah* would add a fourth.[42]

In addition, individual Jews raised objections regarding the festival. They felt that it might become an unnecessary burden on the people and that it might cause bad feeling from the gentile nations. They would not understand how the Jewish nation, famous for its mercy and compassion, could harbor such a long-standing antagonism toward Amalek. They would wonder why the Jews could not simply forgive and forget and move forward.[43]

But Mordechai and Esther prevailed.

Hashem enlightened the eyes of the elders by showing them references in the Torah to the festival of Purim. Purim, it turned out, was already implied at Sinai and accepted there by the Jewish people.[44] The elders then understood that the *Megillah* was written

41. *Ramban* to *Shabbos* 88a. Others attribute this thought to *Rashba*. Some say that the acceptance of *Na'aseh v'nishma* was a verbal one, stemming from fear, but was not meant in the heart. This behavior was typical of Eisav, who spoke with his mouth but not with his heart. Thus Haman, a descendant of Eisav, had the power to decree death to the Jews, for their behavior did not render them special in any way. When the Jews accepted the Torah with all their hearts on Purim, this elevated them to a higher level than the Amalekites, and they could then prevail over Haman (*Ya'aros Devash*).

42. *Megillah* 7a; *Rashi*; *Turei Even*; *Pnei Yehoshua*; *Kedushas Levi*; see *Mishlei* 22:20; see *Seder Olam* 29. Some suggest that since Esther initiated the recording of the *Megillah* (in her request *Kisvuni l'doros*, to write her story for posterity), therefore it is called *Megillas Esther* (*Einei HaEidah*; *Midrash Eliyahu*).

43. *Yerushalmi Megillah* 1:5; *Ruth* 4:5; *Pirush Megillas Achashverosh*; *Megillah* 6b-7a with *Rashi*; *Pnei Yehoshua*; *Ya'aros Devash*.

44. See *Ruth Rabbah* 4:5 and *Maharzu*; *Ran* to *Megillah* 2b and 19a; *Yerushalmi Megillah* 1:5; *Korban Eidah*; *Pnei Moshe*; *Menos HaLevi*; *Shemos Rabbah* to *Parashas Yisro*.

with the divine spirit and was worthy of inclusion in the Written Torah.[45] They also agreed that the reading of the *Megillah* should be mandatory on Purim, since this would take the place of saying *Hallel* on the festival. If being freed from slavery called for songs of praise to Hashem, being spared death certainly did as well.

Once the elders joined ranks in support of the festival and the *Megillah*, they also reassured the people on all accounts. As for their concerns about the public opinion of the gentiles, they pointed out that the entire story already appeared in the annals of the Persian and Medean kings; the gentiles knew it all already even without the *Megillah*. It was highly unusual for the royal chronicles to record the greatness of anyone other than the king, but an exception was made for Mordechai out of gratitude and also to highlight and explain the precipitous rise in Achashverosh's fortunes.[46]

With all this settled, Esther sent letters of harmony and sincerity to all the Jews confirming the agreement of the elders that the celebration of Purim would be obligatory rather than just customary and that the *Megillah* would become part of the Written Torah. She also gave details of the dates of the observance.[47]

Mordechai and Esther knew that the slackening of Torah study among the Jews had brought on their troubles. Their spiritual weakness in the desert had made them vulnerable to attack by Amalek, and their spiritual weakness in Persia had opened the door to Haman. They hoped that Purim would serve as a continual stimulus to inspired Torah learning.[48] Therefore, they rewrote the *Megillah*,

---

45. *Megillah* 7a; *Gra; Me'am Loez;* see *Tikunei Zohar* 3:183b; *Rambam* 1 *Megillah* 14b. Some question why a *megillah* was written to record the miracle of Purim for posterity, but not for the miracle of Chanukah. Esther specifically asked that the Purim miracle be recorded; on Purim the Jewish people accepted the Torah anew, and the lives of the entire Jewish population were threatened. Regarding Chanukah, however, Yehudis had never requested that it be recorded, the Jews did not accept Torah anew at that time, and the decrees were not against the Jews' lives but on practices of Judaism (*Midrash Eliyahu*).

46. *Yerushalmi Megillah* 1:5. As mentioned earlier, this is why Hashem's name does not appear in the *Megillah* (*Taz, Orach Chaim* 364, *s'if katan* 11). See *Midrash Eliyahu* for a detailed discussion of the recording of the *Megillah* and the establishment of Purim for all generations.

47. *Megillah* 6b; *Targum Rishon; Rokeach; R' Elisha Galico; Menos HaLevi; D'na Pishra.* Some suggest that the first letters were to establish the holiday of Purim, while the second ones were to institute the reading of the *megillah* (*Megillas Sesarim*). In her letter Esther also provided halachic justification for her marriage to Achashverosh so that future generations would not question the permissibility of it (*R' Elisha Galico; D'na Pishra*).

48. See *Megillah* 11a; *Maharsha; Me'am Loez.*

fleshing out the story with more details and adding the decisions of
the elders to institute the festival as an obligatory *mitzvah*. Since the
Purim celebration was already becoming somewhat lax, they also
had all the Jewish people swear an oath that they would always
honor the festival properly. The detailed story and the oath would
ensure that the festival would forever be celebrated with great joy
and enthusiasm.[49]

Our Sages tell us that only Purim and Yom Kippur, among all the
holidays, will continue to be celebrated eternally; the Jewish people
accepted Purim on the condition that it remain forever. What exactly does this mean?[50]

Some understand this literally. They take note that before the
destruction of the first *Beis HaMikdash* the celebration of the festivals
had virtually lapsed. Yom Kippur and Purim, however, would
always be celebrated no matter how badly the Jewish people lapse
in their observance.[51]

Some see this as a reference to the times of *Mashiach*. All other festivals will indeed continue to be observed.[52] Some suggest that the
other festivals will continue but with no specific date reserved for
their celebration, while Yom Kippur and Purim will always be cele-

49. See *Targum Rishon; Bava Basra* 15a with *Rashi; Einei HaEidah; Eshkol HaKofer; Ibn
Ezra; Menos HaLevi; Yosef Lekach; Alshich; Gra; Yedei Moshe; R' Shmuel di Uzidah*. There
are various views on who actually wrote the *Megillah*: Esther herself, Mordechai, or
other members of the *Anshei Knesses HaGedolah* (Men of the Great Assembly).

50. *Midrash Mishlei* 9:2; *Yerushalmi Megillah* 1:5; *Midrash Lekach Tov; Rambam, Hilchos
Megillah* 2:18; *Megillas Sesarim; D'na Pishra; Malbim; Yotzer* to *Parashas Zachor*. In fact,
Purim and Yom HaKippurim are similar in more than name. On Yom Kippur we are
commanded to fast, while on Purim it is a *mitzvah* to eat and drink. We are required to
eat the day before the fast of *Yom Kippur*, while the day before the Purim feast is a fast
day. On *Erev Yom Kippur* we rejoice at the meal before the fast, while on Purim we rejoice
at the meal following the fast. On the first Yom Kippur the Jews accepted the second set
of *luchos*, and on Purim the Jews reaccepted the Torah willingly. See *Tikkunei Zohar* 57b;
Likutei Gra 154b; *Midrash Eliyahu; Chiddushei HaRim. Midrash Eliyahu* points out that Yom
Kippur atones for the sin of the *Egel* (Golden Calf), while Purim atones for the sin of participating in Achashverosh's feast. On Yom Kippur we fast since the sin of the *Egel* came
about after the Jews indulged in food, while the celebration of Purim followed the fasts
Esther had mandated.

51. *Sh'eilos U'Teshuvos Rashba* 93; see *Ra'avad* to *Rambam, Hilchos Megillah* 2:18; see
Sh'eilos U'Teshuvos Radvaz 666.

52. *Menos HaLevi*. Some question why Purim would be considered greater than the
Exodus from Egypt, which was marked by the Ten Plagues and the Splitting of the
Sea. Some explain that the Exodus was indeed the greatest of all miracles until the
Jewish people were exiled. However, after the exile from the second *Beis HaMikdash*
(which was built soon after the Purim story took place) the Purim miracle stands as
the last Cannonically documented miracle celebrated nationally by the Jewish people.
See also *HaKosev* cited in *Ein Yaakov* to *Shabbos* 88a; *Sefer Chassidim* 369.

brated on the original date.[53] Others suggest that, since the Jewish people will be in a state of perpetual happiness then, most festivals will no longer stand out as they did throughout history. Only Yom Kippur, as the great Day of Atonement, and Purim, as the celebration of the deliverance from total obliteration, will retain their former glory and become the focal points of the annual calendar cycle of observances.[54]

According to some opinions, Purim stands out as the festival that represents the voluntary acceptance of the Oral Law. This alone makes it worthy of being remembered forever.[55]

---

53. *Sh'eilos U'Teshuvos Rashba.*
Some suggest that since the *megillah* may be read from 11 Adar until 15 Adar, this alone guarantees that it will never be abolished. It is a unique holiday since the *mitzvah* of the day – the reading of the *megillah* – may be done even on other days than the actual date of the holiday (*Likutei Maharil*).

54. See *Sh'eilos U'Teshuvos Radvaz* 828.

55. The combination of the commemoration of the great miracle and the Jews' voluntary acceptance of the Torah makes Purim the greatest of all holidays in certain respects. See *Ya'aros Devash; Midrash Eliyahu.* Some point out that the word Purim alludes to all the festivals. The *peh* stands for Pesach; the *vav* denotes an additional holiday, namely, Succos. The *Resh* is for Rosh Hashanah; the *yud*, Yom Kippur; and the *mem, Matan Torah,* is for Shavuos. Purim includes aspects of all the holidays. Like Pesach, the holiday of freedom, the Jews were freed from Haman's authority. Just as Shavuos commemorates the giving of the Torah, on Purim the Jews accepted the Torah anew. Like the judgment of Rosh Hashanah, the lives of the Jewish people hung in balance on Purim, and just as Yom Kippur is a Day of Atonement, on Purim the sins of the Jewish people were forgiven. Just as Succos celebrates Hashem's *Shechinah* surrounding us, so on Purim many converted to Judaism, seeking refuge under the wings of the *Shechinah* (*Midrash Eliyahu; Bnei Yissaschar*).

Epilogue:
The Aftermath

For most of the people in the Persian Empire, life returned to normal after the downfall of Haman and the deliverance of the Jewish people from his death decree.[1] Achashverosh, however, enjoyed a great improvement in his situation. His appointment of Mordechai as prime minister also enhanced his position greatly.[2] He regained all the lands he had lost to rebellion in the early years of his reign and even gained some lands and islands he had never before controlled. His opposition to the reconstruction of the *Beis HaMikdash* had caused the downturn in his fortunes, but now that he had been kind to Esther, Mordechai and the Jewish people, Hashem restored his losses.[3]

1. *Gra* to *Seder Olam* 29.
2. *Yad HaMelech.*
3. See *Midrash Tehillim* 22; *Aggadas Esther; R' Elisha Galico; Menos HaLevi; Yishai Elokim; Eshkol HaKofer; Tzuf Devash; R' Yosef ibn Yachia; Yad HaMelech.* Many suggest that he acquired an additional one hundred lands and twenty-seven islands, doubling his realm (see *Gra; Nachal Eshkol*).

Furthermore, Hashem honors the Jewish people by elevating the kings who rule over them.[4]

More secure than ever in his power, Achashverosh reinstated the taxes he had suspended in honor of Esther becoming queen. In fact, he raised the taxes even higher than they had been before to punish the provinces for not speaking out against Haman's injustice against the Jews and to replenish the imperial treasuries, which had long been deprived of the revenues.[5] No longer would anyone be exempt from taxes, not even high palace officials and dignitaries. Cemetery taxes were instituted and made mandatory; with all the deaths this was a great source of revenue for the king. So great was his power that even nations outside his empire paid him annual tribute.[6] Once again, everyone under Achashverosh's rule was impoverished by the large taxes they had to pay.[7]

The only exception was the Jews, who now got a tax exemption for the first time. Achashverosh considered it only fair that the Jews, who had paid taxes for seven years while everyone else had not, should not get a respite of their own.[8]

As time went on, Mordechai grew in stature and power, but his new station did not corrupt him. He remained a humble, sensitive man, always responsive to the needs of all the people of the Persian Empire and of the Jewish people in particular. When he walked through the streets, he greeted even the simplest people with honor and grace. Throughout the empire, people respected, loved and feared him both for his own qualities and because Hashem had performed miracles for him.[9] They compared him favorably not only with Haman but also with Achashverosh, because they knew he genuinely had their interests at heart.[10]

---

4. See *Mechilta Shemos* 14. Some suggest that he did not rule over the entire world in fact. Rather, his power was so great that all nations sent him tribute, even those who were not part of the empire.

5. *Targum Rishon; D'na Pishra; Chasam Sofer; Yosef Lekach; Melo HaOmer; R' Shmuel di Uzidah; Menos HaLevi; Eshkol HaKofer.*

6. *Targum Rishon; Ibn Ezra; R' Yosef ibn Nachmiash; Menos HaLevi; D'na Pishra; Chasam Sofer; Yishai Elokim; Maharal;* see *Chagigah* 8a with *Tosafos.*

7. *Megillah* 11a.

8. *R' Elisha Galico; Menos HaLevi; Eshkol HaKofer.*

9. *Targum Rishon; R' Yosef ibn Yachia; R' Shmuel di Uzidah; R' Chaim Abulafia; Menos HaLevi; Alshich; Megillas Sesarim; Gra; Yedei Moshe.* The *Maharal* interprets *mishneh lamelech* as *meshunah lamelech*, different than the King.

10. *R' Yosef ibn Yachia; R' Elisha Galico.*

Mordechai took advantage of his position to improve relations between the Jewish people and all the other peoples. He always spoke well of them and defended them.[11]

Among the Jews themselves, Mordechai showed no favoritism to any one tribe or group. He cared for the needs of even the humblest of the Jews, just as Moshe had embraced all the Jewish people with his boundless love.[12]

All the money he acquired did not cause him to swerve in the slightest from the way of the Torah.[13] He had no personal interest in the wealth, giving a third to Esther, a third to the sages and scholars and a third for the reconstruction of the *Beis HaMikdash*. He continued to be an exemplary sage in his prayer and his Torah scholarship.[14]

Despite his immense popularity, there were some people who did not approve of him completely.[15] His fellow Sages on the Sanhedrin distanced themselves from him, because his political responsibilities had caused his Torah study to suffer.[16] There is no doubt that Mordechai continued to learn diligently, but the need to attend to matters of life and death drew him away from his studies and perhaps lowered the level of his learning to a certain extent.[17] Others suggest that in times of actual crisis rescue operations take precedence over everything, even learning Torah. But learning Torah takes precedence over preventive action. As long as there was no immediate danger, they felt, Mordechai should have resigned and devoted himself exclusively to Torah. Mordechai disagreed.[18]

There were also some members of the tribe of Binyamin who were upset that Mordechai did not show them special favor.[19] He was also

---

11. *Ibn Ezra; Maharal.*

12. See *Shemos Rabbah* 1:27; *R' Elisha Galico; D'na Pishra; Yishai Elokim; Maharal; Chasam Sofer; Alshich.*

13. *R' Shmuel di Uzidah; Eshkol HaKofer.*

14. This too was a result of the proposals put forth by Haman in an attempt to avoid the embarrassment of parading Mordechai through the streets of Shushan. The King assured Haman that he would accept the suggestion to give Mordechai wealth, in addition to the honor he would receive in the parade. The events which occurred to Haman, and the reward Mordechai received, all came about through Haman's own doing.

15. *R' Elisha Galico.*

16. *Megillah* 16b with *Rashi; Maharsha; Rashi* to *Esther.* Some say that the *Sanhedrin* were not pleased that Mordechai made a leap year that year against their wishes (*Tzofnas Paneach*).

17. *Taz, Tzedakah* 251, *s'if katan* 6. See *R' Yaakov Yisrael Kanievsky* in *Karyana D'Igarta, Kimu V'kiblu.*

18. *Ben Yehoyada* to *Megillah* 16a.

19. *Alshich.*

not very popular among the less righteous Jews, whom he rebuked and whose tax exemption he removed. Of course, some people were simply jealous of his great wealth and power, but this was unavoidable.[20]

In the end, Mordechai did not serve as prime minister for very long. Achashverosh's entire reign lasted only fourteen years. He died young, in retribution for having stopped the reconstruction of the *Beis HaMikdash* and the torment to which he had subjected the Jews, but he did gain a share in the world to come by emerging as their champion and protector.

After Achashverosh died, Darius II, his son by Esther, ascended to the throne and eventually authorized the resumption of the reconstruction of the *Beis HaMikdash*. When Darius became king, Mordechai resigned. He would eventually have an important role in preparing the bird offering in the *Beis HaMikdash*.[21]

The first word in the *Megillah, vayehi,* has a numerical value of 31, and the last, *zar'o,* has a value of 283, for a total of 314 — which is the numerical value of Shad-dai, the Almighty. From the beginning to the end, it appeared that events were caused by the protagonists — Achashverosh, Vashti, Haman, Mordechai and Esther — but we must never forget that the hand of the Almighty is the one and only guide of events.[22] And we pray to the Almighty that He take pity on the Jewish people and bring an end to our suffering and sorrow speedily in our days.[23]

---

20. *Rokeach; Yedei Moshe; R' Shmuel di Uzidah; Yad HaMelech.*

21. *Shekalim,* ch. 5; see *Gra; Tzemach David* to *Seder Olam* 29; see *Rashi* to *Megillah* 11b; *Targum Rishon* 1:1; *Eshkol HaKofer.*

22. *Nachal Eshkol.*

23. *Me'am Loez.* See *Ruth Rabbah* 4:5; *Yerushalmi Megillah* 1:5; *Taz, Orach Chaim* 364 *s'if katan* 11 regarding the absence of Hashem's Name in the *Megillah.*